Encyclopedia of the Sixties

Encyclopedia of the Sixties

A Decade of Culture and Counterculture

VOLUME 2: N–Z

James S. Baugess and Abbe Allen DeBolt, Editors

GREENWOOD

AN IMPRINT OF ABC-CLIO, LLC
Santa Barbara, California • Denver, Colorado • Oxford, England

Library of Congress Cataloging-in-Publication Data

Encyclopedia of the sixties : a decade of culture and counterculture / James S. Baugess and Abbe Allen DeBolt, editors.
  p. cm.
Includes bibliographical references and index.
  ISBN 978–0–313–32944–9 (set : alk. paper) — ISBN 978–1–4408–0102–0 (ebook (set)) — ISBN 978–0–313–32945–6 (v. 1 : alk. paper) — ISBN 978–0–313–32946–3 (v. 2 : alk. paper)
1. United States—Civilization—20th century—Encyclopedias. 2. Counterculture—United States—History—Encyclopedias. 3. United States—History—1961–1969—Encyclopedias. 4. United States—Biography—Encyclopedias. 5. Nineteen-sixties—Encyclopedias. 6. Counterculture—History—Encyclopedias. 7. Biography—Encyclopedias. I. Baugess, James S. II. DeBolt, Abbe Allen.
E169.12.E525   2012
973.9—dc23   2011031666

ISBN: 978–0–313–32944–9
EISBN: 978–1–4408–0102–0

16 15 14 13 12   1 2 3 4 5

This book is also available on the World Wide Web as an eBook.
Visit www.abc-clio.com for details.

Greenwood
An Imprint of ABC-CLIO, LLC

ABC-CLIO, LLC
130 Cremona Drive, P.O. Box 1911
Santa Barbara, California 93116-1911

This book is printed on acid-free paper ∞

Manufactured in the United States of America

James S. Baugess: For Leo and Gloria Baugess,
beloved parents who raised me during this turbulent period, and
Rev. Tommy Thurston, who survived Vietnam.

Abbe Allen DeBolt: Dedicated with love and respect
to my grandparents, Rollin Allen and Ruth Wilson Sims.

Contents

Guide to Related Topics

Art and Architecture

Avedon, Richard

Calder, Alexander

Frankenthaler, Helen

Gropius, Walter

Johns, Jasper

Judd, Donald

Lichtenstein, Roy

Max, Peter

Minimalism

Op Art

Pei, I. M.

Performance Art

Pop Art

Skidmore, Owings & Merrill

Smithson, Robert

Stella, Frank

Venturi, Robert Charles

Civil Rights

Abernathy, Ralph

Albany Movement

Angelou, Maya

Birmingham, Alabama

Bond, Horace Julian

Carmichael, Stokely

Chisholm, Shirley

Civil Disobedience

Civil Rights Act of 1960

Civil Rights Act of 1964

Civil Rights Movement

Congress of Racial Equality (CORE)

Council of Federated Organizations (COFO)

Detroit Riots

Evers, Medgar

Forman, James

Freedom Rides

Freedom Summer

Greensboro Sit-In

Hamer, Fannie Lou

Height, Dorothy Irene

Jackson, Jesse

King, Martin Luther, Jr.

Kozol, Jonathan

March on Washington (1963)

March on Washington (1968)

March to Selma

Marshall, Thurgood

Meredith, James

Mississippi Burning Murders

Mississippi Freedom Democratic Party

Motley, Constance Baker

National Association for the Advancement of Colored People (NAACP)

Randolph, Asa Philip

Rustin, Bayard

Shuttlesworth, Fred

Southern Christian Leadership Conference (SCLS)

Student Nonviolent Coordination Committee (SNCC)

United Klans of America (UKA)

Voting Rights Act of 1965

White Citizens' Councils

Cold War

Berlin Crisis

Brandt, Willy

Brezhnev, Leonid Ilich

Castro, Fidel

Cuban Missile Crisis

Guevara, Ernesto "Che"

Glassboro Summit

Kosygin, Alexi

Nuclear Test Ban Treaty

Prague Spring Movement

Pueblo Incident

Tito, Josip Broz

Government and Politics

Abzug, Bella

Agnew, Spiro

Alliance for Progress

American Communist Party

Bundy Brothers

Central Intelligence Agency (CIA) (1960–1969)

Clean Air Act

Clean Water Act

Daley, Richard

Democratic Party (1960–1969)

Democratic Party National Convention of 1968

Dirksen, Everett

Dulles, Allen Welsh

Federal Bureau of Investigation (1960–1969)

Freedom of Information Act of 1966

Fulbright, James William

Goldwater, Barry

Great Society

Head Start

Humphrey, Hubert H.

"Ich Bin Ein Berliner" Speech

Immigration and Naturalization Amendment Acts of 1965

Job Corps

Johnson, Lyndon Baines

Kennedy, Edward Moore

Kennedy, John F.

Kennedy, Robert F.

Kennedy's Inaugural Address

Kissinger, Henry

Lodge, Henry Cabot

Mansfield, Michael Joseph

McCarthy, Eugene

Medicare/Medicaid

Mink, Patsy Takemoto

Model Cities Program

New Frontier

Nixon, Richard Milhous

Nixon-Kennedy Debates

Paris Peace Talks

Pentagon Papers

Reagan's Speech on Behalf of Barry Goldwater: "A Time for Choosing"

Republican Party

Rusk, Dean

Silent Majority

Smith, Margret Chase

War on Poverty

Young, Andrew

Moratorium to End the War in Vietnam
My Lai
Operation Mongoose
Operation Phoenix
Operation Rolling Thunder
Paris Peace Talks
Pleiku
17th Parallel
Taylor, Maxwell
Tet Offensive
Thieu, Nguyen Van
Viet Cong
Viet Minh
Vietnam Veterans Against the War (VVAW)
Vietnam War
Vietnamization

Women

Abzug, Bella
Angelou, Maya
Baez, Joan Chandos
Ball, Lucille
Bra Burning
Brooks, Gwendolyn
Callas, Maria
Child, Julia
Fleming, Peggy

Friedan, Betty
Funicello, Annette
Graham, Katharine
Griffiths, Martha
Height, Dorothy
Hepburn, Audrey
Johnson, Claudia Alta Taylor
Joplin, Janis
King, Billie Jean
Liuzzo, Viola
Lynn, Loretta
Mansfield, Jayne
Miss America (1960–1969)
Mitchell, Joni
Monroe, Marilyn
National Organization for Women (NOW)
National Women's Political Caucus (NWPC)
Rigg, Diana
Roosevelt, Eleanor
Schlafly, Phyllis
Smith, Margaret Chase
Steinem, Gloria
Susann, Jacqueline
Twiggy
Vreeland, Diana
Wynette, Tammy

Preface

The *Encyclopedia of the Sixties: A Decade of Culture and Counterculture* examines individuals, groups, movements, and ideas that made the 1960s unique. The decade was a turbulent period that has had momentous consequences for all subsequent decades. The generation that occupied the campuses of the period now runs the Western world, and though the values of some have changed or turned rightward, many are as flamboyant and radicalized now as in the years 1964–1969. The difference between this volume and others on the 1960s is marked. Most books on the period stress the life and times of the New Left and the eccentricities of the period, but we have elected to stress both counterculture and *traditional* culture.

Not all citizens of the period wore flamboyant clothes, practiced free love, and consumed illegal substances. The era is famous for acid rock and protest songs, but this was also the decade of Elvis Presley's stunning comeback, and was a renaissance for legendary country performers, such as Merle Haggard, who wrote and sang "antiprotest" anthems with lyrics about pride in traditional values. The decade began with the eloquence of John Kennedy, but also the directness of Barry Goldwater and the populism of Lyndon Johnson. Hence, culture is as large a part of the content of these volumes as is counterculture. Conservatism was also cool on many college campuses, hence the growth of Campus Crusade for Christ and the Young Americans for Freedom. The Port Huron Statement of the Students for a Democratic Society (SDS) was a manifesto for the New Left, but the Sharon Statement served the same function for students who looked to William F. Buckley and Barry Goldwater as their mentors.

This work is designed to provide readers at all levels of interest with the beginning or rudimentary knowledge of movements, issues, and upheavals in American history in the 1960s. The encyclopedia contains almost 500 alphabetically arranged entries. Cross-references connect related terms and entries, a chronology of *key* events (not exhaustive or day-by-day) provides a thorough overview, and an annotated bibliography facilitates further research. The annotated bibliography is one of the strengths of the book because we sought to target adolescents, community college students,

Bibliography

Berg, Manfred. *The Ticket to Freedom: The NAACP and the Struggle for Black Political Integration.* Tampa: University of Florida Press, 2005.

Hughes, Langston. *Fight for Freedom: The Story of the NAACP.* New York: W. W. Norton, 1962.

Janken, Kenneth Robert. *Walter White: Mr. NAACP.* Chapel Hill: University of North Carolina Press, 2006.

Jonas, Gilbert. *Freedom's Sword: The NAACP and the Struggle Against Racism in America, 1909–1969.* New York: Taylor and Francis, 2004.

Reed, Christopher Robert. *The Chicago NAACP and the Rise of Black Professional Leadership, 1910–1966.* Bloomington: University of Indiana Press, 1997.

Sullivan, Patricia. *Lift Every Voice: The NAACP and the Making of the Civil Rights Movement.* New York: New Press, 2009.

Tushnet, Mark V. *The NAACP's Legal Strategy Against Segregated Education, 1925–1950.* Chapel Hill: University of North Carolina Press, 1987.

Verney, Kevern, ed. *Long Is the Way and Hard: One Hundred Years of the NAACP.* Little Rock: University of Arkansas Press, 2009.

Wedin, Carolyn. *Inheritors of the Spirit: Mary White Ovington and the Founding of the NAACP.* New York: John Wiley, 1998.

HETTIE V. WILLIAMS

NADER, RALPH (1934–). Ralph Nader was born on February 27, 1934, in Winsted, Connecticut. The son of Lebanese immigrants to the United States, Nader famously arrived on the American political scene with his 1965 indictment of the American auto industry, *Unsafe at Any Speed.* A graduate of Princeton University and Harvard Law School, Nader began to practice law in Hartford, Connecticut, in 1959. In the early 1960s, he became increasingly interested in automobile accidents for which the drivers were blamed but that he believed caused by the automobiles themselves.

Unsafe at Any Speed immediately became a best seller. Although the book attacked the U.S. auto industry in general for designing and manufacturing unsafe vehicles, Nader singled out General Motors and its Corvair for special censure. *Unsafe at Any Speed* became a national phenomenon and led to a series of new laws, most importantly the 1966 National Traffic and Motor Vehicle Safety Act. In this act, Congress gave the federal government the responsibility to enact nationally uniform safety standards for automobiles.

Leading up to the congressional vote on the Safety Act, General Motors went to extreme measures to damage Nader's reputation. In 1966, when Nader learned that the automobile company had hired a private investigator to dig into his personal life, he sued. In 1970, General Motors settled out of court for $425,000, money that Nader reinvested in his growing public advocacy empire.

In 1968, *Newsweek* depicted Nader as the nation's foremost "consumer crusader" and featured him on its cover dressed in a suit of armor. The public interest in Nader's personality, which included extensive interviews in *Time* and the *New Yorker*, emphasized his rejection of the trappings of modern society. The ascetic Nader—who refused to drive a car or live in expensive housing—was embraced as a selfless advocate dedicated to his causes.

And, although some commentators argued that the straight-laced Nader lacked humility, by the late 1960s and early 1970s, the many organizations linked to his Public Interest Research Group became known as the "Nader network." This network included several different public advocacy organizations, which took strong stands on a number of issues, including nuclear safety, the protection of Native Americans, and the regulation of insecticides. Several pieces of legislation emerged from these efforts, most importantly the Wholesale Meat Act, the Cigarette Labeling Act, the Child Protection and Toy Safety Act, and the Occupational Safety and Health Act.

Nader also mobilized a generation of young lawyers and civil advocates, known collectively as "Nader's raiders," in groups established as state and local members of the Public Interest Research Group. These organizations, now working on all levels of government, continued to pressure officials to improve regulation.

Nader's ascendant popularity in many circles and ubiquitous presence in U.S. politics pointed toward a trend in the 1960s. As an expansive middle class developed an activist stance on many social issues, most importantly civil rights and peace protest, the public interest politics promoted by Nader became equated with a broad critique of corporate power. Nader himself most clearly articulated this critique in his 1986 book, coauthored with William Taylor, *The Big Boys: Power and Position in American Business*. Corporations, according to this critique, had become self-serving profiteers that no longer responded to their customers' needs nor were true representatives of the American ideal of free enterprise.

In the late 1990s, although an extended period of antiregulatory politics succeeding in depicting Naderism as an encroachment on the free market, Nader continued in the national spotlight as the Green Party's presidential candidate. In 2000, his campaign not only emphasized consumer protections, but also called for campaign finance reform and universal health care. Although he received only 2.7 percent of the national vote, many commentators argued that he aided the Republican candidate, George W. Bush, by attracting votes in key states, especially Florida, that would have gone to the Democratic candidate, Al Gore.

See also Corvair; *Unsafe at Any Speed* (1965).

Bibliography

Hilton, Matthew. *Prosperity for All: Consumer Activism in the Era of Globalization*. Ithaca, NY: Cornell University Press, 2009.

Nader, Ralph, and William Taylor. *The Big Boys: Power and Position in American Business*. New York: Pantheon, 1986.

Nader, Ralph. *The Ralph Nader Reader*. New York: Seven Stories, 2000.

CHRISTOPHER DIETRICH

NAMATH, JOE (1943–). Born on May 31, 1943, to a Hungarian immigrant family in hardscrabble Beaver Falls, Pennsylvania, Joseph William Namath defined the modern NFL quarterback and sports celebrity. Extraordinary athleticism enabled Namath to transcend a broken home, shattered childhood, and delinquent proclivities.

Defying convention and authority, the beret wearing, chain-smoking Namath played college football for the notoriously authoritarian Paul "Bear" Bryant at the University of Alabama. Namath, surprisingly, took to Bryant's fatherly yet dictatorial style. On the field, the famously conservative Bryant allowed Namath to throw the football, set records, and most importantly, win games.

Upon graduation, Namath seemed destined for stardom in the National Football League (NFL). David Abraham "Sonny" Werblin, owner of the American Football League (AFL) New York Jets, drafted and awarded Namath a $400,000 contract. In tune with America's swirling cultural winds, Namath took New York and the national media by storm. Quotable and colorful, Namath took full advantage of New York's nightlife, which only added to his legend. Telling one reporter, "I don't date so much as I just, you know, run into something, man," Namath earned his place in the city tabloids.

In a sport where stars, at least publicly, followed their coach's dictates and refused the limelight, Namath came to define sports celebrity. With Namath and other young stars building the AFL's popularity in 1966, the NFL was forced to merge with its junior upstart. Despite the ratings gold, AFL president Milt Woodward once suggested that Namath and his teammates shave their facial hair and "conform with the generally accepted idea of an American athlete's appearance."

While every other Jets player shaved, Namath refused to shear his Fu Manchu moustache—until the Schick razor company paid him $10,000 as part of a promotion. Combining the era's rebellious zeitgeist with a nose for media and advertising, Namath became the NFL's most marketable young quarterback.

On the field, Namath led the Jets to respectability and beyond. In 1967, he became the first NFL quarterback to pass for more than 4,000 yards in a single season. More importantly, he starred in two of the league's most important games ever.

In November 1968, Namath's Jets were locked in a close and hard-fought game against the Oakland Raiders. After Namath put the Jets up by three points with a minute left to play, NBC switched from the game to its regularly scheduled broadcast of the movie, *Heidi*. Angry callers so swamped NBC's switchboard that broadcasters now televise games in their entirety.

In the same season, Namath also led the Jets to the AFL championship and a berth in Super Bowl III. Three nights before the game, Namath famously "guaranteed" a Jets victory. With his team a significant underdog compared to the Baltimore Colts, most observers expected Namath to eat his words. Instead, Namath's Jets defeated Baltimore, 16–7, in one of professional sports most celebrated upsets. Finally, quieting critics who questioned his toughness and ability to lead his team to a Super Bowl victory, Namath was unquestionably *the* sports icon of the rebellious and raucous 1960s.

Bibliography

Anderson, David. "Namath Takes It Off—at $10 a Clip." New York *Times*, December 12, 1968.

Lake, John. "Two for the Football Show: The Swinger and the Square." *New York Times*, November 5, 1967.

JEFFREY H. BLOODWORTH

NAPALM. As part of a program by the U.S. Army Chemical Warfare Service to develop a useful incendiary, an organic chemist at Harvard University invented napalm during World War II. A gelatinous flammable explosive based on gasoline, napalm was named for the aluminum salts naphthenate and palmate, which were originally used to thicken gasoline into a gel. Widely used in both World War II and the Korean War, it attracted more media attention during the Vietnam War.

A flame-throwing tank of the U.S. 1st Tank Battalion, 1st Marine Division. The M67A1 (nicknamed the "Zippo") was the M48 variant employed in Vietnam. It had an effective range of 100 to 150 yards. (National Archives)

During Vietnam, a new, more portent formulation known as napalm-B, or super-napalm, was used in place of the original napalm mixture. Super-napalm could burn up to 10 minutes at 2,000 degrees Fahrenheit, adhered to human skin, and sucked the oxygen out of the air. Principally used in air-dropped munitions, napalm could kill or wound persons by immolation or by asphyxiation and remove vegetative cover. On human skin napalm caused intensely painful and disfiguring injuries that required advanced medical resources to prevent infection and death. While incendiary munitions had long been used in warfare for antipersonnel and defoliant effects, and the American rules of engagement did not prohibit its use, napalm became a subject of moral debate.

In 1965, concerns about napalm were attributed to effective communist propaganda, and most of the public had never heard of the substance. Increasingly, media reports about napalm galvanized protest because it was seen to be indiscriminate in its effects and to inflict horrifying wounds on noncombatants. Napalm protests were most often aimed at the Dow Chemical Company, a relatively minor defense contractor that manufactured napalm for the military from 1965 to 1969. Segments of the antiwar movement boycotted Dow's consumer goods, including Saran Wrap. In addition to boycotts, activists also participated in acts of civil disobedience. In May 1966, four women dressed as homemakers—in high heels, dresses, and pearls—obstructed the transport of napalm. Beginning in October 1966, when Dow's recruiters came to college campuses, they faced protests, including placards reading, "Dow Shalt Not Kill."

In January 1967, the antiwar magazine *Ramparts* ran an article, "The Children of Vietnam," claiming that a million Vietnamese children had been killed in the war, many by napalm, and illustrated it with shocking photos of young napalm victims. An article in *Ladies' Home Journal* the same month described the melted flesh on children burned by napalm in a provincial hospital. Such stories catalyzed antiwar sentiment, and anti-Dow demonstrations multiplied. The antiwar movement often employed photographs of children burned by napalm. After a particularly eventful demonstration at the University of Wisconsin in October 1967, the company launched a public relations campaign to refute the charges leveled against it by the antiwar movement. When Dow's napalm contract came up for renewal in 1969, the company (perhaps purposely) lost the bid to American Electric, Inc. for the remainder of the war.

Perhaps the most iconic photo of the war was that of a terrified, severely burned nine-year-old Vietnamese girl, Kim Phuc, who was pictured running down a road naked among other children after South Vietnamese forces dropped napalm on her village. The photograph ran on the cover of newspapers around the world. In America, "napalm" came to represent much that was inhumane about the American war effort—the indiscriminate use of American firepower and the horrific, disproportionate suffering this caused to South Vietnamese civilians.

Due to the widespread media attention napalm received during the Vietnam War, it became an issue among the international community. Studies of napalm conducted by the United Nations Secretary General and the International Committee of the Red Cross catalyzed UN resolutions that proposed a ban on napalm and other incendiaries. Each time the votes passed, but the U.S. abstained from all such votes, and is not, therefore, bound by them. The U.S. Army Manual continues to permit its use against military targets without technically violating international law.

See also Vietnam War.

Bibliography

Chomsky, Noam. "Dow Shalt Not Kill." In Howard Zinn, ed. *The Zinn Reader: Writings on Disobedience and Democracy*. New York: Seven Stories, 1997, pp. 314–21.

Chong, Denise. *The Girl in the Picture: The Story of Kim Phuc, the Photograph, and the Vietnam War*. New York: Viking, 2000.

Conway-Lanz, Sahr. *Collateral Damage: Americans, Noncombat Immunity, and Atrocity after World War II*. New York: Routledge, 2006.

Franklin, H. Bruce. "Burning Illusions: The Napalm Campaign." In Mary Susannah Robbins, ed. *Against the Vietnam War: Writings by Activist*. Syracuse, NY: Syracuse University Press, 1999, pp. 62–75.

Gellhorn, Martha. "Suffer the Little Children . . . " *Ladies' Home Journal* 84, no. 1 (January 1967): 57, 107–110.

Maraniss, David. *They Marched into Sunlight: War and Peace, Vietnam and America, October 1967*. New York: Simon & Schuster, 2003.

Pepper, William F. "The Children of Vietnam." *Ramparts* (January 1967): 46–68.

United Nations. *Report by the Secretary General on Napalm and Other Incendiary Weapons and All Aspects of their Possible Use*. New York: United Nations, 1972.

KEVIN WILSON

NATIONAL ASSOCIATION FOR THE ADVANCEMENT OF COLORED PEOPLE. *See* NAACP (1960–1969)

NATIONAL ORGANIZATION FOR WOMEN (NOW). Founded in 1966, the National Organization for Women (NOW) became a leading civil rights group pursing social, legal, economic, and political equality for women. Growing out of a Washington, D.C., meeting of representatives from the state and federal Commissions on the Status of Women, NOW intended "to take action to bring women into full participation in the mainstream of American society now, assuming all the privileges and responsibilities thereof in truly equal partnership with men" ("The National Organization for Women's 1966 Founding Statement").

Founding members included white journalist Betty Friedan, white union activists Caroline Davis and Dorothy Haener from the United Auto Workers, and the African American lawyer Pauline Murray. Despite the relative diversity represented at its founding, NOW's membership and leadership were drawn overwhelmingly from middle-class and professional white women. In 1966, for example, the board included university administrators and professors, state and national labor union officials, government workers, business leaders, physicians, and members of religious clergy.

NOW was self-consciously modeled as an agent to create a "civil rights movement for women." Borrowing its leadership structure, philosophy, and tactics from the African American civil rights movement, the organization sought to reconcile changes in postwar society as increasing numbers of women moved into the labor force. Thus, the organization directed its earliest efforts toward combating gender discrimination in the workplace and in media depictions.

In 1966, NOW's "targets for action" focused on expanding equal employment opportunities, particularly in positions funded by federal contracts. It also concentrated its efforts on making child care more affordable, increasing the enforcement powers of the Equal Employment Opportunity Commission (EEOC), lobbying for equal educational resources for women, and creating job training for women reentering the labor force after years of homemaking. In the late 1960s and 1970s, the organization broadened its agenda to include improving women's health care, supporting expressions of sexuality, and ending violence against women.

During much of the 1960s, NOW largely kept matters of sexuality out of its agenda. Its founding statement included no mention of homosexuality or reproductive rights. This omission reflected the policy concerns of its founders and an assumption that restructured gender and family roles were not within the purview of a lobbying group. Nevertheless, the organization's founders rejected the notion that "a man must carry the sole burden of supporting himself, his wife and family ... or that marriage, home and family are primarily woman's world and responsibility— hers to dominate—his to support." They believed "that a true partnership between the sexes demands a different concept of marriage, an equitable sharing of the responsibilities of home and children and of the economic burdens of their support."

Throughout the decade, NOW's membership grew rapidly across the nation. Within one year of its founding, the organization claimed 1,200 members organizing in local and state chapters. Even so, NOW's influence was wider than its membership. The organization benefitted tremendously from leaders who had experience lobbying the federal government and dealing with the media.

NOW's notable achievements in the 1960s included campaigns to end sex-segregated want ads in newspapers across the country, efforts to pressure federal officials to include sex as a class of discrimination in federal contracts, and fights to push the EEOC to enforce Title VII of the 1964 Civil Rights Act, which prohibited discrimination on the basis of race, religion, national origin, and sex. In 1969, Marguerite Rawalt and Sylvia Roberts, members of NOW's Legal Committee, successfully argued the *Weeks v. Southern Bell* case before the Supreme Court, which overturned protective labor laws premised on gender differences.

NOW's early years witnessed a number of internal disputes and conflicts. In 1967, the organization's support for the Equal Rights Amendment led to the resignation of several union members. Other women left NOW after it endorsed legalized abortion in 1968 because they feared such a position would deflect attention from employment and education discrimination. (They went on to form WEAL, the Women's Equity Action League.)

More fundamentally, NOW often drew criticism from younger, more radical feminists who rejected its emphasis on political activism. Differences in strategy, philosophy, and organizing separated NOW's liberal reform efforts with those of more radical women's liberationists. Women's liberationists derided the organization as too hierarchical, too reliant on "expert" leadership, and too moderate. These activists hoped to overthrow social and political systems rather than reform them as NOW sought to do.

In the 1970s and beyond, however, NOW and the radical feminists found common ground on a number of issues and increasingly shared membership. NOW has remained one of the longest-lasting and most influential civil rights organizations of the 1960s.

See also Friedan, Betty (1921–2006).

Bibliography

Barakso, Maryann. *Governing NOW: Grassroots Activism in the National Organization for Women*. Ithaca, NY: Cornell University Press, 2004.

Evans, Sara M. *Tidal Wave: How Women Changed America at Century's End*. New York: Free Press, 2003.

Harrison, Cynthia. *On Account of Sex: The Politics of Women's Issues, 1945–1968*. Berkeley: University of California Press, 1988.

National Organization for Women. "The National Organization for Women's 1966 Founding Statement." Available at http://www.now.org/history/purpos66.html.

Rosen, Ruth. *The World Split Open: How the Modern Women's Movement Changed America*. New York: Viking, 2003.

KATE KEANE

NATIONAL WOMEN'S POLITICAL CAUCUS (NWPC) (1971). Discrimination against women in credit laws, educational opportunities, and health—especially the high rate of infant mortality—brought together feminists Betty Friedan and Bella Abzug along with Shirley Anita St. Hill, the first African American woman in Congress; American Indian activist LaDonna Harris; Beulah Sanders of the National Welfare Rights Organization; and Fannie Lou Hamer, one of the founders of the Mississippi Freedom Democratic Party, in Washington, D.C. in July 1971 to form the National Women's Political Caucus (NWPC). The NWPC supported women running for office at civic, municipal, county, state and territorial, Congress, and Senate levels. The founders believed—and their supporters and candidates knew—that improvement in representation would raise the profile of women's issues. The NWPC became a political action committee with local and state caucuses in 38 states and a national 21-member steering committee in an atmosphere of women's consciousness raising and activism gaining in momentum in the late 1960s and early 1970s.

The NWPC believes in the power of people to change incrementally the American political system for women; members provided campaign training. In 1977, the caucus started to financially support candidates running for political office, and its steering committee expected primarily women, but in Santa Clara County, California, men too, to be in favor of abortion rights, flex-time for federal government employees, information on family planning, daycare, increases in the federal minimum wage, and lesbian and gay rights. Until the failure of the Equal Rights Amendment in 1982, the NWPC only endorsed candidates who supported the passage of the amendment. After 1977, contenders were expected to campaign for Medicaid funding for abortion and expansion of the federal food stamp program. Overall political allies would be committed to arresting sexism, racism, classism, and ageism. The NWPC has always supported both Democrat and Republican candidates, although the majority are Democrats (more than twice as likely as Republican candidates to receive endorsement and financial support) despite attempts to divide leadership through separate Democratic and Republican Women's Task Forces. From 1977 to 1981 the caucus's Coalition for Women's Appointments submitted candidates to President Jimmy Carter for cabinet secretaries, undersecretaries, and judgeships and was able to get 42 women appointed as judges in federal courts.

In addition to helping women get elected and appointed to political offices, the NWPC has researched the goals of women candidates and attitudes toward women and has tracked the voting records of politicians on women's issues. Its 1974 survey of women candidates found that all placed women's issues in their campaigns. Later on it sought to understand the barriers identified by citizens to full participation of women in politics as a means to advance women from the state legislatures to Congress. Surveys conducted in 1987 and 1992 found that women were thought of as weaker in terms of political literacy. These same surveys noted that women politicians—both Republican and Democrat—were thought to be more honest than men, less susceptible to sway from special interest groups, and cared more for individuals, but these same respondents doubted women's effectiveness and toughness. From the Ninety-fifth Congress of 1977–1978 until the 101st Congress of 1989–1990, the NWPC monitored support of women in Congress for policy priority areas and found that women across the two parties supported women's issues consistently and more often than did congressmen.

The Republican-dominated Congress and Senate from the early 1980s and into the 1990s attracted women to the membership of the organization, and its numbers grew as legal abortion was put in jeopardy by motions from the federal government to restrict access or recriminalize abortion as well as birth control and court rulings in favor of such policy directions. In 1982, the NWPC grew from 13,000 to 73,000 members, and Republican Kathy Wilson was president from 1981 to 1989. The growth in membership aggravated conflicts between the white, middle-class women and women of African American and Hispanic backgrounds who believed the caucus concentrated exclusively on abortion rights to the detriment of campaigns to stimulate governmental investment in early childhood programs and health.

The NWPC continues to encourage women through education and financial support to run for all political offices in the United States. Its focus continues to be on women's issues, especially maintaining abortion rights (National Women's Political Caucus, para. 1). Its leaders and stakeholders, however, have never deviated from the belief in the power of women to effect change through participation in political office.

Bibliography

Berry, Mary Frances. *Why ERA Failed: Politics, Women's Rights, and the Amending Process of the Constitution.* Everywoman: Studies in History, Literature, & Culture. Bloomington: Indiana University Press, 1988.

Burrell, Barbara C. *A Woman's Place Is in the House: Campaigning for Congress in the Feminist Era.* Ann Arbor: University of Michigan Press, 1994.

Davis, Flora. *Moving the Mountain: The Women's Movement in America since 1960.* Urbana: University of Illinois Press, 1999.

Ferree, Myra Marx, and Beth B. Hess. *Controversy and Coalition: The New Feminist Movement.* 3rd ed. New York: Routledge, 1995.

Flammang, Janet A. *Women's Political Voice: How Women Are Transforming the Practice and Study of Politics.* Philadelphia: Temple University Press, 1997.

Gill, Laverne McCain. *African American Women in Congress: Forming and Transforming History.* Rutgers, NJ: Rutgers University Press, 1997.

Mills, Kay. *This Little Light of Mine: The Life of Fannie Lou Hamer.* Toronto: Penguin Books, 1994.

National Women's Political Caucus. "About Us." 2010. Available at http://www.nwpc.org/ht/d/CaucusDetails/i/178/aboutus/Y/pid/937 (accessed January 18, 2010).

National Women's Political Caucus. "National Women's Political Caucus." 2010. Available at http://www.nwpc.org/.(accessed January 18, 2010).

National Women's Political Caucus. "National Women's Political Caucus." 2010. Available at http://nwpc.org/ht/d/Faqs/pid/945. (accessed January 18, 2010).

National Women's Political Caucus. "NWPC Past Presidents." 2010. Available at http://www.nwpc.org/ht/d/sp/i/42652/pid/42652. (accessed January 18, 2010).

Rymph, Catherine E. *Republican Women: Feminism and Conservatism from Suffrage through the Rise of the New Right. Gender & American Culture.* Chapel Hill: University of North Carolina Press, 2006.

Steiner, Gilbert Yale. *Constitutional Inequality: The Political Fortunes of the Equal Rights Amendment.* Washington, DC: Brookings Institution, 1985.

JONATHAN ANUIK

NEW FRONTIER, THE. The "New Frontier" was a set of legislative priorities of the Kennedy administration that were geared toward updating liberalism beyond the New Deal. It rested on three fundamental assumptions: an internationalist foreign policy, the necessity of domestic reform, and a liberalism that was committed to human freedom abroad and national greatness at home.

The New Frontier was a product of the cultural, intellectual, and social milieu of the 1950s. Intellectuals such as Daniel Bell embraced and feared the era's "end of ideology" zeitgeist. Championing the liberal welfare state's modest goals and skepticism, Bell, nevertheless, feared the West would sink into an abyss of complacency and mediocrity. While intellectuals fretted, the Soviet's 1957 launch of the world's first Earth-orbiting satellite, *Sputnik*, not only created mass consternation but seemingly validated Bell's worries. Thus, the late 1950s featured the convergence of popular and elite opinion, as both expressed a fear of American drift and decline. Believing he needed to "jump-start" America from the staid Eisenhower years, Kennedy called the New Frontier a "set of challenges" rather than promises.

The catchphrase "New Frontier" began as John F. Kennedy's presidential campaign slogan, unveiled at the 1960 Democratic National Convention in Los Angeles. Linking his program to Woodrow Wilson's New Freedom and Franklin Roosevelt's New Deal, Kennedy also tried to make his theme distinct. Rather than represent a "set of [campaign] promises," in his acceptance speech, Kennedy claimed the New Frontier symbolized the challenges of a new era rather than the "safe mediocrity of the past." As a public relations tool, the New Frontier effectively communicated the Kennedy campaign's essence by reminding voters of the senator's youth and vigor. As part of the campaign, Kennedy launched a New Frontier "style offensive," which included a carefully orchestrated media campaign that sold the Kennedy image. Appearing in the pages of *Redbook* and *Life* with his wife Jackie, the smiling and attractive image of the couple was designed to appeal to an increasingly affluent and middle-class electorate.

In his inaugural address, Kennedy evoked the New Frontier's sense of mission that a generation of Americans had come to associate with activist Democratic presidents. Central to the New Frontier was Kennedy's commitment to reviving an activist executive branch. Believing that the president was more than a moral and political leader, Kennedy wanted nothing less than to "unleash the president from the office of the presidency."

While Kennedy was a traditional Cold Warrior, his New Frontier foreign policy employed an array of innovative policies to combat communism. Unlike the Eisenhower administration, which relied heavily on nuclear deterrence, Kennedy endorsed a number of programs that were part foreign aid and part public diplomacy. Three programs in particular—Food for Peace, the Alliance for Progress, and the Peace Corps—underline the multipronged strategy the administration employed to combat communist expansion in the Third World.

Kennedy's most iconic program, launched by executive order in 1961, was the Peace Corps. While the Peace Corps's concrete achievements in the developing world were uneven, the program enhanced America's image abroad and changed the lives of tens of thousands of the volunteers, many of whom returned to the United States recommitted to achieving reform and social justice at home. For liberal intellectuals, the New Frontier was designed to achieve "national greatness." Thus, from a strictly political perspective, the New Frontier offered traditional domestic liberal initiatives, or quantitative liberalism, designed to delight the party faithful while also updating liberalism for an age of affluence.

Constrained by Congress in domestic matters, Kennedy's New Frontier was reflected in the administration's novel "style." In this way, Kennedy changed the office of the president by establishing a number of precedents that his successors seized on with varying results. Persuaded by his press secretary, Pierre Salinger, Kennedy became the first president to hold live press conferences on television. With an engaging wit and ready reply, the president's press conferences were an immediate sensation. Part and parcel of the style offensive was the First Lady. Aloof and uninterested in performing traditional roles, Jackie Kennedy became instrumental in making the White House a cultural center. Though she was infamously more interested in water-skiing off Cape Cod than meeting with the Girl Scouts of America or the Red Cross, Jackie Kennedy labored tirelessly on her best-selling book *The White House: An Historic Guide*. In this way, the New Frontier's significance transcended legislative accomplishments.

Like the truncated Kennedy administration, the New Frontier's legacy is based more on style than substance. Despite the president's paltry legislative achievements, the New Frontier's attempt at modernization looms significant due to Lyndon Johnson's significant failings.

See also Kennedy, John F. (1917–1963).

Bibliography

Dallek, Robert. *An Unfinished Life: John F. Kennedy, 1917–1963*. New York: Little, Brown, 2003.

Giglio, James. *The Presidency of John F. Kennedy*. 2nd ed. Lawrence: University of Kansas Press, 2006.

Hamby, Alonzo. *Liberalism and Its Challengers: From F.D.R. to Bush*. New York: Oxford University Press, 1985.

Mattson, Kevin. *When America Was Great: The Fighting Faith of Postwar Liberalism*. New York: Routledge, 2004.

JEFFREY H. BLOODWORTH

NEW YORK WORLD'S FAIR (1964–1965). The New York World's Fair of 1964–1965 is best remembered as a showcase of mid-twentieth-century American culture and technology and for the autocratic style of Robert Moses, the well-known builder who headed the corporation that ran the fair. Although it offered unprecedented exhibitions of architecture, rides, and films all created especially for it, the New York World's Fair did not live up to expectations, which included a potential 73 million visitors and $28 million in advance ticket sales. During its run, which was actually two six-month seasons (April 22–October 18, 1964, and April 21–October 17, 1965), the fair suffered from difficult public relations, financial blunders, and the lack of international support.

This 1964–1965 event was the third major world's fair to be held in New York City. It was constructed on 646-acre site in Flushing Meadows, in the borough of Queens, which had also been the site of the classic 1939–1940 New York World's Fair. The 1964–1965 theme, "Peace Through Understanding," commemorated the 300th anniversary of the founding of New York as an English colony. The fair was dedicated to "Man's Achievement on a Shrinking Globe in an Expanding Universe," and it was symbolized by a 12-story, stainless-steel model of the Earth called Unisphere, the largest representation of the Earth ever made, which remains today the principal symbol of the fair.

The 1964–1965 Fair was conceived in the late 1950s by a group of New York businessmen, led by lawyer Robert Kopple; they were reminiscing about the 1939–1940 fair and decided to provide that same experience for others. To obtain the private financing and sell bonds to fund the project, the organizers appointed

Visitors to the second day of the New York World's Fair fill the roadway under a cloudless sky in New York on April 23, 1964. By mid-afternoon more than 100,000 people were on the fairgrounds enjoying the attractions, which included a view from the towers of the New York state pavilion, left background; a ride on the Swiss sky-ride cable cars; and a look at the giant Unisphere, the dominant structure of the fair. (AP/Wide World Photos)

Robert Moses—chairman of the Triborough Bridge and Transit Authority and the promoter of the 1939–1940 fair—to run this event through his World's Fair Corporation. Moses had overseen construction of much of the city's highway infrastructure and, in his capacity as parks commissioner, had spearheaded creation of much of the city's park system. However, the ultimate success or failure of the fair came to depend on Moses's autocratic nature and the authorities that he controlled. Moses and his staff had many public projects under development at the time, and they had no experience in organizing a world's fair, nor did they consult with outsiders. The Fair Corporation granted monopolies and expensive cost-plus contracts without competitive bidding. Exhibitors were required to use insurance, maintenance, garbage collection, trucking, and other services at inflated prices, while restaurant concessions were given to fair directors.

These decisions antagonized all involved or interested parties, including local governments, private participants, the press, and the Bureau of International Expositions (BIE), the international body in Paris that sanctions world's fairs. When the BIE refused to sanction the fair, a domino effect developed. The BIE formally requested its members not to participate in the 1964 season, a decision that undoubtedly hurt the fair. Canada, Australia, most of the major European nations (except Spain), and the Soviet Union, all BIE members, did not officially participate, although private European exhibits came from Belgium, Berlin, France, Sweden, and Switzerland, while Austria, Denmark, Greece, Ireland, and Spain had government support. The nations (approximately 80) that did participate were represented in 37 pavilions, of which about 14 were privately sponsored. Other privately sponsored exhibits represented Israel, Hong Kong, and multinational pavilions from Polynesia, Africa, the Caribbean, and Central America. This was the first U.S. fair to have significant participation from developing nations, but there were also sponsored pavilions from Japan, Mexico, Thailand, Philippines, Greece, Pakistan, and the Vatican State (Holy See). One of the most significant exhibits at the fair, the Vatican pavilion displayed Michelangelo's *Pietà*, his 465-year-old marble sculpture masterpiece, the only time it was shown outside the Vatican. Second to the *Pietà* was Spain's art display of classic and contemporary paintings by El Greco, Goya, Picasso, Miro, and Dali. Beside the Vatican, seven other religious organizations or groups had art and films on exhibit: Protestant-Orthodox, Mormon, Sermons from Science, Billy Graham, Russian Orthodox, Wycliffe Bible, and Christian Science.

More political was Jordan's pavilion, which presented a mural emphasizing the plight of the Palestinian people, but the absence of major European countries and the Fair Corporation's abdication of design theme control allowed commercialism to dominate over internationalism, with the resulting disorganization of individual pavilions competing among themselves for attention as exhibit signs and music conflicted with those of the fair. Recurring design themes were Andy Warhol-style pop art images, buildings floating above the ground, and pavilions set in reflecting pools.

The United States Pavilion, titled "Challenge to Greatness," highlighted President Lyndon Johnson's "Great Society" proposals, while the main show in the pavilion was a filmed presentation of American history along with tributes to the late President John F. Kennedy, who had broken ground for the pavilion in December 1962.

The emerging space program was honored with a two-acre United States Space Park, jointly sponsored by the National Aeronautics Space Administration (NASA), the U.S. Department of Defense, and the Fair Corporation. The Space park exhibits included a full-scale model of the aft skirt and five F-1 engines of the first stage of a Saturn V rocket; a Titan II booster with a Gemini capsule; an Atlas rocket with a Mercury capsule; a Thor-Delta rocket; and Aurora 7, the Mercury capsule flown on the second U.S. manned orbital flight.

The New York State open-air pavilion, "Tent of Tomorrow," was designed by famed modernist architect Philip Johnson. Its highlights included high spot observation towers and a large-scale design of a Texaco highway map of New York State.

The most popular exhibit in terms of attendance was General Motors' Futurama, a moving chair ride that was an updated version of the 1939–1940 Futurama, while Westinghouse provided a new version of the earlier fair's time capsule. Another popular exhibit was IBM's giant 500-seat grandstand propelled by hydraulic rams high up into a rooftop theater where a film showed the workings of computer logic. The Bell System gave visitors a ride in moving armchairs and presented an exhibit that depicted the history of communications in dioramas and film. DuPont's theme was chemistry; its exhibit featured a musical review by composer Michael Brown ("The Wonderful World of Chemistry"). Ford Motor Company plugged into the overall commercialism of the fair by introducing the Ford Mustang at its pavilion on April 17, 1964.

The surprise hit of the fair was a noncommercial movie short presented by S. C. Johnson Wax, *To Be Alive!*, which celebrated the joy of life worldwide as manifested in diverse cultures; it won the 1966 Academy Award for best documentary (short subject) and a special award from the New York Film Critics Circle.

The Walt Disney Company used the fair to develop "audio-animatronics" (automated robotic figures), a combination of sound, mechanical electronics, and computers that controlled the movement of lifelike robots to act out scenes. Disney introduced these figures in four pavilions, including the Pepsi pavilion, where dancing dolls created by Richard and Robert Sherman sang "It's a Small World." After the fair, Disney reproduced many of these figures at its theme parks.

When the fair ended, controversy erupted over allegations of financial mismanagement, though it took accountants a long time to realize that revenues were 40 percent below predictions. Eleven exhibitors filed for bankruptcy due to low attendance and high costs, and the fair coporation had to loan them money to keep them running until the end of the fair's run.

Fair finances looked better than they actually were because unused advance ticket sales were credited to the 1964 season, an accounting mistake realized when

15 million visitors in the 1965 season had prepaid tickets. News of financial problems plagued the fair's second year as Moses and the press began to realize that the fair was almost bankrupt. Moses was the focus of most of the anger and conflict because he tried to use the fair to ensure his personal legacy. The fair's total loss was $21 million, with attendance finally determined at 51 million.

Despite this, the fair achieved its own legacy. The fair site, in Flushing Meadows Park, was much improved, although not in the grand style that Moses wanted, He was, however, able to complete the botanical garden, zoo, and the roads he had promised. The city took possession of the site in June 1967. The fair also succeeded in developing unique architecture and exhibit rides, films, and shows that were much imitated by other commercial and entertainment enterprises.

See also Pop Art.

Bibliography

Bletter, Rosemarie Haag, et al. *Remembering the Future: The New York World's Fair from 1939–1964*. New York: Rizzoli, 1989.

Caro, Robert A. *The Power Broker: Robert Moses and the Fall of New York*. New York: Knopf, 1974.

Findling, John E., and Kimberly D. Pelle, eds. *Encyclopedia of World's Fairs and Expositions*. Jefferson, NC: McFarland, 2008.

Nicholson, Bruce. *Hi, Ho, Come to the Fair: Tales of the New York World's Fair of 1964–1965*. Huntington Beach, CA: Pelagian, 1989.

Samuel, Lawrence R. *The End of the Innocence: The 1964–1965 New York World's Fair*. Syracuse, NY: Syracuse University Press, 2007.

MARTIN J. MANNING

NEWTON, HUEY (1942–1989). Huey Newton is best known as the cofounder and leader of the Black Panther Party. He had a socialist political philosophy, which he used to try and serve Oakland's poor black community. Born on February 17, 1942 in Monroe, Louisiana, Newton was the youngest of seven children. His family moved to Oakland, California, in 1945, hoping to find jobs. Instead, they were met with racism and lived a life of poverty. Though he graduated high school essentially illiterate, he attended Merritt College. There he met Bobby Seale, and the two men founded the Black Panther Party for Self-Defense. The organization's goal was to protect the black community from police brutality. They also cowrote the Black Panther Party's Ten Point Plan, which had such goals as to have trials with juries of their peers and military exemption for African Americans, since they did not want to fight on behalf of a racist nation.

The Black Panther Party was seen as a militant organization since many of its members carried weapons. Newton was familiar with California's penal code and laws in the state regarding weapons, and wanted to make sure that African Americans could exercise their right to carry guns. Since many members were armed, the Panthers immediately caught the attention of both the local police and the Federal Bureau of Investigation (FBI). The Panthers had many conflicts with authority, with the most notorious occurring on October 28, 1967, when Newton, who had been involved in a shoot-out with police, was accused of murdering police officer John Frey. Newton was convinced that he could not get a fair trial for these charges, and the Black

Panthers rallied around him, launching a "Free Huey" campaign. In September 1968, he was convicted of voluntary manslaughter, though the California Supreme Court dismissed the charges in 1970. While the state held two more trials, Newton was never convicted, and the state finally dropped the charges against him.

Following this ordeal, Newton moved away from the program of violence that the Panthers had initially advocated. Noting that police had killed 24 members of the Panthers in less than six years, he believed that the group could do more to help the community than simply to engage authorities in violence. He began to advocate social programs such as providing children with free breakfasts, helping the homeless, and organizing free medical clinics in poor communities. He also returned to school, earning his BA from the University of California-Santa Cruz in 1974.

Even though Newton had seemingly changed, trouble continued to follow him. In 1974, he was arrested for the murder of Kathleen Smith. While he was released on bail, Newton, again believing that he would never get a fair trial, fled to Cuba, where Fidel Castro's socialist policies closely mirrored his own. It was not until 1977 that he returned to the United States, believing that conditions had improved enough that he could receive a fair trial. With little solid evidence against him, Newton was acquitted of Smith's murder. He went on to earn a PhD from the University of California-Santa Cruz in 1980.

In 1985, Newton was charged with embezzling state and local funds that had been given to finance the Black Panthers' community projects. He was convicted in 1989. Before he could serve any jail time, Tyrone Robinson murdered Newton on August 22, 1989.

See also Black Panther Party.

Bibliography

Hillard, David, and Donald Weise. *The Huey P. Newton Reader.* New York: Seven Stories, 2002.

Hillard, David, with Keith and Kent Zimmerman. *Huey: Spirit of the Panther.* New York: Thunder's Mouth, 2006.

Jeffries, Judson L. *Huey P Newton: The Radical Theorist.* Jackson: University Press of Mississippi, 2002.

ELIZABETH BRYANT MORGENSTERN

NICKLAUS, JACK (1940–). Sharing the golfing spotlight with Arnold Palmer and Gary Player throughout the 1960s, Jack Nicklaus was the dominant golfer of that decade, an era when he won an astonishing 30 tour events and seven major championships.

Born in Columbus, Ohio, on January 21, 1940, Nicklaus attended Ohio State University, where he won an NCAA championship (1961) and two U.S. Amateur titles (1959, 1961). Nicklaus turned professional in 1961, his winning ways continuing throughout the 1960s. He won the first of his record 18 major championships (Masters, U.S. Open, British Open, and the PGA) in 1962, his first full year on the professional tour. The 1962 Open came down to an 18-hole playoff between the legendary and wildly popular Palmer and the younger Nicklaus—Jack won by three shots at the famed Oakmont Country Club, often one of the most difficult courses to play. Winning three PGA tour events in 1962 and in the process earning in excess of $60,000, Nicklaus claimed the number three ranking among professional golfers.

He followed his early success with wins at golf's hallowed Masters in 1963 and his third career major at the PGA in Dallas. For the 1963 season, he won five tournaments and topped $100,000 winnings, a mark he would continue to exceed each year of his career (this was during a period when golfers rarely earned more than $50,000 a year on tour).

During his early career, the rather large and muscular Nicklaus was nicknamed the Golden Bear by an Australian writer—the name stuck. His rivalry with Palmer introduced golf's most popular decade before Tiger Woods turned professional in 1996. Nicklaus followed his early success with a decade of triumphs and titles, although he never matched the popular appeal of Palmer. But Nicklaus won two more Masters titles (1965 and 1966), another Open championship in 1967 at Baltusrol in New Jersey, still another of golf's hallowed courses, defeating veteran golfers Tommy Jacobs and Gay Brewer in yet another 18-hole playoff. He completed the career "grand slam"—all four major golf titles—in 1966 at the British Open's historic Muirfield course in Scotland, winning by a single stroke over Doug Sanders and Dave Thomas.

Further testament to Nicklaus's dominance during the decade is his 30 tour championships to go with seven major titles. His tour earnings continued to rise each year, and he approached the unheard-of $200,000 mark in 1968 (five titles, one major, and over $188,000). He led the tour earnings list three times. Nicklaus closed the decade as a pivotal member of the U.S. Ryder Cup team, and became involved in golf course design during that period. If Arnold Palmer rescued golf as a spectator and television sport, Jack Nicklaus led the charge into golf's most successful and popular era.

His golfing career continuing well beyond the 1960s, Nicklaus won a total of 73 PGA tour events, 18 majors, with career earnings in excess of $5.7 million. Honored by numerous halls of fame and other noteworthy awards, including male athlete of the century by *Sports Illustrated* and golfer of the century by virtually all golf publications, Nicklaus is the author of countless books and an unmatched course designer.

Bibliography

Bowden, Ken. *Jack Nicklaus: My Story*. New York: Simon & Schuster, 1997.

O'Connor, Ian. *Arnie & Jack: Palmer, Nicklaus, and Golf's Greatest Rivalry*. Boston: Houghton Mifflin, 2008.

Sampson, Curt. *The Eternal Summer: Palmer, Nicklaus, and Hogan in 1960, Golf's Golden Year*. Dallas: Taylor Publishing, 1992.

BOYD CHILDRESS

NIGHT OF THE LIVING DEAD (1968). George Romero's low-budget, black-and-white film *Night of the Living Dead* was not well received by critics upon first release in 1968 but became a cult film and eventually won respect for its effective use of horror elements in an allegorical film that critiques many aspects of American society. It is also credited as the first modern zombie movie, portraying hordes of zombies attacking living people without making reference to voodoo or witchcraft.

The screenplay was written by Romero and John A. Russo. The film begins with Barbra (Judith O'Dea) and her brother Johnny (Russell Streiner), who have come to a cemetery in rural Pennsylvania to lay a wreath on their father's grave. They are followed by a tall stumbling man (S. William Hinzman), who turns out to be the first of many zombies (or ghouls, as the film refers to them). Johnny is killed, but Barbara flees and is rescued by a young African American man named Ben (Duane Jones). Together they seek refuge in an abandoned farmhouse, where they attempt to fend off the ever-increasing number of zombies (in this film, a person killed by a zombie becomes a zombie himself, has a seemingly unlimited appetite for human flesh, is afraid of fire, and can be killed by a bullet through or blow to the brain).

Several dramas play out within the night of siege. Ben and an older white man named Harry (Karl Hardman) argue over the best strategy for survival, and Harry clearly expects to be in charge because of his age and race. Radio broadcasts sensationalize the killings (particularly that corpses have been partially eaten) but also offer the speculation that the dead have become reanimated due to release of radiation into the atmosphere. One survivor locks the others out of the house (a scenario also used in contemporary stories about fallout shelters). A zombie girl attacks and eats her parents (the film is quite graphic in its portrayal of violence). Finally, only Ben remains. Coming out of the house the next morning, he is mistaken for a zombie and shot through the head. Because he is African American and his assailant is white, this recalls other assaults including the shooting of James Meredith and the assassination of Martin Luther King Jr.

Night of the Living Dead was added to the National Film Registry in 1999. It was remade in 1990 by Tom Savini with a revised screenplay by Romero and was also the first in a series of "Dead" movies by Romero, including *Dawn of the Dead* (1978), *Day of the Dead* (1985), *Land of the Dead* (2005), *Diary of the Dead* (2007), and *Survival of the Dead* (2009).

See also Black Power.

Bibliography

Harvey, Ben. *Night of the Living Dead*. New York: Palgrave Macmillan, 2008.
Paffenroth, Kim. *Gospel of the Living Dead: George Romero's Visions of Hell on Earth*. Waco, TX: Baylor University Press, 2006.
Phillips, Kendall R. *Projected Fears: Horror Films and American Culture*. Westport, CT: Praeger, 2005.
Williams, Tony. *The Cinema of George A. Romero, Knight of the Living Dead*. New York: Wallflower, 2003.

SARAH BOSLAUGH

NIXON, RICHARD MILHOUS (1913–1994). Richard Milhous Nixon, the 37th president of the United States, was a man with a long and complex career in national service. While his legacy will forever be linked with the Watergate scandal that led him to resign the presidency in 1974, he also served in both houses of Congress and as vice president under President Dwight Eisenhower. An ambitious man with a deep and abiding interest in foreign affairs, perhaps Nixon's greatest legacy beyond Watergate was his role in opening the doors to diplomatic relations with Communist China in the early 1970s.

Richard Nixon was born on January 9, 1913, in Yorba Linda, California, to Frank Nixon and Hannah Milhous Nixon. Both parents formed part of the stream of Midwestern migrants populating southern California in the early twentieth century, but Hannah's stridently Quaker family was the dominant influence in young

Richard's life. Frank's attempt to develop a viable lemon orchard in Yorba Linda was not a success, and the family moved in Richard's early childhood to nearby Whittier, where his father operated a grocery store. Young Nixon's childhood years were further colored by the loss of two of his brothers to tuberculosis.

Economic circumstances forced Nixon to earn his undergraduate degree at nearby Whittier College, a Quaker institution, despite high school accomplishments that qualified him for a place at Harvard. Following his graduation, he entered the newly formed law school at Duke University in North Carolina, where he was noted for his work ethic and graduated third in his class. Duke's status was not sufficient to secure Nixon a position at a New York law firm, forcing his return to Southern California in 1937.

Many biographers have speculated that Nixon's, poor, western upbringing and his college and law school experiences combined to stimulate a distrust of the Eastern Establishment that followed him throughout his political career. Subsequent experiences would continue to develop in him a tendency toward identification with the "common American"—an affinity that would lead over time to Nixon's outreach to the "silent majority" during his presidential years. Membership in an amateur dramatics society was one of Nixon's many interests while living in Southern California in the late 1930s, and it was during a production of *The Dark Tower* in 1938 that he met Thelma Catherine "Pat" Ryan. The two would marry in 1940 and later have two children, Patricia (born 1946) and Julie (born 1948).

In early 1942, the Nixons moved to Washington, D.C., so Richard could take a job in the Office of Price Administration (OPA). Nixon later commented that his experiences at the OPA deeply impacted the policies he would advocate in his political career. By the end of his eight months in Washington, he was severely disenchanted by his experience of the wartime bureaucracy. Later in 1942, Nixon learned that the U.S. Navy was looking for young lawyers to serve as commissioned officers. Despite his eligibility for conscientious objector status as a Quaker, he was eager to serve in World War II. He served in the Pacific with the South Pacific Combat Air Transport Command and in Washington D.C., working on Navy contract terminations.

Following the war, Nixon came to the attention of a group of Republican leaders in his home district in California who were looking for a candidate to run for Congress against incumbent Democrat Jerry Voorhis. Following a spirited campaign during which he first demonstrated his instinct to go for the political jugular, tying the popular incumbent to a communist-infiltrated political action committee, Nixon won election to Congress in the Republican landslide of 1946.

Nixon's time in the House forged significant foundations for the rest of his career. In 1947, he was appointed to the Herter Committee, a congressional committee charged with preparing a report in connection with the Marshall Plan under consideration before Congress. His trip to Europe with the committee was an eye-opening experience for the young Californian. Exposure to Communist mobs and firsthand knowledge of the devastation wrought in Europe by World War II converted Nixon into an internationalist, and foreign affairs would be his greatest area of interest throughout the rest of his political career.

The episode that brought the young congressman to national attention, however, was a domestic case with international implications. Nixon was appointed to the House Un-American Activities Committee, and in the summer of 1948, he became a major figure in the case against accused Soviet spy Alger Hiss. Nixon recognized that over the course of his first testimony before HUAC, Hiss failed to categorically state that he had not known his accuser, *Time* editor and avowed ex-communist Whittaker Chambers. Nixon befriended Chambers and pursued the case to its conclusion, demonstrating with some veracity that the two men had known each other.

Nixon was now firmly established as a national figure and a Red hunter on the front lines against communism. These attributes served him well in his next step up the political ladder. In 1950, he ran for the Senate against incumbent Helen Gahagan Douglas, casting her as distressingly friendly toward communists and fellow travelers in a campaign that earned him the approbation of his supporters—and the sobriquet of "Tricky Dick" among his opponents. Indeed, Nixon was becoming one of the more polarizing political figures of the 1950s, demonized by political cartoonists like the *Washington Post*'s Herblock but admired by the Republican political establishment for his dogged devotion to party.

It was the latter characteristic that brought Nixon to the attention of Eisenhower and his advisors in 1952, when he was selected as the popular former general's running mate for the presidency. Nixon's vice presidential campaign was not an easy one; he was charged with accepting monetary gifts and nearly dropped from the Republican ticket. Nixon responded in true postwar populist style, with an appeal to the nation via live television broadcast. He laid bare the family's modest finances on national television, concluding with the comment that the only political gift he'd ever kept was a cocker spaniel puppy that his daughters had named Checkers—and that gift he intended to keep. While critics dismissed the "Checkers" speech as maudlin, Nixon had demonstrated his ability to appeal to the masses. Antiestablishment appeals to the common American would become a staple of his political program, used with great effectiveness in his second run for the presidency in 1968.

As vice president, Nixon spent much of his time in two roles: chief political campaigner in the Republican Party and representative of the U.S. government abroad. Beginning with a trip to Asia in 1953 and continuing through notable journeys to Latin America in 1958 and the Soviet Union in 1959, Nixon was able to indulge his love of foreign affairs and become expert in the dynamics of the international Cold War. His experiences in Latin America, where the Nixons and the rest of the American delegation nearly fell prey to communist-affiliated protestors, furthered his inclination to support U.S. aid efforts abroad. The vice president's trip to the USSR culminated in his famous "Kitchen Debate" with Soviet Premier Nikita Khrushchev.

Nixon's duties as chief campaigner, however, had perhaps the largest impact on his subsequent run for the presidency in 1960. Eisenhower treasured his own status as a man above politics and a hero to the American people. Accordingly, he sent his vice president on campaign tours throughout the country, supporting candidates—and gathering chits—throughout his eight years in the number two role. Nixon was a dedicated party leader who doggedly supported Republicans even during the dismal 1958 midterm election, and party operatives throughout the country would remember his support when it came time for the 1960 campaign.

What might have been heir apparent status for Nixon in 1960 was sullied by Eisenhower's distinctly lukewarm support for his loyal vice president. The former general disliked Nixon's partisan tendencies, even as he made good use of them, and never warmed to the vice president on a personal level. Eisenhower was famously quoted in August 1960 as answering a question about Nixon's contributions to the administration with the quip, "If you give me a week I might think of one." Fortunately for the vice president, his long history of dedication to the party gave him sufficient support to overcome putative challenges to his candidacy from conservative supporters of an effort to draft Arizona senator Barry Goldwater on the right and from liberal New York governor Nelson Rockefeller on the left.

Normally an astute interpreter of party opinion, Nixon's instincts nearly let him down in the summer of 1960. Shortly before the Republican nominating convention in Chicago, the vice president attempted to smooth over differences in opinion with the liberal wing of the party via a clandestine conference with Rockefeller at his Fifth Avenue apartment. The resulting agreement, known to history as the "Compact of Fifth Avenue," angered conservatives in the party and carried an aura of indignity among those who believed a person in Nixon's position should not have traveled to New York and put forth so much effort to placate a restive state governor. Despite murmurs of insurrection by Goldwater and other conservatives, Nixon was able to conciliate the party and gain the nomination, selecting UN ambassador Henry Cabot Lodge as his running mate.

Over the course of his 1960 campaign, Nixon adopted a forerunner of the 1968 approach that tactician Kevin Phillips famously named the "southern strategy." He pledged in his nomination speech to visit every state in the newly 50-state union, a decision that endeared him to some southerners even as it stretched his campaign extremely thinly. Among other results, a knee infection that forced cancellation of several visits meant Nixon wound up in Alaska, home to a mere three electoral votes, the day before the general election. This marked the first time since Reconstruction, however, that a Republican candidate had specifically reached out to the South through personal campaign visits. Inroads he made over the course of this campaign would bear fruit eight years later.

Despite his aptitude for working within the party, Nixon demonstrated tone-deafness toward several groups, including African Americans. His campaign lacked responsiveness to minority concerns, and he failed to intervene in the October 1960 jailing of Martin Luther King Jr. He later argued it would have been improper for him to do so, citing his status as a lawyer and the American Bar Association's *Canon of Professional Ethics* injunction against communicating with a judge regarding the merits of a pending case. John F. Kennedy was able to make political hay of this with his own outreach to Coretta Scott King and brother Robert Kennedy's legal intervention.

Nixon's campaign was also slow to understand the importance image would play in an age of television, a deficiency all the more curious in light of his notable success with the Checkers speech in 1952. At the time of his first televised debate with Kennedy, Nixon was recovering from a knee infection that left him underweight and tired. Rather than resting, Nixon continued his frenetic campaign schedule right up to the morning of the telecast and refused makeup proffered to improve his appearance before the television cameras. Consequently, the vice president appeared tired, drawn, and bearded in contrast to the dapper Kennedy. The disparity in reactions to the debate between radio listeners and television viewers was striking: those who heard the debate on the radio cast Nixon as the winner, but television views overwhelmingly selected Kennedy as the victor. Nixon learned an important lesson.

Nixon lost the 1960 election by the closest of margins, with allegations of fraud in Illinois and Texas. Despite the efforts of some of his supporters, Nixon refused to contest the election, arguing that a prolonged recount battle would be bad for the country. His experiences in 1960, however, colored the rest of his political career, heightening his distrust of the Establishment and his feelings of besiegement. He returned to California, where he joined the Los Angeles law firm of Adams, Duque, and Hazeltine and published his first memoir, titled *Six Crises* (1962).

By the summer of 1961, however, Nixon was growing restless in private life. Following a protracted period of agonizing, he decided to enter the 1962 race for California governor, a decision many observers then and now speculated had more to do with a desire to be part of political life than with innate interest in the position. Nixon was, after all, fascinated first and foremost by international affairs, and despite the prominence of his home state, he was not a man easily absorbed by the minutia of state-level government.

Nixon also failed to account for the growing power of the right-wing conservative movement in the state of California. Challenged in the primary election by conservative state assembly leader Joe Shell, Nixon was barely able to eke out a victory. In the general election, he found his support in conservative circles decidedly lacking. Far from demonstrating the party loyalty that had characterized his own political identity or even that of Arizona senator Barry Goldwater, California conservatives no longer felt bound to party above ideology. Nixon lost the general election to incumbent governor Edmund "Pat" Brown—in the same year that California senator Thomas Kuchel won his own reelection contest by over 100,000 votes.

Angry and disappointed, the former vice president appeared the next morning before a press conference at the Ambassador Hotel and let lose his flood of frustrations. The press had enjoyed a lot of fun at his expense over the past 16 years, "and I think I've given as good as I've taken." Now, however, he admonished them to consider how much they would be missing with him gone: "You won't have Nixon to kick around anymore, because gentlemen, this is my last press conference. . . . I hope that what I have said today will at least make television, radio, the press . . . recognize that they have a right and a responsibility, if they're against a candidate, give him the shaft, but also recognize if they give him the shaft put one lonely reporter on the campaign who will report what the candidate says now and then."

Nixon's outburst seemed at the time to place the final nail in his political coffin. ABC News went so far as to run a half-hour special the Sunday following the election titled "The Political Obituary of Richard Nixon." In a crowning indignity for the former vice president, one of the invited commentators who spoke with host Howard K. Smith was none other than Alger Hiss. Shortly afterward, the Nixon family moved to New York—Rockefeller territory—where the former vice president took a position with the Wall Street firm thenceforth known as Nixon, Mudge, Rose, Guthrie, and Alexander. Such a geographical move seemed to confirm that Nixon was no longer interested in pursuing political office. A quarter-century after he first pursued work on Wall Street, Nixon had fulfilled his first life's dream, but by this juncture it likely was limited consolation for a man whose political career was viewed as over.

Nixon and other have referred to the mid-1960s as his "wilderness years," but in truth the former vice president never entirely left the political arena. Among his duties with Nixon, Mudge were extensive foreign travels, and he made the most of such trips by meeting with old friends and continuing to make new ones in regions including South and Southeast Asia. In 1964, when many party stalwarts stepped back in the wake of Barry Goldwater's nomination, Nixon volunteered to present the nominee to the Republican National Convention and took the opportunity to stridently advocate party unity. While he liked Goldwater personally, he later recounted feeling "almost physically sick" at what he termed the divisive nature of Goldwater's acceptance speech. Goldwater's use of the phrase "Extremism in the defense of liberty is no vice! . . . Moderation in the pursuit of justice is no virtue!" in particular was credited by Nixon as allowing Johnson and the Democratic Party to "put the skids" under the Republican's campaign. Nonetheless, he made over 150 appearances in 36 states for various candidates and for Goldwater—a show of party loyalty that would be remembered by grateful candidates and party operatives following this disastrous election.

The disarray left by Goldwater's defeat in 1964 left Nixon with some shreds of personal optimism. The discrediting of extremism left hope, he believed, for a moderate candidate to enter the spectrum and achieve a victory as involvement in Vietnam and the growing prominence of the New Left whittled away at President Lyndon Johnson's popularity. Nixon determined that the party's best hope might well be none other than a certain Richard Milhous Nixon. While financially rewarding, he found his legal work personally unfulfilling. Meanwhile, Republicans across the spectrum respected the work he had undertaken in 1964. Goldwater introduced him with gratitude at a Republican National Committee meeting following the campaign as the person "who worked harder than any one person for the ticket."

Nixon followed his 1964 performances with wide-ranging dedication to Republican races across the nation in 1966. Nixon aides began raising money to fund his involvement the year before, and he crisscrossed the country over the course of the 1966 election. The midterm race was a triumph for the GOP, netting 47 House seats, three seats in the Senate, eight governorships, and 700 seats in state legislatures. Nixon also increased his visibility in the foreign policy debates of the late 1960s, taking special interest in Vietnam and Asia as a whole. In 1967, he penned an article published in *Foreign Affairs* titled "America After Viet Nam" that argued for greater engagement with Communist China. "There is no place on this small planet," he argued, "for a billion of its potentially most able people to live in angry isolation." In domestic circles, he increasingly positioned himself as a proponent of law and order in the wake of inner-city riots and increasing student unrest.

By 1968, then, Nixon had positioned himself well to become the Republican Party nominee for the presidency once again. He managed to fend off challenges from perennial hopeful Nelson Rockefeller, Michigan governor George Romney, and the newest star of the revitalizing conservative movement, California governor Ronald Reagan, to claim the 1968 nomination in Miami. Nixon selected Maryland governor Spiro Agnew, who had distinguished himself with hard-line policies in the wake of riots in Baltimore, as his running mate, a decision that appealed to both southerners and urban northerners unnerved by racial unrest.

Nixon's political coalition reflected many of the themes he first explored in 1960. Southerners, most notably South Carolina senator Strom Thurmond, played an important role even in an election that featured a third-party run by Alabama segregationist George Wallace. Nixon strove to mobilize mainstream voters disenchanted by student demonstrations and race riots—citizens his administration would come to label the "Silent Majority." He also famously argued that he could enact a Vietnam policy that combined "peace with honor." Historians have debated the degree to which Nixon and his supporters attempted to influence peace negotiations ongoing in Paris in an effort to delay significant progress until after the 1968 election.

November 8, 1968, brought the results Nixon had hoped for eight years before: he had won the election over Democratic nominee Hubert Humphrey and American Independent Party candidate Wallace. He had gained the presidency but faced a deeply divided country, with Democratic majorities in both houses of Congress and a war in Vietnam so seemingly intractable that it drove Lyndon Johnson from office.

Nixon's first term would be characterized by moderation in domestic policy and secretive attempts to influence the international situation. Domestically, his administration attempted to set in place price controls to deal with spiraling inflation in the summer of 1971, but it soon reversed course. Monetary policy became Nixon's preferred method of economic intervention. His advisor Daniel Patrick Moynihan even went so far as to propose a radical overhaul of welfare policy with the Family Assistance Plan (FAP), which would replace specific payments with a negative taxation scheme. Nixon established the Environmental Protection Agency (EPA) and supported legislation that led to Clean Air and Clean Water Acts. He attempted outreach to southerners and northern urbanites with legislative proposals to prohibit school segregation through the use of forced busing. Although his efforts to do so failed, Nixon did bar the Department of Health, Education and Welfare from cutting off funds to school districts that failed to comply with court orders to desegregate. His attempts to give the Supreme Court a more conservative cast by appointing a southerner were a failure. At the same time, however, Nixon also ordered the first affirmative action program for workers on federally funded projects. In short, his administration left a decidedly mixed economic and racial legacy.

Some historians, most notably Bruce Schulman, have argued that these actions were seemingly liberal decisions that in fact cut the bureaucratic framework from under programs that owed their genesis to the Great Society or even the New Deal. replacing administrative bureaucracies with block grants and tax policy would relieve generations of liberal civil servants of their positions. At the time, however, conservatives were not pleased with aspects of Nixon's economic policy, the FAP, or the EPA, and even party liberals like Nelson Rockefeller attempted rightward moves to capitalize on these sentiments. Nixon was able to cast the 1970 midterm elections as a victory, with a "working majority of four" in the Senate including conservative Democrats who could be counted on to support much of the president's legislative agenda, but it was far from an overwhelming endorsement of his agenda.

Nixon and the Republicans doubtless suffered not only from continuing domestic woes that saw 1970 become the first year in over a decade when U.S. production of real goods and services declined, but from an electorate increasingly unnerved by American policy in Vietnam. Nixon adopted a policy of "Vietnamization" during the first year of his presidency, advocating that the United States draw down its troops while stepping up training of the South Vietnamese Army. Meanwhile, however, the United States substantially increased its bombing campaigns, including initially secret expansion of the war to Cambodia and Laos to take out Viet Cong supply networks. News of these efforts brought increased protest against the war, including the tragic events of May 4, 1970, at Kent State University in Ohio, where four innocent bystanders were killed by National Guard troops. Nixon's administration increasingly came to resemble a body under siege, and access to the president was highly restricted.

The president's feelings of besiegement increased following the publication in June 1971 of the Pentagon Papers, reams of classified documents collected by former Defense Department employee Daniel Ellsberg that revealed in shocking detail the way in which previous administrations had issued upbeat interpretations about the war to the American public while concealing the ineffectiveness of American military efforts. The Pentagon Papers pertained largely to the Kennedy and Johnson administrations, but Nixon soon became convinced that they represented a danger to his foreign policy efforts, revealing Americans' inability to control internal leaks. For a president preparing to undertake one of the greatest foreign policy transformations of the modern era, this was an alarming turn of events.

The year 1972 witnessed arguably the greatest achievement of Nixon's political career, as well as his deepest failure. In February 1972, Nixon went to China, opening a diplomatic door to the world's largest national population that had been closed since Mao drove nationalist forces from the Chinese mainland in 1949. While some conservatives looked on this trip as kowtowing to the forces behind such atrocities as the recently ended Cultural Revolution, most international opinion was shocked and gratified by the magnitude of this gesture toward Cold War détente. During the same year, however, Nixon's fears about the 1972 election stimulated the below-the-belt activities of the Committee to Re-Elect the President (CREEP), culminating with the May 28 break-in at Democratic National Committee headquarters in Washington, D.C.'s Watergate complex.

Nixon won the 1972 election in a landslide over the Democratic nominee, South Dakota senator George McGovern. As 1973 began, however, revelations over the course of the burglars' trial led Congress to begin asking increasingly strident questions about the events surrounding the Watergate burglary. As early as October 1972, *Washington Post* reporters Carl Bernstein and Bob Woodward had started to document connections between the Watergate incident and CREEP. In the spring of 1973, the Senate convened a special committee chaired by Senator Sam Ervin of Texas to investigate a growing flood of allegations, including payment of cover-up money to the burglars. A turning point in the investigation came when presidential staffer Alexander Butterfield let slip that Nixon routinely taped telephone calls and in-person meetings in the Oval Office. In October 1973, over the course of what became known as the "Saturday Night Massacre," Attorney General Elliot Richardson and deputy William Ruckelshaus resigned rather than follow Nixon's order to fire special prosecutor Archibald Cox. Justice Department employee Robert Bork finally carried out the termination order. Meanwhile, scandal rocked other quarters of the executive branch; Spiro Agnew resigned his office on October 15 in the wake of a no-contest plea to bribery charges dating from his time as Maryland governor.

Over the next few months, the White House released edited transcripts of many of the Oval Office tapes, but it became clear that an 18-and-a-half-minute deletion marred one very significant tape. The White House explained away the deletion by arguing that Nixon's secretary, Rose Mary Woods, had inadvertently erased it when she answered the telephone while preparing a transcription. Over the summer of 1974, the House Judiciary Committee agreed upon three resolutions of impeachment on the charges of obstruction of justice, abuse of presidential powers, and violation of his oath of office by the president. Meanwhile, three additional transcripts dating back to June 1972 seemed to provide the "smoking gun" indicating Nixon's involvement in a Watergate cover-up.

On August 8, 1974, Nixon informed the American people in a televised address that he would resign the office of the presidency at noon the next day. On August 9, he left the White House grounds via helicopter, leaving a new vice president, Gerald Ford, to assume the office of the presidency. Nixon would spend a few years in San Clemente, California, before returning east to live out the rest of his days in New Jersey.

In his later years, Nixon regained some of his status as a foreign policy expert and elder statesman. Presidents ranging from Ronald Reagan to Bill Clinton called on him for advice prior to his death in 1994. Nixon was an early public figure to recognize that a changing world would bring the United States into a position where it would be one of many players in the international realm. Unfortunately, the distrust of government that has characterized the last generation of American political life is also a significant part of his legacy.

See also Agnew, Spiro Theodore (1918–1996); Nixon-Kennedy Debates (1960); Presidential Election of 1960; Presidential Election of 1968.

Bibliography

Ambrose, Stephen E. *Nixon Volume I: The Education of a Politician 1913–1962.* New York: Touchstone, 1987.

Gifford, Laura Jane. *The Center Cannot Hold: The 1960 Presidential Election and the Rise of Modern Conservatism.* DeKalb: Northern Illinois University Press, 2009.

Nixon, Richard. *RN: The Memoirs of Richard Nixon.* New York: Grosset and Dunlap, 1978.

Nixon, Richard. *Six Crises.* Garden City, NY: Doubleday, 1962.

Parmet, Herbert S. *Nixon and His America.* Boston: Little, Brown, 1990.

Perlstein, Rick. *Nixonland: The Rise of a President and the Fracturing of America.* New York: Scribners, 2008.

Schulman, Bruce. *The Seventies: The Great Shift in American Culture, Society, and Politics.* New York: Da Capo, 2001.

LAURA JANE GIFFORD

NIXON-KENNEDY DEBATES (1960). During the 1960 presidential campaign in the United States, the two main candidates, Richard Nixon and John Kennedy, participated in a series of four televised debates in September and October. These debates were the first in U.S. history to be televised to a national audience. The debates may have helped Kennedy win a close election. More importantly, they marked the start of an era in which television would play a major role in the political process.

The campaign leading up to the November 1960 election was closely contested. Heading into the debates, polls showed Nixon with a very slight lead. Nixon seemed to have some advantages that would help him win, especially the fact that he was a two-term incumbent vice president. Furthermore, he had a reputation of successfully fighting communism, an important issue at the height of the Cold War. Kennedy in contrast had served only a single term as the senator from Massachusetts and had little experience in foreign affairs. Kennedy also faced opposition to his Roman Catholic faith.

The first of the four debates took place on September 26, 1960, in Chicago and focused mainly on domestic issues. An estimated 75–80 million viewers—more than 60 percent of the adult population—watched the two candidates discuss the issues, while millions more listened on the radio. In terms of the substance of their comments, the two candidates seemed almost evenly matched. In fact, a majority of those listening on the radio felt that Nixon had won the debate, based on what they heard.

However, those watching on television gave Kennedy the edge based on what they saw. The visual contrast between the two candidates in the first debate was striking. Nixon had recently spent two weeks in the hospital and had lost 20 pounds. He was thin and pale. His shirt did not fit well due to his weight loss, and his gray suit blended in with the background. He refused to wear makeup, and his famous five

Sen. John F. Kennedy gestures during a nationally televised debate with Richard Nixon on October 21, 1960. (AP/Wide World Photos)

o'clock shadow was noticeable. Furthermore, while he had studied the key issues before the debate, he had not actually practiced delivering his answers.

Kennedy on the other hand had recently campaigned in California and was well tanned. He looked young, fit, and handsome on television. Unlike Nixon, Kennedy not only prepared for possible debate topics, he also repeatedly rehearsed the delivery of his answers. Already a poised and gifted speaker, Kennedy knew to look directly into the camera when answering questions, making viewers at home feel as if he were speaking to them. Nixon looked at the questioners in the studio and did not achieve the same intimate feeling that Kennedy gave the home audience.

After the debate, polls indicated the Kennedy had taken a slight lead over Nixon. In the subsequent three debates, Nixon was better prepared, looked healthier, and performed very well. However, significantly fewer voters watched these other debates. Some voters at the time indicated the first debate influenced their choice in the elections. More common was the role of the first debate in solidifying the choice of voters who were considering voting for Kennedy. Kennedy's youth and inexperience concerned many voters, and the debates served to put those doubts at ease, as Kennedy came across as confident and competent. In the end, Kennedy narrowly won the election by only one-tenth of 1 percent of the popular vote, although his margin of victory in the Electoral College was somewhat more comfortable at 303 to 219.

In the long term, these first televised presidential debates played a very important role in politics in the United States. While squabbles over laws about equal airtime and Nixon's refusal to participate in debates in 1968 and 1972 meant that it would not be until 1976 that televised debates would again be significant, during the last quarter of the twentieth century, such debates had become a cornerstone of the presidential electoral politics. Perhaps more importantly, the 1960 presidential debates clearly made television the key medium through which candidates would reach the electorate, surpassing newspapers and radio. This situation raised questions about the role of television in politics. The medium had become a powerful tool that could be used to influence the outcome of elections. Many observers even began to ask how it might impact democracy. Some were concerned that television would place too much emphasis on the visual and physical aspects of candidates, rather than their actual competency on issues. Furthermore, as candidates began to also place more advertisements on television, it required them to raise even more money, leading to escalating campaign costs. At the same time, others argued that television could strengthen democracy by making political debate more open for all to see from their own homes.

Bibliography

Jamieson, Kathleen Hall, and David S. Birdsell. *Presidential Debates: The Challenge of Creating an Informed Electorate.* New York: Oxford University Press, 1988.

Matthews, Christopher. *Kennedy and Nixon: The Rivalry That Shaped Postwar America.* New York: Simon & Schuster, 1996.

Schroeder, Alan. *Presidential Debates: Fifty Years of High-Risk.* 2nd ed. New York: Columbia University Press, 2008.

RONALD E. YOUNG JR

NUCLEAR TEST BAN TREATY (1963). The Nuclear Test Ban Treaty (NTBT) banned nuclear weapons tests in the atmosphere, under water, and in outer space. The signing of the treaty, also called the Limited Test Ban Treaty (LTBT) or Partial Test Ban Treaty (PTBT), on August 5, 1963, represented the first major breakthrough in postwar arms control negotiations between the Western and the communist bloc nations and laid the groundwork for a series of subsequent agreements attempting to limit nuclear dissemination and the arms race. The treaty was both a product and a symbol of the détente of relations between the two superpowers.

Discussions of arms control and disarmament and, in particular, control of the military use of nuclear energy had started shortly after the end of World War II. Although there was widespread recognition of the danger of an uncontrolled arms race and of the need to reduce the likelihood of a nuclear war, international negotiations had until 1963 led to no binding agreement limiting or controlling the buildup of the military arsenal of the nuclear powers. Negotiations within the UN framework and in particular the Eighteen Nation Committee on Disarmament (ENDC) had led to a stalemate. The deadlock was in large part due to the insistence of the United States and the United Kingdom on on-site inspection-based control systems to verify compliance and avoid clandestine testing, and the opposition of the Soviet Union to these intrusive inspections.

The Berlin and Cuban missile crises of 1961 and 1962, which brought the world to the brink of nuclear war, helped relax Cold War tensions and provided an incentive to reach agreement. The subsequent establishment of a "hot line" between the Kremlin and the White House in April 1963 and U.S. president John F. Kennedy's speech at American University on June 10, 1963, in which he announced a unilateral suspension of American nuclear tests and called for a détente in East-West relations, contributed to unlock arms control negotiations. Although the continued hostility of Soviet General Secretary Khrushchev to on-site inspections precluded any agreement on an underground nuclear test ban, a ban in the noncontroversial atmosphere, under water, and in outer space remained on the table.

High-level discussions among the United States, the Soviet Union, and the United Kingdom resumed in July 1963 in Moscow and were concluded rapidly at the beginning of August. Within a few months after its signature by the three original signatories, most countries with the notable exceptions of France and China signed the treaty. The treaty went into effect on October 10, 1963. It banned nuclear weapon tests in the atmosphere, in outer space, and under water, but underground testing remained permissible. As a result, testing of nuclear weapons continued almost unabated after the signature of the NTBT and was accompanied by substantial qualitative improvements such as the deployment of multiple warheads on missiles and the improvement of guidance systems.

After the NTBT was ratified, the next step to nuclear disarmament shifted from negotiating an unlimited test ban to preventing the proliferation of nuclear weapons. Negotiations eventually led to the signing of the Non Proliferation Treaty (NPT) in 1968 and to the Strategic Arms Limitations Discussions in 1972 (SALT I) and 1979 (SALT II), which sought to limit the spread of nuclear weapons.

Negotiations for a Comprehensive Nuclear Test Ban Treaty (CNTBT) prohibiting underground testing started only in 1977 but was eventually abandoned by the Reagan administration early in the 1980s. In September 1996, the General Assembly of the United Nations passed a treaty banning all military and peaceful (i.e., civilian) nuclear testing. The CTBT has not become law because it has not been ratified by prominent nuclear powers such as the United States, China, Pakistan, and North Korea.

See also Berlin Crisis (1958–1962); Cuban Missile Crisis.

Bibliography

Beschloss, Michael. *The Crisis Years: Kennedy and Khrushchev, 1960–1963*. New York: HarperCollins, 1991.

Firestone, Bernard J. "Kennedy and the Test Ban: Presidential Leadership and Arms Control." In Douglas Binkley and Richard T. Griffiths, eds. *Kennedy and Europe*. Baton Rouge: Louisiana State University, 1999, pp. 66–94.

Mary Milling. *Foreign Policy Formulation: A Case Study of the Nuclear Test Ban Treaty*. Columbus, OH: C. E. Merrill, 1971.

Seaborg, Glenn T., and Benjamin S. Loeb. *Kennedy, Khrushchev and the Test Ban*. Berkeley: University of California Press, 1983.

CARINE S. GERMOND

NUCLEAR TESTING. Nuclear testing refers to the process of determining the characteristics of a nuclear weapon by creating a test explosion. Testing is considered a demonstration of a country's nuclear capabilities. The first atomic bomb was built in the United States under the auspices of the Manhattan Project, which was a collaboration during World War II with the United Kingdom and Canada to develop a nuclear capability before Nazi Germany. The first nuclear test was conducted in the United States at Trinity Site in New Mexico on July 16, 1945, with a yield of 20 kilotons with a bomb involving nuclear fission technology. Less than a month after the first test, the world witnessed the first and so far only deployment of nuclear bombs on enemy targets, when the Japanese cities of Hiroshima and Nagasaki were bombed on August 6 and 9. In the ensuing Cold War climate, an arms race began between the Soviet Union and the United States, which also included nuclear weapons and led to the first Soviet nuclear test on August 29, 1949. Because the Soviet Union had successfully developed and tested an atomic bomb, the United States developed and tested the much more powerful hydrogen bomb using nuclear fusion and reaching yields of many megatons. The first American test took place November 1, 1952, on the Marshall Islands. Another test at the same location on March 1, 1954, codenamed "Castle Bravo," produced a horrific incident of nuclear fallout that polluted the environment of the test site and killed the crew of a nearby Japanese fishing boat.

In 1958, an informal moratorium on nuclear testing was agreed on between the Soviet Union, the United States, and Great Britain during talks in Geneva. The moratorium lasted until September 1961, when the Soviet Union detonated the largest nuclear device ever recorded, the Tsar Bomba, with a yield of 50 megatons. The Soviets cited increased international tension, most notably the ongoing Berlin Crisis, as well as the French nuclear testing of 1960 as their reason for test resumption. It followed from the Cold War logic that the United States had to resume its test program as well. Despite public opposition, test explosions were conducted in Nevada shortly after the Soviet test, but to prove the difference between the United States and the Soviet tests, the American one was conducted underground and consequently generating less fallout than the Soviets' atmospheric test. Both East and West continued to test nuclear devices, but also pursued the negotiating track that had produced the test moratorium in Geneva. This eventually culminated in the 1963 Limited Test Ban Treaty that banned all nuclear tests in the atmosphere, outer space, and under water and was initially signed by the Soviet Union, Great Britain, and the United States. Underground nuclear testing was permitted in the treaty, and both the Soviet Union and the United States continued such testing until 1990 and 1992, respectively. The latest nuclear test was conducted by North Korea in 2009.

Bibliography

Gaddis, John Lewis, ed. *Cold War Statesmen Confront the Bomb: Nuclear Diplomacy since 1945.* Oxford: Oxford University Press, 1999.

KASPER GROTLE RASMUSSEN

PEANUTS (1950–2000). *Peanuts* was a long-running American comic strip created, written and drawn by cartoonist Charles Schulz (1922–2000). Although the strip's later popularity and the ubiquity of the comic-intelligent beagle Snoopy would later eclipse its original message, *Peanuts* was in reality one of the most heartbreakingly melancholy, and in some ways most realistic, looks at the innocence and sadness of childhood in popular culture. The strip started in 1947 in the *St. Paul Pioneer Press* and ran until 1950. *Li'l Folks* was the first strip to feature a character named Charlie Brown (who at first did not speak) and a dog that resembled Snoopy. When United Feature Syndicate picked up the strip, they changed the name to *Peanuts* (presumably after the popular Peanut Gallery of cheering children on *Howdy Doody*) and after deciding *Li'l Folks* was too close to the popular *Li'l Abner* strip. The first strip featured two female characters talking about "good old" Charlie Brown walking by, before one character remarks on how much she hates him, setting up from the start how the strip would address the complex nature of children's lives.

While *Peanuts* had started in 1950, it was during the '60s that it became popular as Schulz grew as a storyteller. The strip was rooted in the innocence of childhood, but it expanded to take on contemporary events such as the moon landing and introduced a new character, a bumbling bird friend of Snoopy named Woodstock. *Peanuts* was also integrated during the '60s with the arrival of new characters such as the tomboy Peppermint Patti and her constant companion Marcy (who keeps calling her "Sir") as well as the first African American character, Franklin, and the strangely named "5" (who also had brothers named 3 and 4). During the '60s, Peanuts maintained its wide appeal not only through numerous collections of the strips sold in bookstores, but also in other mediums such as the popular cartoon specials, especially *A Charlie Brown Christmas* (1965) and *It's the Great Pumpkin, Charlie Brown* (1966). It was also the subject of two theatrical productions, most notably the Off-Broadway musical *You're a Good Man, Charlie Brown*, which ran from 1967 to 1971. In addition, Schulz licensed the characters for numerous commercials, and Snoopy repped Metropolitan Life among other products. The strip maintained its quality through the '60s and throughout the next three decades. While *Peanuts* was not specifically relevant to the social upheavals of the 1960s, it maintained its popularity, mostly because of its comedic consistency and Schulz's keen eye for how even an abject failure such as Charlie Brown is the quintessential everyman, not unlike favorite counterculture characters such as Holden Caulfield. *Peanuts* is among the most influential comic strips of the twentieth century.

Bibliography

Gherman, Beverley. *Sparky: The Life and Art of Charles Schulz*. San Francisco: Chronicle Books, 2010.

Michaelis, David. *Schulz and Peanuts: A Biography*. New York: Harper, 2007.

Schulz, Charles. *Everything I Need to Know I Learned from Peanuts*. Jackson, TN: Running Press, 2010.

Schulz, Charles. *My Life with Charlie Brown*. Jackson: University Press of Mississippi, 2010.

BRIAN COGAN

PEI, I. M. (1917–). From his earliest projects to most recent work, architect I. M. Pei has been credited with blending the Western ideals of engineering with the cultural and traditional ideals of his Eastern roots, using modernist principles. Pei (born in

National Center for Atmospheric Research, designed by I. M. Pei in 1961, Boulder, Colorado. (Dreamstime.com)

Shangzhou, China, on April 26, 1917) is an internationally reputed architect for several seminal modernist works such as the iconic entrance pyramid at the Louvre, Paris (1983). Inspired by design traditions of Chinese gardens from his early childhood, Pei is distinguished as an architect of clarity of geometrical order, engaging physical conditions of the site as well as experiential qualities of the built environment. He was trained at the MIT School of Design in 1940 and was inspired by prominent European and American modernists of the twentieth century from Le Corbusier to Walter Gropius. Pei has built upon this style along other styles to create a body of work characterized not only by how humans engage space, but also by an understanding of how innovation in materials and construction techniques can create sculptural forms and experientially rich interior spaces.

Although Pei already had many notable projects to his credit prior to the 1960s, in that decade he created some of his most significant works, including the National Center for Atmospheric Research, in Boulder, Colorado, begun in 1961. This project, consisting of striking geometric forms, is one example of Pei's skill at balancing the built environment with the existing landscape of the site. Embedded in the slopes of Colorado's Rocky Mountains, the center was built on the remains of ancient architecture and presents an artistic dialogue between the human activities in the structure and its natural setting. The John F. Kennedy Library (1964) is another prestigious project in Pei's career that has received considerable critical attention. The signature atrium volume is defined and celebrated by the massive glass curtain wall supported by steel space frame members that offers vast views out onto the Boston Harbor. Once again, Pei combines the programmatic components of a project (the research center, museum, and memorial) by expressing form through the interplay of geometries, material transitions, and a dynamic treatment of natural light, to evoke a sense of memory and reflection on the eminent American leader.

Another renowned work of this decade is the East Wing of the National Gallery of Art in Washington, D.C. Located among prominent monuments along the National Mall and serving as an addition to the existing National Gallery, this structure has become as iconic as the other national monuments in the mall. Pei built on various precedents and refined certain design tendencies employing triangular geometries as an ordering principle to create diverse spatial conditions that encourage movement and enrich the museum experience. Marked by a network of skylights that illuminate the grand atrium, the structure is considered an engineering feat of construction in steel and glass. From the ingenuity in design and construction to the redefinition of formal and spatial relationships, Pei created a new museum experience by highlighting the dynamism of public space.

Through a variety of projects including skyscrapers and civic buildings as well as master plans, Pei continues to define architecture as a merging of art, history, and engineering ideals in every work. His creations of form exhibit a strict devotion to geometry, but also are strongly dependent on how space can define function and heighten the experience of occupants through variations of light and structure. Each of his works is influenced by various international styles and design sensibilities, and yet is deeply rooted in cultural and technological contexts as well as site-specific responses to the surrounding environment. The recipient of many honors in the field, Pei remains a seminal figure in modern architecture because of his unique ability to combine art, architecture, engineering, and innovation.

Bibliography

Cannell, Michael. *I. M. Pei: Mandarin of Modernism*. New York: Carol Southern Books, 1995.

Jodidio, Philip, and Janet Adams Strong. *I. M. Pei: Complete Works*. New York: Rizzoli, 2008.

Wiseman, Carter. *I. M. Pei: A Profile in American Architecture*. Revised ed. New York: Harry N. Abrams, 2001.

MOHAMMAD GHARIPOUR AND ANITHA DESHAMUDRE

PENTAGON PAPERS (1971). The *Pentagon Papers* was part of a study conducted by the Pentagon on the war in Vietnam that was released by the *New York Times* and the *Washington Post* with the assistance of RAND corporation analyst Daniel Ellsberg in 1971. The ensuing attempt by President Richard Nixon to discredit Ellsberg resulted in Ellsberg's lack of punishment and the downfall of the Nixon administration.

Initiated by Secretary of Defense Robert McNamara, the *Pentagon Papers* was based on a study prepared between June 1967 and January 1969, officially entitled "History of U.S. Decision Making Process on Vietnam Policy from from 1945 to 1968." The 47-volume, 7,000-page, two-and-a-half-million-word, sixty-pound document was classified "top secret-sensitive" and dispensed to only 15 individuals within the government. The report confirmed the suspicion of antiwar protesters that the government had lied about its operations in Vietnam to the American people. The documents contained the truth about the war: that covert military operations had been executed against North Vietnam and Laos, that John F. Kennedy had approved the coup d'état against South Vietnamese president Ngo Dinh Diem, and that the Gulf of Tonkin incident had been misrepresented by the Johnson administration as an excuse to escalate the war. The papers revealed the deceptiveness of presidents John F. Kennedy and Lyndon Baines Johnson, increasing the American public's distrust of the government.

Daniel Ellsberg had served in Vietnam as a company commander in the Marines and as a State Department civilian. After Ellsberg's five years at the RAND Corporation, McNamara recruited him to work at the Pentagon in 1964. Ellsberg became increasingly disillusioned with the war; his sentiments increasingly transformed into a conviction that the war was a political and moral disaster and a crime. With the assistance of a RAND associate and Vietnam veteran Anthony Russo, Ellsberg copied the study from 1969 to 1970, releasing his findings to antiwar critic Senator William Fulbright and the newspapers *New York Times* and *Washington Post* in 1971. The first article, written by Neil Sheehan, was printed on Sunday, June 13, 1971 in the *Times*, beginning the largest unauthorized disclosure of classified material in the history of the United States.

President Richard Nixon and his administration, caught off-guard by the release of the information, decided to halt the reports through court action. Although the study did not reference Nixon, the president and his secretary of state, Henry Kissinger, rationalized that it could prove harmful to their own administration and filed an injunction on June 14, 1971, to enjoin the *Times* from publishing further reports, marking the first time the federal government had sued the press to limit their publication of material pertaining to national security since the adoption of the U.S. Constitution. On June 18, the same day as the trial in New York, the *Washington Post* also released segments of the study, resulting in a second lawsuit, against the *Post*. Although both newspapers initially abided by the restraining orders given them by the courts, both U.S. District Judges Murray I. Gurfein in New York and Gerhard A. Gesell in Washington, D.C., ruled in favor of the newspapers due to lack of evidence that further printed reports would be a threat to national security. An appeal by both President Nixon and the *New York Times* elevated the case to the U.S. Supreme Court on June 30, resulting in a six-to-three ruling in favor of the newspaper and the quick resumption of the publication of more of the *Pentagon Papers*. The importance of the decision lay in the precedence the court set in establishing the publishing right of newspapers.

In the process of the newspaper trials, Daniel Ellsberg and Anthony Russo were criminally charged—Ellsberg with 12 federal felony counts for violating the Espionage Act and unauthorized possession of government documents, adding up to 115 years in prison. Desperate to discredit Ellsberg, President Nixon formed an extralegal investigative unit he called "the plumbers" to stop the information leaks, and commissioned them to recover files from the office of Ellsberg's psychiatrist, Dr. Lewis Fielding. Their effort failed to find personal information on Ellsberg, and in combination with the revealing of the illegal wiretap of Ellsberg, resulted in the charges being dropped against him. On July 12, 1974, a court found John Ehrlichman, Gordon Liddy, and their Cuban assistants guilty of conspiracy to violate Dr. Fielding's civil rights. Only Russo served jail time for his connection with the *Pentagon Papers* for his refusal to testify in secret before a federal grand jury in Los Angeles. Ellsberg and Russo, to their dismay, were never formally acquitted of the charges against them.

Instead, attention turned to the televised spectacle of the further actions of the plumbers in their involvement in the Watergate affair. The clandestine actions initiated by President Richard Nixon in the *Pentagon Papers* resulted in his resignation of the presidency in August 1974.

See also Fulbright, James William (1905–1995); Vietnam War.

Bibliography

DeBenedetti, Charles. *An American Ordeal: The Antiwar Movement of the Vietnam Era.* Syracuse, NY: Syracuse University Press, 1990.

Ellsberg, Daniel. *Secrets: A Memoir of Vietnam and the Pentagon Papers.* New York: Penguin, 2002.

Rudenstine, David. *The Day the Presses Stopped: A History of the Pentagon Papers Case.* Berkeley: University of California Press, 1996.

Ungar, Sanford J. *The Papers & the Papers: An Account of the Legal and Political Battle Over the Pentagon Papers.* New York: Columbia University Press, 1972, 1989.

ANCA GATA

PEPSI GENERATION, THE. "The Pepsi Generation" was a fictional youth movement created by Pepsi-Cola in the 1960s, used in advertising the Pepsi product in a pioneering appeal to consumers to identify themselves with the product. The concept, created by Pepsi-Cola advertising executive Alan Pottasch, attempted to unify brand image and consumer identity through lifestyle marketing, describing the consumer rather than the product in advertisements.

The roots of the Pepsi Generation campaign began in 1961, a time when the monotonous commercial advertising strategies of the 1950s were being scrutinized and rejected on the grounds of their emphasis on "mass society." In the 1950s, consumerism appeared to stress the importance of fitting in with the ideal, or buying a product for the sole purpose of impressing one's neighbour. Pepsi-Cola itself used the same formula in their 1950s advertisements featuring a well-to-do group called "The Sociables." The derogatory notion of mass society seeped into consumerism toward the end of the 1950s, portraying postwar U.S. capitalism as a soulless machine bent on limiting individual freedom by dictating what the consumer needed.

Sensing this rejection of traditional advertisement, Pepsi decided to change their advertising methods. Their rivals, Coca-Cola, were at the time the brand beyond competition, a veritable symbol of America; whereas Pepsi was considered the cheaper option. Pepsi decided to base their advertising on denouncing the conservative aspects of the past and embraced the new, different, nonconformist perspective that was being established in American youth. Pepsi cast itself between 1961 and 1963 as the drink for "those who think young." Youth was marketed as a philosophy, not a chronological age; a generation in which membership could be bought in the product of Pepsi. Consumers became the ultimate individual through the act of choosing Pepsi.

Throughout the decade, Pepsi's ads contained images of the Pepsi Generation engaged in dangerous or exotic entertainment, with visual effects that were previously unknown on American television such as characteristics of French New Wave Cinema. Ranging from music concerts to motorbike rides, Pepsi ads attempted to cover all symbols of the counterculture, displaying its up-to-date knowledge of what was hip. However, as the decade progressed, the concept of the Pepsi Generation hit a problem—youth no longer looked like the Pepsi Generation portrayed in Pepsi ads. As the counterculture became increasingly viewed as hostile or dangerous, the Pepsi

Generation soon looked, in comparison, like advertising anachronisms of everything they originally rebelled against—safe, established, square. Pepsi was trapped between the need to appeal to the counterculture and its reluctance to be viewed as condoning the violent protests, drug taking, and other antisocial activities stereotypically equated with late 1960s counterculture. Despite campaigns such as the "Live/Give" ads that ran from 1969 to 1972, the Pepsi Generation failed to fully reclaim their image as the hip trendsetters they were in the early 1960s.

Although the Pepsi Generation was remarketed in the 1980s, the main legacy of the 1960s campaign was one of innovation in advertising and consumer segmentation. It helped redefine the consumer from one who desires conformity to one who is expressing their individuality by what they desire. Ultimately, the Pepsi Generation's transformation—from organized, harmless rebellion to an apparent uncontrollable, inaccurate movement—parallels the changing perspective on the counterculture itself in the 1960s.

Bibliography

Frank, Thomas. *The Conquest of Cool: Business Culture, Counterculture, and the Rise of Hip Consumerism.* Chicago: University of Chicago Press, 1997.
Rutherford, Paul. *The New Icons? The Art of Television Advertising.* Toronto: University of Toronto Press, 1994.

ADAM PEARSON

PERFORMANCE ART. Performance art refers to a conceptual form of art that involved live, often improvisatory pieces that played with the expectations of the audience. Unlike regular art with its strict rules and structure, performance art is a time-based experience that often cannot be recreated, and happens once in a specific place for a specific time (although that time can last as long as several months or even a year), and is meant in some cases to test the endurance of both the performer and the audience.

Many trace the start of performance art to the Italian futurists and the surrealists and dada movements of the late nineteenth and early twentieth centuries, where traditional notions of art and dance were combined in often groundbreaking ways. Other scholars look at the mid-1960s "happenings," largely attributed to Allan Kaprow, who developed many of the tropes of modern performance art by leading audiences though set tableaus where musicians were playing or other kinds of performances were happening. Many were inspired by Kaprow's approach to letting the audience be as much a part of the art as the work itself, and soon happenings were widespread by the late '60s.

One of the most influential performance artists of the last three decades is Tehching Hsieh, who is most notable for his "one year" performances in which he dedicates himself to a singular activity for duration of one year. Hseih started in the 1960s, but created several important pieces in the '80s and '90s. They include the 1985–1986 No/Art Piece, where he produced no new works and did not view any art; the 1983–1984 Art/Life Piece, where he was attached to fellow artist Linda Montano by an eight-foot piece of rope for a year; and most famously his 1978–1979 Cage Piece, where he was imprisoned for a year in a small cage and did not talk, read, or watch TV (this was open to the public for select viewings as well).

Notable performance artists of the last three decades include Genesis P-Orridge and Cosey Fan Tutti of the live performance collective COUM and later the industrial noise band Throbbing Gristle, who did improvisational pieces involving nudity, penetration, and ritual scarification. Others who mixed performance with a wide variety of artistic endeavors included the Velvet Underground and Andy Warhol's Exploding Plastic Inevitable. Other examples include the Fluxus group, particularly Yoko Ono, who—along with her husband Beatle John Lennon—famously staged a "bed-in" for peace for two different weeks in Amsterdam and Montreal in 1969.

Performance art continues to this day, most notably realized in a recent project by long running conceptualists who started in the '60s, such as Marina Abramovic, who in 2010 completed a piece that lasted over 700 hours in which she sat in a chair in the Museum of Modern Art, staring silently for eight hours a day at any interested parities who wished to either stare at her or involve themselves in the piece.

Bibliography

Goldberg, Rosalee. *Performance Art: From Futurism to the Present*. London: Thames & Hudson, 2001.
Goldberg, Rosalee. *Performance: Live Art Since the '60s*. London: Thames & Hudson, 2004.

BRIAN COGAN

PETER, PAUL, AND MARY (1962–2009). Peter Yarrow, Noel (Paul) Stookey, and Mary Travers released their debut album, *Peter, Paul and Mary*, in 1962. The album marked a critical joining of a nation recovering from the McCarthy era, forming the civil rights movement, heating up the Cold War, and stoking the spirit of social activism. It took Peter, Paul, and Mary to merge these events into an indelible imprint of folk music as an instrument of social change.

Trailblazers like Woody Guthrie and Pete Seeger and the Weavers had linked folk music with social and political activism, but during the McCarthy witch-hunting era of the late 1950s, folk music was forced underground. By the time Peter, Paul, and Mary appeared, most people viewed American folk as a sidebar to the heavily acoustical pop and rock music. Peter, Paul, and Mary's more lightly accented guitar and musical message of humanity, hope, and activism arrived at exactly the right time and resonated with generations.

Peter, Paul, and Mary met as individuals in the early 1960s in New York's Greenwich Village. Peter Yarrow arrived at the Village with a psychology degree from Cornell. Paul Stookey met Yarrow, who played as a solo act at the Village coffeehouses. They met Mary Travers, who had grown up in the Village and had already gained some fame for her work in the Song Swappers, a folk group that had sung with Pete Seeger. With the encouragement of folk music impresario Albert Grossman, the trio decided to work together and made their debut at the Bitter End in the Village in late 1961.

In 1962, Warner Bros. Records produced their album *Peter, Paul and Mary*, and with the help of enormous hits like "Lemon Tree" and "If I Had a Hammer," it shot to the top of the Billboard charts. It remained number one on the Billboard Top 10 for 10 months and in the top 20 for two years, enjoying a three-and-a-half-year run on the charts. In 1963, they released the albums *Moving*, which hit number two, and *In The Wind*, which reached number one, and both continued to hold top 20 positions beside their first album. Their recording of "Puff the Magic Dragon" achieved great popularity and went on to become a children's classic.

In 1963, Peter, Paul, and Mary sang at the March on Washington, and in 1965 at the Selma-Montgomery March, under the threat of violence and personal injury. The trio's music awakened America and helped it unite in song and spirit to fulfill its promise to afford liberty and justice to everyone. They reached out with their music of conscience to personally touch the lives of millions of Americans and use folk music as a tool of social change. Their song "If I Had A Hammer" became the anthem of the civil rights movement, and again in 1969, the group sang at a march on Washington.

In 1970, Peter, Paul, and Mary disbanded to pursue individual interests. They reunited at an antinuclear benefit at the Hollywood Bowl in 1978, and went on to create more popular albums and Public Broadcasting System specials. Their 50 years of working and recording together provided an inspiring example of what united talent and determination can accomplish. Mary Travers died in 2009, but Peter and Paul continue to work together musically.

Bibliography

Peter, Paul, and Mary. *Peter, Paul & Mary, Deluxe Anthology*. Van Nuys, CA: Alfred Publishing, 1990.

Peter, Paul and Mary. *The Peter, Paul, and Mary Song Book*. Indianapolis: Warner Bros. Publications, 1990.

Peter, Paul, and Mary. *Peter, Paul and Mary on Tour: Songbook*. n.p., 1964.

Roy, William G. *Reds, Whites, and Blues: Social Movements, Folk Music, and Race in the United States*. Princeton, NJ: Princeton University Press, ebook, 2010.

KATHY WARNES

PLANET OF THE APES (1968). Director Franklin J. Schaffner's *Planet of the Apes* presents a dystopian morality tale that spoke directly to the 1960s counterculture's concerns about the future of humanity, commenting on social ills such as violence, greed, racism, social hierarchy, and environmental destruction. Filmed largely in the southwestern United States, the story is set on an unknown planet where the conventional roles of humans and apes are reversed. Apes have evolved into the dominant species, possessing all the traits and social organization normally associated with humans; humans, meanwhile, are held in captivity as animal-like slaves and laborers and considered incapable of higher intellect or speech. The film is loosely based on the novel *La planete de singes* by Pierre Boulle (1963), following a screenplay initially written by the *Twilight Zone*'s Rod Serling.

The film tells the story of four Earth astronauts: Taylor (Charlton Heston), Landon (Robert Gunner), Dodge (Jeff Burton), and Stewart (Dianne Stanley), who embark on a deep space journey, most of which will occur in hibernation to prevent aging. Just prior to his entry into the medically induced sleep, Taylor, the captain, contemplates the vastness of space and the finite nature of the human condition. He records in his final log: "Seen from out here, everything is different. Time bends. Space is … boundless. It squashes a man's ego. I feel lonely." This proves to be the first of many thinly veiled messages about human nature and humanity's failure to comprehend its place in a vast, interdependent universe.

The three male astronauts are awakened prematurely by their ship's crash landing in the year 3978 A.D. Stewart, however, dies in-flight. As they venture across the planet's alien landscape, they discover a group of primitive humans, who appear to have developed only enough to hunt, gather, and scavenge for food. When mounted gorilla patrols descend on the group, most are either captured or killed, including the astronauts. Dodge is fatally wounded; Landon and Taylor are taken prisoner and brought to Ape City, where Landon is lobotomized—a victim of the apes' all-too-human ignorance and objectification. Taylor thus becomes the central character. He rapidly learns of the apes' prejudices against humans, clearly reminiscent of the unconsidered racism in Earth's history, and throughout the remainder of the film's narrative, he negotiates his captivity, release, and status as a sentient being, finally convincing ape scientist Zira (Kim Hunter) and her fiancé, archaeologist Cornelius (Roddy McDowell), of human beings' capacities. In the final scenes, Taylor and his "mate," Nova (Linda Harrison), are released to discover their "destiny" as freed slaves, but they discover the past, instead, in the half-buried form of the Statue of Liberty. Taylor realizes that his ship did not crash on a planet in some remote galaxy, but rather, returned to Earth 2,000 years in the future—a planet that had been destroyed by human folly and reclaimed by the apes that now risked following in humanity's footsteps.

Planet of the Apes received an honorary Academy Award for its pathbreaking use of prosthetic makeup techniques, and its score, by Jerry Goldsmith, was ranked in the American Film Institute's "100 Years of Film Scores" as the 18th best film score in American cinema. In 2001, the film was selected for preservation in the Library of Congress's National Film Registry, an honor bestowed annually on films deemed "culturally, historically, or aesthetically significant."

Bibliography

Greene, Eric. *Planet of the Apes as American Myth: Race, Politics, and Popular Culture.* Middletown, CT: Wesleyan University Press, 1998.

CYNTHIA J. MILLER

PLAYBOY MAGAZINE. The first issue of *Playboy* was composed at the kitchen table of Hugh Hefner's small Southside-Chicago apartment in 1953. It was to be "an entertainment magazine for the young, urban male," in Hefner's words, "devoted to men's dreams and fantasies." With a total sale of almost 54,000 copies and the first full-color, nude photograph of Marilyn Monroe, the magazine proved not only successful but revolutionary. During the 1960s, an encompassing "Playboy Empire"—including mansions, nightclubs, television shows, a multimillion-dollar jet, as well as the magazine—occupied a significant niche within the decade's cultural scene.

If, as Hefner claimed, "sex is the primary motivating factor in the course of human history," then *Playboy* certainly tapped into and produced such a factor. By 1960, monthly sales of the magazine were over one million. Intended for men "between 18 and 80," the large sales of *Playboy* reflected a common and popular interest. It was more than pictures of nude women, however, that appealed to '60s consumers. *Playboy* offered a particular depiction of female beauty as well as a total lifestyle that spoke to the heterosexual male imaginary.

The image of beauty *Playboy* sought to cultivate was that of the "girl next door." The "Playmate of the Month" centerfolds were to be sexualized versions of the everyday woman captured in everyday scenes, like the June 1963 Playmate, Jayne

Mansfield, in a bubble bath. The cute, all-American Playmate was accessible, ideal, and best of all, supposedly commonplace and awaiting discovery.

Much more than a magazine, *Playboy* offered its readers an entire world, a lifestyle, "an empire of dreams," as Hefner claimed. In issues like May 1962, *Playboy* granted readers access to such a place, as editors gave "The Playboy Townhouse" a nine-page illustrated article detailing the inner opulence of the mansion as well as the sexy activities that took place therein. It was an unrestricted sexual haven, an alternative to the '50s single-family home, full of viewable and available "bunnies." The mansion was where *Playboy* was made and where the Playboy lifestyle was enjoyed, the perfect blend of business and pleasure.

In addition to being a medium for fantasy, *Playboy* was a forum for '60s culture and counterculture. As African Americans in the Jim Crow South struggled for overdue freedoms, *Playboy* provided a particularly liberal, progressive medium and an extensive readership. In 1962 and 1963, the magazine included interviews with Miles Davis, Malcolm X, and Martin Luther King Jr.—all providing commentary on the current state of the union for African Americans.

On the cover of *Time* in 1966, Hefner and his magazine were (and are) "a major American business success story." By 1969, *Playboy* sold about 4.5 million copies a month. Worthy of imitation, magazines like *Nugget, Dude, Swank, Gent, Rogue, Fury, Caper, Cavalcade, Gay Blade,* and *Scamp* sought to replicate the cultural phenomenon *Playboy* represented. *Playboy* captured, and in many ways led, the '60s countercultural reassessment of sexuality, beauty, gender roles, the home, and even politics.

Bibliography

Edgren, Gretchen. *Inside the Playboy Mansion: If You Don't Swing, Don't Ring.* Los Angeles: Playboy Enterprises, 1998.
Miller, Russell. *Bunny: The Real Story of Playboy.* New York: Holt, Rinehart, and Winston, 1984.

MILES ADAM PARK

PLEIKU. Pleiku is the capital of Gia Lai Province located in Vietnam's Central Highlands. Most of its inhabitants are Montagnards or Degar peoples. Situated near highways 14 and 19, Pleiku was of economic and strategic value throughout the Vietnam War. During the war, it served as a hub for westward bound traffic coming from South Vietnam's port of Qui Nhon. Strategically positioned between American and South Vietnamese bases at Kon Tum and Buon Ma Thuot, as well as North Vietnamese staging areas in Cambodia, control of Pleiku was essential to the defense of South Vietnam.

Throughout the Vietnam War, Pleiku hosted the U.S. Army's Camp Holloway, a vital helicopter base that provided mobility to units of both the U.S. Army and the Army of the Republic of Vietnam (ARVN). Pleiku served as the headquarters for the ARVN's II Corps and the home for U.S. Air Force (USAF) and Vietnamese Air Force (VNAF) units. USAF units at Pleiku included the 21st Tactical Air Support Squadron, 663d Special Operations Wing, 6th Air Commando Squadron, 9th Air Commando Squadron, and 362d Tactical Electronic Warfare Squadron. The 6th Air Division of the Vietnamese Air Force (VNAF) also operated out of Pleiku.

During the early hours of February 7, 1965, a Viet Cong (VC) force assaulted Camp Holloway. Spotted before they placed explosives on the barracks' walls, the

VC threw their explosives on to the barracks' roof, resulting in fewer causalities. Nevertheless, the engagement left over 100 Americans wounded, 8 Americans killed, and the loss of five helicopters. The assault on Pleiku exposed the vulnerability of U.S. installations in South Vietnam and thus resulted in the deployment of American combat troops to act as security. In retaliation for the attack, the Lyndon B. Johnson administration sanctioned Operation Flaming Dart, which consisted of air strikes against North Vietnamese military targets. Ultimately, the attack at Pleiku pushed the Johnson administration to escalate the war in Vietnam.

Pleiku figured prominently in the battles of the Ia Drang Valley, also referred to as the Pleiku Campaign. Due to the city's economic and strategic value, NVA and VC forces sought to capture it. In a series of battles to secure the area surrounding Pleiku, from October 19 to November 25, 1965, U.S. Army forces fought units of the North Vietnamese Army (NVA) for the first time during the war. Pleiku provided substantial air mobility and fire support to the American units participating in the operations against the NVA.

North Vietnam's 1975 invasion of South Vietnam called for the capture of Pleiku. Under orders from South Vietnamese president Nguyen Van Thieu, ARVN forces abandoned the central highlands, including Pleiku, in an effort to consolidate forces around Saigon. NVA units quickly occupied the city and overran the retreating ARVN troops, thus opening the road to Saigon.

See also Montagnards; Thieu, Nguyen Van (1924–2001); Viet Cong; Vietnam War.

Bibliography

Coleman, J. D. *Pleiku: The Dawn of Helicopter Warfare in Vietnam.* New York: St. Martin's, 1988.

Herring, George C. *America's Longest War: The United States and Vietnam, 1950–1975.* 4th ed. New York: McGraw-Hill, 2002.

Prados, John. *Vietnam: The History of an Unwinnable War, 1945–1975.* Lawrence: University Press of Kansas, 2009.

ROBERT J. THOMPSON III

POLANSKI, ROMAN (1933–). Film director Roman Polanski was born on August 18, 1933, in Paris to Polish-Jewish parents but was taken to Poland at age three by his parents. When he was eight, his parents were taken to a concentration camp, while he was left alone in the Kraków ghetto. Polanski escaped shortly before most of the Jewish population were killed or sent to concentration camps and spent the remainder of the war hiding out in the countryside. The horrors and terrors of that period have informed Polanski's films, which often feature acts of extreme violence or horror, an atmosphere of alienation and estrangement, and an interest in human aberrations and obsessions.

Polanski began acting as a teenager and attended film school in Lodz, graduating in 1959. His first feature, *Nóz w wodzie* (*Knife in the Water*, 1962), is notable for its unsettling exploration of jealousy and spite among three characters (a married couple and young hitchhiker) who spend most of the film in the claustrophobic confines of a small yacht. The film won the critics' (FIPRESCI) prize at the Venice Film Festival and was nominated for the Oscar for Best Foreign Language Film.

Polanski's next two films were also critically acclaimed: *Repulsion* (1965; his first film in English) and *Cul-de-Sac* (1966). However, it was his 1968 film *Rosemary's*

Baby, with a screenplay adapted by Polanski from a novel by Ira Levin, that made him famous among popular film audiences as well as with critics and connoisseurs of art-house cinema. Rosemary (Mia Farrow) is a young woman whose husband (John Cassavetes) becomes involved with a group of devil worshippers, and a series of strange events lead her to believe she is carrying a child fathered by Satan. The success of *Rosemary's Baby* spawned a number of big-budget American films dealing with the occult (a topic previously more associated with exploitation films), including *The Exorcist* (William Friedkin, 1973) and *The Omen* (Richard Donner, 1976).

In August 1969, Polanski's pregnant wife Sharon Tate was among several people murdered in Polanski's home by members of the Charles Manson family. The murders received a great deal of public attention, both because they were particularly gruesome and also because the popularity of *Rosemary's Baby* associated Polanski with devil worship in the public mind, leading some to suggest that the killings were part of a Satanic ritual.

Polanski returned to directing in 1971 with *Macbeth* and produced a number of notable films including *Chinatown* (1977) and *The Pianist* (2002; winner of the Oscar for Best Picture). In 1977, he was accused of statutory rape in California and was convicted in absentia after he fled the country. He has lived in Europe since that time, although extradition proceedings begun in 2009 which may force him to return to the United States.

See also Manson, Charles (1934–); *Rosemary's Baby* (1968).

Bibliography

Cronin, Paul. *Roman Polanski: Interviews*. Jackson: University Press of Mississippi, 2005.

Morrison, James. *Roman Polanski*. Urbana: University of Illinois Press, 2007.

Orr, John, and Elzbieta Ostrowska, eds. *The Cinema of Roman Polanski: Dark Spaces of the World*. New York: Wallflower, 2006.

Sandford, Christopher. *Polanski*. New York: Palgrave Macmillan, 2008.

SARAH BOSLAUGH

POLAROID. Under the leadership of owner Edwin H. Land, the Polaroid Corporation achieved global fame as the creator of instant photography. The immediate thrill offered by Polaroid cameras seized the imagination of amateur and professional photographers across the United States, securing its widespread popularity. Although the subsequent advent of digital photography was in part responsible for the near-bankruptcy of the company in 2001, Polaroid has nonetheless helped to shape photographic history in the twentieth century, both capturing and captivating the modern age.

Having founded the Polaroid Corporation in 1937, Harvard graduate Edwin H. Land grounded his fledging business in the principle that scientific innovation was the foundation of artistic photographic practice. The company consequently adopted a pioneering laboratory-based structure that sought to deliver new innovations in camera technology. Although Land's personal interests lay initially in reducing the glare on developed images, his attention quickly switched to the possibility of instant photography after his young daughter wanted to see a photograph immediately while on family vacation in Mexico. After several intense years of groundbreaking research, Land introduced instant imaging to the Optical Society of America in 1947, with the first Polaroid camera hitting the shelves the following year.

After generating significant profit through the sale of sepia and black-and-white Polaroid film throughout the 1950s, the heyday of instant photography undoubtedly commenced in the '60s with the release of Positive/Negative Land film in 1961, which produced an additional peel-away negative that could be either reused or enlarged. This was quickly followed by the introduction of color Polaroid film in 1963. The combination of color imagery and the instant gratification of the Polaroid camera provoked such excitement among camera users that by the end of the decade it was estimated that over half of all American families owned a Polaroid camera. However, while the cameras were certainly an affordable pleasure for the average amateur camera user, many artists were equally enraptured with the new technology, with a number—including Andy Warhol—subsequently producing work based on Polaroid images.

Although the unrivalled popularity of Polaroid cameras assured the commercial success of the corporation into the 1990s, Land nonetheless became somewhat resentful of the link between Polaroid and instant photography in the popular imagination (Hitchcock and Kao 1999). For Land, this profit-making association obscured other technological achievements by the company, including its advances in the fields of military surveillance and x-ray film. This fear proved well founded as the grounding of Polaroid's profits primarily in instant imaging led to the company's economic downfall as the emerging digital photography market rendered Polaroid obsolete by the late 1990s. Amidst growing debts and plummeting profits, the Polaroid Corporation was forced to file for bankruptcy in 2001. In 2007, it announced the cessation of production of Polaroid cameras and film, to the consternation of many long-standing devotees.

Polaroid cameras have been increasingly commercially marginalized in the current digital age, serving primarily as a nostalgic novelty for subsequent generations. Yet, if these cameras promised to capture memories instantly in time, Land's innovations undoubtedly also captured a groundbreaking moment in photographic history in the twentieth century.

Bibliography

Haig, Matt. "Polaroid." In Matt Haig, ed. *Brand Failures: The Truth About the 100 Biggest Branding Mistakes of All Time*. London: Kogan Page, 2003, pp. 228–34.
Hitchcock, Barbara, Deborah Klochko, and Deborah Martin Kao. *Innovation/Imagination: 50 Years of Polaroid Photography*. New York: Harry N. Abrams, 1999.

ROSEMARY DELLER

POOR PEOPLE'S CAMPAIGN (1967). In the waning months of 1967, Martin Luther King Jr. and the leaders of the Southern Christian Leadership Conference (SCLC) decided that the civil rights movement needed to go beyond a call for racial equality. In the early years of the movement, King viewed the North as a shining example of the racial egalitarianism he was working so hard to achieve in the South. Yet after seeing the rampant racism and unofficial segregation of the northern cities, King began to believe that the civil rights movement had set its standards too low. Additionally, in the latter half of the 1960s, King and many other civil rights leaders began to link racial inequality with economic inequality. They believed that the suppression of blacks was not only a racial issue, but rather one example of an economic system that privileged the rich and subjugated the poor. Many leaders even saw the

Poor People's March in Washington, D.C., on June 18, 1968. (Library of Congress)

overt racism of poor, rural, southern whites as a symptom of their own economic oppression. Subsequently, King broadened the SCLC's goals and began what he called the "second phase" of the civil rights crusade.

This second phase sought to combat the economic disparity between rich and poor Americans. King and the SCLC planned to fight this oppression with many of the same tactics they had been using for over a decade: nonviolent protest and a call for legislative action. In December 1967, the SCLC began planning what they called a Poor People's Campaign. The campaign would involve a march on Washington, D.C., to dramatize the plight of America's poor. The protesters would visit various government agencies, advocating on behalf of the poor and refusing to leave the city until action was taken. The goal of the campaign would be the passage of an "economic bill of rights" that emphasized adequate housing for the poor and a guaranteed annual income for all Americans. The campaign was planned for the spring of 1968. However, weeks before the planned march, King's shift to economic in addition to racial concerns brought him to Memphis, Tennessee to support a local sanitation workers' strike. On April 4, he was assassinated on the balcony of the Lorraine Motel.

Following King's death, his widow, Coretta, and his chief lieutenants, particularly Ralph Abernathy and Jesse Jackson, decided to continue with the planned march on Washington in honor of King. The first protesters began arriving in Washington on May 12. One week later, a settlement of shacks and tents was erected on the National Mall to house the protesters. The new settlement was named Resurrection City. The protesters stayed in Washington for almost six weeks. The news coverage of the event tended to be negative, and a number of people picketed the campaign. The assassination of presidential candidate Robert Kennedy further disheartened the protesters, and the campaign ended without an economic bill of rights being passed and little noticeable difference being made in the public's concern over the plight of America's poor. As a result, the Poor People's Campaign was seen as a failure, though the movement was later resurrected in Chicago in 2003.

See also Abernathy, Ralph (1926–1990); Jackson, Jesse (1941–); Kennedy, Robert F. (1925–1968); King, Martin Luther Jr. (1929–1968); March on Washington (1968); Southern Christian Leadership Conference (SCLC).

Bibliography

Branch, Taylor. *At Canaan's Edge: America in the King Years, 1965–1968.* New York: Simon & Schuster, 2006.
Jackson, Thomas F. *From Civil Rights to Human Rights: Martin Luther King, Jr., and the Struggle for Economic Justice.* Philadelphia: University of Pennsylvania Press, 2006.
McKnight, Gerald D. *The Last Crusade: Martin Luther King Jr., the FBI, and the Poor People's Campaign.* New York: Basic Books, 1998.

ANDREW POLK

POP ART. Pop art, short for "popular" art, was a term coined by Lawrence Alloway to define the form that emerged in the late 1950s as a refutation of abstract expressionism. Based on popular cultural elements such as comic books and consumer items, pop art borrowed from American media and advertising as a reflection of mass consumerism in postwar society, beginning the shift toward postmodernism.

Although remembered as an American style, pop art as a movement began in Britain in the mid-1950s as the Independent Group combined art with science fiction, comic books, and consumable products, many from America. Although the British artists influenced American ones, the American style was distinct. Some artists played on common objects such as flags, soup cans, and beer bottles or combined them with unrelated items to produce an ironic effect, usually on a very large scale. Strengthened by the upheavals of the '60s, this artistic movement protested the "plastic" nature of society.

Pop art both baffled and awed critics. Hilton Kramer and John Canaday believed the style signified the decline of art in general. However, those in favor of it included Thomas Hess and Gene Swenson from *Art News magazine*, the brilliant young critic Barbara Rose, West Coast artist Peter Plagens, and prominent figures of the New York art world like Harold Rosenberg, Leo Steinberg, Max Kozloff, and Susan Sontag, all of whom recognized the cheekiness and freedom of pop art. Due to the relationship of pop to the culture of mass advertising, the popular press accepted the style with ease and wrote glowing reviews of it. Pop art infiltrated *Life* and *Vogue*, using the magazines as a vehicle to reach the public, creating its quick ascent into popular culture promote.

The artists of pop art furthered its fame, as their creative and distinctive styles permeated the art scene. Main artists included Andy Warhol, Roy Lichtenstein, Claes Oldenberg, Jasper Johns, and Robert Rauschenberg. Less famous artists included Allan D'Arcangelo, Jim Dine, Öyvind Fahlström, Robert Indiana, Mel Ramos, Edward Ruscha, George Segal, Peter Saul, Wayne Thiebaud, John Wesley, Tom Wesselman, Billy Al Bengston, Stephen Durkee, Joe Goode, Red Grooms, Philip Hefferton, Marisol, Robert Watts, and Richard Artschwager.

Pop artist and underground film producer Andy Warhol, November 12, 1969. (AP/Wide World Photos)

Andy Warhol (1928–1987), born Andrew Warhola, was the leading artist of American pop art, known as the "Pope of Pop." Known mostly for his silk screens of consumer culture and celebrities, he also produced drawings, sculptures, audio recordings, television shows, films, fashion, performance art, theater, photography, and early digital art. His first exhibition featured his famous cans of Campbell's Soup, and he later created art pieces of Coca-Cola cans and Brillo boxes at his "Factory" studio in New York City. His most famous pieces are 10 silk-screen prints of Marilyn Monroe entitled *Marilyn* and eight prints of Elvis Presley, *Eight Elvises*. Warhol also coined the term "fifteen minutes of fame." His works shocked audiences accustomed to appreciating art in an emotional and sentimental way.

Roy Lichtenstein (1923–1997) was a painter, sculptor, printmaker, and decorative artist. His work is most distinctive for its use of comic book and advertisement style and content involving the patterns of colored circles that replicate benday dots used in newspapers. His most popular paintings are *Spray*, *Whaam!*, *As I Opened Fire*, and *Drowning Girl*. His *Mirrors* series questioned whether representational art directly represented reality.

Claes Oldenburg (1929–) is a sculptor, draughtsman, printmaker, performance artist, and writer of Swedish birth. He was involved in happenings, a form of performance art with his first canvas sculptures. As a form of installation art, he preferred commercial fabrication by using soft canvas props to represent monumental and sagging common objects, as seen in *Floor Cone*, *Floor-burger*, and *The Home—Bedroom Ensemble* being the largest and most complex of the series. He moved on to permanent outdoor installation art monuments such as *Giant Three-way Plug, Scale A, 1/3, Giant*

Trowel, Crusoe Umbrella, Screwarch, and *Stake Hitch*. His monumental sculptures, sometimes fragmented, add to the abstract element of his version of art.

Jasper Johns and Robert Rauschenberg shared the title "Neo Dadaist," although their work often included images from popular culture. Johns (1930–) was primarily involved in painting and printmaking, and is best known for his painting *Flag* and *Map*. Robert Rauschenberg (1925–2008) was an American painter, sculptor, printmaker, photographer, and performance artist and is well-known for his "Combines," which involved the mixture of nontraditional materials and objects. Pop art, like the counterculture, critiqued mass consumerism and thus became a significant part of the social upheaval of the 1960s.

See also Minimalism; Op Art; Performance Art; Warhol, Andy (1928–1987).

Bibliography

Doris, Sara. *Pop Art and the Contest Over American Culture*. New York: Cambridge University Press, 2007.
Lippard, Lucy R. *Pop Art*. New York: Praeger, 1966.
Madoff, Steven Henry, ed. *Pop Art: A Critical History*. Los Angeles: University of California Press, 1997.

BRITTANY BOUNDS

POPE JOHN XXIII. *See* John XXIII

POPE PAUL VI. *See* Paul VI

POWERS, FRANCIS GARY (1929–1977). Powers was an American pilot best known for commandeering the U-2 spy plane that was shot down over the Soviet Union on May 1, 1960. Born into a working-class family in Kentucky, Powers was fascinated by airplanes. Following his graduation from Milligan College in Tennessee in 1950, he enlisted in the Air Force and was commissioned a second lieutenant in 1952. From the mid 1950s he was involved with the CIA's secret U-2 program, flying high-altitude (70,000 feet) reconnaissance missions out of Turkey and Pakistan. He officially resigned his Air Force commission in 1956, and became an employee of the Lockheed Corporation—the manufacturer of the aircrafts used—in order to maintain a cover as a civilian pilot. His initial missions consisted of mapping the Middle East and observing naval movements during the Suez Crisis. He subsequently moved on to Eastern Europe and the Soviet Union.

On May 1, 1960, he was making a flight from Peshawar Airbase in Pakistan to Bodø in Norway, when his plane came under fire over the southern Soviet city of Sverdlovsk. His U-2 aircraft out of control, Powers ejected and landed in a rural area, where he was taken to the authorities. The self-destruct mechanism on the airplane was defunct, and Powers chose not to use his "suicide-needle." The official U.S. cover story was that a weather observation plane had crashed near the Soviet border, but as the Soviets could produce both the wreckage and the pilot, that story was quickly abandoned. The incident occurred just before a summit between Soviet chairman Nikita S. Khrushchev and U.S. president Dwight D. Eisenhower in Paris beginning on May 16, where the two leaders were to discuss Cold War issues. Khrushchev, however, announced that he would leave the summit if Eisenhower did not apologize for the U-2 incident. Eisenhower refused, and Khrushchev left. Some have claimed that the U-2 incident was directly responsible for the breakdown of the summit and the beginning détente between the two nations. It is much more plausible, however, that Khrushchev deliberately used the incident to make the summit collapse in order to obtain a potentially better deal with a new American president, who was to be elected in the fall of 1960.

Powers confessed to espionage and was sentenced to three years imprisonment and seven years hard labor. He served nearly two years of the sentence and was exchanged for Soviet spy Rudolf Abel in Berlin in 1962. When he returned to the United States, he was criticized by the government for talking to the Soviets and for not committing suicide before capture, but Powers held that he was trained as a pilot and not a spy. He escaped further sanctions and was awarded the CIA's Intelligence Star for Valor, but solely for actions until 1960.

He was fired from his job at Lockheed in 1970 for publishing his memoirs, although he had received unofficial CIA approval to do so. During the 1970s, he worked as a traffic pilot for various Los Angeles-based media outlets, but died in 1977, when his helicopter ran out of fuel and crashed.

Bibliography

Powers, Francis Gary, and Curt Gentry. *Operation Overflight: A Memoir of the U2 Incident.* Dulles, VA: Potomac Books, 2002.

KASPER GROTLE RASMUSSEN

PRAGUE SPRING MOVEMENT (1968). The Western media coined the term "Prague Spring" to describe the short period of liberalization of the communist regime in Czechoslovakia in 1968. The reforms included the granting of freedom of speech, civil rights, autonomy of Slovakia, and other liberal transformations, which led to an increasing democratization of Czechoslovakia from January 5 to August 20, 1968, when the process was stopped by a Soviet-led invasion of the Warsaw Pact armies.

In the late 1960s, there was increasing discontent among the general population of Czechoslovakia with the rigid communist regime of President Antonin Novotny, who was also first secretary of the Communist Party. On January 5, 1968, the Central Committee of the Communist Party replaced Novotny with the young Slovak communist Alexander Dubček.

Dubček had little political experience, but he became very popular due to his willingness to comply with the public demands for more freedom. He propelled the Prague Spring Movement with a series of reforms and the message that he wanted to build "socialism with a human face." Meanwhile, by April 1968, other reformers replaced the high-ranking old-guard communists. Ludvik Svoboda became president of Czechoslovakia in March 1968, and Oldřich Černík became prime minister in April 1968.

That same month, the new reformist government adopted the Action Program, which included the recognition of Slovakia as an equal member within a new Czechoslovak federation, a revised constitution with guarantees to civil rights and liberties including the rehabilitation of all former political prisoners, the transfer of

Young Czechs holding a Czechoslovakian flag stand atop an overturned truck in Prague amid Soviet tanks in August 1968, while other youths surround the tanks. (AFP/Getty Images)

power over the government from the Communist Party to the National Assembly, wider media freedom and urgent economic reforms. The reformist government even allowed the Communist Party members to express their opposition and criticism to the party policies. The general public was fascinated with their newly acquired freedom. The press started to expose government and party corruption; intellectuals formed clubs, human rights groups, Christian and other noncommunist associations; and farmers and workers started to bargain for more rights. In June 1968, a group of dissidents led by Ludvik Vaculik published the "Two Thousand Words Manifesto," which demanded the transformation of Czechoslovakia into a full-fledged democratic country.

Dubček was confident that he could manage well the reforms in his country, but Soviet leader Leonid Brezhnev and the leaders of the other communist countries in the Warsaw Pact considered these reforms an attempt at an anticommunist counter-revolution. After two meetings of Dubček with the other Eastern European communist leaders and Brezhnev on August 3 and August 15, 1968, Dubček still thought he would be left to complete his reform program. On the evening of August 20, 1968, however, Soviet armed forces, supported by small detachments of Polish, Hungarian, and Bulgarian troops and aided logistically by the East German army, invaded Czechoslovakia to put an end to the Prague Spring Movement.

The invasion was not resisted by the Czechoslovak army even though the population tried acts of passive resistance and road blockades. Seventy-two Czechs and Slovaks were killed during the invasion, and hundreds of others were injured. Over

200,000 Czechs and Slovaks emigrated from the country during and shortly after the invasion. Dubček and the other reformers were deposed, and the new government of Gustav Husak curtailed the Prague Spring reforms.

See also Brezhnev, Leonid Ilich (1906–1982).

Bibliography

Navratil, Jaromir, et al. *The Prague Spring 1968: A National Security Archive Documents Reader*. Budapest: Central European University Press, 1998.
Stolarik, M. Mark, comp. and ed. *The Prague Spring and the Warsaw Pact Invasion of Czechoslovakia, 1968: Forty Years Later*. Mundelein, IL: Bolchazy-Carducci, 2010.

CHRIS KOSTOV

PRESIDENT'S COMMISSION ON THE STATUS OF WOMEN (PCSW) (1963).

On December 14, 1961, President John F. Kennedy signed Executive Order 10980 creating the President's Commission on the Status of Women (PCSW) to be administered by the Labor Department. Chaired by Eleanor Roosevelt, the commission brought visibility and legitimacy to women's concerns.

The PCSW aimed to design proposals to combat sex discrimination in government and private employment, and to recommend services that would enable women to contribute economically to society. It reviewed progress and made recommendations in six areas: employment policies and practices; federal social insurance and tax laws; federal and state labor laws, differences in legal treatment of men and women; new and expanded services that may be required for women as wives, mothers, and workers; and the employment policies and practices of the U.S. government. To explore these areas in depth, the PCSW established committees on civil and political rights, education, federal employment, private employment, home and community, protective labor legislation, and social insurance and taxes.

On October 11, 1963, the PCSW gave its report, *American Women*, to Kennedy. The commission noted that many mothers, particularly African American mothers, had to work and that most women who worked were married. The report pointed out that women's earnings were less than men's and that women in federal service were in the lower grades. Seeing women primarily as wives and mothers rather than wage-earners, the PCSW declared that the adoption of its proposals would directly benefit men as well as women.

American Women avoided an analysis of the ideological roots of women's oppression, focusing instead on specific policy recommendations designed to create opportunities for working women. Although the PCSW ignored the contradiction between greater opportunities for women in the public sphere and their primary responsibilities for the home and family, it did recommend significant changes in government policies and employment and educational practices. One of the major clashes within the PCSW occurred over regulations on the hours that women may work, with the commission refusing to endorse maximum-hours legislation.

The PCSW achieved a number of successes. When the Civil Service Commission accepted its recommendation to end the practice of stipulating the sex of applicants, the placement of larger numbers of women became a possibility overnight. Commissions on the Status of Women also formed within a few years in 49 states, with Texas

The success of Project Mercury shaped the U.S. manned space program for the rest of the 1960s. Grissom, Schirra, and Cooper commanded three of the first four Gemini flights; Grissom died, along with two crewmates, while preparing for the first flight of Project Apollo, and Schirra took his place, commanding the first test flight of the Apollo spacecraft in Earth orbit. Deke Slayton, denied a Mercury flight because of a heart murmur, became a NASA administrator and chose the crews for the lunar landing missions, one of which was commanded by Shepard. The Gemini and Apollo spacecraft—blunted cones perched atop missile-like launch vehicles—were direct descendents of the Mercury design. The United States ended Project Mercury as they began it: behind the Soviet Union in the space race. Mercury's success, however, set the stage for far greater successes later in the decade.

See also Glenn, John (1921–); Project Apollo; Project Gemini; Shepard, Alan (1923–1998); Space Race.

Bibliography

Carpenter, M. Scott, et. al. *We Seven*. New York: Simon & Schuster, 1962.
McDougall, Walter A. *The Heavens and the Earth: A Political History of the Space Age*. New York: Basic Books, 1985.
Swenson, Loyd, James M. Grimwood, and Charles C. Alexander. *This New Ocean: A History of Project Mercury* [SP-4201]. Washington, DC: National Aeronautics and Space Administrations, 1966. Available at http://history.nasa.gov/SP-4201/toc.htm.
Wolfe, Tom. *The Right Stuff*. New York: Farrar, Straus, and Giroux, 1979.

A. BOWDOIN VAN RIPER

PROTEST MUSIC. Throughout the 1960s, music provided an innovative and creative outlet for social protest movements, and the civil rights movement and the antiwar movement were the two main manifestations of this strategy. In both of these examples, music was more than lyrics set to a melody; rather, it was a force to unite and strengthen those involved.

Music in the antiwar movement was more than hippies singing about peace. In the early 1960s, renowned American musician Bob Dylan released popular protest songs such as "The Times, They Are A-Changin," "Masters of War," and "Blowin' in the Wind." Lyrics full of social commentary and criticism on American malaise, inequality, consumerism, and the Vietnam War filled Dylan's records. Some radio stations banned P. F. Sloan's "Eve of Destruction," one of 1965's best-selling records, for its pointed criticism against the Vietnam War. Using a foolish World War II Army captain as a metaphor, Pete Seeger's 1965 "Waist Deep in the Big Muddy" criticized President Johnson's choice to continue American involvement in the Vietnam War.

Also voicing their criticisms with American culture in addition to war, protest music commented on society's general indifference. Simon and Garfunkel told Americans to open themselves up and make the "moment last," in their 1966 record "The 59th Street Bridge Song." Frustrated with conformity, social repression, and American society's contentment with the status quo, for some musicians America's role in the Vietnam War was indicative of bigger issues. During the 1969 music festival Woodstock, 400,000 attendees participated in a group chant against the military's presence in Southeast Asia and the draft. Furthermore, the music of Dylan, Joan Baez, and Seeger was popular, demonstrating both its pervasive influence in the antiwar movement and the general public's familiarity with socially inspired music and its relevance.

Some historians have argued that the civil rights movement would not have been successful had it not been for the use of music. Slave spirituals, such as "We Shall Overcome," and the gospel blues, with songs like "This Little Light of Mine," provided the soundtrack to marches, meetings, and rallies. Lyrics concerned with freedom and democracy struck a chord with protesters. Movement leader Fannie Lou Hamer often adapted lyrics of popular slave spirituals to the civil rights context. More than just religious songs, Nina Simone's pointed 1964 hit "Mississippi Goddam" also demonstrated intense frustration with inequality and exploitation. James Brown's empowering 1968 record "Say It Loud (I'm Black and I'm Proud)" indicated the commercial popularity of many of such songs.

Additionally, popular songs from white musicians also addressed the challenges of the African American population and their struggle for social equality. Dylan's "The Lonesome Death of Hattie Carroll" engaged the reality of the civil rights struggle. Singer-songwriter Frank Zappa's 1965 song "Trouble Coming Everyday," sympathetically addressed the exploitation and hardships faced by African Americans. Seeger and Baez's recordings of Depression-era Woody Guthrie songs linked the struggles of 1930s farmworkers with the contemporary situation. Connecting social struggles and criticisms, Dylan and Baez also sang during King's March on Washington.

Bibliography

Carawan, Guy, and Candie Carawan, eds. *Sing for Freedom: The Story of the Civil Rights Movement Through Its Songs*. Montgomery: New South Books, 2007.

Perone, James E. *Music of the Counterculture Era*. Westport, CT: Greenwood, 2004.

Rodnitzky, Jerome L. "The Sixties Between Microgrooves: Using Folk and Protest Music to Understand American History, 1963–1973." *Popular Music and Society* 23, no. 4 (1999): 105–22.

Rogovoy, Seth. *Bob Dylan: Prophet, Mystic, Poet*. New York: Scribners, 2009.

Rosenstone, Robert A. "'The Times They Are A-Changin': The Music of Protest." *Annals of the American Academy of Political and Social Science* 382, Protest in the Sixties (March 1969): 131–44.

EMILY SUZANNE CLARK

PSYCHEDELIC. "Psychedelic"—a term originating from the Greek and meaning "mind-manifesting"—describes the sensations felt and seen from the ingestion of hallucinogenic (or psychedelic) drugs such as lysergic acid diethylamide (or LSD-25), psilocybin, mescaline, and, though far less potent, cannabis or marijuana. In this state, the user experiences a disruption of the senses, an altered condition of understanding reality—in short, they take a mind-manifesting trip from their old sense of construing the world to a new sense in which they identify connections beyond those they had recognized before the trip. From the perspective of the 1960s, psychedelic may be seen as an adjectival lens for interpreting one's surroundings, identifying "fellow travelers," or even creating objects, sounds, or images that engage with the new set of codes established in the psychedelic community.

A good description of what psychedelic means—or an idea of its experience—can be found in the observations of early experimenters such as British author Aldous Huxley and LSD's creator Albert Hofmann. *The Doors of Perception*, written by Huxley in the mid-1950s—and immortalized in the name of the psychedelic rock band the Doors—explains the breakdown of various commonsense values such as spatial and time relationships to one's surroundings: "Place and distance cease to be of much interest. The mind does its perceiving in terms of intensity of existence, profundity of significance, relationships within a pattern. . . . [And] an even more complete indifference to time"—with the latter escaping the conventional notions of understandings. Visually, Huxley observed: "The field of vision was filled with brightly colored, constantly changing structures that seemed to be made of plastic or enameled tin: solid material appeared to move in a pliable, liquid manner." Sound, according to Hofmann, "generated a vividly changing image with its own consistent form and color." Combined, these characteristics were incorporated into consumer products or events that allowed users to step into a world where their intoxicated state intersected with a created psychedelic environment.

Creating an atmosphere conducive to the label "psychedelic" characterizes many products of the 1960s counterculture. Music and rock concerts became venues for "freaks"—those embracing the altered state and countercultural lifestyle (see *Woodstock*, 1970)—to enter a world outside their parent's and "straight" society. The rock band The Grateful Dead pioneered the aural construction of this environment, with San Francisco becoming an important center for the increasingly multimedia presentation of psychedelic rock (Andy Warhol and the Velvet Underground were also important in New York City as well) that combined projected images of shifting liquid and dancing lights to the beat of the music. Space and time were affected by both the visual sensations and the music, which often involved shifting tempos, repetition, and free-form improvisations that produced a hypnotic synthesis with the light show. Effects on instruments also provided the music with an ethereal characteristic, including reverberation that gave guitars the sense of space through its deep echo. Volume played a role as well, with the bands' music enveloping the audience with their sound as the light show entranced their vision.

Bibliography

Bromell, Nick. *Tomorrow Never Knows: Rock and Psychedelics in the 1960s*. Chicago: University of Chicago Press, 2000.

DeRogatis, Jim. *Turn on Your Mind: Four Decades of Great Psychedelic Rock*. Milwaukee: Hal Leonard, 2003.

Farber, David. "The Intoxicated State/Illegal Nation: Drugs in the Sixties Counterculture." In Peter Braunstein and Michael William Doyle, eds. *Imagine Nation: The American Counterculture of the 1960s and '70s*. New York: Routledge, 2002.

Hicks, Michael. *Sixties Rock: Garage, Psychedelic & Other Satisfactions*. Urbana: University of Illinois Press, 1999.

Huxley, Aldous. *The Doors of Perception/Heaven and Hell*. New York: Harper Colophon Books, 1963.

JEFFREY T. MANUEL

PSYCHO (1960). Shocking cinema audiences in 1960 with its bag of narrative twists, *Psycho* has earned itself a long-standing place in the Hollywood film canon, having established the terms for subsequent movie horror. Generating tremendous profit for its director, *Psycho* and its infamous shower scene continue to hold legendary status in contemporary popular culture.

In 1959, author Robert Bloch published a slice of horror fiction entitled *Psycho*, with its main character, Norman Bates, based loosely on 1950s serial killer Ed Gein.

Janet Leigh screams in the shower in the famous scene from the film *Psycho* directed by Alfred Hitchcock, 1960. (Paramount Pictures/Getty Images)

Later that year, the screen rights were bought for $9,000 by British director Alfred Hitchcock as material for his 47th film. Joseph Stefano's adapted screenplay follows secretary Marion Crane (played by Hollywood golden girl Janet Leigh) as she impulsively steals thousands of dollars from her workplace. Fleeing on the highway, Marion makes the fateful decision to stop for a night at the Bates Motel, run by the shy and somewhat awkward Norman Bates (a career-defining role for Anthony Perkins), seemingly living under the tyrannical rule of his invalid mother. The rest, as they say, is (murderous) movie history.

While Hitchcock was wholeheartedly committed to adapting *Psycho*, Paramount, his studio, was contrastingly appalled. When Paramount refused to provide money or even a set for the director, Hitchcock waived his usual fee in exchange for distribution and 60 percent ownership of the film. This gamble paid off as the very horror that provoked the studio's distaste was precisely what caused audiences to flock to showings throughout the early '60s, making Hitchcock over $20 million in profit.

What Paramount appears to have missed was the technical mastery with which Hitchcock handled *Psycho*'s violent terror. While the decision to shoot in black and white was partly financial, it nonetheless created the film's potent claustrophobia. Moreover, Hitchcock's use of a 50mm film lens, offering the closest resemblance to human vision, stylistically emphasized the theme of voyeurism at the heart of *Psycho*.

In addition to Hitchcock's masterful directing, the commercial success of the movie was also bolstered by cunning pre-publicity. Already sensing the shock power of Janet Leigh's early death in the now-notorious shower scene, Hitchcock stirred intrigue by declaring that no one would be allowed to enter screenings once the film had started. While this ensured that the release of *Psycho* was "event" cinema, its subsequent popularity showed that the film was more than capable of selling itself on its own terms.

Although the public success of *Psycho* made it an instant classic, it nonetheless received a mixed reception with reviewers and failed to capitalize on any of its Oscar nominations, a slight that Hitchcock felt deeply. This initial critical ambivalence provides a notable contrast with the almost universal condemnation received by Gus Van Sant upon the release of his 1998 shot-by-shot color remake of *Psycho*. The level of ire directed at Van Sant confirms the rarefied status that *Psycho* now holds in the eyes of the public and critics alike, continuing to offer not only one but two of the most chilling and adept film twists in cinematic history.

Bibliography

Baer, William. "Psycho (1960): A Conversation with Joseph Stefano." In William Baer, ed. *Classic American Films: Conversations with the Screenwriters*. Westport, CT: Greenwood, 2008, pp. 79–94.

Rebello, Stephen. *Alfred Hitchcock and the Making of Psycho.* London: Boyars, 1990.

ROSEMARY DELLER

PUEBLO INCIDENT (1968). The *Pueblo* Incident (alternately known as the *Pueblo* affair or *Pueblo* crisis) occurred on January 23, 1968, near the North Korean port of Wonsan in the Sea of Japan, creating a major event in the Cold War. Claiming the Americans strayed into territorial waters, the North Koreans captured the USS *Pueblo* and imprisoned the crew as suspected spies for 11 months. The incident was declared a failure for U.S. diplomacy and the protection of intelligence, and its slogan "Remember the Pueblo!" has since served as a warning.

Named after Pueblo, Colorado, the USS *Pueblo* was a designated Navy auxiliary general environmental research ship, or AGER 2, converted in 1966 at the Puget Sound Naval Shipyard in Bremerton, Washington, into an intelligence vessel equipped with $2 million worth of listening equipment. Aboard ship to operate the equipment were the communications technicians (CTs), or "the Spooks," a slang name given to them due to their secretive nature. Commander Lloyd Bucher as Skipper led a crew of 75 enlisted men, two Marines who spoke Korean, six officers, and two civilian oceanographers from the Oceanographic Office in Suitland, Maryland as a cover for their real mission, of which most of the 75 enlisted crewmen were not told.

The ship received its operational orders from ComNav 4, Japan in December to leave Sasebo, Japan; proceed north through the Tsushima Strait to a point just off the North Korean-Russian border and opposite the Russian port of Vladivostok; cruise 13 to 15 miles off the coast to collect intelligence; then turn south and cruise at the direction of the captain. The closest the ship came to the mainland was 12.8 nautical miles, a distance greater than the standard for international waters of 12 nautical miles.

However, around noon on January 23, 1968, a North Korean SOG-1 subchaser, accompanied by three torpedo boats, approached the ship with warning flags to follow them to the port of Wonsan for violating their territorial waters. Commander Bucher attempted delays of response flags and maintaining half-speed to allow his crew to destroy the equipment and documents. However, most of the classified material and personnel records fell into the hands of the North Koreans. The North Koreans became impatient and fired on the *Pueblo* with 57mm cannon, killing one crewman (Duane Hodges) and injuring three others (Steve E. Woelk, Robert J. Chicca, and Charles H. Crandell). After they boarded the ship, the North Koreans navigated the ship into the port of Wonsan and transported the 82 crewmembers inland to a compound outside of Pyongyang. Lt. General Seth J. McKee, commander of the U.S. Fifth Air Force, was notified of the *Pueblo*'s predicament approximately two hours after first spotting the subchaser. He sent the USS *Enterprise* in the direction of the *Pueblo*, although it would not arrive until the next afternoon, and held off on sending two F-105 fighter-bombers due to approaching darkness.

In March 1968, the crewmen were moved to a larger facility after being forced to sign detailed confessions of espionage following prolonged sessions of torture. The men suffered for 11 months before Major General Gilbert H. Woodward assumed negotiations with North Korean major general Pak Chung Kuk, meeting on December 17, when Woodward agreed to sign the confession of U.S. guilt. The men were released the morning of December 23, allowed to cross the bridge into South Korea, and were reunited with their families for Christmas. Although a Navy court of inquiry suggested punishment for failing to evade capture and destroy classified material, the Secretary of the Navy, John B. Chafee, decided that they had suffered enough punishment as POWs.

Bibliography

Brandt, Ed. *The Last Voyage of USS Pueblo.* New York: W. W. Norton, 1969.
Lerner, Mitchell B. *The Pueblo Incident: A Spy Ship and the Failure of American Foreign Policy.* Lawrence: University Press of Kansas, 2003.
Liston, Robert A. *The* Pueblo *Surrender—A Covert Action by the National Security Agency.* New York: Bantam, 1991.

BRITTANY BOUNDS

R

RAMPARTS MAGAZINE (1962–1975). Founded in 1962 by Helen and Ed Keating, *Ramparts* magazine was published until 1975. Ed Keating's original vision for the periodical was a literary vehicle for discussion on Catholicism. This vision was broadened to include issues of social justice by the participation of Thomas Merton and John Howard Griffin. The racist policies of the Catholic Church were addressed in articles such as "The Sorrowful Mysteries of the Negro Catholic" by Warren Hinckle (November 1964) and "Magnolia Ghetto" by John Beecher (December 1964). The condition of race relations in the South and the battle for civil rights were examined through the *Ramparts* lens of social justice in articles by John Beecher and a special report titled "Five Battles of Selma" by Warren Hinckle and David Welsh in the May and June 1965 issues. At the same time, *Ramparts* was questioning segregated Catholic churches and the treatment of civil rights workers, seminal articles on the Vietnam War were also appearing in the magazine. The January 1965 issue included an interview with Senator Frank Church of Idaho, a member of the U.S. Senate Foreign Relations Committee. Former Green Beret Donald Duncan's memoir, "The Whole Thing Was a Lie" was excerpted in the February 1966 issue. The editors and writers of Ramparts chronicled and participated in the changes taking place in the San Francisco Bay Area as well as nationally. With the publication of Eldridge Cleaver's writings and his subsequent role as an editor, *Ramparts* became a channel for black activism and brought the realities of racial inequality on the West Coast to a national audience.

The magazine faced internal turmoil in terms of financing and editorial control throughout most of its existence. Financing, as well as editorial personalities, was responsible for the frequent shifts in organizational structure. The first major reorganization took place in April 1967 when Ed Keating was voted out as president and publisher. Warren Hinckle took over as editor and in the following two years, with the close collaboration of Robert Scheer, raised the circulation and national profile of *Ramparts*. While the magazine was originally conceived as a quarterly publication, the editors and writers adjusted the publication schedule as public interest grew and financing allowed. The number of issues per year grew to 10 then 12, with Warren Hinckle announcing its new role as a "twelfthly" in volume 5, no. 1. The graphic design and illustrations were a signature part of the *Ramparts* essence, overseen for many years by Dugald Stermer. Clever political cartoons featured the work of artists such as Seymour Chwast and Edward Sorel.

Generating cash for operating costs was difficult, since advertisers were wary of the magazine's self-proclaimed vision as a promoter of dissent. The concept of a reader-financed periodical was advocated by Hinckle and proposed to the readership in the June 15, 1968, issue. Hinckle resigned in the early months of 1969, and Robert Scheer is listed as the editor beginning with the April 1969 issue. Scheer's name remained on the masthead through October 1969. The November 1969 issue lists Jan Austin, Peter Collier, David Horowitz, and David Kolodney as the collective editors. The magazine struggled in the early 1970s with its identity and the growing competition from other media outlets and published its last issue in 1975.

Bibliography

Hinckle, Warren. *If You Have a Lemon, Make Lemonade*. New York: Putnam, 1974.
Richardson, Peter. *A Bomb in Every Issue: How the Short, Unruly Life of Ramparts Magazine Changed America*. New York: New Press, 2009.

REBECCA S. FEIND

RANDOLPH, ASA PHILIP (1889–1979). Asa Philip Randolph was an important figure in the civil rights movement, leading the Brotherhood of Sleeping Car Porters, organizing the 1941 and 1963 Marches on Washington, and founding the Leadership Conference on Civil Rights.

Randolph was born on April 15, 1889, in Crescent City, Florida. In 1891, his family moved to Jacksonville, Florida, where there was a flourishing African American community. Randolph's parents were huge proponents of education, and Randolph attended the Cookman Institute, where he was valedictorian of his graduating class. After high school, he moved to New York, where he hoped to become an actor, though he never won his parents' support, so he gave up on this goal.

In 1925, Randolph organized the Brotherhood of Sleeping Car Porters, the first effort to organize Pullman workers. The workers wanted Randolph as their leader because he did not work for the company, which meant that he could not be fired for his actions. In 1935, the Brotherhood became the exclusive bargaining agent of Pullman workers. This was a victory not only for Randolph, but for African Americans in general as this was the first time that a black union had achieved this sort of victory. Randolph was able to secure a contract for the sleeping car porters in 1937, which included over $2 million in raises, overtime, pay, and a shorter workweek. Randolph's nonviolent actions and use of mass protest to achieve his goals inspired many of the civil rights leaders of the 1950s and 1960s. Randolph served as leader of the brotherhood until 1968.

In 1941, Randolph again made history by organizing a 100,000 man March on Washington to protest racial discrimination in war industry jobs and also to advocate the desegregation of the armed forces. President Franklin Delano Roosevelt was worried about the effect this march would have on the country and convinced Randolph to call it off by issuing Executive Order 8802, which prevented discrimination in hiring for war industry jobs and led to the creation of the Fair Employment Practices Commission. Though some African Americans criticized Randolph's decision to cancel the march since there was still segregation in the military, Executive Order 8802 is seen as a success.

During the 1950s and 1960s, Randolph continued to work toward gaining equality for African Americans, appearing often on the news in support of desegregation. He is often referred to as the father of the civil rights movement since he utilized nonviolent actions throughout his career. In 1950, he founded the Leadership Conference on Civil Rights and has coordinated national lobbying efforts for every civil rights bill since 1957. He organized the March on Washington for Jobs and Freedom, along with Dr. Martin Luther King, on August 28, 1963. Though Randolph wanted the focus to be more on employment than on the plight of southern blacks, he still considered the march to be a success. The March on Washington is thought to have contributed to the passage of the Civil Rights Act of 1964, which forbade discrimination on the basis of sex or race in the hiring, promoting, or firing of employees.

Randolph also remained active in labor issues throughout the 1950s and 1960s. In 1955, he was named vice president of the AFL-CIO. Believing that there was discrimination within that union, in 1960 he founded the Negro American Labor Council. In 1964, following the March on Washington, he founded the A. Philip Randolph Institute to promote cooperation between the black community and labor. He remained active in labor and civil rights issues until his death on May 16, 1979.

See also March on Washington (1963).

Bibliography

Anderson, Jervis. *A. Philip Randolph: A Biographical Portrait*. New York: Harcourt Brace Jovanovich, 1973.
Leadership Conference on Civil Rights. "About LCCR and LCCREF." Available at http://www.civilrights.org/about/ (accessed January 11, 2010).
Pfeffer, Paula F. *A. Philip Randolph: Pioneer of the Civil Rights Movement*. Baton Rouge: Louisiana State University Press, 1996.

ELIZABETH BRYANT MORGENSTERN

RAT PACK. The "Rat Pack" was a nickname given to a group of Las Vegas–based entertainers during the early 1960s. The name had been previously used by writers to describe the antics of actor Humphrey Bogart and his drinking buddies such as Sinatra, and actors David Niven and Cary Grant. It was later identified with the group that included leader Frank Sinatra, singers Sammy Davis Jr. and Dean Martin, actor Peter Lawford and comedian Joey Bishop (actress Shirley MacLaine was sometimes considered an un-official member).

The group, formed in January 1960 as a group of Sinatra's friends he usually referred to as the Rat Pack, was a way for Sinatra to enlist others to help him during his largely ad-libbed show at the Copa Room in the Sands Casino. The group also appeared together in several movies (*Ocean's Eleven*, their best and most successful group collaboration, was filmed at the same time the group was performing at nights at the casino), and in 1962, *Sergeants Three*. They went on to perform together in the film *Robin and the Seven Hoods* (1964). While the group had genuine chemistry,

Sinatra was deeply insecure and anxious to become a close associate with the newly elected president John F. Kennedy. The shows were a huge draw and even with just a chance that the entire group would be onstage at the same time led to massive crowds.

By late 1960, the group began to fracture when President Kennedy, worried about Sinatra's mob ties, declined an invitation to stay with him, leading to Lawford's dismissal from the group. However, even without Lawford, the other members of the group found no problem in attracting record crowds to both their live act and the movies in which they appeared together. When the group made *Robin and the Seven Hoods*, Bing Crosby took the role originally intended for Lawford. As the Rat Pack members continued to become more in demand as individual performers and actors, they began to perform together much less often.

After 1965, the group gave one last live concert and then went their separate ways. Sinatra, Martin, and Davis reunited for a group tour in 1987, but Martin soon left the tour and was replaced by Liza Minnelli. Lawford and Sinatra never spoke again, and most of the members remained estranged from each other later in life. While the tenure of the group was relatively brief, it has come to signify in pop culture a certain nostalgic attitude toward a mythical age where men were hard=drinking swingers (endlessly proclaiming "a-ring-a-ding ding!") and women were "dames."

Bibliography

Levy, Sean. *Rat Pack Confidential: Frank, Dean, Sammy, Peter, Joey and the Last Great Show Biz Party*. St. Charles, MO: Main Street Books, 1999.

Quirk, Lawrence, and William Schoell. *The Rat Pack: Neon Nights with the Kings of Cool*. New York: It Books, 1999.

Starr, Michael. *Mouse in the Rat Pack: The Joey Bishop Story*. Lanham, MD: Taylor Trade, 2002.

BRIAN COGAN

REAGAN, RONALD WILSON (1911–2004). Born in Tampico, Illinois, the son of Irish-Catholic shoe salesman John Edward "Jack" Reagan and Protestant homemaker and shop clerk Nelle Wilson, Ronald Reagan climbed from lifeguard, to sportscaster, movie actor, television host, union boss, governor, and finally, president of the United States (1981–1989). The 1960s proved to be the turning point of Reagan's life.

By that decade, Reagan's film and television career were in decline. During the previous decade and into the early 1960s, he hosted a weekly television drama, *General Electric Theater*, and after leaving that show, moved to *Death Valley Days*, a Western with different performers (sometimes including himself) each week. In his last film, *The Killers* (1964), he starred as gangster Jack Browning, a thug betrayed by his wife played by Angie Dickinson. Clu Gulager and Lee Marvin starred as equally bad criminal types. The film, originally planned as made as a television movie, shifted to theaters because of the intense violence.

Reagan had always been interested in politics. He was president of his class at his alma mater, Eureka College; supported Franklin Roosevelt and Harry Truman for president; and on several occasions served as president of the heavily Democratic Screen Actors Guild (SAG). Nevertheless, the leftward shift of the Democratic Party toward socialism troubled him greatly. Though registered as Democrat, he voted for Eisenhower in 1952 and 1956 and Richard Nixon in 1960. He officially changed his registration to Republican in 1962.

In 1964, Reagan made a televised speech for Barry Goldwater broadcast on NBC entitled "A Time for Choosing," in which he declared that the nation had a "rendezvous with destiny." It was an enthralling oratorical effort, in which Reagan used his folksy storytelling to communicate with the average listener. In the speech he warned of the dangers of government power and encroachment, themes that later guided his course as governor and as president. As a result of the speech, Goldwater's campaign took in $8 million, an enormous sum at that time. That address was the start of Reagan's career as a candidate.

After watching the speech, enthusiastic conservative supporters, many very wealthy, began coming to Reagan's Pacific Palisades home and begging him to run against Edmund G. "Pat" Brown, the Democrat who defeated Richard Nixon for governor in 1962. Reagan, shocked by the requests, continued to turn a deaf ear to them, but he finally decided to acquiesce to their entreaties and ran as a Republican for governor of California in 1966. In the end, Reagan buried Brown with more than 58 percent of the vote. He won the hearts of traditional Californians with his description of hippies as those who "act like Tarzan, look like Jane, and smell like Cheetah." Most of Reagan's jokes were self-deprecating, such as when asked what he would do as governor, he quipped, "I don't know, I never played a governor." He won reelection handily again in 1970 and served until 1975. As governor, Reagan's style foreshadowed that of his presidency. He implemented tax cuts, slowed the growth of the state government, reformed welfare, and on the four occasions when he had to raise taxes, he quickly rebated the money to the citizens of the state when the treasury had a surplus.

In 1968, the California delegation at the Republican convention supported him as a favorite-son candidate for the presidential nomination, but he placed third to Richard Nixon, who won the nomination and the presidency in November. After completing his second term as governor, he once again tried to win the nomination, and in 1976 entered the Republican primary against incumbent Republican president Gerald R. Ford, but lost narrowly in a close race. After Ford's defeat by Governor Jimmy Carter of Georgia, Reagan prepared for the 1980 nomination, which he won, and went on to defeat Jimmy Carter by a stunning electoral margin. After serving eight years as president, Reagan retired to his ranch in California, where he died at age 93 in June 2004, from pneumonia related to Alzheimer's disease.

See also Reagan's Speech on Behalf of Barry Goldwater: "A Time for Choosing."

Bibliography

Buckley, William F. Jr. *The Reagan I Knew*. New York: Basic Books, 2008.
Reagan, Ronald. *An American Life*. New York: Simon & Schuster, 1990.

JAMES S. BAUGESS

REAGAN'S SPEECH ON BEHALF OF BARRY GOLDWATER: "A TIME FOR CHOOSING." On the evening of October 27, 1964, a former B-movie actor and union president of the Screen Actors Guild, Ronald Reagan (1911–2004), gave a stirring speech on behalf of the Republican presidential nominee, Senator Barry Goldwater of Arizona. Goldwater experienced an uphill battle from the start. The Johnson campaign played dirty tricks, accused Goldwater of being a warmonger, and portrayed him as unstable. He needed a jolt, and a handsome, eloquent actor with a golden voice and folksy manner was just the person he needed.

The speech was scheduled for prime time and delivered to an audience at the NBC studios. Reagan peppered his speech with ideological dictums, personal anecdotes, stories about common people, and examples of government fraud and waste. One example was about a Cuban exile recently escaped from Castro:

> Not too long ago two friends of mine were talking to a Cuban refugee, a businessman who had escaped from Castro, and in the midst of his story one of my friends turned to the other and said, "We don't know how lucky we are." And the Cuban stopped and said, "How lucky you are?! I had someplace to escape to." In that sentence he told us the entire story. If we lose freedom here, there is no place to escape to. This is the last stand on Earth.

For Reagan, the descent into liberalism, despite all its humanitarian pronouncements, could result in the abyss of totalitarianism:

> You and I are told increasingly that we have to choose between a left or right, but I would like to suggest that there is no such thing as a left or right. There is only an up or down—up to a man's age-old dream, the ultimate in individual freedom consistent with law and order—or down to the ant heap totalitarianism, and regardless of their sincerity, their humanitarian motives, those who would trade our freedom for security have embarked on this downward course.

In a short discourse, he railed about the left wing's contempt for the Constitution:

> Another voice says that the profit motive has become outmoded, it must be replaced by the incentives of the welfare state; or our traditional system of individual freedom is incapable of solving the complex problems of the twentieth century. Senator Fulbright has said at Stanford University that the Constitution is outmoded. He referred to the president as our moral teacher and our leader, and he said he is hobbled in his task by the restrictions in power imposed on him by this antiquated document. He must be freed so that he can do for us what he knows is best. And Senator Clark of Pennsylvania, another articulate spokesman, defines liberalism as "meeting the material needs of the masses through the full power of centralized government."

Presaging twenty-first-century America, Reagan gave the nation an ominous warning:

> A government can't control the economy without controlling people. And they know when a government sets out to do that, it must use force and coercion to achieve its purpose. ... Yet anytime you and I question the schemes of the do-gooders, we are denounced as being against their humanitarian goals. They say we are always "against" things, never "for" anything. Well, the trouble with our liberal friends is not that they are ignorant, but that they know so much that isn't so.

Socialized medicine came under attack as well:

> I think we are for telling our senior citizens that no one in this country should be denied medical care because of a lack of funds. But I think we are against forcing all citizens, regardless of need, into a compulsory government program, especially when we have such examples, as announced last week, when France admitted that their Medicare program was now bankrupt. They've come to the end of the road.

In the end, in keeping with his support of Goldwater, near the end of his speech he offered a paragraph that spoke to millions:

> No government ever voluntarily reduces itself in size. Government programs, once launched, never disappear. Actually, a government bureau is the nearest thing to eternal life we'll ever see on this Earth.

Before he closed with an endorsement with Goldwater, he reminded his audience:

> You and I have a rendezvous with destiny. We will preserve for our children this, the last best hope of man on Earth, or we will sentence them to take the last step into a thousand years of darkness.

The Goldwater campaign was ecstatic. Reagan's speech, broadcast nationally and then locally, raised $8 million in the last week of the campaign. More importantly, it made Reagan a political star, and soon Republican operatives came to his home in suburban Los Angeles begging him to run against Edmund G. "Pat" Brown, the incumbent Democrat governor who defeated Richard Nixon for the office in 1962.

In 1966, after much pleading, Reagan gave in and defeated Brown with 58 percent of the vote. Reelected in 1970 with 53 percent against California House Assembly leader, Jesse Unruh, Reagan was poised to run for president. In 1980, at the third national Republican convention in which his name was offered, he won the nomination and then the presidency in a landslide vote against James Earl "Jimmy" Carter. The "Time of Choosing" did indeed culminate in a "rendezvous with destiny" for the Great Communicator.

See also Goldwater, Barry (1909–1998); Presidential Election of 1964; Reagan, Ronald Wilson (1911–2004).

Bibliography

Buckley, William F. Jr., *The Reagan I Knew*. New York: Basic Books, 2008.
Cannon, Lou. *Governor Reagan: His Rise to Power*. New York: Public Affairs, 2003.
Reagan, Ronald. *An American Life*. New York: Simon & Schuster, 1990.

JAMES S. BAUGESS

REPUBLICAN PARTY (1960–1969). The 1960s were a period of transformative change for the Republican Party. The GOP entered the decade as the party of Eisenhower and "Modern Republicanism." Party stalwart Richard Nixon was the 1960 presidential nominee, and consensus ideals remained in fashion. Conservative discontent would surface over the course of the 1960 election and grow in strength as the right wing of the party took over the presidential nominating apparatus and secured the 1964 nomination for its own candidate, Arizona senator Barry Goldwater. Goldwater's overwhelming loss in 1964 led to a period of retrenchment, self-examination and purging of extremist elements within the party. On the whole, however, external events and internal organizing continued to combine in a manner that encouraged rightward growth. Richard Nixon demonstrated his mastery of this approach in 1968. While the final consolidation of conservative sentiments that would lead to Ronald Reagan's presidential election in 1980 remained to be completed, the Republican Party ended the 1960s a far more conservative organization than it began.

The midterm elections of 1958 were a nearly unqualified disaster for Republicans. Americans voiced their disapproval of an economic downturn and their anxiety over recent demonstrations of Soviet technological prowess by voting Republicans out of office across the country. Democrats gained 13 Senate seats, a record victory, and 47 seats in the House of Representatives for their largest gain in 10 years. Even the traditionally Republican farm states of the Midwest voted against the party, ousting 19 Republicans from the House and electing two Democratic senators and three governors in the midst of a wave of anger over agriculture secretary Ezra Taft Benson's policies. In two states, however, two very different Republicans claimed important electoral victories. In New York, liberal Republican and Standard Oil heir Nelson A. Rockefeller won a massive victory in his first electoral campaign, gaining the governorship over Democratic incumbent Averell Harriman. In Arizona, stridently conservative senator Barry Goldwater won reelection to a second term on an antilabor platform.

These exceptional victories presented the Republican Party with a decidedly mixed message. Rockefeller was a liberal; Goldwater was an unapologetic conservative. As pundits attempted to read the results of the elections, both men vaulted into the position of potential contenders for the 1960 presidential nomination. The front-runner for this nomination was, of course, Vice President Richard M. Nixon. A loyal party stalwart and two-term vice president under Dwight Eisenhower, Nixon nonetheless suffered under the neglect and even outright disapprobation of his boss. Eisenhower was famously quoted in August 1960 as answering a question about Nixon's contributions to the administration with the quip, "If you give me a week I might think of one." Fortunately for the vice president, he had a strong base of support within the national party organization following years of dedicated service as the GOP's chief campaigner.

Over the course of 1959, Rockefeller sent out a series of feelers regarding a potential challenge to Nixon, and even went so far as to help underwrite organization of a Rockefeller for President Citizens Information Committee. The New York governor failed to garner sufficient support to forge a candidacy, and he formally disavowed any such intentions at the end of 1959. Rockefeller would continue to harbor hopes of a "draft" through the first half of 1960, continuing to make public statements and otherwise constitute a significant thorn in Nixon's left side.

Goldwater, on the other hand, actually was the target of a draft attempt, despite a personal lack of interest in challenging Nixon for the nomination. Conservatives including former University of Notre Dame Law School dean and radio host Clarence Manion spearheaded the formation of a "Committee of 100" to promote Goldwater, and even directed the ghostwriting of the Arizona senator's paradigmatic 1960 book *The Conscience of a Conservative*. Goldwater inspired significant support in conservative circles across the country, securing the votes of the South Carolina Republican delegation and those of his own state.

Shortly before the Republican National Convention, Nixon moved to placate the left flank of his party with a secret mission to Rockefeller's Fifth Avenue apartment. The two men hammered out a 14-point agreement on domestic and foreign policy principles for distribution to the GOP platform committee, and Nixon even went so far as to allow Rockefeller to issue the first public news of this agreement. Nixon's readiness to cater to Rockefeller demonstrated where the party apparatus believed its strongest center of support would be. Liberal Republicanism—what Eisenhower administration official Arthur Larson termed "Modern Republicanism"—was viewed as the wave of the future.

Events would prove, however, that Nixon had substantially misread the situation. Conservatives erupted in fury, with Goldwater referring to what became known as the "Compact of Fifth Avenue" and the "Munich of the Republican Party." In the end, Goldwater was cognizant of his lack of strength within the party apparatus, and he stepped aside—but first he issued a call to arms: "If we want to take this Party back," he told his followers in his withdrawal speech, "and I think we can someday, let's get to work."

Get to work they did. Nixon went on to lose the 1960 election by the slimmest of margins, with allegations of fraud in Illinois and Texas. His pledge to campaign in all 50 states following the convention cost him the ability to focus on tight races in swing states, although it was an important early indication that Nixon and the party were beginning to see the South as a potential opportunity for expansion. Democrats actually lost a few seats in the House and Senate in 1960; Kennedy's victory was far from a sweeping consensus for Democrats. Conservatives, for their part, quickly moved their attentions to 1964. Immediately following the 1960 convention, conservative elders urged their youthful counterparts to organize for the future, and in September 1960, Young Americans for Freedom was established in a founding conference held at William F. Buckley Jr.'s home in Sharon, Connecticut. This activist organization would become a proving ground for a number of young conservatives who later went on to occupy important roles in government. In the summer of 1961, *National Review* publisher and former Young Republican activist William Rusher, freshman Ohio congressman John Ashbrook, and longtime Young Republican political operative F. Clifton White became a new, successor organization to what Manion had first attempted in 1960.

White conceived of a strategy that ignored the Northeast, the traditional stronghold of the Eastern Establishment and the power base of officials like Nelson Rockefeller. Instead, he focused on organizing other states beginning at the precinct level. After all, control of precincts accumulated to control of counties and then congressional districts. In nonprimary states, control of congressional districts translated to control of the delegates to the 1964 Republican National Convention. It was the ultimate grassroots strategy, and with the support of networks developed over the course of the 1960 campaign, conservatives were developing the foundation necessary to carry the strategy through to completion.

While conservatives consolidated their efforts and worked to create suitable conditions for a nomination triumph in 1960, party liberals failed to recognize growing changes in the political landscape. Historian Nicol C. Rae has convincingly argued that a combination of tactical ineptitude, indiscipline, and lack of foresight hobbled liberals' attempts to maintain power within the Republican Party over the course of the 1960s. Liberal Republicans failed to construct grassroots organizations that could successfully compete with emerging conservative networks. Over the next decade, conservative networks organized in the 1960s could take full advantage of reforms in the party nomination process that increasingly favored political primaries—contests that rewarded partisan political organization.

Nixon ran for the governorship in California in 1962, lost in part due to the growth of a strain of conservatism in his home state that privileged ideology over party loyalty, and famously appeared to exit the political scene with a comment to the press that they wouldn't have "Nixon to kick around anymore." Rockefeller won reelection in 1962, but he hobbled his chances at a successful run in 1964 with a public divorce and hasty remarriage. While he would forge an attempt for the

1964 nomination, his new wife gave birth to their son, Nelson Jr., immediately before the important California party primary, reawakening concerns about his personal life and contributing to his loss. Other contenders, including Michigan governor George Romney, Pennsylvania governor William Scranton, and former Nixon running mate Henry Cabot Lodge—by 1964 the U.S. ambassador to Vietnam—were unable to forge networks that could successfully challenge the Goldwaterites.

Outside the presidential arena, conservative Republicans began to open new inroads across the country. Increasingly, the party's center of gravity was moving away from the Northeast and toward the nation's "Sunbelt," the states of the South and Southwest where rapid population growth via migration from the traditionally Republican Midwest and heavy reliance on the defense industry combined to form potent new conservative alliances. In 1961, young conservative John Tower won an astonishing Senate victory in Texas to fill Lyndon Johnson's old seat. Republicans stepped up their organizing efforts throughout the South, making the argument that the true party of conservatism was the GOP and encouraging a process of increasing ideological polarization that would come to characterize party affiliation by the end of the twentieth century. The civil rights movement and landmark legislation signed into law by President Lyndon Johnson in 1964 and 1965 moved southerners further toward presidential Republicanism. These inclinations would filter down over the years to the local level. Civil rights and the appeal of Goldwater would also move some prominent Democrats into the Republican column, most famously South Carolina senator and former Dixiecrat Strom Thurmond.

The efforts of the Draft Goldwater movement paid off; their hero garnered the presidential nomination in a triumphal display at the 1964 Republican National Convention in San Francisco. Longtime party officials were stunned by the massive transformation in the body of delegates between 1960 and 1964. Conservatives had been overwhelmingly successful in taking over the machinery of the GOP. Henry Cabot Lodge, for example, had chaired the Platform Committee in 1952, but following his presentation in 1964 of plans for a "Republican-sponsored Marshall Plan for our cities and schools," he received standing ovations from 30 of the committee's 100 members—and complete silence from the other 70. Scanning the sea of unfamiliar faces on the convention floor, Lodge was later heard to exclaim, "What in God's name has happened to the Republican Party! I hardly know any of these people!"

The 1964 general election was a disaster for Goldwater. The Arizonan started the general election campaign on anything but a conciliatory note, famously proclaiming in his acceptance speech, "Extremism in the defense of liberty is no vice! . . . Moderation in the pursuit of justice is no virtue!" Rather than pursue a balanced ticket, Goldwater chose Congressman William Miller of New York as his running mate. A fellow conservative and the chair of the Republican National Committee—further evidence of the degree to which the right wing had taken over the party—his chief attribute was that, in Goldwater's words, his strident partisan speeches would drive Lyndon Johnson "nuts."

The Johnson campaign successfully cast the Goldwater-Miller ticket as dangerously extremist, most infamously with an advertisement featuring a little girl counting daisy petals as an ominous voice counted down toward a nuclear explosion. While the advertisement ran only once, its prominence on news programs and in print coverage far outstripped the original broadcast in terms of importance. This and many other episodes resulted in an overwhelming win for Johnson; Goldwater won the electoral votes of only six states. Significantly, however, five of those six states were in the Deep South: Alabama, Georgia, Louisiana, Mississippi, and South Carolina. He ran well in Florida and elsewhere in the South. Goldwater's lack of popularity had negative ramifications for the party as a whole. Republicans lost 38 House seats, including 19 in the traditional stronghold of the Midwest.

Many commentators have noted that in the wake of John F. Kennedy's assassination, a traumatized nation would have been loath to change chief executives once again even if the Republican nominee had been a more moderate candidate. However, liberal Republicans basking in feelings of relief failed to learn the lessons of 1964. Conservatives had achieved notable successes with their development of a national campaign organization and their remarkable network of volunteer activists. They also managed to form an ideologically coherent framework—even if it had been repudiated on the national level. Republican liberals who were elected over the course of the decade tended to be elected based on their individual merits and not because they were part of a larger party program. Liberals ranging from Romney to Scranton to Rockefeller also tended to be jealous of their counterparts' successes, failing to forge the cooperative networks that could have given them collective strength against conservatives.

Post-1964, Republican conservatives did move to eliminate extremist forces such as the John Birch Society from positions of influence in the party. Meanwhile, party moderates successfully replaced Goldwater's choice for Republican National Committee chairman, Arizona attorney and strident conservative Dean Burch, with Ohio GOP chairman Ray Bliss. Perhaps the most positive outcome of 1964, however, was the emergence of a new figure to lead the conservative insurgency within the GOP. In the closing days of the race, former actor and General Electric company spokesman Ronald Reagan delivered an engaging televised address titled "A Time for Choosing." The speech catapulted Reagan into the national political arena. He went on to easily defeat incumbent Democrat Edmund "Pat" Brown for the governorship of California in 1966.

More broadly, by the time of the 1966 midterm elections, Democrats' seemingly overwhelming mandate to govern was crumbling in the face of growing upheaval on college campuses, widespread racial unrest, and the nascent antiwar movement. Republicans were well positioned to take advantage of these developments. Reagan, for example, memorably referred to California hippies as those who "act like Tarzan, look like Jane, and smell like Cheetah." Ray Bliss proved to be a good fund-raiser and ideologically tolerant party man who helped shepherd the GOP to a gain of 47 House seats, three new senators, and wins in eight gubernatorial contests. Meanwhile, traditional southern support for the Democratic Party was becoming further fractured by the growing popularity of former Alabama governor George Wallace. Wallace had made a strong showing in northern primaries running as a Democrat in 1964; in 1968, he would leave the party to forge a third-party campaign as leader of the American Independent Party.

Four years earlier, in 1962, Richard Nixon appeared to have come to the end of a long and already distinguished political career. By 1966, however, he had astutely studied political trends within the GOP and in society as a whole. He was one of the few party stalwarts to actually extend his support to Goldwater, making over 150 appearances in 36 states on behalf of party candidates in a year when most moderate and liberal Republicans stayed out of the public eye to avoid association. He was a stalwart campaigner once again in 1966, and by 1967 was reaping the benefits of this dedication. Nixon appeared moderate in comparison to Goldwater, but his growing attention to law-and-order arguments and other subjects of increasing importance to the middle-class Americans he would famously label the "Silent Majority" in 1969 meant Nixon could creditably offer himself as a more conservative alternative to figures like Rockefeller or Romney.

As the 1968 convention approached, Nixon's position appeared secure. Some conservatives, however, feared the former vice president would reveal his liberal colors once nominated, and an insurgent campaign mounted in support of Ronald Reagan. Nixon placated his putative supporters in the increasingly vital region of the South with a pledge of opposition for enforced busing. Over a series of private meetings with southern delegates, he also stated his opposition to federal judges who interfered in local schools. In the end, strong pro-Nixon support by southern political figures, including South Carolina's Strom Thurmond, and his own adept handling of the situation garnered Nixon the nomination. As his running mate, Nixon chose Maryland governor Spiro Agnew, who had distinguished himself with his hard-line racial policies in the wake of riots in Baltimore.

While George Wallace constituted a third-party threat in the South for Nixon as well as for the Democrats, Nixon's campaign doubtless benefited greatly from the tremendous violence showcased on national television throughout the course of the Democratic National Convention in Chicago. Johnson's vice president, Hubert Humphrey, was unable to overcome widespread dissatisfaction with the course of the war in Vietnam and concern over unrest throughout the nation. Nixon won the presidency by 110 electoral votes, although he ran less than a percentage point ahead of Humphrey in the popular vote.

The 1968 election as a whole was not a massive repudiation of Democrats; Nixon took office with Democratic majorities in both houses of Congress. The more significant transformation came in terms of the parties' racial support. White voters were increasingly moving away from the Democratic Party, especially in previous strongholds like the South. As well, 1968 marked the last year in which Democrats could count on equal support in the fight for campaign donations. Nixon had created an organization of political operatives that would grow and thrive after 1968 into a formidable fundraising force that Democrats would remain unable to match. Importantly, some of the most significant figures in this process had their start in the conservative youth activism of the 1960s. Computerized mailing-list mastermind Richard Viguerie, for example, was the first executive secretary of Young Americans for Freedom in 1961.

In some ways, the end of the 1960s looked very much like the beginning of the 1960s for the Republican Party. Richard Nixon was the party's nominee, winning a close election in 1968 after a razor-thin loss in 1960. Republicans were the minority party in both houses of Congress. Under the surface, however, the party had witnessed transformative change. Liberal Republicans were on the defensive, well on their way to elimination from consideration in national party affairs; by the time of the 1970 midterm elections, even Nelson Rockefeller was running toward the right. Meanwhile, new, conservative politicians, most notably Ronald Reagan, were on the ascent. The conservative activists forging new political networks in the early 1960s were becoming primary players in the national political arena. The ideological polarization of the two major political parties in the United States was well underway.

See also Goldwater, Barry (1909–1998); Nixon, Richard Milhous (1913–1994); Presidential Election of 1960; Presidential Election of 1964; Presidential Election of 1968; Reagan, Ronald Wilson (1911–2004).

Bibliography

Critchlow, Donald T. *The Conservative Ascendancy: How the GOP Right Made Political History.* Cambridge, MA: Harvard University Press, 2007.

Gifford, Laura Jane. *The Center Cannot Hold: The 1960 Presidential Election and the Rise of Modern Conservatism.* DeKalb: Northern Illinois University Press, 2009.

Gould, Lewis L. *Grand Old Party: A History of the Republicans.* New York: Random House, 2003.

Perlstein, Rick. *Before the Storm: Barry Goldwater and the Unmaking of the American Consensus.* New York: Hill and Wang, 2001.

Rae, Nicol C. *The Decline and Fall of the Liberal Republicans from 1952 to the Present.* New York: Oxford University Press, 1989.

Schoenwald, Jonathan. *A Time For Choosing: The Rise of Modern American Conservatism.* New York: Oxford University Press, 2001.

LAURA JANE GIFFORD

REUTHER, WALTER P. (1907–1970). Walter P. Reuther was one of the most influential leaders of organized labor in the United States throughout the mid-twentieth century. He served as the president of the United Auto Workers (UAW) from 1946 to 1970, and also as the president of the Congress of Industrial Organizations from 1952 to 1955. At the height of his career, the UAW's ranks swelled to more than 1.5 million workers, making him one of the nation's most formidable power brokers, able to command the ear of leading figures within the business community, the Democratic Party, and the federal government, including a long line of presidents extending from Harry S Truman to Richard M. Nixon.

Reuther was born on September 1, 1907, into a working-class German family residing in Wheeling, West Virginia. It was there that he was apprenticed in a tool-and-die shop, but once he had mastered skilled metal work, he sought to go elsewhere. In 1927, he landed a position with the Ford Company in Detroit, where he also became involved in the local Socialist Party. Throughout the early years of the Great Depression, Reuther's ties to radical movements deepened. In 1931, he joined the Auto Workers Union, an organization with ties to the local Communist Party, and then from 1933 to 1935, he and his brother Victor traveled to the Soviet Union, where they worked together in an automobile plant. Upon his return to Detroit in 1935, he once more became active in socialist politics, and was rumored to have paid dues to the Communist Party as well. This same period witnessed the beginning of his rise within the ranks of the newly founded UAW, as he was elected to the organization's executive board in 1936.

By the time Reuther was named director of the UAW's General Motors Department in 1938, however, he had turned sharply against the radical leanings of his youth. He resigned from the Socialist Party that same year, and in 1940—even as he was elected vice president of the UAW—strongly supported Franklin D. Roosevelt's bid for reelection. This trend back toward the center continued following Reuther's assumption of the presidency of the UAW in 1946, and in the years that followed, he became one of the chief players within a postwar Democratic coalition that dominated the nation's political life for the better part of a quarter-century.

Throughout this era, Reuther championed an ideal of industrial democracy. He believed that advances in technology had made permanent prosperity possible, if the American people would only empower their government to discipline the free enterprise system in accord with their interests. While Reuther rejected the Soviet model of total centralization, he fought for increased government control of pricing and production. He embraced the interest-group politics of the New Deal era and worked with other leading representatives from the business, labor, agricultural, consumer, and government sectors to advance the interests of "the people." In the early 1960s, Reuther's quest for economic justice earned him the early respect of important constituencies within the New Left, including Students for a Democratic Society (SDS) and the civil rights movement, and in 1963, he stood behind Martin Luther King Jr. as King delivered his "I Have a Dream" speech from the steps of the Lincoln Memorial. But in the years following Lyndon B. Johnson's landslide 1964 victory, which seemed to betoken the eminent triumph of a liberal governing coalition, Reuther's embrace of a top-down, establishmentarian style of politics rendered him increasingly out-of-step with the changing culture of the Democratic Party. His refusal to break with the Johnson administration on the Vietnam War was, for many within the Party's progressive wing, particularly damning. As a result of these dynamics, and of Richard Nixon's victory in the 1968 election, Reuther's influence was on the wane by the time of his death in 1970. Yet by that point his legacy as an advocate of the nation's industrial workers and as an architect of postwar liberalism was already secure.

Bibliography

Barnard, John. *American Vanguard: The United Auto Workers during the Reuther Years, 1935–1970*. Detroit: Wayne State University Press, 2004.

Boyle, Kevin. *The UAW and the Heyday of American Liberalism, 1945–1968*. Ithaca, NY: Cornell University Press, 1995.

Lichtenstein, Nelson. *The Most Dangerous Man in Detroit: Walter Reuther and the Fate of American Labor*. New York: Basic Books, 1995.

HEATH W. CARTER

RIGG, DIANA (1938–). Although initially a classical actress, Diana Rigg would become internationally famed for her role as Mrs. Emma Peel in the popular television series *The Avengers*. Stylishly garbed in the latest London fashions, Rigg became a veritable 1960s icon, a status only bolstered by her subsequent role as a "Bond girl" in 1969.

Born in the north of England on July 20, 1938, Rigg began her acting career at the Royal Academy of Dramatic Arts, making her stage debut in 1955. This theatrical experience, bolstered by her subsequent position in the Royal Shakespeare Company, provided Rigg with her initial reputation as a talented classical actress.

In light of this early stage promise, Rigg's appointment as Mrs. Emma Peel in television's *The Avengers* in 1965 certainly marked a contrast. Although Elizabeth Shepherd was originally chosen to replace Honor Blackman, who had left the show to play Pussy Galore in the James Bond thriller *Goldfinger* (1964), it was Diana Rigg who would become the most iconic of agent John Steed's female sidekicks. Over 10 years younger than Blackman, Rigg was a willful force behind the decision for Peel to sport '60s fashions as *The Avengers* switched to color. Although U.S. producers initially objected to them, Peel's miniskirts would become a heralded part of her *Avengers* uniform, alongside her tight catsuits known as "Emma-peelers."

Channeling the latest sartorial trends of "Swinging London," Peel's clothes emphasized the avant-garde nature of a show that always carried an air of unmistakable "Britishness."

The role of Emma Peel was, however, more than decorative. While Peel's name was a pun on her "M-appeal," that is, her "Man Appeal," perhaps more than any other *Avengers* girl, Diana Rigg brought a feistiness to the character that exemplified the changing representation of women in the 1960s. Rather than being relegated to the role of secretary or dispensable lover, the widow Peel was a resourceful and self-sufficient woman; a female transposition of the "man-about-town." Behind the scenes, however, Rigg was growing increasingly frustrated by the fact that she was paid little more than the cameraman, and certainly less than her costar Patrick MacNee in the role of agent John Steed. Although a renegotiated contract in 1967 would temporarily quell her desire to leave *The Avengers*, it was in part this unbalanced treatment that would eventually provoke Rigg's departure.

Although nominated for an Emmy award for her performance in *The Avengers*, Diana Rigg left the show in 1968 after 51 episodes. After a brief return to the stage, Rigg, like Blackman before her, played a Bond girl in *On Her Majesty's Secret Service* in 1969. Her role as Teresa "Tracy" di Vicenzo is notable for being the only Bond girl to date to secure the screen Bond's hand in marriage.

Since the 1960s, Rigg has continued to pursue a successful career spanning television, film and stage. Nonetheless, it is her role as Emma Peel in *The Avengers* that has arguably enshrined her as an icon of 1960s visual culture.

See also Avengers, The (1961–1969).

Bibliography

Britton, Wesley. *Spy Television*. Westport, CT: Praeger, 2004.
Carraze, Alain, and Putheaud, Jean-Luc. *The Avengers Companion*. London: Titan, 1997.

ROSEMARY DELLER

ROCKEFELLER, NELSON ALDRICH (1908–1979). Nelson Aldrich Rockefeller, was born July 8, 1908. The grandson of Standard Oil tycoon John D. Rockefeller, he was perhaps the greatest representative of post–World War II liberal Republicanism. Years after rejecting the vice presidency under Richard Nixon, he attained the same position under Nixon successor Gerald Ford. Despite several efforts, however, he never grasped the golden ring of the presidency. Meanwhile, he transformed New York State during his 15 years as governor and played important roles in foreign and domestic affairs under four presidents.

John D. Rockefeller Jr.'s second-born son was the natural leader among his five brothers. He served as director of Rockefeller Center during the 1930s and 1940s, and he used his staggering financial resources to, among other things, expand and develop the Museum of Modern Art that his mother helped to found. His experiences investing in Standard Oil's Venezuelan subsidiary led Rockefeller to become interested in South American development. He and some friends formed a company in the late 1930s to finance local industrial development in Venezuela, hoping to raise the general standard of living through responsible capitalist expansion. This theme was to remain prominent in Rockefeller's involvement with foreign aid throughout the 1940s and 1950s. In 1941, he was appointed to the position of coordinator of inter-American affairs in Franklin Roosevelt's administration. Later in the war, he became assistant secretary of state for Latin American affairs.

Rockefeller remained involved in South America following his return to private life in 1945. He believed that the best way to fight the Cold War was through non-military means like foreign aid, and he continued to promote his cause in the halls of government. President Truman's Point Four program had its origins in a conversation between Rockefeller and a State Department speechwriter, and the president appointed him chairman of the International Development Advisory Board in 1950.

In 1952, President Dwight Eisenhower named Rockefeller chair of his Special Committee on Government Reorganization. He also became undersecretary of the new Department of Health, Education and Welfare. Resigning in December 1954 to reenter the field of foreign relations, he served for a time as special assistant to the president for foreign affairs. Determining, however, that elective office was the key to achieving real power, Rockefeller resigned this office as well and returned to New York to lay the groundwork for a 1958 gubernatorial campaign.

Rockefeller's first electoral victory came in a very poor year for Republican candidates across the country. This notable success, coupled with the fact that the New York governorship was generally considered the most powerful in the nation, instantly propelled him into consideration for the 1960 presidential nomination. Newspapers and magazines—and the Republican Party—speculated for months about whether he would run. Following a series of polls and a lengthy probe of national opinion, however, Rockefeller withdrew from consideration at the end of December 1959.

In succeeding months, however, the governor continued to sound like a candidate. A month before the Republican National Convention, he let loose a string of statements criticizing the probable nominee, Vice President Richard Nixon. Intending to placate the New York governor, Nixon traveled to Manhattan to meet with Rockefeller and discuss the Republican platform. The two came to an agreement on 14 largely progressive recommendations to the GOP platform, but brought down the wrath of the conservative wing of the GOP in the process. It took all of Nixon's considerable political skills to reestablish order. While Rockefeller did stump for Nixon during the general campaign, his actions had solidified conservative Republican sentiment against him.

Rockefeller went on to attempt presidential runs in 1964 and 1968, but faced the wrath of conservatives within the party organization and was unable to achieve success. Meanwhile, however, he continued to govern New York, and his administration wrought major changes to the fabric of state government over the course of his 15-year tenure.

Rockefeller's administration of New York has been described as a prime example of increases in executive power at the state level in the 1950s and 1960s, as well as a paradigmatic example of "pragmatic liberalism." Rockefeller shied away from ideology, going so far as to say in a profoundly inaccurate 1968 prediction that he felt the country was becoming less ideological and more pragmatic. Despite having won election in 1958 on a promise of "pay as you go" government, no other governor in the twentieth century submitted so many requests for tax increases, and no other New York governor spent so freely to meet societal needs.

Rockefeller's accomplishments included massive improvements to New York's infrastructure, including 90,000 new low- and moderate-income housing units, four-and-a-half miles of new highway every day he was in office, space for 208,000 new students in the State University system, and the construction of a billion-dollar marble-clad government complex in Albany. He pioneered the use of public benefit corporations to take on large tasks including construction, power, and transportation. His administrations also saw New York's debt rise from $900 million in 1959 to $3.4 billion by 1973, and he presided over the enactment of harsh "lock 'em up for life" drug policies and the 1971 tragedy at Attica State Prison.

A fiscal crisis hit the state in late 1973, and the federal government proved unwilling to provide as much assistance as Rockefeller requested. Rockefeller argued that the ability to meet the needs of New Yorkers was no longer in the hands of the state, but rested with the federal government—and he resigned the office of governor. Following Nixon's resignation in 1974, President Ford selected Rockefeller as his vice president. By the end of 1975, however, the same conservatives he had angered 15 years earlier effectively forced him off the 1976 ticket. Rockefeller died on January 26, 1979, in New York.

See also Presidential Election of 1960; Presidential Election of 1964; Presidential Election of 1968.

Bibliography

Connery, Robert H., and Gerald Benjamin. *Rockefeller of New York: Executive Power in the Statehouse*. Ithaca, NY: Cornell University Press, 1979.

Morris, Joe Alex. *Nelson Rockefeller: A Biography*. New York: Harper, 1960.

Reich, Cary. *The Life of Nelson A. Rockefeller: Worlds to Conquer, 1908–1958*. New York: Doubleday, 1996.

Rockefeller, Nelson. *Unity, Freedom and Peace: A Blueprint for Tomorrow*. New York: Random House, 1968.

Underwood, James E., and William J. Daniels. *Governor Rockefeller in New York: The Apex of Pragmatic Liberalism in the United States*. Westport, CT: Greenwood, 1982.

LAURA JANE GIFFORD

RODDENBERRY, GENE (1921–1991). Gene Roddenberry was an American television writer and producer who created the popular science fiction series *Star Trek* (1966–69). Eugene Wesley Roddenberry was born August 19, 1921, in El Paso, Texas, and grew up in Los Angeles. He was educated in local public schools and majored in police studies at Los Angeles City College. A licensed pilot at the time of the attack on Pearl Harbor, he flew B-17 bombers for the U.S. Army Air Force during World War II and airliners for Pan-American Airways from 1945 to 1949. Roddenberry began selling stories to magazines while still in the army, and in 1949 he moved to Los Angeles to break into the television industry, taking a job with the Los Angeles Police Department to support himself.

Roddenberrry's first sale as a screenwriter was a 1953 script, "Defense Plant Gambling," for the series *Mr. District Attorney*. He went on to write additional scripts for that and other series such as *Dragnet, Highway Patrol, West Point*, and *The Kaiser Aluminum Hour*. He resigned from the police force in 1957 to write full-time, becoming head writer for the popular Western series *Have Gun, Will Travel* and creating an hour-long drama about the peacetime Marine Corps titled *The Lieutenant* (1963–1964).

Star Trek, a drama about a giant starship exploring "strange new worlds," followed. Roddenberry described it as "*Wagon Train* to the stars," invoking a then-popular Western adventure, but his original pilot failed to live up to that promise and was rejected by NBC as "too cerebral." The second pilot blended traditional TV tropes—including romance, murder, and a fistfight—with a science-fiction plot about crew members who acquire superhuman powers when they pass through an energy field at the edge of the galaxy. It sold the series and established the template for *Star Trek* and the franchise it spawned: five subsequent series, 11 feature films, and hundreds of print stories. Roddenberry contributed a few scripts to *Star Trek*, which ran for three seasons (1966–1969), but his primary contribution to the series was his optimistic vision of a future in which war and poverty are distant memories and harmonious cooperation between members of different sexes, races, and even species is taken for granted.

Roddenberry produced other television pilots, as well as three movies, in the 1970s, but none was successful. He returned to the *Star Trek* universe at the end of the decade as producer for *Star Trek: The Motion Picture* (1979), and it remained his creative focus until his death on October 24, 1991. He was credited as "executive consultant" on four subsequent films featuring the cast of the original series, as executive producer on the sequel series *Star Trek: The Next Generation* (1987–94), and as creator of the franchise on every subsequent *Star Trek* series and feature film. He was beloved by millions of *Star Trek* fans, who (adopting a nickname bestowed on him during the original series) referred to him fondly as "the Great Bird of the Galaxy."

Bibliography

Alexander, David. *Star Trek Creator: The Authorized Biography of Gene Roddenberry*. New York: Roc, 2004.
Engel, Joel. *Gene Roddenberry: The Myth and the Man Behind Star Trek*. New York: Hyperion, 2004.
Whitfield, Stephen E., and Gene Roddenberry. *The Making of Star Trek*. New York: Ballantine, 1968.

A. BOWDOIN VAN RIPER

ROLLING STONES, THE. With the exception of the Beatles, no other rock-and-roll band of the 1960s was more influential than the Rolling Stones. The band helped lead the so-called British Invasion of the United States during which British groups came to dominate the American music scene. Named for an old Muddy Waters blues song, the Rolling Stones came together in London in 1962 with a lineup that included Mick Jagger (1943–) as lead vocalist, his childhood friend Keith Richards (1943–) and musical prodigy Brian Jones (1942–1969) on guitars, Bill Wyman (1936–) on bass, Charlie Watts (1941–) on drums, and Ian Stewart (1938–1985) on piano. The band's first official manager Andrew Loog Oldham, who was concerned as much with the group's image as their music, deemed that Stewart did not fit in and relegated him to road manager and part-time accompanist, a role he filled until his death in the 1980s. The Rolling Stones began as a blues band that revered blues artists such as Muddy Waters, Chester "Howlin' Wolf" Burnett, and Jimmy Reed but was also influenced by American rock-and-roll stars like Elvis Presley, Little Richard, Buddy Holly, Chuck Berry, and Bo Diddley. Among their first recordings were covers of Chuck Berry's "Come On" and Buddy Holly's "Not Fade Away."

The Rolling Stones are shown during rehearsal on April 8, 1964, at an unknown location. The British band members, from left, are, Brian Jones, guitar; Bill Wyman, bass; Charlie Watts, drums; Mick Jagger, vocals; and Keith Richards, guitar. (AP/Wide World Photos)

Pushed by Oldham, Jagger and Richards formed a songwriting partnership that eventually produced a huge string of rock classics. In 1964, "The Last Time" was the first Jagger/Richards song to reach the top 10 on the American charts, and the next year the Stones skyrocketed to international fame with the release of "Satisfaction." Oldham, an excellent promoter with an irreverent sense of humor, began to push an image of the Stones as a somewhat darker, more dangerous version of the Beatles, who at the time were viewed as more clean and polished. Major tours and television appearances followed, and as they became more popular, the group generated more controversy. In 1967, when they appeared on American television's *Ed Sullivan Show*, network executives and Sullivan himself forced the group to change the refrain of their current hit record "Let's Spend the Night Together" to "let's spend some *time* together." That same year Jagger, Richards, and Jones were arrested in Britain on drug charges, although none served significant jail time. Jones's drug use and erratic behavior escalated to the point that the Stones kicked him out of the band in 1969, and not long afterwards he drowned in his swimming pool. Blues guitarist Mick Taylor replaced Jones and remained with the band for the next five years.

As the 1960s drew to a close, the Stones continued to produce hit singles like "Jumpin' Jack Flash" and "Honky Tonk Women" along with well received albums such as *Beggar's Banquet* and *Let It Bleed*. They produced a film titled *The Rolling Stones Rock and Roll Circus* that included performances by the Stones as well as other acts such as the Who, John Lennon, Marianne Faithfull, and Jethro Tull. The Stones also sponsored a notorious, ill-conceived free concert at Altamont Speedway near San Francisco on December 6, 1969, during which one man was murdered and a number of others injured by members of the Hells Angels motorcycle gang, who had been hired as security for the show. To some, the violence at Altamont marked the ideological end of the "peace and love" experiment that had colored much of the 1960s. The Rolling Stones would survive the Altamont affair, of course, and they remain one of rock music's most powerful and popular acts.

See also Altamont (1969).

Bibliography

Booth, Stanley. *Dance with the Devil: The Rolling Stones and Their Times*. New York: Random House, 1985.

Russell, Ethan A. *Let It Bleed: The Rolling Stones, Altamont, and the End of the Sixties*. Boston: Hachette Book Group, 2009.

Wyman, Bill. *Rolling with the Stones*. New York: DK Publishing, 2002.

BEN WYNNE

ROMEO AND JULIET (1968). William Shakespeare's play *Romeo and Juliet*, first published in 1597, has inspired countless films, ballets, and other artistic expressions. Although earlier writers also told the story of the doomed love of two teens, separated by the violent feud of their respective families, Shakespeare's script has remained the classic version. Few modern adaptations of his work have succeeded as completely as Franco Zeffirelli's 1968 movie.

Zeffirelli had already directed a stage production of *Romeo and Juliet* in London in 1960. The cast included, in the title roles, John Stride and Judi Dench, young performers rather than seasoned veterans of the stage. Zeffirelli also had directed four movies, including Shakespeare's *The Taming of the Shrew*, starring Richard Burton and Elizabeth Taylor, which was released in 1967. Studio executives were reluctant to finance a second Shakespeare production for the screen, but Zeffirelli promised to complete the project for $800,000. Permission was granted, although the film ran over budget and in the end cost $1.5 million.

As he had done for the London stage version, Zeffirelli sought young performers for the title roles. He selected Leonard Whiting to play Romeo Montague and Olivia Hussey to play Juliet Capulet. He persuaded Michael York to play Tybalt and chose John McEnery for Mercutio. Filming in several locations in Italy, Zeffirelli put his cast in medieval clothing and featured streets and buildings of the same time frame. Laurence Olivier, who was in Italy filming *The Shoes of the Fisherman*, offered his voice for several roles, including the dubbed-in voice of Lord Montague and the narrator at the beginning and end of the movie; Olivier's name was not included in the film's credits. The script followed Shakespeare's original closely, with most changes or omissions a result of the difference between stage and cinema.

The movie opened in American theaters October 8, 1968, and was generally well received. Some critics protested the youth of Whiting and Hussey, criticizing their acting skills, but in general the movie was highly praised. Ironically, because of her youth, Hussey was not allowed to attend the movie's premiere in England due to one scene that contained brief nudity—this in spite of the fact that she and Whiting were the performers shown unclothed. McEnery's portrayal of Mercutio frequently won special praise, as it epitomized Zeffirelli's conception of how a script several centuries old could be convincingly portrayed in a modern medium.

Romeo and Juliet grossed nearly $40 million for Paramount, a spectacular return on their investment. The movie received two Academy Awards, for costuming and for cinematography. It was also nominated for best picture, and Zeffirelli was nominated for best director, but in both cases the award went to *Oliver!*, directed by Carol Reed. Whiting and Hussey received Golden Globe awards as most promising new actor and actress of the year. Several versions of the "Love Theme from Romeo and Juliet" were released, including one orchestrated by Henry Mancini that reached number one on the *Billboard* music charts in May 1969. Zeffirelli's version of *Romeo and Juliet* continues to be regarded as one of the best screen treatments of Shakespeare's play.

Bibliography

Adler, Renata. "The Screen: Zeffirelli's 'Romeo and Juliet' Opens." *New York Times*, October 9, 1968, p. 41.
"New Movies: Virtuoso in Verona." *Time*, October 11, 1968, p. 104.
Zeffirelli, Franco. *Zeffirelli: An Autobiography*. New York: Weidenfeld & Nicolson, 1986.

STEVEN WAYNE TESKE

ROOSEVELT, ELEANOR (1884–1962). Anna Eleanor Roosevelt was a former First Lady and noted social activist, fighting for the rights of women, African Americans, and the poor.

Born October 11, 1884, in New York City, Roosevelt faced a tumultuous childhood. Her mother died in 1892, and her father was sent to a mental institution, leaving Roosevelt to live with her grandmother. In 1899, Roosevelt was sent to the Allenswood Academy in England, where she first developed an interest in social activism, before returning to America in 1901. In 1903, she became engaged to Franklin Delano Roosevelt, her fifth cousin once removed, and the pair had six children, one of whom died in infancy. When Franklin contracted polio in 1921, Roosevelt supported him, becoming more active in politics not only to keep his interests alive but also to further her own agenda, which included abolishing child labor and pushing for a minimum wage law.

In 1932, when Franklin was elected president, Roosevelt used this opportunity to transform the role of the First Lady. Though she still worked as a gracious hostess, she also became more politically involved than any First Lady before her. She wrote a column, "My Day," six days a week; held all-female press conferences, which helped increase the number of jobs at news stations for women; gave speeches on the radio; and traveled the United States extensively serving as Franklin's eyes and ears into the lives of ordinary Americans. She used her position to push for the causes of civil rights, labor issues, as well as expressing a special concern for the plight of women. During the U.S. involvement in World War II (1941–1945), Roosevelt traveled abroad to raise morale among troops and advocated for soldiers' benefits at home.

With Franklin's death in April 1945, Roosevelt initially contemplated retiring from public life, which she did for a few months. Later that year, President Harry Truman appointed Roosevelt to be a delegate of the United States to the United Nations. From 1946 to 1951, she chaired the UN Commission on Human Rights, helping to pass the United Nations Universal Declaration on Human Rights in 1948. In 1951, she resigned from the position to go into retirement, but she still remained active. She continued to support the Democratic Party, campaigning for Adlai Stephenson during the 1952 and 1956 presidential elections, and attended the Democratic National Convention in 1960. In 1960, President John F. Kennedy reappointed Roosevelt to the United Nations. She also was named chair of the President's Commission on the Status of Women and served as a member of the National Advisory Committee of the Peace Corps. She continued publishing "My Day" six days a week, taking only four days off for Franklin's death, until her death, lending her support to various social and political causes. During the 1960s, she sustained her support of the civil rights movement, and especially championed the National Association for the Advancement of Colored People (NAACP), a group with which she had worked for many years, and also continued to advocate for the rights of women and the poor. On November 7, 1962, she died of tuberculosis.

Bibliography

Black, Allida M. *Casting Her Own Shadow: Eleanor Roosevelt and the Shaping of Post-War Liberalism*. New York: Columbia University Press, 1997.

Roosevelt, Eleanor. *My Day: The Best of Eleanor Roosevelt's Acclaimed Newspaper Columns, 1936–1962*. New York: Da Capo, 2001.

Roosevelt, Eleanor. *The Autobiography of Eleanor Roosevelt*. New York: Da Capo Press, 2000.

ELIZABETH BRYANT MORGENSTERN

ROSEMARY'S BABY (1968). In 1968, Paramount Pictures released *Rosemary's Baby*, a psychological horror film starring Mia Farrow, John Cassavetes, and Ruth Gordon. It was director Roman Polanski's first American film and Mia Farrow's first major role.

The screenplay, adapted by Polanski from an Ira Levin novel of the same name, centers on a young couple, Rosemary (Farrow) and Guy Woodhouse (Cassavetes), who move into a classically spooky apartment building (the Dakota, in New York City). They are warned about the sinister history of the building—infanticide, witchcraft, and cannibalism are said to have occurred there—but move in anyway. They are quickly befriended by an elderly couple, Minnie and Roman Castevet (Ruth Gordon and Sidney Blackmer), and shortly thereafter, Guy's stalled acting career takes a turn for the better.

Rosemary becomes pregnant but under circumstances that make her suspicious: she was unconscious (it is later revealed she was drugged by Minnie) and had hallucinations suggesting she was impregnated by the devil. Guy and the Castevets become more controlling toward her, limiting her contact with other people, requiring her to drink potions brewed by Minnie, and insisting she see only the obstetrician they recommend. Strange coincidences continue to mount, and Rosemary becomes convinced that the Castevets are part of a coven that intends to use her baby in their rituals. The film is deliberately ambiguous until its final scene as to whether Rosemary is suffering from paranoid delusions or actually is being used as part of a satanic plot.

Part of the horror of *Rosemary's Baby*, particularly to a modern audience, is the extreme sexism displayed toward Rosemary. Her husband belittles her fears, destroys her possessions, and apparently values his career more than either her or any children they might have. He displays the characteristics of an abusive husband, isolating her from her friends and treating her rational requests as infantile, an attitude that would be inconceivable if he were dealing with a male peer. Similarly, the suppression of her right to control her body (she is treated as a baby machine, without even the right to know who the father of her child is) parallel a concern voiced by abortion rights activists, while her obstetrician also refuses to take her description of her experiences seriously.

Mia Farrow, wearing a plaid maternity dress, holds a book in a still from the film *Rosemary's Baby*, directed by Roman Polanski, 1968. (Paramount Pictures/Getty Images)

Rosemary's Baby includes religious imagery that heightens the horror: the Satanists greet Rosemary's baby with language similar to that used in Christian ritual; the film makes reference to Rosemary's Catholicism; religious imagery appears in Rosemary's hallucination while she is being impregnated; and the Pope's visit to New York (which took place in 1965) is referenced several times. *Rosemary's Baby* was nominated for two Academy Awards and won one, Best Actress in a Supporting Role (Ruth Gordon).

See also Polanski, Roman (1933–).

Bibliography

Lyman, Rick. *Watching Movies: The Biggest Names in Cinema Talk About the Films that Matter.* New York: Times Books, 2002.

Orr, John, and Elzbieta Ostrowska, eds. *The Cinema of Roman Polanski: Dark Spaces of the World.* New York: Wallflower, 2006.

Tropiano, Stephen. *Obscene, Indecent, Immoral and Offensive: 100+ Years of Censored, Banned and Controversial Films.* New York: Limelight, 2009.

SARAH BOSLAUGH

ROSTOW, WALT WHITMAN (1916–2003).

Born in New York City on October 7, 1916, Walt Whitman Rostow attended Yale University and then won a

Rhodes scholarship to Oxford University. During World War II, he was employed in the Office of Strategic Services, the predecessor of the Central Intelligence Agency.

In 1960, as a history professor at the Massachusetts Institute for Technology, Rostow published *The Stages of Economic Growth: A Non-Communist Manifesto*. Upon its publication, the book became the elemental text of modernization theory, a largely academic model that, as the intellectual underpinning for the U.S. involvement in Vietnam and U.S. foreign policy toward former colonial nations in general, had profound material and moral consequences for U.S. foreign policy in the 1960s and 1970s.

In 1961, President John F. Kennedy hired Rostow as his deputy special assistant for national security affairs. In this position, working directly under McGeorge Bundy, Rostow chaired the State Department's Policy Planning Council until 1966. In 1966, Lyndon B. Johnson made Rostow the White House special assistant for national security affairs, a position that soon became known as the national security advisor.

As Rostow and other theorists of modernization believed, it was important to protect the economic and political development of recently independent nations from communist influence. By creating aid programs that encouraged the improvement of agriculture, transportation, and communications in these nations, the Kennedy and Johnson administrations believed they could usher these states into a modern, pro-Western existence. As the first country to experience a modern revolution, the United States held the responsibility of assisting others. In this context of post–World War II decolonization, modernization theory and state building increasingly imposed this view of Cold War geopolitics on the developing world.

The Stages of Economic Growth, with its commitment to modernization through a combination of government aid and private enterprise, was the most vivid expression of this Cold War logic. Assuming that the U.S. model of capitalism and representative government could be imposed successfully on foreign cultures, Rostow effusively supported the American involvement in Vietnam as a theorist and policymaker. In 1965, when the Johnson administration began to escalate the U.S. presence in Vietnam in earnest, he developed the "Rostow thesis," which argued that an insurgency supported by outside powers could only be defeated by increased military pressure against that external support. As the number of American ground troops in Vietnam increased in the next two years, Rostow became the leading advocate of the administration's Vietnam policy. Even in 1968, after many other officials, including Defense Secretary Robert McNamara, had privately pronounced the war unwinnable, Rostow maintained his faith in the ability of the United States to create a modern state in South Vietnam.

Rostow's conviction regarding Vietnam derived largely from his strong belief in modernization as a force for good in the world. An ardent anticommunist, he strongly believed that defeating the communist-nationalist forces of North Vietnam under Ho Chi Minh was a requirement for modernization to take hold in Southeast Asia. This ideological belief in modernization led him to become the most aggressive civilian supporter of the Vietnam policy of the Johnson and Kennedy administrations.

As one of the chief architects of the ever-more unpopular war in Vietnam, Rostow was shunned by many of his fellow academics at the end of the Johnson administration. In 1969, he returned to academia at the University of Texas at Austin, where he continued to teach and write until his death in February 2003. His brother, Eugene Rostow, served as the undersecretary of state for political affairs for the Johnson administration, and his wife Elspeth Rostow was the chairwoman of the United States Institute for Peace and Dean of the LBJ School of Public Affairs at the University of Texas.

See also Johnson, Lyndon Baines (1908–1973); Kennedy, John F. (1917–1963); Vietnam War.

Bibliography

Engerman, David C., Nils Gilman, Mark H. Haefele, and Michael E. Latham. *Staging Growth: Modernization, Development and the Global Cold War*. Amherst: University of Massachusetts Press, 2003.

Milne, David. *America's Rasputin: Walt Rostow and the Vietnam War*. New York: Hill and Wang, 2008.

Rostow, W. W. *The Stages of Economic Growth: A Non-Communist Manifesto*. Cambridge: Cambridge University Press, 1960.

CHRISTOPHER DIETRICH

ROSZAK, THEODORE (1933–2011). After becoming an early opponent of U.S. militarism, Theodore Roszak offered an influential exploration of the rising tide of revolutionary youth with his 1969 work *The Making of a Counter Culture*. Roszak's empathetic reflection on the 1960s counterculture has not only become a canonized text of the era, but it also secured Roszak's reputation as a valuable social commentator committed to probing the human consequences of technological development.

A graduate of Princeton University, Theodore Roszak was an active participant in the emerging U.S. peace movement, working as an editor of *Peace News* at the start of the '60s. As this growing terrain of grassroots political struggle looked to British antinuclear protests for inspiration, the pressing question of nuclear militarism shaped Roszak's increasingly critical perspective on the changing relationship between humans and technology. Yet it was not until his early thirties that his beliefs became crystallized in the form of a book, written during a 1967 visit to London.

Predating another countercultural analysis, *The Greening of America* (1970), by a year, *The Making of a Counter Culture* argued that a scientific world-view had pervaded American society, fostering a "technocracy" grounded in the alienating tenets of rationalized capitalism. While Roszak warned that the dictates of this prevailing technocracy threatened to expunge emotionality, imagination, and individual freedom from social life, he nonetheless acknowledged an odd by-product of this very system; namely, the flourishing of a dissenting counterculture. As middle-class youth formed a new market force primed with disposable incomes and college educations, these very privileges provided the social and economic freedom necessary to form a dissident subculture. Although quantitatively speaking the counterculture may have been a social minority, Roszak nonetheless believed that it represented a potent expression of political discontent to counteract the stultifying values increasingly propagated by mainstream American society.

Although Roszak undoubtedly welcomed the countercultural valuation of imagination over reason, Roszak nonetheless retained a degree of skepticism regarding the revolutionary potential of revolting youth. While *Life* magazine may have suggested that Roszak's work had overinvested in the counterculture's tendency to seek salvation primarily through the individual, the personal, and the private, Roszak's work offered sufficient examination of the overarching political and social context of the decade to warn that dissent risked becoming a commodity lifestyle to be packaged, bought, and consumed by affluent youth. His awareness of the ever-present tension between the demands of sincere political commitment and mere "dropping out' provided vital nuance to *The Making of a Counter Culture*, as Roszak reexamined the work of countercultural heroes such as Herbert Marcuse, Allen Ginsberg, and Timothy Leary with a sympathetic yet critical eye.

Certainly, *The Making of a Counter Culture* may have overemphasized a somewhat reductive polarity between mainstream society and the emergent counterculture that occasionally threatened to veer into caricature. Nonetheless, in largely avoiding the trap of sycophantism, Roszak's favorable yet undoubtedly reflective exploration of the counterculture set the foundations for his successful and long-standing academic career, grounded in the continued critical interrogation of the evolving relationship between society and technology. Theodore Roszak died on July 5, 2011, at his home in Berkeley, California. He was 77.

See also Greening of America, The (1970).

Bibliography

Chedd, Graham. "Theodore Roszak: Romantic in Reason's Court." *New Scientist* 49, no. 741 (March 4, 1971): 484–86.

Keniston, K. "Review: Counter-Culture: Cop Out . . . " *Life* 67, no. 19 (November 7, 1969): 10–11.

Roszak, Theodore. *The Making of a Counter Culture: Reflections on the Technocratic Society and Its Youthful Opposition.* London: Faber & Faber, 1969.

ROSEMARY DELLER

RUBY, JACK (1911–1967). Jack Ruby murdered Lee Harvey Oswald on November 24, 1963, as the Dallas Police were transferring the accused Kennedy assassin from the police station to the county jail. Ruby's single bullet hit Oswald in the stomach, causing massive internal and fatal injuries. With one squeeze of the trigger, captured live on television as the nation watched in horror, Ruby did more to fuel conspiracy theories than even the most dedicated conspiracist. Oswald's motive for killing John F. Kennedy died with him, as did all definitive answers about the plotting of the assassination itself.

Jack Ruby was born on March 25, 1911, in Chicago to an Orthodox Jewish family. Originally named Jacob Rubenstein, Ruby changed his name as an adult. He had a difficult childhood and an abusive father. His parents eventually separated, and his mother was eventually committed to a mental institution. Ruby was a violent, short-tempered child who barely managed to acquire a sixth-grade education. After a short stint with his siblings in foster care, Ruby became a low-level hustler and street fighter. He drifted from Chicago to California and back, scraping out a living. He worked briefly with the Scrap Iron and Junk Handlers Union until the mob took over the union and edged him out. His association with this union and his background in Chicago would form the basis for the belief that he was connected to the mafia.

After serving in the Army Air Force in World War II and earning an honorable discharge, Ruby moved to Dallas, where his sister managed a nightclub. After several failed attempts in business, Ruby found marginal success running a strip club, the Carousel, yet he was still perpetually in debt. Thought of in Dallas as a loser and a poseur, Ruby was moody and mentally unstable, and racked up a string of minor arrests in a little over a dozen years.

Ruby was a great admirer of President Kennedy. The morning of the assassination he was at the *Dallas Morning News* putting in his weekend ads for his club. He noticed an anti-Kennedy ad supposedly placed by a Bernard Weissman. Ruby was upset that another Jew would defame the president in print. Shortly thereafter, he heard the news that Kennedy had been shot. Distraught, Ruby decided to close his clubs. The assassination affected him deeply, and there is evidence he went to the hospital where Kennedy and Texas governor John Connally had been taken. According to his sister and his friends, his grief and shock had overwhelmed him. He attended Oswald's press conference, posing as a journalist. Over the next day he visited the police station, talked to reporters, and inserted himself into the investigation wherever possible. He was the kind of man who liked to be in the middle of the action, and the Kennedy assassination was the biggest action in Dallas.

On Sunday, November 24, Oswald was supposed to be transferred from police headquarters at 9:00 a.m.; however, unforeseen delays caused the event to take place over two hours later. Ruby, who was running errands that morning and had actually left his dog in the car, walked unnoticed into the basement of the police station seconds before Oswald was brought through. Ruby shot Oswald at 11:21 a.m., and was immediately arrested. Convicted and sentenced to death, he maintained he never was part of a conspiracy; most lone gunman advocates believe that Ruby, mentally unstable to begin with, was never affiliated with the mafia in any meaningful way, and was too talkative to be an effective conspirator. A Warren Commission–ordered polygraph supported Ruby's insistence that shooting Oswald was a spur-of-the-moment decision resulting from his grief and anger over the president's death. Suffering from cancer, he died in prison of a blood clot on January 3, 1967. His impulsive act of revenge has inspired speculation ever since.

See also Owald, Lee Harvey (1939–1963); Warren Commission.

Bibliography

Bugliosi, Vincent. *Reclaiming History: The Assassination of President John F. Kennedy.* New York: W. W. Norton, 2007.

Epstein, Edward Jay. *Inquest: The Warren Commission and the Establishment of Truth.* New York: Viking, 1966.

Kantor, Seth. *Who Was Jack Ruby?* New York: Everest House, 1978.

Manchester, William. *The Death of a President: November 20–November 25.* New York: Harper & Row, 1967.

McAdams, John. *JFK Assassination Logic: How to Think About Claims of Conspiracy.* Washington, DC: Potomac Books, 2011.

McKnight, Gerald D. *Breach of Trust: How the Warren Commission Failed the Nation and Why.* Lawrence: University Press of Kansas, 2005.

Meagher, Sylvia. *Accessories After the Fact: The Warren Commission, the Authorities, and the Report.* New York: Vintage Books, 1992.

Posner, Gerald. *Case Closed: Lee Harvey Oswald and the Assassination of JFK.* New York: Doubleday, 1993.

Report of the President's Commission on the Assassination of President Kennedy. Available at http://www.archives.gov/research/jfk/warren-commission-report/.

ELIZABETH DEMERS

RUDOLPH, WILMA (1940–1994). Wilma Rudolph was an African American Olympic athlete who became the first American woman to win three gold medals in the Olympics. Known as "the fastest woman in the world," she was celebrated the United States and internationally. Rudolph's model paved the way for other women to break the gender barrier in track and field events. Her examples of resilience in the face of tremendous physical and social obstacles remain an inspirational expression of the American Dream.

Born prematurely on June 23, 1940, to Ed and Blanche Rudolph of St. Bethlehem, Tennessee, Rudolph contracted polio at age four and lost use of her left leg. Regular massage helped her regain her strength. Rudolph survived double pneumonia and scarlet fever as well with help from her large family. At age nine, she walked without her braces but used an orthopedic shoe for the next two years. By the time she was 12, she played basketball and outran every child in her neighborhood. After convincing her high school basketball coach to keep her on the team, Rudolph set a new state record for girls' teams: she scored 803 points in 25 games. Her talents caught the eye of the women's track coach at Tennessee State University, who let her practice with his team.

At 16, Rudolph qualified for the Summer Olympic Games in Melbourne, Australia, and returned home with a Bronze medal. She was voted the United Press Athlete of the Year in 1960, the same year Rudolph joined the Olympic track and field team in Rome, Italy, where she set a record for winning three gold medals. The Italians dubbed her "La Gazella Nera," the black gazelle, for her graceful form on the track. British and Italian sprinters came in behind Rudolph in the 100-meter final. She defeated Britain again, as well as Germany in the 200-meter event. Her third gold was for the 4 X 100-meter relay team comprised of her Tennessee teammates; they set a world record in the semi-final with a time of 44.4. Besides winning the medals, she tied the world record in the 100-meter and managed it all on a sprained and swollen ankle. Her achievements at the Olympics catapulted Rudolph into the public spotlight. Two years running the Associated Press named her Woman Athlete of the Year (1960, 1961). An integrated parade, which she insisted on, welcomed her home to Clarksville, Tennessee —the first integrated event in the town's history. In 1961, she was given the AAU Sullivan Award, an honor exceeding that of the Heisman, as the most outstanding amateur athlete in the United States. In 1962, she received the Babe Didrikson Zaharias Award. Rudolph bowed out of the 1964 Olympics. She retired in 1963 from professional competition because she didn't want to disappoint herself or her fans if she could not duplicate or exceed her initial achievements. Rudolph died of brain cancer in Nashville on November 12, 1994, after a long career as a public school teacher and her work on behalf of youth.

Bibliography

Rudolph, Wilma. *Wilma*. New York: New American Library, 1977.

                                                    REBECCA TOLLEY-STOKES

RUSK, DEAN (1909–1994). Dean Rusk served as secretary of state from 1961 to 1969 under the administrations of Presidents John F. Kennedy and Lyndon B. Johnson. He is primarily known as a proponent and architect of the Vietnam War, but he was also crucial in diffusing the tense climate of the Cuban Missile Crisis

Dean Rusk was secretary of state in the administrations of presidents John F. Kennedy and Lyndon B. Johnson and a strong supporter of U.S. involvement in Vietnam. (Yoichi R. Okamoto/Lyndon B. Johnson Presidential Library)

and negotiating the Nuclear Test Ban Treaty with the Soviet Union. Rusk was much maligned by the American antiwar movement during the 1960s and 1970s, but garnered a great deal of respect in the later years of his life in his teaching position at the University of Georgia.

Rusk was born on February 9, 1909, in Cherokee County, Georgia. He excelled in school and attended Oxford University on a Rhodes scholarship, earning BS and MA degrees. While attending Oxford, Rusk developed his lifelong opposition to political appeasement when students at the university debated the proper approach to the rising Nazi party in Germany. Rusk felt that dictators such as Adolf Hitler could not be appeased, and, therefore, had to be ardently opposed even if it meant outright war. This belief drove many of Rusk's later policy decisions in his career as secretary of state.

Upon returning to the United States, Rusk accepted a position teaching government and international relations at Mills College in Oakland, California. He also took classes at the University of California, Berkeley Law School, but he never completed a degree there. Anticipating the U.S.'s entry into World War II, Rusk joined the army in 1940, serving with the Third Infantry Division and then the Military Intelligence Service. Rusk planned on a long military career after the war but was asked in 1947 to lead the Office of Special Political Affairs in the State Department by General, and then Secretary of State, George Marshall. Rusk became friends with Marshall's successor, Dean Acheson, when Rusk supported President Truman's highly criticized policy toward Asia. Acheson appointed Rusk assistant secretary of state for Far Eastern Affairs in 1950. Rusk left the government in 1952 to become president of the Rockefeller Foundation, where he focused on development programs for poor nations and eliminating the testing of nuclear bombs in the atmosphere.

Rusk returned to public service when newly elected President John Kennedy asked him to become secretary of state in 1961. Rusk did not have a close relationship with Kennedy, but his advice did dramatically alter the two largest international incidents in Kennedy's presidency: the failed Bay of Pigs invasion and the Cuban Missile Crisis. After invasion forces supplied and trained by the Central Intelligence Agency met resistance by the Cuban military in April 1961, Rusk adamantly opposed offering U.S. air support to the forces. Kennedy took his advice, and the operation ended in utter failure, greatly embarrassing the young administration. Rusk's advice during the Cuban Missile Crisis of October 1962 proved to be far superior. After U-2 spy planes discovered Soviet-supplied nuclear missile sites on Cuba, Rusk counseled against a military invasion of the island. He helped convince the president to establish a "quarantine" against Soviet vessels headed to the island rather than any direct military action. Rusk then helped negotiate a behind-the-scenes diplomatic solution to the crisis with the Soviets.

However, Rusk's support of the Vietnam War has far overshadowed his vital role in the successful end to the Cuban Missile Crisis. After President Kennedy's assassination in 1963, Rusk continued as secretary of state under President Johnson. As the violence in Vietnam increased, Rusk was wary of escalating the conflict to the point of Chinese intervention. However, his antiappeasement philosophy demanded a direct resistance against the spread of communism. Rusk ultimately lobbied for the escalation of U.S. forces in the region, and he became one of the more outspoken proponents of the war. This support created a great deal of animosity amongst antiwar advocates, and Rusk became much maligned across America's college campuses, in particular.

When Republican Richard Nixon won the presidency in 1969, Rusk left the Department of State and accepted a job at the University of Georgia in Athens. He taught international law at the university and refused to follow the example of most of his predecessors and travel on the lucrative lecture circuit. Rusk became quite popular among the students at the university, where he taught until his death on December 20, 1994, of congestive heart failure. Although his long career was certainly controversial, he was a key figure in the political intrigue of the 1960s, and his influence, for good or ill, cannot be denied.

See also Bay of Pigs Invasion (1961); Cuban Missile Crisis; Johnson, Lyndon Baines (1908–1973); Kennedy, John F. (1917–1963); Vietnam War.

Bibliography

Rusk, Dean. *The Winds of Freedom: Selections from the Speeches and Statements of Secretary of State Dean Rusk, January 1961–August 1962.* Boston: Beacon Press, 1963.

Schoenbaum, Thomas J. *Waging Peace and War: Dean Rusk in the Truman, Kennedy and Johnson Years.* New York: Simon & Schuster, 1988.

Zeiler, Thomas W. *Dean Rusk: Defending the American Mission Abroad.* Wilmington, DE: SR Books, 1999.

ANDREW POLK

RUSSELL, WILLIAM FELTON (1934–). Arguably the greatest professional basketball player in the history of the game, Bill Russell played for the University of San Francisco, leading it to back-to-back NCAA championships, and spent his professional career as a center for the Boston Celtics of the National Basketball Association (NBA). He was the first black player to become a national superstar.

Russell was born on February 12, 1934, in West Monroe, Louisiana, a bastion of racial segregation. During the second black Great Migration, his father moved the family to Oakland, California, where initially he struggled to support the family. Russell was extremely close to his mother, who died unexpectedly when he was 12. The athletic Russell was cut from his junior high school basketball team and barely escaped the same fate in high school. During his junior year, his basketball game solidified and he became an outstanding defensive player, primarily because he ignored conventional wisdom and jumped rather than play with his feet flat on the ground. That technique alone profoundly changed the game of basketball. Russell was recruited by coach Hal DeJulio of the University of San Francisco, where he honed his skills as a primarily defensive player.

DeJulio had three black starters on the team, and as such it was often the recipient of racism. Their teammates, however, were fairly supportive. During his junior year in college, he led the team to a national championship, averaged more than 20 points and 20 rebounds per game, was named a first-team All American and the most valuable player in the Final Four. However, he was passed over as Player of the Year for Northern California. In 1956, he declared his eligibility for the NBA draft. He was drafted by the Boston Celtics and played his first game for them in December of that year. Also in 1956, Russell led the Celtics to their second-best record since the 1946–1947 season. He became the first NBA player to average more than 20 rebounds per game for the whole season, an accomplishment he reached in 10 of his 13 professional seasons. In 1966, he became the first black coach in the NBA when he performed as player-coach for the Celtics. From 1973 through 1977, he coached the Seattle SuperSonics, leading them to their first playoff appearance ever. He also coached the Sacramento Kings from 1987 through 1988.

Russell had a problematic relationship with fans, especially those in Boston. He was subjected to racial taunts and incidents all his life, and was especially critical of the racial atmosphere in Boston. Thus, he refused to sign autographs for fans or respond to their acclamation. He also had a difficult relationship with the Boston press corps, calling them corrupt and racist. Russell apparently mellowed when he grew older; in 1999, the Celtics re-retired his jersey, an event attended by his daughter, his favorite rival Wilt Chamberlain, Celtics star Larry Bird, and Los Angeles Lakers star Kareem Abdul-Jabbar. He received a long-standing ovation, which moved him to tears.

Russell garnered more awards than almost any other professional basketball player. He twice led his team to the NCAA Championships, and won an Olympic gold medal in 1956. He owns 11 NBA Championship rings, was five times named the most valuable player of the regular season, and was selected 12 times as an All Star. In 2009, NBA Commissioner David Stern announced that the MVP Award of given during the NBA Finals would be renamed in honor of Bill Russell.

Bibliography

Goudsouzian, Aram. *King of the Court: Bill Russell and the Basketball Revolution.* Berkeley: University of California Press, 2010.

Russell, Bill, and Alan Steinberg. *Red and Me: My Coach, My Lifelong Friend.* New York: HarperCollins, 2010.

MARILYN K. HOWARD

RUSTIN, BAYARD (1910–1987). Bayard Rustin was born March 17, 1910, in Westchester, Pennsylvania. The son and grandson of pacifists, he would be active with the National Association for the Advancement for Colored People (NAACP) campaigning against Jim Crow segregation laws. Rustin emerged as one of the most influential leaders and strategists of the civil rights movement and was an architect of the 1963 March on Washington for Jobs and Freedom. His influence was considerable in several areas of civil rights and human rights in American history. Rustin was especially important in the domains of labor, civil rights and the gay rights movement.

Rustin was a member of the Communist Party and later learned how to effectively organize people under the tutelage of black labor leader A. Philip Randolph. Rustin's talent as an organizer emerged out of the union activism of the 1930s and '40s during the era of New Deal Democratic politics. As an activist, he had to frequently face hostility and persecution as a homosexual, ultimately being arrested and incarcerated for an encounter with a man. However, despite these obstacles, Rustin was able to critically evaluate the goals and objectives of the freedom movement in relation to the American political landscape and advise Martin Luther King Jr., its most prominent leader, on tactics and strategy in the struggle for civil rights.

Rustin persuasively argued for a new strategy following the passage of civil rights legislation, in his essay "From Protest to Politics: The Future of the Civil Rights Movement." In it he asserted that African Americans in the pursuit of equality were behaving in a revolutionary fashion because, although their demand was middle class in nature, it could only be met through a reordering of American political and economic relations and achieved by progressive coalition forces that became the governing majority. Rustin influenced Martin Luther King Jr.'s incorporation of economic ideas into speeches to secure civil rights gains and worked with economists to develop what was later called the "Freedom Budget." The Freedom Budget was based on the idea that a government jobs program would be the guarantee of work for those willing and able to work and a minimum wage that would lift families out of poverty. Many of the ideas of the Freedom Budget were incorporated into a bill passed in 1978 as the Full employment and Balanced Growth Act, although it was stripped of the guaranteed job provision articulated by the Freedom Budget.

Rustin emerged as a leader at an important time in American history, during the dismantling of segregation and the legalization of interracial marriage by the U.S. Supreme court. Following the successes of the civil rights movement in the '60s, Rustin's stance against the Vietnam War and nuclear weapons, support for gay rights, the recognition of same-sex unions, and his work related to the A. Philip Randolph Labor Institute would keep him active in progressive causes until the end of his life. He died on August 24, 1987.

Bibliography

Forstater, Mathew. "From Civil Rights to Economic Security: Bayard Rustin and the African American Struggle for Full Employment, 1945–1978." *International Journal of Political Economy* 36 (Fall 2007): 63–74.

Rustin, Bayard. "From Protest to Politics: The Future of the Civil Rights Movement." *Commentary* (1964).

REYNALDO ANDERSON

S

SAINT, THE (1962–1969). Often compared to a modern-day Robin Hood (Britton 2004), *The Saint* offered a popular '60s television equivalent to the emerging James Bond cinema franchise, bringing fame to actor Roger Moore in the title role.

Unlike other secret agent shows of the 1960s, *The Saint* was notable for originating in a preexisting literary character. Based on Simon Templar, the gentleman detective created by Leslie Charteris, *The Saint* was not only a regular on library shelves between the 1930s and 1960s, but Templar had also made his screen debut in eight films based on *The Saint*, released between 1938 and 1941. These existing depictions of Charteris's charming hero on a personal crusade against "the ungodly" would provide the basis for the subsequent television series.

With British producers securing the rights to *The Saint* in 1961, the show went into production in June 1962. Thirty one-hour episodes were produced for the first season, with 32 following in the second series. Two more seasons would appear, in color, until its eventual demise in 1969. Although Patrick McGoohan had been the alleged first choice to play Templar during his hiatus from *Danger Man*, producers sought a less earnest presence. Known as a romantic action hero from his roles in *Ivanhoe* and *Maverick* in the 1950s, Roger Moore seemed an apt choice for the hero of *The Saint*.

Despite featuring a more humorous actor for the role of Templar, *The Saint* nonetheless possessed a distinct moral thrust, as demonstrated in the quasireligious overtones of its title. Its grounding in contemporary current affairs, in particular the Cold War context of the era, also brought the show closer to the realist path forged by *Danger Man* than the more surreal *The Avengers*. Yet, for all its interest in topical plot-lines, *The Saint* was undeniably glossy; the use of a white Volvo as signature product of the series shows how its surface values aligned with the emerging consumerism of the '60s. In addition, the show pandered to national, racial and gendered stereotypes, with many female stars having little more than a decorative role. *The Saint* also attracted a certain degree of affectionate mockery due to Moore's acting technique being seemingly orientated around a particularly expressive right eyebrow. Nonetheless, despite these causes for derision, the program proved highly popular, with the chivalrous Simon Templar considered an engaging hero for the 1960s.

While *The Saint* was an undoubted hit, serving as reliable filler for NBC between 1967 and 1969, it was very much a product of its era. Subsequent attempts to revive the show, whether in a television remake in the 1970s or the 1997 film starring Val Kilmer, have proved considerable failures. As Chapman (2002) suggests, this can in part be attributed to the anachronistic nature of its hero, the 1930s mold of gentleman detective no longer appearing relevant to contemporary audiences. Despite this charge, *The Saint* not only served as a successful television counterpart to James Bond (Moore, of course, going on to play Bond throughout the 1970s), but also proved a highly popular example of the '60s secret agent genre.

See also Avengers, The (1961–1969); *Danger Man* (1960); *Prisoner, The* (1966).

Bibliography

Britton, Wesley. *Spy Television* Westport, CT: Praeger, 2004.
Chapman, James. *Saints and Avengers: British Adventure Series of the Sixties*. London: I. B. Tauris, 2002.

ROSEMARY DELLER

SASSOON, VIDAL (1928–). Vidal Sassoon is a hairstylist whose philosophy of "wash and go" freed women from time-consuming styling. He influenced hairstyling trends of the 1960s when he promoted very short and very long cuts at each spectrum of the decade. He was one of the first beauty entrepreneurs when he parlayed his celebrity into selling a line of hair care and beauty products as well as franchising salons and hairdressing academies.

Born on January 17, 1928, in London to Nathan Sassoon and Betty Bellin, he was placed in a Jewish orphanage for several years after his father abandoned the family. At 11, Betty remarried and brought Sassoon and his brother home. He dropped out of school at 14, and his mother suggested he work at a beauty salon for Adolph Cohen as an alternative. He fought with the elite fighting force Palmach in Israel's War of Independence in 1948 at age 20. When Sassoon returned to London and hairstyling, he adopted an adventurous sensibility to his approach and technique.

London was swinging in the 1960s, and thanks to Sassoon's experimentation, so were women's hairstyles. His first salon was established on Bond Street in 1954. He restructured and modernized the bob and introduced geometric styles that featured his trademark blunt-cut technique. Sassoon's easy hairdos liberated women from regular visits to the beauty parlor for a shampoo and set. Key to his styles was a natural approach to styling and care with minimal products. Free-flowing hair mimicked the free-flowing vibe of the decade. He employed young, mod stylists in his salon, which attracted a similar clientele. Word of mouth spread quickly, and his customers included models and actresses, and eventually caught the eye of the Beatles, who adopted his shaggy look for men's hair. In 1963, Mary Quant's models' hair featured Sassoon's bob. His bob differed from the iconic bob of the 1920s; it was cropped closely at the nape of the neck and fell to chin or shoulder length in the front. The next year, British fashion magazines adopted his bob as their favorite style, and

Poetry magazine and a Guggenheim Foundation fellowship. In 1969, Snyder released a collection of prose, *Earth House Hold*, which further explored the deep, primeval connection between humankind and nature.

Turtle Island, which appeared in 1974, was Snyder's most celebrated work and contained favorites such as "I Went into the Maverick Bar." As a whole, *Turtle Island* challenged Americans to think about their place in nature, not as an invasive species but as a part of the land. Snyder continued to publish through the 80s and 90s, and most recently in 2007 with *Back on the Fire: Essays*. In 2010, the University of California–Davis, where Snyder was a professor of English, announced the pending creation of the Gary Snyder Endowed Chair in Science and Humanities.

See also Ecology; Ginsberg, Allen (1926–1997); Kerouac, Jack (1922–1969).

Bibliography

Gray, Timothy. *Gary Snyder and the Pacific Rim: Creating Countercultural Community*. Contemporary North American Poetry Series. Iowa City: University of Iowa Press, 2006.
Murphy, Patrick D. *A Place for Wayfaring: The Poetry and Prose of Gary Snyder*. Corvallis: Oregon State University Press, 2000.
Steuding, Bob. *Gary Snyder*. Twayne's United States Authors Series. Boston: Twayne, 1976.

DARRON R. DARBY

SOUND OF MUSIC, THE (1965). The film *The Sound of Music*, an adaptation of the Broadway musical of the same name, was released in 1965 by Twentieth Century-Fox. It became the top-grossing film of the year in the American market and as of February 2010 remains the number three film of all time in terms of domestic box office gross, adjusted for inflation.

The screenplay by Ernest Lehman was adapted from the book of the musical by Howard Lindsay and Russel Crouse, which was based on Maria von Trapp's 1949 book *The Story of the Trapp Family Singers*. The film capitalized on the popularity of the Broadway production (which ran for 1,443 performances in 1959–1963), and while a few songs were added for the film, most are from the musical (music by Richard Rodgers, lyrics by Oscar Hammerstein II) including "The Sound of Music," "My Favorite Things," "Do-Re-Mi," "Edelweiss," and "Climb Ev'ry Mountain." The serious subject matter was unusual but not unprecedented for a musical film: similar material had served as the basis for other Rodgers and Hammerstein musicals that were later filmed, including *South Pacific* and *Carousel*.

The story begins in the late 1930s, shortly before the Nazi annexation (*Anschluss*) of Austria. Maria (Julie Andrews), a novitiate in a Salzburg abbey, is sent to be a governess in the household of the widower Captain von Trapp (Christopher Plummer). Her high spirits bring her into conflict with the captain's strict ideas about child rearing but she wins over the captain's seven children: in a famous scene, she makes them playclothes from the curtains so they won't tear up the uniforms the captain insists they wear. She also wins over the captain, who breaks off with his wealthy fiancée (Eleanor Parker) in favor of Maria.

Over the course of the film, the encroachment of the Nazis into Austrian life becomes increasingly obvious. In an early scene, after Rolf (suitor of the captain's eldest daughter) greets them with a Nazi salute, the captain and family friend Max Dettweiler (Richard Haydn) argue about the growing influence of the Nazis. As an

Austrian patriot, the captain opposes them openly, while the apolitical Dettweiler refuses to take a stand. A dinner party guest questions why the captain displays the Austrian flag, and later, after the *Anschluss* is official, the same person returns as a Nazi official to demand the captain fly the Nazi flag instead. When the captain is ordered to report for duty in the German Navy, the entire family is forced to flee to Switzerland.

The Sound of Music was nominated for 10 Academy Awards and won 5: Best Picture, Best Director (Wise), Best Film Editing (William Reynolds), Best Music (Irwin Kostal), and Best Sound (James Corcoran and Fred Hynes). It was added to the National Film Registry in 2001.

See also Camelot (1960); *Cabaret* (1966); *Hair* (1967–1972); *Man of La Mancha* (1965).

Bibliography

Maslon, Laurence. *The Sound of Music Companion*. New York: Fireside, 2007.
Nolan, Frederick. *The Sound of Their Music: The Story of Rodgers and Hammerstein*. New York: Applause Theatre & Cinema Books, 2002.
Wilk, Max. *The Making of The Sound of Music*. New York: Routledge, 2007.

SARAH BOSLAUGH

SOUTHERN CHRISTIAN LEADERSHIP CONFERENCE (SCLC). Founded in 1957, the Southern Christian Leadership Conference (SCLC) was the organizational mechanism that helped propel the African American struggle for civil rights onto the national stage. The organization focused its efforts on increasing black political participation and protesting discriminatory segregation laws in transportation, suffrage, and housing. Although not novel at the time, the SCLC's commitment on a massive scale to nonviolent direct action made the sit-in and the peaceful march synonymous with the civil rights movement. The SCLC is still in operation today, with headquarters in Atlanta, Georgia.

Formation. The SCLC coalesced in the wake of the Montgomery Bus Boycott of 1955–1956, and most of its leaders being Baptist ministers, brought an intentional and visible religious leadership to the fore of the movement. Among its founders were Ralph Abernathy, Ella Baker, Martin Luther King Jr., Stanley Levinson, Bayard Rustin, and Fred Shuttlesworth. Resistance to the organization was strong from its earliest days, as Abernathy's home and church were bombed during a formational Atlanta meeting on January 10, 1957. This meeting at Ebenezer Baptist Church was attended by some 60 people and largely determined the course of SCLC, though it would not be fully organized and named until in a meeting in Montgomery, August 7–8, 1957. Its earliest leaders were veterans of the civil rights movement, affiliated with the Congress of Racial Equality, (CORE) the National Association for the Advancement of Colored People (NAACP), and the Fellowship of Reconciliation.

The SCLC differed from other civil rights organizations of the time in its overt linking of racial equality with evangelical religion, its dedication to nonviolent direct action, and its locally driven campaign strategy. The organization was implemented as a coalition of civil rights interest groups and therefore did not compete with these other organizations for members. Although often referred to as the organizational arm of Martin Luther King Jr.'s civil rights work, the SCLC involved many high-profile civil rights leaders and boasted the dedication of countless activists. Individual members of SCLC affiliated with their local chapter—usually through their church—rather than a national office, and the loose national structure of the organization would be a cause of criticism as well as its principal strength. What centralized power there was in the SCLC could easily jump from one campaign to another. A common complaint against the organization was that it planned events it did not see through, which may have been precisely why it was so often able to direct its resources toward causes that were more likely to receive media attention. The SCLC rarely fought losing battles.

Tactics. During the 1960s, the approach of the organization was to lend national attention and resources to local campaigns of protest. Through their efforts, a lunch counter sit-in in Greensboro, North Carolina, could become an event of national interest. In that particular instance, it was the organizing of a conference in the spring of 1960 at Shaw University in Raleigh, North Carolina, that lent rhetorical force and wider attention to a series of student-initiated nonviolent protests. These events led to the formation of the Student Nonviolent Coordinating Committee (SNCC), a separate organization with close ties but a rocky relationship to the SCLC. The SCLC borrowed intentionally from Mohandas Gandhi's teaching of nonviolence protest as an agent of social change and, working alongside organizations such as CORE, trained black youths in the art of nonviolent resistance. In addition to pushing for legal reforms, the SCLC directed much effort toward educating blacks on the American political system and organizing voter drives. These workshops and the Citizenship Schools of the SCLC made it as formidable on the grassroots level as it was effective on the national scene. In 1965, the SCLC helped to register 85,000 voters.

The scenes of calm black resistance and the eloquence of its leaders did much to change the national sentiment regarding segregation. With the group's efforts focused early on the South, the common perception that blacks were content with Jim Crow law in the region was shattered on a national level. No longer was segregation an issue peculiar to the North.

Major Campaigns. The SCLC led or participated in many memorable campaigns for civil rights during the 1960s. Virtually all of the iconic scenes of the civil rights movement involved the ubiquitous organization. The organization's first official campaign was the Crusade for Citizenship begun in 1958, a colossal effort to double the number of blacks registered to vote. In part, the notoriety of this effort gained King and other SCLC members a meeting with President Eisenhower. The SCLC also led the Birmingham Campaign of 1963, in which King was arrested and wrote his famous "Letter from Birmingham Jail." This struggle involved 65 consecutive days of mass meetings, sit-ins, and boycotts and left an indelible impression on the nation as televisions across the country relayed scenes of black children being blasted with fire hoses by local police. The March on Washington on August 28, 1963 was headed by SCLC leaders fresh from their victory in Birmingham, in cooperation with leaders from the NAACP, CORE, and other groups. This rally attracted nearly a quarter of a million marchers and set the scene in which King delivered his "I Have a Dream" speech, an eloquent and moving piece of oratory that defined the movement.

Although the SCLC was committed to nonviolence, their marches and rallies had a knack for attracting violent reaction. Such was the case with their work on the issue of voting rights in and around Selma, Alabama, in the early days of 1965. The peaceful march of January 19 led to the arrests of 62 participants who had been ordered to enter the courthouse through a side entrance. Less than two weeks later, King and

Abernathy, along with 500 other youths, were also arrested for violating a parade ordinance. In nearby Marion, violence erupted over the imprisonment of SCLC worker James Orange, leading to the shooting and death of marcher Jimmy Lee Jackson. Weeks later back in Selma, protestors were met with violence on what became known as "Bloody Sunday." Hundreds of marchers were sprayed with tear gas and clubbed by state troopers as they attempted to cross the Edmund Pettus Bridge. These well-publicized events helped garner white liberal support for the movement, and led to the Civil Rights Act of 1964 and the Voting Rights Act of 1965.

As the organization matured, King and the SCLC increasingly broadened their work from civil rights to human rights from desegregation to economic justice. In 1962, the SCLC launched Operation Breadbasket, a drive for better job opportunities for blacks. Using boycotts and public pressure on businesses with unfair hiring practices, Operation Breadbasket was successful in Atlanta and was expanded to Chicago in 1966. Under the able leadership of Chicago seminary student Jesse Jackson, who had been swept into the SCLC during the Selma campaign, Operation Breadbasket went on to negotiate jobs for blacks in major dairy companies, supermarket chains, and even Pepsi and Coca-Cola bottlers. The last major crusade of the SCLC was the Poor People's Campaign, which was planned as a march from Marks, Mississippi, to Washington, D.C., and centered on the issue of economic justice for all poor people. King would not live to see the outcome of this march, as he was assassinated on April 4, 1968. Despite the best efforts of the SCLC, King's death essentially halted the campaign.

Decline. King was the president and national image of the SCLC from its founding until his assassination, at which time Abernathy took leadership. In the late 1960s, in the wake of the assassination of Malcolm X, and especially following King's death, the SCLC's focus on nonviolence and desegregation held less appeal for many civil rights leaders. Instead, groups like the Black Panthers gained power, calling for armed self-defense and reverse discrimination. In this turmoil and with the loss of its iconic leader, the SCLC dwindled in the 1970s. Jesse Jackson split with the SCLC in 1971 over differences with Abernathy, especially regarding the management of Operation Breadbasket. The SCLC boasts a continuous history since its formation in 1957 but never regained the influence it exerted in the early and mid-1960s. Today, the Atlanta-based organization, with Byron C. Clay its most recent president, continues working in a broad range of civil rights and community health issues from drug prevention to criminal justice.

See also Abernathy, Ralph (1926–1990); Civil Disobedience; Congress of Racial Equality (CORE); Jackson, Jesse (1941–); King, Martin Luther Jr. (1929–1968); March to Selma (1965); March on Washington (1963); Rustin, Bayard (1910–1987); Shuttlesworth, Fred (1922–2011).

Bibliography

Fairclough, Adam. *To Redeem the Soul of America: The Southern Christian Leadership Conference and Martin Luther King, Jr.* Athens: University of Georgia Press, 1987.

Garrow, David J. *Martin Luther King, Jr., and the Southern Christian Leadership Conference.* New York: William Morrow, 1986.

Peake, Thomas R. *Keeping the Dream Alive: A History of the Southern Christian Leadership Conference from King to the Nineteen-Eighties.* New York: Peter Lang, 1987.

CHRISTOPHER J. RICHMANN

SPACE RACE. The space race was an intense but undeclared competition between the United States and the Soviet Union in which each tried to outdo the other in achieving milestones in the exploration of space. It began with the launch of *Sputnik 1* in 1957, reached a peak in the first half of the 1960s, and wound down after the first successful lunar landing in 1969. The Apollo-Soyuz test project—a joint U.S.-USSR mission flown in 1975—marked its symbolic end.

The space race had a military dimension. Missiles that could launch satellites could also launch nuclear warheads, and Earth orbit seemed—in the late 1950s and early 1960s—like key strategic ground. Military concerns soon faded into the background, however, and by the early 1960s, the space race was primarily about the superpowers' desire to burnish their national images. Success in space implied, leaders on both sides believed, mastery of cutting-edge fields such as rocketry, electronics, and telecommunications: the stuff of which the future would be constructed. The Soviet Union, traditionally a minor contributor to such fields, wanted to win the space race.

Milestones—going somewhere or doing something in space for the first time in history—became the means by which the superpowers publicly kept score in the space race. Initially, virtually all of them seemed to belong to the Soviets. The United States, meanwhile, seemed permanently consigned to second place. *Sputnik 1* reached orbit on October 4, 1957, and *Sputnik 2*—carrying a dog named Laika on a one-way trip—followed on November 2. The first American attempt to launch a satellite, on December 6, ended in spectacular and highly public failure: Its launch vehicle—a modified Jupiter missile—lifted a few feet off the pad, slumped back down, toppled onto its side, and exploded. The *International Herald Tribune* summed up the result in a one-word headline above a photograph of the explosion: "Kaputnik!" The first successful American satellite, *Explorer 1*, reached orbit on February 1, 1958. The fact that it accomplished more once in orbit—its instruments detected what became known as the Van Allen Radiation Belts—mattered less, in public-image terms, than the fact that it lagged nearly four months behind its Soviet counterpart.

The string of Soviet successes continued, seemingly unabated, for five years after *Sputnik 1*. The robotic *Luna 1* probe, launched in January 1959, became the first spacecraft to leave Earth's orbit, the first to transmit data from space, the first to fly past the moon, and the first to go into orbit around the sun. The same year saw *Luna 2* become the first spacecraft to crash-land on the moon and *Luna 3* take the first pictures of the lunar far side. A pair of dogs named Belka and Strelka—passengers aboard *Sputnik 5*—became the first animals to return safely from orbit in 1960, avoiding Laika's fate. The first robot probes to fly by other planets—*Marsnik 1* in 1960 and *Venera 1* in 1961—were also Soviet projects. American "firsts" in this period were concentrated in Earth orbit: the first weather satellite (*TIROS-1*, 1960), the first navigation satellite (*Transit*, 1961), and the first commercial communication satellite (*Telstar*, 1962).

The Soviets achieved a similar series of milestones in the first five years of human spaceflight (1961–1966). Yuri Gagarin was the first human to fly in space (April 1961), Gherman Titov the first human to spend an entire day in space (December 1961), and Valentina Tereshkova the first woman to fly in space (August 1962). The first launch of multiple manned spacecraft (also August 1962), the first spaceflight by a multiperson crew (October 1964), and the first spacewalk (March 1965) were all Soviet. The United States reached the same milestones months, years, or (in the case of women in space) decades later.

The Soviet Union's lead in the space race was real, but two factors made it seem even greater than it was—especially to observers outside the respective space programs. The first was the USSR's state-controlled media, which trumpeted the Soviet space program's successes and buried its failures. The U.S. space program's successes were equally well publicized, but its failures—from the ill-fated attempt to launch TV-3 in 1957 to the near-loss of *Apollo 13* in 1970—took place in full view of the world, and were reported on in detail. The second was Soviet political leaders' insistence on flight schedules that would ensure a steady stream of firsts, whether or not they made sense in engineering or operational terms. American political leaders generally resisted such demands. President John F. Kennedy's 1961 challenge to execute a successful lunar landing by the end of the decade was a rare—and spectacularly successful—exception to the rule.

Astronaut Buzz Aldrin stands beside a U.S. flag on the moon on July 20, 1969, during the Apollo 11 mission into space. (NASA)

Reaping the benefits of a slow-and-steady approach that subordinated public relations coups to engineering advances, the United States gradually took the lead in the space race beginning around 1966. The American lunar landing program surged forward, while the Soviet lunar program (hurt by the death of Sergei Korolev, the visionary behind it) languished. American astronauts were the first to orbit the moon, the first to land on it, the first to walk on it, and the first to drive on it. The robotic spacecraft that the Soviets sent to the moon between the mid-1960s and the mid-1970s—orbiters, landers, and rovers—were impressive feats of engineering and returned important scientific results, but the words and the human-centered images sent back from the moon by Project Apollo captured the imagination of the American public and much of the wider world.

The space race ended, for all practical purposes, when *Apollo 11* landed on the moon in 1969: the United States achieved the greatest first of all. The formal end of the race, however, came in 1975 with the Apollo-Soyuz Test Project: two space-craft—one Soviet, one American—in Earth orbit for joint scientific experiments and symbolic exchanges of greetings and gifts. The Apollo-Soyuz flight reflected the superpowers' pursuit of détente, just as the space race it ended had reflected the Cold War tensions of the late 1950s and early 1960s.

See also Project Apollo; Project Gemini; Project Mercury.

Bibliography

D'Antonio, Michael. *A Ball, a Dog, and a Monkey: 1957—The Space Race Begins.* New York: Simon & Schuster, 2008.

French, Francis, and Colin Burgess. *Into That Silent Sea: Trailblazers of the Space Era, 1961–1965.* Lincoln: University of Nebraska Press, 2007.

French, Francis, and Colin Burgess. *In The Shadow of the Moon: A Challenging Journey to Tranquility, 1965–1969.* Lincoln: University of Nebraska Press, 2007.

MacDougall, Walter. *The Heavens and the Earth: A Political History of the Space Age.* New York: Basic Books, 1985.

A. BOWDOIN VAN RIPER

SPAGHETTI WESTERNS. The term "Spaghetti Western" is used to describe European Westerns, largely originating in Italy, but often produced in collaboration with Spanish, German, or French studios. From the early 1960s to the late 1970s, over 600 such Westerns were filmed by directors such as Sergio Leone, Sergio Corbucci, Duccio Tessari, and Sergio Sollima. These Euro-Westerns were modeled after those filmed in the United States, using classic Western themes, symbolism, and character types, but often created through production methods and moral complexities that undermined the conventions of traditional Westerns.

In the early 1960s, Spaghetti Westerns were produced on low budgets similar to North American B-grade movies, and typically featured international casts consisting of actors from the United States, Italy, and Spain. Michael Carreras's *The Savage Guns* (European title: *Tierra Brutal*), produced in 1961, is considered by many to be the first Spaghetti Western, despite its lack of association with Italy, because of its low production values and European cinematographic influence. Shot on location in Almeria, Spain, the film showcased an American lead cast (headed by Richard Basehart), with Spanish actors in supporting roles.

The mid-1960s marked a shift in styles that established the conventions for Spaghetti Westerns as a genre unto themselves. That shift was brought about by director Sergio Leone, who along with composer Ennio Morricone, cinematographer Massimo Dallamano, and film star Clint Eastwood, crafted a trilogy of films—*A Fistful of Dollars* (1964), *For a Few Dollars More* (1965), and *The Good, the Bad, and the Ugly* (1966)—that quickly became the defining works of the genre. These became formula films for a generation of new directors, as well as giving rise to popular series based on the exploits of a single character, such as "Django," first played by Franco Nero, and introduced in Sergio Corbucci's *Django*, and revisited in nearly a dozen sequels and spin-offs, associated with various actors and directors.

Spaghetti Westerns are primarily set in the barren landscapes resembling those found in the Mexican border region of the American Southwest. Unlike the frontier of the mainstream Western, which typically signifies a combination of freedom and wildness, the rugged desert landscapes of Spaghetti Westerns speak of unrelenting harshness and isolation. Heat rising from the desert sands threatens to choke out all life; wilderness and towns alike are filmed in muted shades of dusty tan and gray; no vibrant visual contrast exists between life and death. The moral landscape of the Spaghetti Western's characters mirrors this lack of contrast, with no clear divide between "good" and "bad" as in traditional Westerns. Rather than presenting a morality tale of "civilized justice" brought to a wild frontier, the world of the Spaghetti Western is one of retribution, where the instrument of justice, the hero, is as untamed as the villain and the landscape that surrounds them both. Not all good wins out, and evil-doers are made to suffer penalties in accordance with their damage to others.

This absence of clear-cut good and evil and the films' simplistic moral character clearly reflected the moral conflict experienced in Western Europe and the United States during the Cold War era, and also aligned Spaghetti Westerns with the revisionist trend that characterized mainstream American Westerns in the 1970s and beyond.

Bibliography

Weisser, Thomas. *Spaghetti Westerns: The Good, the Bad, and the Violent.* Jefferson, NC: McFarland, 1992.

CYNTHIA J. MILLER

SPELLING, AARON (1923–2006). Aaron Spelling was a writer, actor, and producer of film and television best known for his televised series, which were popular culture touchstones for several generations of viewers, such as *Charlie's Angels* (1976–1981), *The Love Boat* (1977–1986), *Dynasty* (1981–1989), and *Beverly Hills, 90210* (1990–2000). Spelling's ability to discern the zeitgeist of America as it moved through the latter half of the twentieth century led to television and film productions that persist as icons of the decades in which they were created.

Spelling began his career writing for television in the mid-1950s, contributing to several series that spanned the decade and continued into the 1960s, such as the CBS drama series *Playhouse 90* (1956–1961), *Zane Grey Theatre* (1956–1961), and *Wagon Train* (1957–1965). In 1959, he became a producer for Four Star Studios, where he would remain until 1965, creating programming such as *The*

Lloyd Bridges Show (1962–1963), the award-winning *Burke's Law* (1963), and *Honey West* (1965). At Four Star, he also contributed to the development of the situation comedy *The Smothers Brothers Show* (1965–1966), which launched the careers of two brothers, Tom and Dick Smothers, who would go on to host the popular variety show *The Smothers Brothers Comedy Hour* (1967–1969).

In the late 1960s, Spelling began a four-year partnership with actor Danny Thomas, creating Thomas-Spelling Productions. Between 1968 and 1972, the pair produced the iconic counterculture detective drama *The Mod Squad* (1968–1973), which earned six Emmy Award nominations for Outstanding Drama Series. Based on the experiences of the series' creator, Bud Ruskin, the series featured a trio of troubled young characters, all recently arrested and on probation, who are offered the opportunity to work undercover for the police. Each of the three represented mainstream society's chief fears involving youth in the 1960s: wealthy, bored, and out-of-control Pete Cochran (Michael Cole) was kicked out of his Beverly Hills home and arrested after stealing a car; African American Linc Hayes (Clarence Williams III) was arrested during the Watts riots—one of the longest and most violent real-life race riots in the city of Los Angeles; and Julie Barnes (Peggy Lipton) was a runaway arrested for vagrancy while fleeing from her prostitute mother. The three became members of a special squad intended to infiltrate the underbelly of the counterculture and arrest the adult criminals who victimized and manipulated their fellow youth. With *Mod Squad*, Spelling not only created a space for 1960s counterculture music, fashion, language, and art, but also introduced positive images of the era's young people, as well as featuring one of television's first female police officers in a leading role.

Spelling continued to produce timely and insightful entertainment—both televised programming and films—throughout the next three decades, until his death in 2006, earning Emmy Awards for his television films *Day One* (1989) and *And the Band Played On* (1993), along with a host of other honors, including a Lifetime Achievement Award from the Producers Guild of America and a star on the Hollywood Walk of Fame.

Bibliography

Bodroghkozy, Aniko, and Lynn Spigel. *Groove Tube: Sixties Television and the Youth Rebellion*. Durham, NC: Duke University Press, 2001.
Spelling, Aaron, and Jefferson Graham. *Aaron Spelling: A Prime-Time Life*. New York: St. Martin's, 2002.

CYNTHIA J. MILLER

SPOCK, BENJAMIN (1903–1998). Born in 1903 into a comfortable Connecticut home, Benjamin Spock was the eldest of six children. An accomplished student and athlete, he excelled at Yale and continued on to medical school, specializing in pediatrics. His study of parents' and children's psychological needs convinced him that accepted theories about child rearing were ill founded. In 1946, he published his iconoclastic views in *The Common Sense Book of Baby and Child Care*. In a culture that favored parental authoritarianism, he emphasized the benefits of expressing affection for children. In a postwar culture that honored expertise, he convinced parents that they were experts on their own children, who were themselves individuals with particular needs. The book became one of the best-selling books of all time, and Dr. Spock became the nation's preeminent authority on family issues.

Despite his celebrity, Dr. Spock remained initially apolitical and, outside pediatric circles, likewise uncontroversial. He was optimistic about human nature, and his enlightened, nonideological liberalism supported the notion that people could make the world a better and more humane place. As his fame grew, he began to feel that a degree of public responsibility came along with his celebrity. He supported Kennedy in 1960 because of the candidate's staunch anticommunism, but his hawkishness was soon overcome by his conscience when, in 1962, the Kennedy administration resumed the testing of nuclear weapons. Spock joined SANE, the Committee for a Sane Nuclear Policy, in order to oppose the nuclear arms race. Spock also opposed the Kennedy administration's involvement in the Vietnam conflict. When the bombing of Vietnam began in February 1965, Spock joined in SANE's denunciation and subsequent protests.

In contrast to other early opponents of the Vietnam War, Dr. Spock appeared remarkably pragmatic. Perceived as a mainstream liberal and a legitimate public figure, even his political advice appeared as common sense. Spock was the first major celebrity who was seen as credible by "Middle America" to oppose the war publicly. But because he took an unpopular position, his activism also damaged his reputation. Viewed as a father figure to a whole generation of young Americans, Spock, critics charged, led, or misled, these same young Americans into antiwar protest. In order to explain the popularity of protest among youth, critics even cited his child care techniques—particularly the misconception that he advocated permissiveness—to charge that they spoiled young Americans and taught them instant gratification.

Spock had been a supporter of the Johnson administration's war on poverty and a personal acquaintance of the president, and he wrote Johnson telegrams and letters expressing his moral opposition to the war. He specifically opposed the violence the American military unintentionally visited upon Vietnamese civilians, and particularly children, his subject of expertise. Despite Spock's celebrity, the Johnson administration had little trouble ignoring foreign policy advice from a baby doctor. However, Spock saw pediatrics and politics as inherently linked. He saw his antiwar activity as yet another way of protecting the young people—in America and Vietnam—to whom he devoted his life and career.

Spock knew his usefulness to the peace movement lay in recruiting people from the middle of the road, but he did not restrict himself to so-called responsible protests. In the spring of 1967, Spock signed "A Call to Resist Illegitimate Authority," an argument in support of draft resistance, and he and four other signers were charged with conspiracy to counsel young men to resist the draft. Spock was convicted on charges of conspiracy to counsel, aid, and abet draft resistance, though his conviction was overturned on appeal. He remained popular among the antiwar movement. He considered a vice presidential candidacy on a ticket with Martin Luther King Jr. in 1968, and in 1972, he ran for president on the People's Party ticket. Dr. Spock died at his home on March 15, 1998 after a lengthy battle with cancer.

Bibliography

Bloom, Lynn Z. *Doctor Spock: Biography of a Conservative Radical.* Indianapolis: Bobbs-Merrill, 1972.

Foley, Michael S. *Dear Dr. Spock: Letters about the Vietnam War to America's Favorite Baby Doctor.* New York: New York University Press, 2005.

Hall, Mitchell K. *Because of Their Faith: CALCAV and Religious Opposition to the Vietnam War*. New York: Columbia University Press, 1990.

Maier, Thomas. *Dr. Spock: An American Life*. New York: Harcourt, Brace, 1998.

Mitford, Jessica. *The Trial of Dr. Spock: The Rev. William Sloane Coffin, Jr., Michael Ferber, Mitchell Goodman, and Marcus Raskin*. New York: Alfred A. Knopf, 1969.

Spock, Benjamin, and Mitchell Zimmerman. *Dr. Spock on Vietnam*. New York: Dell, 1968.

KEVIN WILSON

STAR TREK (1966–1969). *Star Trek* was first run on NBC Television from 1966 to 1969. Created by Gene Roddenberry, *Star Trek* was a space adventure series with a social message. The cast of the original series included William Shatner as Captain Kirk, Leonard Nimoy's as Spock, DeForest Kelley as Dr. McCoy, James Doohan as Montgomery Scott, Nichelle Nichols as Uhura, George Takei as Hikaru Sulu, and Walter Koenig as Pavel Chekov. All 79 episodes of this series were set in the twenty-third century on the starship *Enterprise*, on alien planets, or both, and explored themes of adventure, futurism, and progress.

Star Trek's imaginary world sees Earth as part of an interplanetary coalition, the United Federation of Planets. Its diplomatic and military arm is Starfleet, whose flagship is the starship *Enterprise*. Launched into deep space, its five-year mission is to "explore strange new worlds; to seek out new life and new civilizations; to boldly go where no man has gone before" (*Star Trek* narrative lead-in). Elements of science fiction—space travel, alien contact, and futurism—set the stage for adventure, camaraderie, exotic romance, and exploration of alternate worlds.

The series offered cheap sets, cheesy humor, and women in mini-skirts, but it also had a serious side. Props used on the show included gadgets like a flip-top communicator and a transporter that dematerialized matter. Aliens included humanoids, shape shifters, silicon creatures, androids, immortals, energy beings, and telepaths, some benevolent and altruistic, some evil, and all strange. *Star Trek* also explored serious themes. As America's war with Vietnam dragged on and antiwar movement sped up, *Star Trek* took a subtle antiwar stance. Combining this with themes of multiculturalism and civil rights, the series came to be viewed as offering a reasonable exploration of American social and political problems.

For example, the episodes "Let That Be Your Last Battlefield" and "The Cloud Minders" combined themes of peace and civil rights. In "Battlefield," a civilization is destroyed by a war that is fueled by racism. In "Cloud Minders," violence erupts between working-class miners and elites living in a floating city. In both episodes, one group believes it is superior and controls and oppresses the other, but the

William Shatner (left), DeForest Kelley (center), and Leonard Nimoy (left) pose on the set of the television series *Star Trek*. (AP/Wide World Photos)

Enterprise crew finds no meaningful difference between them. The only difference in "Battlefield," for example, is skin color; one race has white on the right and black on the left side of its body, while the other has the opposite. In "Cloud Minders," the working class does suffer from diminished intellect and lack of self-control, but these are caused by exposure to gas during mining operations, to which elites are also susceptible.

Numerous other episodes explored war and peace, benevolence and self-interest, a variety of alternative social/political arrangements, as well as the space race and the hippie movement. Although the series was canceled after its third season, its fan base grew as the series was continuously rerun. It was eventually followed by 11 full-length films and four spin-off series.

See also Roddenberry, Gene (1921–1991).

Bibliography

Alexander, David. "Gene Roddenberry: Writer, Producer, Philosopher, Humanist." *The Humanist* (March/April 1991): 5–30.

Asherman, Allan. *The Star Trek Compendium.* New York: Simon & Schuster, 1981.

Barrett, Michele, and Barrett, Duncan. *Star Trek: The Human Frontier.* New York: Routledge, 2001.

SUSAN DE GAIA

STEINEM, GLORIA (1934–). Gloria Steinem is an American feminist, journalist, and political activist who is nationally recognized as a spokesperson for the second-wave feminist movement in the late 1960s and '70s. Steinem founded *Ms.* magazine as well as organizations like the Ms. Foundation for Women, the Women's Action Alliance, the National Women's Political Caucus, the Coalition of Labor Union Women, Choice USA, and the Women's Media Center, and has been the recipient of many awards and honors.

Gloria Marie Steinem was born on March 25, 1934 in Clarklake, Ohio. She is the second daughter of Leo and Ruth Steinem; her older sister is Susanne (b. 1925). Her parents separated in 1944 and Steinem lived with her mother in Toledo, Ohio. She wrote compassionately about her mother's struggles with acute anxiety and depression in the essay "Ruth's Song (Because She Could Not Sing It)," published in *Outrageous Acts and Everyday Rebellions* (1983).

Steinem won a scholarship to attend Smith College and graduated in 1956 with a degree in government. Following her graduation, she traveled in India for one year. This experience culminated in her first book, *The Thousand Indias* (1957), a travel guide published by the Indian government and designed for the American tourist. She became increasingly interested in Mohandas Gandhi's principles of nonviolent resistance and spoke to a number of his followers, many of whom still used his methods of peaceful protest to resist unfair laws.

Upon her return from India, Steinem worked with youth organizations and foundations like the National Student Association (NSA) in Cambridge, Massachusetts, and New York. However, her true passion was for journalism, and by 1960, she found a way to support herself as a freelance journalist in New York. The story of her assignment to write about the life of a Playboy Bunny at the New York Playboy Club is a notable example of her work at the time. Posing as a Bunny, Steinem worked undercover for several weeks as a cocktail waitress. She wrote about her experience in a two-part article entitled "A Bunny's Tale," published in *Show* magazine in May and June 1963. The assignment was integral to her growing interest in feminism, while the article series brought her recognition and assignments from *Glamour, Ladies' Home Journal, Vogue*, the *Herald Tribune*, and the *New York Times Magazine*.

Steinem's life in the 1960s was marked by her ambition to be a respected journalist and writer. It was not until the late '60s when the anti-Vietnam War movement reached its zenith that she fully immersed herself in the political ferment of the times. In 1968, Steinem's friend and colleague Clay Felker founded *New York* magazine and invited her to be a part of the new enterprise. As a journalist and media spokesperson, she became a prominent figure in the antiwar movement and a vocal adherent of Cesar Chavez's efforts to organize migrant labor through the United Farm Workers. She followed the presidential campaigns of Eugene McCarthy, Shirley Chisholm, George McGovern, and Richard Nixon. Her regular column, "The City Politic," in *New York* magazine covered politics on the local and national level. In 1969, Steinem wrote her first feminist article, "After Black Power, Women's Liberation," predicting a mass movement for women's liberation. She began to take part in speaking tours to encourage an inclusive brand of feminism, partnering with African American activists like Dorothy Pittman Hughes, Florynce Kennedy, and Margaret Sloan. Their speaking tours amassed diverse audiences, including supporters of the civil rights movement and peace activists. Steinem wanted to offer women (and men) an alternative to the National Organization for Women, founded by Betty Friedan, which spoke to the concerns of white, middle-class women. On July 10, 1971, Steinem and Friedan, Fannie Lou Hamer, Myrlie Evers, Chisholm, and Bella Abzug founded the National Women's Political Caucus (NWPC). A coconvener of the caucus, she delivered her celebrated "Address to the Women of America."

In 1972, Steinem started the first magazine controlled editorially and financially by its female staff. The cofounders chose the title *Ms.* because it applied to all women regardless of marital status. *Ms.* magazine was a success and attracted upwards of 26,000 subscriptions in its first year. Steinem edited and wrote for the magazine while continuing to speak on women's issues, testify before Congress, and support other political causes. She was particularly active in the campaign for the Equal Rights Amendment (ERA) to end discriminatory laws based on sex. *Ms.* magazine was sold for financial reasons in 1987 and then acquired by the Feminist Majority Foundation in 2001. Steinem continues to serve on the magazine's advisory board and appears in the masthead as one of the six founding editors.

In recent years, Steinem has been involved in the 2008 presidential race as a supporter of Senator Hillary Rodham Clinton in the primaries and the Democratic nominee, Senator Barack Obama, in the general election. She was outspoken about the widely perceived misogyny in the media surrounding Clinton's candidacy. Gloria Steinem married David Bale, the South African activist in 2000. He died in 2003 of a brain lymphoma.

See also Freidan, Betty (1921–2006); National Organization for Women (NOW); National Women's Political Caucus (NWPC) (1971).

Bibliography

Conway, Jill Ker, ed. *Written by Herself: Autobiographies of American Women: An Anthology.* New York: Vintage, 1992.

Echols, Alice. *Daring to Be Bad: Radical Feminism in America, 1967–1975.* Foreword by Ellen Willis. Minneapolis: University of Minneapolis Press, 1989.

Feminist.com, "Gloria Steinem News." Available at http://www.feminist.com/gloriasteinem (accessed April 25, 2010).

Heilbrun, Carolyn G. *The Education of a Woman: The Life of Gloria Steinem.* New York: Dial, 1995.

Mankiller, Barbara Smith. *The Reader's Companion to U.S. Women's History.* New York: Houghton Mifflin Harcourt, 1999.

Steinem, Gloria. *Moving Beyond Words.* New York: Simon & Schuster, 1994.

Steinem, Gloria. *Outrageous Acts and Everyday Rebellions.* New York: Holt, Rinehart, and Winston, 1983.

Steinem, Gloria. *The Revolution from Within.* Boston: Little, Brown, 1992.

CAROLINE E. KELLEY

STELLA, FRANK (1936–). Frank Stella is an abstract painter, mixed-media sculptor, printmaker, and architectural designer who is associated with color field painting of the late 1950s and 1960s. He pioneered the creation of shaped paintings around 1960. Although this innovation was not unprecedented in modernist art (Pablo Picasso, Kurt Schwitters, and others made them earlier in the twentieth century), they became widespread in the 1960s and after largely because of Stella. He is best known for abstract imagery that is extremely linear, geometric, smooth surfaced, and symmetrical and for using canvases of complex geometric, organic, or irregular shapes that deviate sharply from traditional rectangular, oval, and circular painting surfaces. Stella's paintings merge the flatness of the painted abstracted imagery and the surface of the canvas so that they become one and the same. They fulfill some of the central intentions and tenets of modernist art, including completely nonrepresentational imagery, extreme flatness, the elimination of any special focus or emphasis within compositions, and the revelation of the self-evident qualities of artistic materials and techniques, such as paints applied with brushes or other implements to canvas.

Born and raised in Malden, Massachusetts, Stella became interested in art as a teenager while a student at Phillips Academy in Andover. He studied history and art at Princeton University, and upon graduating in 1958 moved to New York City to paint. Coming into artistic maturity in the late 1950s, Stella was very familiar with abstract expressionism, which had dominated American art for 15 years. At this time, he also became familiar and intrigued with the work of Jasper Johns. It was the combined result of these divergent styles and ideas, of pursuing flatness and literalness and eliminating personal, emotive expression while continuing to paint abstractly, that led to Stella's characteristic geometrically abstract painting, which he produced from the late 1950s until the 1970s.

Stella's first important paintings were his Black Paintings of 1958–1959, such as *Die Fahne Hoch!* and *The Marriage of Reason and Squalor*, in which long black lines of equal width separated by narrow unpainted strips of canvas are repeated sequentially across rectangular canvases, emphasizing the flat, two-dimensional surface of painting and achieving the total elimination of compositional emphasis and focus for absolute regularity, symmetry, and flatness. In the Aluminum Series of 1960, with paintings such as *Avicenna*, Stella used metallic paint to create rhythmic, sequential, flat images with bilateral symmetry that led him to cut the corners of the canvases to maintain this symmetry. This quickly led Stella to experiment further with more radically shaped picture surfaces in his Copper Series of 1960–1961, arranging large rectangular areas of sequential bands of metallic color in right-angled combinations of L's, T's, H's, X's, crosses, triangles, and the like, as in *Ophir* (1961) and *Pagosa Springs* (1962). By 1960, Stella was represented by the Leo Castelli Gallery, one of the most important galleries in the world at the time for modernist art, and his works were being included in major museum exhibitions internationally.

By the mid-1960s, Stella's paintings became more diverse and complex in their shapes and colors. In the Notched V Series of the mid-1960s, Stella arranged chevron shapes at various angles with their sides adjacent, and he began to combine large areas of different muted, often metallic hues. *Empress of India* (1965) consists of four chevrons, each one painted a somber brown. Stella also began to work with bright, vivid, saturated spectrum hues in complex geometric and circular shapes. He often used bright, vivid alkyd, epoxy, and acrylic paints in his Irregular Polygon Series of 1965–1967. In the Irregular Polygons, which include *Conway I* and *Moultonville II* (both 1966), shaped canvases were constructed with large, varied, and adjoining geometric shapes and painted with diverse, bright, saturated hues that fill large areas or outline broad geometric shapes. In his Protractor Series of 1967–1971, he used an even wider variety of hues, tones, and shades, often making them somewhat pale and translucent. This allowed greater variety and subtlety with color than he had ever achieved before. The Protractor Series repeatedly used three complex geometric shapes of canvases that he divided up in various ways with large protractor shapes that overlap, abut, and intersect, achieving a total of 93 works in the series. Some of them are as large as gallery walls, approaching 10 by 25 feet, and thus are the largest works of his career up to that time. Works such as *Tahkt-i-Sulayman I* (1967), *Harran II* (1967), and *Agbatana III* (1968) feature circles, semicircles, and other fragments of circles comprised of colorful protractor shapes arranged in complex ways and painted in diverse, vibrant, but carefully modified hues.

Around 1970, Stella began making many prints, often using them to explore themes from earlier paintings. He also started to create painted relief sculptures with metal, wood, and various found objects; and like his early paintings, these have often been conceived as groups and given intriguing titles, such as his Indian Birds Series of the 1980s. However, they are often gaudy and brash in their colors, rough and irritating in their textures, and asymmetrical and uneven in their arrangement of forms and creation of depth. Since the late 1980s, he has produced many architectural designs.

As a history major and Ivy League graduate, it is not surprising that Stella often gave his works complex, thought-provoking titles that relate to regions, cities, and towns all over the world; famous people; major historical events; and so on. Yet Stella has almost always dismissed claims that there is underlying social, political, philosophical, or spiritual meaning in his work. This makes his work typical of much abstract art of the 1960s but at odds with nearly all earlier abstraction, including abstract expressionism. Early in his career, Stella said, "my painting is based on the fact that only what can be seen there is there" and "all I want anyone to get out of my paintings, and all I ever get out of them, is the fact that you can see the whole idea without any confusion."

Bibliography

Guberman, Sidney. *Frank Stella: An Illustrated Biography*. New York: Rizzoli, 1995.
Rubin, William. *Frank Stella*. New York: Museum of Modern Art, 1970.
Rubin, William. *Frank Stella, 1970–1987*. New York: Museum of Modern Art, 1987.

HERBERT R. HARTEL, JR.

STONEWALL. In the late '60s, the solicitation of homosexual relations was illegal in New York City—as it was in most other parts of the country—but young gay men and women living in the metropolis had created an extensive network of subterranean social outlets. Bars, restaurants, and clubs scattered throughout the city provided spaces for homosexuals to congregate without fear of social approbation. However, these spaces often operated on the fringes of legality and played a constant cat-and-mouse game with the authorities.

The most famous of these establishments in New York City was the Stonewall Inn. When the original Greenwich Village restaurant burned down in 1967, a coalition of local businessmen, largely backed by the mafia, converted the space into a gay bar and dance club. Rather than legally obtain an expensive liquor license, the owners sold liquor under the table and kept the money from sales in cigar boxes rather than cash registers. To maintain this arrangement, the managers routinely bribed local police for their cooperation.

These payoffs, however, did not mean that patrons of the bar avoided harassment. Indeed, the club was raided approximately once a month. Customers were humiliatingly shuffled out into the street while the police arrested bartenders, managers, and owners for operating without a license. Also, pursuant to New York law, an individual had to be wearing at least three articles of gender-appropriate clothing or faced arrest. The transvestites who frequented the Stonewall, therefore, were often arrested. On June 28, 1969, only four days after the last raid, New York police entered the club. Rather than slip quietly away from the bust, as was the norm, the frustrated young men and women clustered around the exit. The crowd initially was lighthearted—catcalling and laughing—but the mood devolved into tension. One woman in men's clothing fought back, and the crowd, incensed at the escalating police violence (especially against a woman) reacted. The banter morphed into shouts of "Pig!' and other insults, and soon, bottles and fists were flying. The wildly outnumbered police, unprepared for such a violent response, barricaded themselves in the bar, waiting for reinforcements. The crowd outside broke windows and used a makeshift battering ram—an uprooted parking meter—to enter the bar. Eventually, more police arrived to defuse the situation. It was too late, though; for the next five days, young gay men and women rebelled throughout Greenwich Village, spray painting the new slogan "Gay Power" on streets and confronting police.

Embracing the influence of the black power movement, the antiwar movement, and feminism, gay men and women asserted that they had a right to be heard and respected as well. In the 1950s, homophile groups such as the Mattachine Society had relied on the rhetoric of respectability to gain tolerance, if not equality. The groups that were born in the Stonewall Inn Rebellion, such as the Gay Liberation Front (GLF) and the Gay Activist's Alliance (GAA), rejected the notion that they had to kowtow to society's mores to be political citizens.

Bibliography

Bloom, Alexander, ed. *Long Time Gone: Sixties America Then and Now*. Oxford: Oxford University Press, 2001.

Carter, David. *Stonewall: The Riots That Sparked the Gay Revolution*. New York: St. Martin's, 2004.

D'Emilio, John. *World Turned: Essays on Gay History, Politics, and Culture*. Durham, NC: Duke University Press, 2002.

Duberman, Martin B. *Stonewall*. New York: Plume, 1994.

CAITLIN CASEY

STRANGER IN A STRANGE LAND (1961). *Stranger in a Strange Land* is a 1961 science fiction novel by Robert A. Heinlein. It tells the story of Valentine Michael Smith—a human raised by Martians—who returns to Earth, founds a new religion, and is martyred. It enjoyed enormous popularity among members of the counterculture, who relished its satire of middle-class mores and embraced its fictional religion as a model for communal living.

Heinlein was the most popular and influential science fiction writer of his generation, and *Stranger* was his most significant work. Its sprawling, discursive social satire of religion and sex was a radical departure for a writer known, in the 1940s and 1950s, for streamlined plots and competent, problem-solving heroes who know How Things Work. Smith (Mike to his friends) is an equally radical departure from Heinlein's usual protagonists. He is both Christ and Candide, and his function, especially in the first half of the story, is to *not* know how things work, so that his friend and mentor Jubal Harshaw—a more typical Heinlein hero—can explain them to him. *Stranger* continued the exploration of religion begun in Heinlein's early novels and heralded the fascination with sex that would dominate his post-*Stranger* work. It won the World Science Fiction Association (Hugo) Award for best science fiction novel in 1962, but subsequently fell out of print.

The emergent counterculture movement discovered and embraced *Stranger in a Strange Land* in the late 1960s, forcing a second printing in 1968 and expanding the book's readership beyond the ranks of science fiction fans. The elements of the fictional religion that Mike founds on Earth—communal living, casual nudity, free love, and water sharing as a sacrament—resonated with the hippie lifestyle, as did Mike's gentle, childlike approach to the world. "Grok," a verb coined by Heinlein to describe the Martians' concept of total understanding, became part of the counterculture's vocabulary, and the underlying concept (understanding so complete and intimate that it leads to oneness with the thing being understood) became part of its intellectual landscape.

Stranger in a Strange Land served as the partial inspiration for the communal Church of All Worlds, which was founded the year after the book was published and took its name from Mike's own religion. In a broader sense, however, it was an inspiration to scores of less formal experiments in communal living, whose members used the communes in the book—the "nests" of believers who follow Mike's religion, and the residents of Jubal's mansion—as models for their own. Hippies who saw the book as an instruction manual made pilgrimages to Heinlein's home in the late 1960s, wanting him to become for their social experiments what Jubal becomes for Mike's religion: an esteemed father figure and wise spiritual guide.

Interest in *Stranger* as a guide to living faded with the counterculture, but interest in it as a novel remained strong. An "uncut" version, restoring 60,000 words that Heinlein trimmed from his original manuscript at the request of his publisher, appeared in 1992.

Bibliography

McFarlane, Scott. "Stranger in a Strange Land: The Ecstasy of Grokking." In *The Hippie Narrative: A Literary Perspective on the Counterculture*. Jefferson, NC: McFarland, 2007.
Patterson, William, ed. *The Martian Named Smith: Critical Perspectives on Robert A. Heinlein's Stranger in a Strange Land*. Citrus Heights, CA: Nitrosyncretic Press, 2001.

A. BOWDOIN VAN RIPER

STUDENT NONVIOLENT COORDINATING COMMITTEE (SNCC). The Student Nonviolent Coordinating Committee (SNCC) was established in April 1960 by students to coordinate the sit-in movement of the 1960s. The sit-in of the Woolworth's counter in Greensboro, NC by four students from North Carolina A&T State University sparked similar protests is over 60 cities throughout the South. SNCC was established to coordinate these activities. Civil rights activist Ella Baker, largely credited with the creation of the organization, was successful in securing funding from the Southern Christian Leadership Conference (SCLC) to coordinate a conference of sit-in movement leaders (which included Julian Bond, who would serve as the organization's communication director and eventually the chairman of the NAACP), on the campus of Shaw University in Raleigh, North Carolina. Over 200 people attended that conference in which the Reverend Martin Luther King Jr. was among its speakers.

After the Freedom Riders of 1961—which sought to assess compliance of another landmark decision, *Boynton v. Virginia* (1960), in which the U.S. Supreme Court held that segregation in public transportation was unconstitutional—were severely beaten by members of the Ku Klux Klan and their bus firebombed in Alabama, members of SNCC reached out to James L. Farmer Jr., the director of the Congress of Racial Equality (CORE), to fill in and join members of CORE in continuing the Freedom Rides. It was the young people of SNCC and CORE who as Freedom Riders promoted "Jail, No Bail," where members remained in jail rather than being bailed out for their activities challenging Jim Crow. John Lewis, who would go on to become the chairman of SNCC in 1963 and a U.S. Representative in 1986, participated in the Freedom Rides. Despite arrests, and sometimes attacks, the Freedom Riders were successful in that then U.S. Attorney General Bobby Kennedy challenged the Interstate Commerce Commission and forced it to implement regulations to enforce Morgan, Boynton, etc. and end Jim Crow in public transportation effective November 1, 1961.

SNCC sought to challenge segregation and civil rights violations in the South. SNCC volunteers, working with the Council of Federated Organizations (COFO), led a massive voter registration drive in Mississippi. Volunteers sought to expose practices to prevent blacks from exercising their right to vote. Despite the efforts of hundreds of volunteers, few blacks were successful in registering to vote. Volunteer attorneys found a Reconstruction-era law that afforded unregistered voters the opportunity to vote if they completed an affidavit asserting that they had a right to do so. Those persons, who were afraid to go to vote, would complete the freedom ballot collected by COFO during the August 1963 gubernatorial primary. Despite threats from the state attorney general that persons seeking to vote this way would be arrested, voters met angry, white crowds, but no arrests were made. Though participants did not cast legally binding votes, the mock election demonstrated the willingness of the people to vote despite the threats and intimidation against them. From this endeavor, the Mississippi Freedom Democratic Party (MFDP) was established to challenge the Mississippi Democratic Party at the Democratic National Convention.

Freedom Summer (also known as the Mississippi Summer Project) involved the establishment of freedom schools to address the educational void for black citizens, as well as the establishment of community centers. Northern whites were active in Freedom Summer, assisting in the establishment of schools and voter registration drives. It was long debated whether SNCC would invite white participants, as there was a question whether it would influence the federal government to afford protection to activists, whether the organization could effectively manage hundreds of volunteers, and whether there were appropriate resources to house them.

During the mid-1960s, the SNCC began to evolve from an organization promoting integration and fighting segregation to one embracing black nationalism, changing its name to Student National Coordinating Committee. Some members thought that the nonviolent philosophies were ineffective and were slow to effect change, and they were disillusioned with the tragic murders in the summer of 1964. The organization adopted the slogan "Black Power" at its 1966 convention. The SNCC even expelled white members from its leadership and, while under the leadership of Stokely Carmichael, alienated women as well. H. Rap Brown succeeded Carmichael as its chairman, ultimately leaving the organization to join the Black Panther Party. The SNCC ceased to exist in 1970.

See also Black Power; Brown, H. Rap (1943–); Carmichael, Stokely (1941–1998); Congress on Racial Equality (CORE); Freedom Rides.

Bibliography

Farmer, James. *Lay the Bare Heart: An Autobiography of the Civil Rights Movement*. Ft. Worth: Texas Christian University, 1998.
Gillespie, J. David. *Politics at the Periphery: Third Parties in Two Party America*. Columbia: University of South Carolina Press, 1993.
Grant, Joanne. *Ella Baker: Freedom Bound*. New York: John Wiley, 1998.
Payne, Charles. M. *I've Got the Light of Freedom: The Organizing Tradition and the Mississippi Freedom Struggle*. Berkeley: University of California Press, 1995.

NICOLA DAVIS BIVENS

STUDENTS FOR A DEMOCRATIC SOCIETY (SDS). A leading organization in the campus-based antiwar movement of the 1960s, the Students for a Democratic Society (SDS) first appeared in January 1960. Its goals were to support the civil rights movement and politically organize the urban poor. Tom Hayden, a University of Michigan student, served as the organization's first secretary and worked hard to popularize its ideas. The SDS grew in size and notoriety in mid-1962 when it issued the Port Huron Statement, which called for "true democracy" in the United States and an end to the arms race. It also energized student activists to increase their involvement with the liberal wing of the Democratic Party.

The involvement of the SDS with traditional politics was short-lived, however. The limited progress of the civil rights movement and America's increasing involvement in Vietnam radicalized Hayden and his colleagues. By 1964, and especially after the Gulf of Tonkin incident, the SDS began to organize more and more campus demonstrations, including "teach-ins," to protest the Vietnam War. SDS members circulated "we won't go" petitions among young men of draft age and developed a militant (and sophisticated) draft resistance program to serve their needs. As a result of these activities, membership in the SDS grew rapidly. In 1965–1966, the number of SDS chapters at U.S. colleges and universities doubled from 124 to 250, with an actual overall membership of some 31,000 people.

Toward the end of the 1960s, dissension began to overtake the organization. Those who saw America's involvement in Vietnam beginning to wind down wanted

Chicago police confront demonstrators in Grant Park during the Democratic National Convention, August 26, 1968. (AP/Wide World Photos)

to shift focus to domestic and cultural issues. Others continued to advocate the importance of politics but in a more violent, revolutionary vein. Antiwar demonstrations soon became more unruly. During the "Stop the Draft" week of October 1967, for example, SDS leader Carl Davidson demanded that protesters burn down government draft centers. Still worse was the 1968 Democratic National Convention in Chicago, where SDS members and their sympathizers fought with, and were battered by, riot police in the streets.

At its peak, SDS had approximately 400 chapters, but Vietnamization, a growing revulsion with student violence, and the fragmentation of the New Left into different political arenas, such as women's liberation, led to its demise. The organization's impact was significant, however. Although it did not change U.S. foreign policy, it did help block or scale back the number of military options Presidents Lyndon Johnson and Richard Nixon were initially prepared to use. As a result, Vietnamization became the only viable option the Nixon administration had left to extricate itself from a political and military dead end.

Bibliography

Gitlin, Todd. *The Sixties: Years of Hope, Days of Rage.* New York: Bantam Books, 1987.

Miller, James. *Democracy Is in the Streets: From Port Huron to the Siege of Chicago.* New York: Simon & Schuster, 1987.

O'Neill, William L. *Coming Apart: An Informal History of America in the 1960s.* New York: Times Books, 1971.
Viorst, Milton. *Fire in the Streets: America in the 1960s.* New York: Simon & Schuster, 1979.

TRACY R. SZCZEPANIAK

SUMMER OF LOVE/SAN FRANCISCO (1967). The "Summer of Love" refers to June through September 1967, when thousands of young Americans migrated to San Francisco, California, to participate in the hippie counterculture of peace, love, and communal living. They gravitated to the Haight-Ashbury district, where cheap Victorian-style houses coexisted alongside Beat-era icons. While hippies shared the antiwar convictions of their New Left counterparts, they generally preferred to experiment with alternative lifestyles rather than to protest directly. Local groups such as the Diggers rejected mass consumption and industrial society. Hippie experiments included interactive street theatre, free stores (in which surplus goods were freely shared), and free health clinics. Prior to a police crackdown in mid-1967, it was common for hippies to sleep in nearby Golden Gate Park, and the overall community ethos rejected traditional jobs and responsibilities in favor of a commitment to finding alternatives to mainstream American culture.

Bands such as the Jefferson Airplane, Big Brother and the Holding Company, and the Grateful Dead, all of whom at one point lived in and mixed with the Haight-Ashbury community, provided much of its creative vitality. The drug LSD also played a key role. In the 1950s, legitimate scientific research focused on LSD's potential use for treatment of alcoholism and depression. Some scientists attested to the drug's ability, in medically supervised doses, to provide intense spiritual experiences. However, the uncontrolled proliferation of LSD, alongside the controversial proselytizing of Timothy Leary, prompted legislators to ban the drug. LSD became illegal in California on October 6, 1966, though hippies, among others, continued to use it routinely.

Hippie spokespersons, such as Peter Coyote and Stephen Levine, warned that the large number of Americans travelling to Haight-Ashbury in the summer of 1967—today estimated between 50,000 and 100,000 people—would severely strain community resources. These newcomers represented a surge of interest in the hippie alternative, but the media attention they brought with them undermined the whole point of the experiment. Stores began selling "hippie souvenirs," while the Gray Line Tour Company offered tourists a ride through Haight-Ashbury, billing it as Cthe only foreign tour in the domestic United States." Most of the early hippies were college educated and in their twenties. However, many of the new arrivals were vulnerable teenaged runaways. As the summer progressed, violence, rape, sexually transmitted diseases, and drug overdoses all escalated. On October 6, 1967, what remained of the hippie movement participated in a mock funeral called "The Death of Hippie," hoping to discourage further migration to a now derelict community.

It is easy to parody the "flower children" of the 1960s due to their rhetoric, drug taking, and clothing styles. Nevertheless, the attempt to construct a peaceful and organic society was sincere. The hippie ideal—more of an orientation than a coherent political ideology—hoped to subvert consumerism, conformity, and war. The Summer of Love suggests that such experiments in communal living work best in small, relatively cohesive groups rather than on a large scale. The impact of drugs —and drug abuse—on American society also remains a highly controversial topic.

Nevertheless, the cultural and political significance of the Summer of Love—seen in popular music, environmentalism, and peace movements—endures.

See also Haight-Ashbury.

Bibliography

Anthony, Gene. *Summer of Love: Haight-Ashbury at Its Highest.* San Francisco: Last Gasp, 1995.
Coyote, Peter. *Sleeping Where I Fall—A Chronicle.* Berkeley, CA: Counterpoint, 1998.
Gitlin, Todd. *The Sixties: Years of Hope, Days of Rage.* New York: Bantam, 1987.
Perry, Charles. *The Haight-Ashbury: A History.* New York: Wenner Media, 2005.
Roszak, Theodore. *The Making of a Counter Culture: Reflections on a Technocratic Society and Its Youthful Opposition.* Berkeley: University of California Press, 1995.

AMY L. FLETCHER

SURFING. Once reserved for kings and royalty, then later banned by Protestant missionaries in Hawaii because it promoted unrestrained intermingling of the sexes, surfing's golden age spanned the late 1950s through the 1960s. The growth in popularity was partly due to film and promotional materials that gave the rest of the United States a peek into a unique coastal culture.

Local authorities in Hawaii and Southern California attempted to regulate surfing by closing beaches and implementing surfboard taxes. Still, the sport grew in the U.S. mainland; the surfing population in California rose from 5,000 in 1956 to 100,000 in 1962. Competitions and federations formed in the United States and abroad to fight off social backlash and provide a public acceptance of the sport. But surfers struggled to embrace the competitive aspect, instead preferring to capture the experience. As the culture grew in the United States, it also was popularized in Australia and South Africa amid a growing split among surfing styles and attitude.

Style was as much a part of surfing as the act itself. Hawaiian style emerged as a smooth, natural movement where surfers rode with the waves. California style was similar but focused on the beauty of a breaking wave. Australian style was much more aggressive than the others, with surfers riding on the wave rather than with it —an attacking style of performance. The aggression spawned a movement toward shortboards that were 6 feet long rather than the traditional Malibu-style boards measuring up to 11 feet long. Also included in the shift in equipment was a change from balsawood boards to sculptured polyurethane and a more rounded edge with fins. Clothing and wetsuit manufacturers noted the trend and created fashions that allowed nonsurfers to be part of the culture by wearing the clothes. The style included Pendleton shirts, white and tight Levi jeans, baggy shorts, sandals, and bleached hair. Musically, more than 800 surf bands recorded one song or more in the early 1960s. Artist Dick Dale helped popularize surf-rock music (referred to as "California Music" or "California Sound") in local venues, while the Beach Boys held their first professional tour in 1962.

Hollywood fueled the surf craze by producing films depicting the antiestablishment lifestyle. The 1959 film *Gidget* initiated a genre that mainly focused on beach stories as opposed to the "pure" surfing films that were being shot by amateur videographers and focused simply on the surfing. The 1964 Bruce Brown-produced film *The Endless Summer* is the best example of a surprisingly popular "pure" film, grossing $8 million worldwide and commonly known as *the* surf movie. John Severson was among the successful "pure" film producers, and his 1960 black-and-white booklet *The Surfer*, created to promote one of his films, went on to become the now-monthly publication *Surfer* magazine.

Social distance grew between surfers and mainstream society in the mid-1960s due to a change in the political world and economy along with the threat of nuclear war. Surfers became seen as outlaws as many films depicted drug use incorporated into the alternative lifestyles. Surfer movie production abruptly slowed in 1965. Critics argue film had a negative effect on the sport's image, but proponents claim it only mirrored societal issues. Political change and music's British Invasion slowed the popularity of surfing culture as a mainstream lifestyle.

Bibliography

Booth, Douglas. "Ambiguities in Pleasure and Discipline: The Development of Competitive Surfing." *Journal of Sport History* 22 (1995): 189–206.
Booth, Douglas. "Surfing Films and Videos: Adolescent Fun, Alternative Lifestyle, Adventure Industry." *Journal of Sport History* 23 (1996): 313–27.
Booth, Douglas. "Surfing: The Cultural and Technological Determinants of a Dance." *Sport in Society* 2 (1999): 36–55.
Carney, George O. "Cowabunga! Surfer Rock and the Five Themes of Geography." *Popular Music and Society* 23 (1999): 3–29.
Lanagan, David. "Surfing in the Third Millennium: Commodifying the Visual Argot." *Australian Journal of Anthropology* 13 (2002): 283–291.

JOSHUA R. PATE

SUSANN, JACQUELINE (1918–1974). Born on August 20, 1918, in Philadelphia, Jacqueline Susann was the daughter of a schoolteacher and a portrait painter. After unsuccessfuly pursuing a movie career in Hollywood, she became a newspaper columnist. Her big break came with the publication of her novel *Valley of the Dolls*, though. Though it had been rejected by several publishers, Susann kept sending it to more publishers until it was finally accepted. When *Valley of the Dolls* came out in 1966, it became an immediate best seller, staying in the *New York Times* best-seller list for 28 weeks. Critics, however, berated the novel for its bold sexual content and called it "trashy." Reviewers attacked the novel because of its popular style and its large readership.

The novel largely drew on Susann's personal experiences and some characters were said to be based on close friends of Susann's such as Judy Garland and Ethel Merman and actresses Marilyn Monroe, Grace Kelly, Marlene Dietrich, and Greta Garbo. Actually, large chunks of *Valley of the Dolls* came from Susann's own private diaries. She and her husband, publicist Irving Mansfield, made innumerable publicity gigs, TV appearances, and promotional tours to advertise *Valley of the Dolls*, beginning a trend to be followed by later writers. The novel has so far sold 30 million copies worldwide, being translated into many foreign languages. It appeared in the *Guinness Book of World Records* as the most popular novel ever to that time.

A film version was released the following year to appalling reviews. Susann shared the negative opinions of the film and actually walked out of the premiere. In 1981 and again in 1994, it was adapted for television. It also spawned a short-lived television show.

Prior to *Valley of the Dolls*, in 1963 Susann had published *Every Night, Josephine!*, in which she described her life with her poodle, Josephine, for which she bought designer clothes and accesories. Though not a best seller, it sold well for a first book.

Susann regularly attended literary and social parties, often appearing in photographs from these events in magazines. She had a very public falling out with writer Truman Capote, who compared her to a transvestite truck driver.

Susann's following novel, *The Love Machine*, came out in 1969 and was also a best seller. Like *Valley of the Dolls*, it is autobiographical to some extent, and the protagonist closely resembled Susann's father's womanizing ways. Her subsequent novels, published in the '70s, all more or less closely followed the approach of *Valley of the Dolls*. She was the first American female author to have three *New York Times* number one best sellers consecutively.

In the early 1960s, Susann was diagnosed with breast cancer, which finally claimed her on September 21, 1974. Her life inspired a made-for-TV movie titled *Scandalous Me: The Jacqueline Susann Story* (1998) and the big-screen *Isn't She Great* (2000).

Bibliography

Doonan, Simon. "Five Best: Books About Fashion." *Wall Street Journal*, September 17 2005, Eastern Edition.

Drukman, Steven. "Oh, You Beautiful Dolls." *American Theatre*, December 1, 2001, p. 7.

Quinn, Judy. "Getting ready for a Susann revival." *Publishers Weekly*, September 22, 1997, p. 24.

Trinidad, David. "The Valley of No Return." *Chronicle of Higher Education*, May 30, 2008, p. B28.

M. CARMEN GOMEZ-GALISTEO

T

TAYLOR, MAXWELL (1901–1987). Maxwell Taylor, born on August 21, 1901, in Keytesville, Missouri, was a U.S. Army general and a key military advisor to Presidents John F. Kennedy and Lyndon B. Johnson. He was a strong supporter of the Republic of Vietnam (South Vietnam) and a consistent defender of America's fight against communism in Southeast Asia. Taylor graduated from the U.S. Military Academy at West Point in 1922. In 1942, he helped found the U.S. Army's first airborne division, the 82nd, and went on to command the 101st Airborne Division during the Normandy landings on D-Day. Following World War II, Taylor served as the commandant of West Point until 1949. From there, he worked for a couple of years as chief of staff of U.S. forces in Europe and then became deputy chief of staff of the army in 1951. In 1953, he took over command of the Eighth Army in Korea and remained there until the end of the Korean conflict. He later became chief of staff of the army in 1955 and served in that capacity until his retirement from active duty in 1959.

In the late 1950s, Taylor became a vocal critic of President Dwight D. Eisenhower's New Look policy that emphasized nuclear weapons in lieu of conventional ground forces. This low-cost defense strategy promised to reduce U.S. military spending and deter communist aggression with the threat of "massive retaliation." Taylor instead favored a policy of "flexible response," which entailed building up U.S. ground forces to provide the nation with the capability to deal with several different military operations ranging from counterinsurgency and limited wars to full-scale conventional and nuclear war. In April 1961, President Kennedy, who supported Taylor's flexible response proposal, recalled him to active duty and selected him as his primary military advisor. The two men developed a close and trusted relationship, leading Kennedy to name Taylor as chairman of the Joint Chiefs of Staff in October 1962.

As chairman, Taylor urged Presidents Kennedy and Johnson to stay the course in Vietnam, arguing that the area was vital to America's military and strategic interests and that failure to do so could lead to an expansion of communism in Southeast Asia. In July 1964, Taylor retired once again to assume a civilian position as U.S.

ambassador to South Vietnam. From Saigon, Taylor reported on the deteriorating situation and advocated increasing military pressure on North Vietnam as a means of halting their support for the Viet Cong insurgency in the south. Following the Gulf of Tonkin incident, the ambassador called for the strategic bombing of North Vietnam, and throughout the war, he remained a proponent of U.S. airpower. Nevertheless, while Taylor supported gradual escalation and the military strategy of attrition, he initially opposed deploying U.S. ground troops to South Vietnam, fearing it would lead to increasing American commitments. On July 30, 1965, Taylor stepped down as ambassador but continued to serve President Johnson as a special consultant and chairman of the Foreign Intelligence Advisory Board. He officially retired from public service in 1969. He died on April 19, 1987.

See also Johnson, Lyndon Baines (1908–1973); Kennedy, John F. (1917–1963); Viet Cong; Vietnam War.

Bibliography

Buzzanco, Robert. *Masters of War: Military Dissent and Politics in the Vietnam Era.* Cambridge: Cambridge University Press, 1996.
Kinnard, Douglas. *The Certain Trumpet: Maxwell Taylor and the American Experience in Vietnam.* Washington, DC: Potomac Books, 1991.
McMaster, H. R. *Dereliction of Duty: Lyndon Johnson, Robert McNamara, the Joint Chiefs of Staff, and the Lies That Led to Vietnam.* New York: HarperCollins, 1997.
Olson, James S., and Randy Roberts. *Where the Domino Fell: America and Vietnam, 1945–1990.* New York: St. Martin's, 1991.
Taylor, Maxwell D. *Swords and Plowshares.* New York: W. W. Norton, 1972.

CHRISTOS G. FRENTZOS

TEACH-IN: UNIVERSITY OF MICHIGAN (1965). The University of Michigan Teach-In was a 12-hour protest against American participation in the Vietnam War. Consisting of speeches, seminars, and a rally, the event took place at the university's Ann Arbor campus on March 24 and 25, 1965. It was the first of more than 100 teach-ins held in the United States and abroad during the 1960s and early 1970s.

The teach-in was organized by Michigan faculty members, many of whom had supported Lyndon B. Johnson, seeing him as the peace candidate, in the presidential election of 1964. They felt betrayed when Johnson began escalating the war in Vietnam in the months after the election, particularly when the United States began sending large numbers of ground troops and initiated Operation Rolling Thunder, the extensive bombing of North Vietnam. On March 11, 1965, several professors, most of them young and without tenure, met to consider ways of protesting U.S. actions in Vietnam. They agreed to organize a one-day work moratorium, a protest in which faculty would teach about the war rather than their regular curriculum. A backlash developed quickly: the governor and state legislature began discussing disciplinary measures against faculty members who participated in such an event. On March 16, the organizers decided to hold the event at night so as not to disrupt regular classes. Relieved, the university administration allowed the teach-in to take place in campus buildings and allowed female students from the dorms to say out after curfew. Organizers adapted a term from the civil rights movement ("sit-in"), to describe an event that was to be part protest, part educational experience.

More than 3,000 students and 300 faculty members showed up for the opening speeches at 8:00 p.m. on March 24. Another 75 students organized a counterdemonstration, picketing the event. One of the speeches was interrupted by a bomb threat, but continued outside in 20 degrees Fahrenheit weather while the police searched the building. Over the teach-in's 12 hours, participants listened to speeches, took part in lively discussions, and participated in a torchlight parade and a final rally. By 8:00 a.m. on March 25, there were still 600 in attendance.

In the next week, campuses across the United States hosted 35 teach-ins. By the end of the year, similar events had taken place in more than 100 locations. The National Teach-In on May 15 and 16, 1965, in Washington, D.C., was broadcast by radio and public address systems to 122 campuses and was carried live on National Educational Television. An estimated 30,000 students (up to 12,000 at a time) took part in the largest teach-in, a 36-hour event at the University of California, Berkeley, on May 21 and 22. The phenomenon then spread abroad, with Tokyo, Toronto, Oslo, and other international cities hosting teach-ins. Although originally intended to foster academic debate, the events increasingly became little more than rants against the Johnson administration's foreign policy.

The teach-ins had a profound impact on many individual college students, but did not substantially alter public opinion or administration policies. Polls showed that most Americans were opposed to the teach-ins and supported the war in Vietnam. Even most college students continued to support the war until the Tet Offensive in early 1968. Still, the teach-ins represented the start of the growing antiwar movement.

See also Antiwar Movement, United States; Civil Disobedience; Vietnam War.

Bibliography

Menashe, Louis, and Ronald Radosh, eds. *Teach-Ins: U.S.A., Reports, Opinions, Documents.* New York: Praeger, 1967.

Wells, Tom. *The War Within: America's Battle Over Vietnam.* Berkeley: University of California Press, 1994.

STEPHEN AZZI

TET OFFENSIVE (1968). The Tet Offensive was a major military campaign during the Second Indochina War, where the forces of the People's Liberation Army, or Viet Cong, and the North Vietnamese army, or People's Army of Vietnam (PAVN), attacked the forces of South Vietnam, the United States, and their allies. The goal of the offensive was to cripple the civilian and military command of South Vietnam and spark a general uprising that would bring down Nguyen Van Thieu's government in Saigon and end the war. While the offensive failed to spark a general uprising and resulted in heavy causalities for the Viet Cong and North Vietnamese, it had a tremendous effect on popular support for the war in the United States. The attack began in the early morning hours of January 31, 1968, the first day of the year on a traditional lunar calendar and the most important Vietnamese holiday. In Vietnamese, the offensive is called *Tong Cong Kich-Tong Khoi Nghia* ("General Offensive—General Uprising") or *Tet Mau Than* (Tet, year of the monkey).

The offensive required a level of coordination beyond any previous Viet Cong or PAVN operation. Planning was finalized in Hanoi in July 1967. Six months of military, political, and diplomatic preparations followed. For the attack, the Central Office for

Refugees flee Tet Offensive attacks in 1968. By the end of the offensive, the Viet Cong and People's Army of Vietnam forces had absorbed immense casualties and had failed to achieve any of their principal objectives, yet in many ways the offensive marked an important turning point in the Vietnam War. (National Archives)

South Vietnam (COSVN), the command center for the Viet Cong and liaison between the broader National Liberation Front (NLF) and North Vietnam, reorganized its command structure in preparation for the attack, shuffled the positions of Viet Cong units, and brought down new reinforcements from North Vietnam. All of this movement attracted attention, and, as result, the Tet Offensive included a series of border skirmishes and a massive siege at the U.S. combat base at Khe Sanh to distract from the general offensive. There is some debate as to whether the Battle of Khe Sanh was a distraction or an attempt to recreate the Battle of Dien Bien Phu, where the Viet Minh defeated a sizable French force holed up in a mountain fortress and forced a diplomatic resolution to the First Indochina War. The siege did not reproduce the success of Dien Bien Phu, and the broader offensive in the South Vietnam had the greater impact. While many historians mark the end of the siege of Khe Sanh as the end of the Tet Offensive, it is more accurate to see the Tet Offensive as occurring in three waves: the first from January to April 1968, the second in May and June 1968, and the third in July and August 1968. The second two waves of the Tet Offensive, often referred to as "Mini-Tet" by Western historians, were planned as part of the general offensive.

The first wave of the offensive struck more than 100 cities and towns, 39 of 44 provincial capitals, and 71 district capitals in South Vietnam. Thirty-five Viet Cong battalions attacked Saigon and targeted the presidential palace, the U.S. Embassy, Tan Son Nhut Air Base and the Joint General Staff headquarters, the Long Binh Naval Headquarters, and the National Radio Station. Major fighting in Saigon continued into early February, and sporadic firefights flared up until March. The second wave of the Tet Offensive included a renewed assault on Saigon and attacks on 119 other cities and towns. The most destructive and bloodiest battle of the Tet Offensive occurred in Hue, the old imperial capital and cultural and intellectual center of Vietnam. The Viet Cong quickly overran the city and, by the morning of January 31, 1968, raised the NLF flag over the Citadel, former seat of the emperors of the Nguyen dynasty. Viet Cong cadres began forming Revolutionary Committees for each neighborhood and rounded up Vietnamese and foreigners known to be loyal to the government of South Vietnam. By February 24, U.S. and South Vietnamese forces had retaken the city. The fighting leveled much of the city, leaving 116,000 people homeless. A total of 5,800 civilians died, including 3,000 found in mass graves, executed by the Viet Cong and PAVN. An estimated 2,400 to 8,000 PAVN and Viet Cong died. South Vietnamese forces lost 384 soldiers with more than 1,800 more wounded, while 221 Americans died and 1,364 were wounded.

The Tet Offensive marked a decisive shift in support for the war in the United States. In March 1968, Gen. William Westmoreland, seniormost U.S. officer in Vietnam, requested 206,000 more troops for Vietnam. While President Lyndon Johnson denied the request, it had tremendous political effects. Two days after the *New York Times* reported the requested increase, Senator Eugene McCarthy, an antiwar Democrat who was challenging Johnson for the nomination in the upcoming presidential elections, won the New Hampshire primary. Four days after the primary, Robert Kennedy entered the race, and on March 31, 1968, President Lyndon Johnson announced he would not seek reelection in November, a shocking decision that many attribute to the impact of the Tet Offensive. On a broader level, the Tet Offensive marked the beginning of the end of U.S. involvement in Vietnam, as Richard Nixon, who won the presidential election in 1968, campaigned with a promise that his "secret plan" could end the war. On an even broader world-historic level, the Tet Offensive is seen as marking the end of traditional Western control the formerly colonized people and places of the world with military force.

See also Johnson, Lyndon Baines (1908–1973); Kennedy, Robert F. (1925–1968); Viet Cong; Viet Minh; Vietnam War.

Bibliography

Arrighi, Giovanni, Terence K Hopkins, and Immanuel Wallerstein. *Antisystemic Movements.* New York: Verso, 1989.

Orberdorfer, Don. *Tet! The Turning Point in the Vietnam War.* Baltimore: Johns Hopkins University Press, 2001.

Prados, John. *Vietnam: The History of an Unwinnable War, 1945–1975.* Lawrence: University Press of Kansas, 2009.

Willibanks, James H. *The Tet Offensive: A Concise History.* New York: Columbia University Press, 2007.

BRENDAN McQUADE

THEY SHOOT HORSES, DON'T THEY? (1969).

They Shoot Horses, Don't They? is an existential film based on the eponymous novel by Horace McCoy. It uses the marathon dances of the Depression era as a metaphor for the violence and greed of American capitalist society and, more specifically, of the Hollywood film industry.

The film was directed by Sydney Pollack and produced by Robert Chartoff, Johnny Green, Theodore B. Sills, and Irwin Winkler. James Poe adapted the novel into a screenplay. The film stars Jane Fonda (Gloria Beatty), Michael Sarrazin (Robert Syverton), Susannah York (Alice LeBlanc), Gig Young (Rocky), Red Buttons (Harry Kline), Bonnie Bedelia (Ruby), Bruce Dern (James), Robert Fields (Joel Girard), Michael Conrad (Rollo), Al Lewis (Turkey), and Madge Kennedy (Mrs. Laydon).

They Shoot Horses takes place in a dismal ballroom perched on a pier in Santa Monica, California, the site of actual marathon dances. During the 1930s, contestants in these competitions would dance until they literally dropped from exhaustion while spectators cheered on their favorite couples. Occasionally, the marathon organizers made contestants race around the ballroom in order to wear them down and speed up eliminations. Winners received modest cash prizes and gifts after weeks, even months, of nonstop dancing. While McCoy's novel did not entirely survive its transition to the screen, the basic metaphor of people exerting themselves to the point of madness, or death, in pursuit of some illusive reward translates well.

Director Sydney Pollack avoids romanticizing his characters who endure this nightmare because they have no other economic means. The film offers no call to arms. Instead, it alludes to the hopelessness of the human condition. A pregnant woman (Bedelia) and her young husband (Dern) barely drag themselves around the ballroom floor; while an aspiring actress (York), dressed up as Jean Harlow, hopes to be discovered by a film industry talent scout. Most effective are the race scenes, in which exhausted dancers sprint around a haphazard race course for 10 minutes, desperately holding onto each other. The couples who finish last are swiftly eliminated. These scenes are heart-wrenching—the first of them is filmed in a kind of whirlwind; the second race is shot in slow motion, suspending the dancers' anguish.

They Shoot Horses introduces a number of changes to the *film noir* genre. Instead of a cynical, reserved hero, the protagonist is an embittered woman, and the story has a clear social context. The two main characters traveled to California to be movie stars; the boy (Sarrazin) possesses a naïveté, while the girl (Fonda) is overcome by her negative experiences. The marathon is a last resort for her. Angry and morose, she expects the worst. Unlike the male *noir* protagonists whom she resembles, however, Gloria aggressively seeks out her own death. Her life exposes the emptiness of the American Dream; she is effectively trapped in a bizarre contest on a decomposing pier at the edge of Los Angeles and is ultimately rescued from this nightmare by her partner, who at her request becomes her murderer.

The film was met with mixed reviews upon its release in 1969. Nevertheless, it received nine Academy Award nominations. Gig Young won the Academy Award for Best Supporting Actor. The film also received a Golden Globe Award (Gig Young, Best Supporting Actor) and a BAFTA (Susannah York, Best Actress in a Supporting Role).

Bibliography

Brode, Douglas. *The Films of the Sixties.* New York: Carol Publishing Group, 1990.
Fonda, Jane. *My Life So Far.* New York: Random House, 2005.
Hirsch, Foster. *The Dark Side of the Screen.* 2nd ed. New York: Da Capo, 2008.
Lopate, Phillip. *American Movie Critics: An Anthology from the Silents until Now.* New York: Library of America, 2008.
Schickel, Richard. "The Dance of Life as a Marathon." *Life* (January 23, 1970): 15.

CAROLINE E. KELLEY

THIEU, NGUYEN VAN (1924–2001). Nguyen Van Thieu was a military general and president of the Republic of (South) Vietnam. He gained control of the government after the elections of 1967 and retained power through a mixture of coercion and mild reform until his resignation shortly before the fall of Saigon. During this period, Thieu consistently resisted American-backed negotiations but proved indecisive in his direction of South Vietnamese military forces.

Nguyen Van Thieu was born on the central coast of Vietnam in 1924 (some sources say April 1923). The son of a minor landowner, he briefly joined Ho Chi Minh's nationalist guerrillas, the Viet Minh, but he left after growing disillusioned with the communist-influenced group. He received a commission in the French-supported Vietnamese army following his attendance at the National Military Academy at Da Lat and, in 1951, converted to the religion of his Roman Catholic bride. An able if cautious soldier, Thieu commanded the strategically important 5th Division, which occupied the presidential palace during the 1963 coup that unseated President Ngo Dinh Diem. He became increasingly influential as the senior member of a loosely affiliated group of generals known as the "Young Turks," serving for two years as head of state behind Prime Minister Nguyen Cao Ky. He outmaneuvered the colorful Ky to earn the presidency of the country in the surprisingly close elections of 1967.

As president, Thieu proved an ardent opponent of a negotiated truce. He adopted a policy that allowed no recognition of the communist forces in the South, no Laotian-style neutralization, no participation in a coalition government, and no surrender of territory. These four tenets made accommodating northern demands difficult, and Thieu proved a thorn in the side of American negotiators. In 1968, he covertly aided Richard Nixon's presidential campaign by refusing to accept National Liberation Front (NLF) participation in the Paris talks, effectively stalling Lyndon Johnson's peace initiative. Henry Kissinger received similar treatment during his negotiations from 1972 to 1973; Thieu vocally objected to any accommodation of communist demands for political and territorial recognition. The recalcitrant general acquiesced to Kissinger's Paris Treaty only after receiving American assurances of military aid, but he disregarded the document in his attempts to reestablish control over communist-held southern territory after the ceasefire.

The regime continued to govern South Vietnam until 1975, though its lack of political legitimacy and Thieu's poor leadership doomed it to failure. Thieu had filled government positions with family members and loyalists, and he ran unopposed in the 1971 elections by barring his political opponents. He struggled to control rampant official corruption and only implemented land reforms under American pressure. Moreover, his cautious nature proved disastrous in the military realm; he hesitated to commit troops without American support and failed to adjust South Vietnamese strategy during the period of Vietnamization. Southern tactics remained cautious until the ceasefire of 1973, when Thieu's attempts to gain additional territory dangerously overextended national forces. The North Vietnamese response two years later convinced a panicked Thieu to order a disastrous retreat, which led to his resignation in April 1975—barely a week before the fall of Saigon and the end of the South Vietnamese state. Thieu escaped into exile, settling first in London before moving to Massachusetts. He remained relatively anonymous and avoided the public denunciations of the communist state popular in Vietnamese exile politics. He died in 2001.

See also Kissinger, Henry (1923–); Nixon, Richard M. (1913–1994); Vietnam War; Vietnamization.

Bibliography

Bui Diem. *In the Jaws of History*. Boston: Houghton Mifflin, 1987.

Gardner, Lloyd C., and Ted Gittinger, eds. *The Search for Peace in Vietnam, 1964–1968*. College Station: Texas A&M University Press, 2004.

Herring, George C. *America's Longest War: The United States and Vietnam, 1950–1975*. 4th ed. Boston: McGraw-Hill, 2002.

Nguyen, Gregory Tien Hung, and Jerrold L. Schecter. *The Palace File*. New York: Harper & Row, 1986.

R. JOSEPH PARROTT

TITO, JOSIP BROZ (1892–1980). Josip Broz Tito was a Yugoslav communist statesman, marshal of Yugoslavia, and president of Yugoslavia from 1953 until his death in 1980. Tito's leadership was marked by the creation of a Yugoslav state with its own socialist regime, known as Titoism, independent from the Soviet Union.

Josip Broz, known by his alias Tito, was born on May 7, 1892, in Kumrovec, Austro-Hungarian Empire (now Croatia) of a Slovenian mother and a Croatian father. During World War I, he served in the Austro-Hungarian army on the Eastern Front, and he was wounded and captured by the Russians. He enlisted in the Red Army in November 1917 and joined the Russian Communist Party in 1918. In 1920, he went back to his country, the Kingdom of Serbs, Croats, and Slovenes (since 1929, Yugoslavia) to organize the local communist party. During this period, he accepted the alias Tito. After he served a prison term from 1928 to 1934 for his illegal communist activities, he went to Moscow to work for the organization Communist International (Comintern). In 1936, Stalin sent him back to Yugoslavia to purge the Communist Party, and in 1937 he became General Secretary of the Communist Party of Yugoslavia.

After the Nazi invasion and occupation of Yugoslavia in 1941, Tito organized a mass communist partisan movement in Yugoslavia. Tito's partisans fought both the Nazis and the royalist guerrillas of Drazha Mihailovic. The successful actions of Tito against the Nazis made him very popular in Yugoslavia, and he was also supported by the Allies. His army made him a marshal in 1943.

In March 1945, Tito became a prime minister of Yugoslavia. He imposed quickly his own communist dictatorship, and many Nazi

One of the most accomplished guerrilla leaders of all time, Josip Broz Tito led Yugoslavia out of World War II and was responsible for reorganizing the country into a socialist republic. An authoritarian president, Tito ruled Yugoslavia from 1945 until his death in 1980. (Library of Congress)

collaborators were executed, including en masse executions such as the Bleiburg massacre.

Initially, Tito was a supporter of Stalin, but in 1948 he refused to follow Stalin's orders, and as a result Yugoslavia was banned from the Cominterm. Tito opted to create his own socialist regime, which he called *self-management socialism* because he allowed workers' councils to manage enterprises and share the profit.

The Yugoslav split with the Soviet Union delighted the West, and Yugoslavia enjoyed western economic and political support until the end of the Cold War. In the 1960s, Tito even opened the borders for the citizens of Yugoslavia to travel abroad, which was unheard of in any other communist country.

In 1953, Tito was elected president of Yugoslavia, and from 1974, he became President for Life. The country was renamed the Socialist Federal Republic of Yugoslavia. It included six federal republics: Slovenia, Croatia, Serbia, Montenegro, Bosnia-Herzegovina, and Macedonia. Vojvodina and Kosovo became autonomous regions within Serbia.

In 1950, Tito created the labor camp Goli Otok and later other labor camps for political prisoners. Half a million political prisoners were killed or served prison terms in these labor camps. Despite these measures, Tito remained very popular among the majority of Yugoslavs.

Tito's foreign policy remained favorable to the West. Yugoslavia became part of the nonaligned countries in the world, and Tito protested against the Soviet invasions of Hungary (1956), Czechoslovakia (1968), and Afghanistan (1979). Tito died on May 4, 1980, after a few months spent in the hospital. His funeral was very lavish and drew throngs of mourners.

Bibliography

Banac, Ivo. *The National Question in Yugoslavia: Origins, History, Politics.* Ithaca, NY: Cornell University Press, 1984.

Haug, Hilde Katrine. *Creating a Socialist Yugoslavia: Tito, Communist Leadership, and the National Question.* London: I. B. Tauris, 2010.

CHRIS KOSTOV

TO KILL A MOCKINGBIRD **(1960).** Few works of fiction published in the 1960s have proven to be as enduring with the public as Harper Lee's semi-autobiographical, Pulitzer Prize–winning novel *To Kill a Mockingbird.* Despite its clear moral stance, popularity, and frequent inclusion in school curriculum, *To Kill a Mockingbird* has also been one of the most frequently banned and challenged books of the era due in large part to the controversial topics it addresses, including racism and gender roles. The novel, which is set in the small town in of Maycomb, Alabama, during the Great Depression, is at root a compelling character study of a heroic statesman, lawyer, and father, Atticus Finch; a man whose extraordinary generosity, sense of justice, integrity, courage, and dignity set him apart from his peers. Published in 1960 and adapted into an Oscar-winning film starring Gregory Peck in 1962, Lee's bestseller explicitly addresses the mentality behind racism and the results of it at a time when the civil rights movement was most active. Lee examines racism through the central story of Finch's noble but ultimately futile defense of a black man falsely accused of raping a white woman in a community so entrenched in bigotry and self-satisfaction that it would rather kill a man than face its own faults.

To Kill a Mockingbird is also a coming-of-age story, which increases its broad appeal, especially among young readers. In fact, Finch's tomboyish young daughter, Jean Louise "Scout" Finch, narrates the tale, both from the perspective of a child and as an adult reflecting on those formative experiences in her past. This approach allows Lee to develop the themes of lost innocence, wisdom, independence, and tolerance in a way that is accessible to children and adults. In particular, the subplot involving Scout and her brother Jem spying on the mysterious and ostensibly frightening town recluse Boo Radley, only to discover that their fear of the stranger is unfounded and based upon hurtful gossip, serves to underscore the prejudices that their father must combat in the courtroom. By exploring this common childhood fear of the unknown and showing that a stranger like Boo Radley may in fact be a misunderstood hero, Lee provokes young readers to question conventional wisdom, and she prompts them to approach others with empathy and respect before passing judgment. Lee also uses Scout to question other societal norms such as prescribed gender roles. Scout, who refuses to embody the ladylike role promoted by her Aunt Alexandra and others, opts for independent thought and embraces her own nature even though it is at variance with the genteel world around her. In this respect, Scout adopts the model of her father, whose moral strength allows him, even in defeat, to remain true to his convictions.

Bibliography

Bloom, Harold. *Harper Lee's "To Kill a Mockingbird."* New York: Bloom's Literary Criticism, 2010.
Lee, Harper. *To Kill a Mockingbird*. New York: Harper Perennial Modern Classics, 2006.
Mancini, Candice. *Racism in Harper Lee's "To Kill a Mockingbird."* Detroit: Greenhaven Press, 2008.

CALEB PUCKETT

TO SIR, WITH LOVE (1967). This is one of the three Sidney Poitier films released in 1967 (along with *In the Heat of the Night* and *Guess Who's Coming to Dinner*). *To Sir, with Love*, adapted from a novel by E. R. Braithwaite, was actually an autobiographical tale based on the author's experiences. Poitier plays British Guinea engineer Mark Thackeray, who is unable to find work in his chosen field, mostly because he is black; instead he accepts a teaching position in a poor school in the East End section of London. He arrives on the first day to find a totally undisciplined class who are poorly educated, rebellious, and downright rude to authority figures. Rather than give up on them, Thackeray tries unorthodox methods; he depends less on textbooks and more on experience. He starts implementing his own brand of classroom discipline: forcing the pupils to treat each other with respect and to address him as "Sir." Along with Poitier, the film starred Christian Roberts, Judy Geeson, Suzy Kendall, Ann Bell, Lulu, Geoffrey Bayldon, Faith Brook, and Patricia Routledge.

James Clavell (1924–1994), himself a novelist, was fascinated by Braithwaite's book. He agreed to write the screenplay and to direct and produce the picture. However, even when Poitier agreed to star, there was so little enthusiasm for its commercial possibilities that it was given what Poitier called a "take it or leave it" budget of only $640,000, although Clavell was given a huge percentage of the profits and Poitier a healthy percentage of the gross. The film eventually grossed over $7.2 million and became the eighth-largest grosser in 1967. This included respectable profits overseas, although the South African Publications Control Board banned the film, claiming that it was "offensive to see a Black male teaching a class of white children."

Poitier did great work in one of his best-known roles, with good support from the rest of the cast, and the title song, sung by Lulu, became a commercial hit. Poitier comes across as a real person, embodying a sense of morality, respect, integrity, and heroism. Because of these traits, he is able to redeem a class of students who would otherwise end up at the bottom of society. By the end of the film, they have started to mature into adults.

In this film, the racial issues were understated or not touched on at all. Poitier's Thackeray is a teacher who happens to be black, not a black teacher. The students in his classroom represent a wide variety of nationalities, and potentially racial situations are underplayed. In fact, the racial overtones in this film were not as fully developed as they were in other 1960s films and certainly not those with Poitier. For example, the budding romance between Thackeray and the Suzy Kendall character was not pursued to any great length (they did not end up together), and he deflected the attempts of Pamela Dare (Geeson), who was attracted to him. In the late 1960s climate of the film, Poitier was not allowed to date a white woman on screen, at least in *To Sir, with Love*. That had to wait until his next film, *Guess Who's Coming to Dinner* (also 1967), in which he courted a white woman and starred against the formidable Spencer Tracy and Katharine Hepburn.

See also Guess Who's Coming to Dinner (1967); *In the Heat of the Night* (1967); Poitier, Sidney.

Bibliography

Magill, Frank N., ed. *Magill's Survey of Cinema: English Language Films; Second Series, Volume 6: The-Z*. Englewood Cliffs, NJ: Salem Press, 1981.
Poitier, Sidney. *This Life*. New York: Alfred A. Knopf, 1980.

MARTIN J. MANNING

TOPLESS BATHING SUIT. In the seventh and eighth centuries, people commonly swam in the nude or with a strip of fabric that covered the genital area. The practice of wearing a costume in which to swim or bathe was not new even then; ancient drawings and murals found in Italy and Greece show women athletes in two-piece suits that cover the breast, hips, and genitalia. In eighteenth-century America, women commonly wore long dresses to swim in known as bathing gowns. These gowns were carefully constructed to ensure that the material could not be seen through when wet and that it would stay in place. During this same period, men wore wool swimming suits that were tightly fitted and had long sleeves and legs. Well into the late nineteenth century, the concept of modesty was still the chief concern, and both women and men remained well covered.

In the early twentieth century, the Australian vaudeville and film star Annette Kellerman traveled to the United States demonstrating a new swimming style often referred to as *underwater ballet*; it is now commonly known as *synchronized swimming*. Her swimming attire was thought to be scandalous: Kellerman had ditched the dress and pantaloons and wore a one-piece, short-sleeved costume under which she sometimes wore tights. Indeed, she was arrested in the United States for indecent exposure, and swimwear for women has never been the same.

By the 1930s, swimsuits had become smaller, showing the arms and legs down to about the middle of the thigh, and hugged the figure. New fabrics developed after World War II meant that the garments were more comfortable than ever, and that they could actually be used to swim in rather than merely for just posing or strolling.

The first *bikini*, so named because it was claimed to have an explosive effect on men that recalled the nuclear weapons being tested on the island of Bikini Atoll, was introduced in the middle of the 1940s. It was a two-piece garment, the top of which fully covered the breasts; the bottom half came up high enough to cover the navel so that some of the midriff was bare.

By the 1960s, the youth quake was taking hold, and clothing for women and men became less formal and less restrictive. Hemlines rose to sometimes dizzying heights, and swimming suits became smaller and smaller, some barely covering the breasts and genitalia.

The Austrian-born designer Rudi Gernreich is generally given credit for the invention of the topless bathing suit in 1964; he dubbed it a *monokini*. The monokini fit perfectly with the desire of Gernreich to make unisex clothing. The reaction of the world was immediate. Many lambasted Gernreich for his lack of morals; perhaps just as many shrugged. Gernreich pointed out that at many European beaches, it was common for women to go topless for swimming and sunbathing, and that his design proposed nothing new.

Approximately 3,000 of the monokinis were sold, a number that surprised even Gernreich. For the most part he did not design the monokini with an eye toward commercial success, but merely as a way to pay homage to youth, encourage minimalism in clothing design, and promote a unisex lifestyle.

Bibliography

Kennedy, Sarah. *The Swimsuit: A History of Twentieth-Century Fashion*. London: Carlton Books. 2010.
Moffitt, Peggy. *Rudi Gernreich*. Cologne, Germany: Taschen America. 1999.

MARILYN K. HOWARD

TRANSCENDENTAL MEDITATION (TM). Transcendental Meditation was introduced to the United States in 1959 when its founder, Maharishi Mahesh Yogi, came to Hawaii and California. Maharishi was an Indian ascetic who began touring the world in 1958, teaching what he professed to be ancient meditative techniques grounded in the Vedantic Hindu tradition. TM reached the peak of its popularity in the mid 1970s, but it burst onto the American cultural scene in the late 1960s when the Beatles became public adherents of the practice. TM's popularity declined in the latter half of the 1970s, but the practice still retains a large following around the world. The movement's U.S. base is in Fairfield, Iowa, where the Maharishi University of Management is located. Maharishi died on February 5, 2008, in Vlodrop, Netherlands.

Transcendental Meditation was established in the early 1960s as a standardized form of mantra mediation. After taking a seven-step course for four to eight weeks at an approved teaching center, an adherent discovers or is given a secret mantra that he or she is to use in the meditation exercises. The mantra is used at least twice a day for 20 to 30 minutes to center the practitioner's mind. TM professes to offer its followers increased energy, concentration, memory, and peace when practiced regularly. TM proponents have also claimed a "Maharishi Effect" where an entire community receives the benefits of reduced crime and increased productivity and peace when only 1 percent of the community regularly mediates using TM techniques.

TM's popularity exploded when numerous celebrities became adherents, including actress Mia Farrow, singer-songwriter Donovan, and especially the Beatles, who joined the movement in 1967. The group became so involved in TM that they traveled to learn directly from Maharishi in Bangor and Wales. In 1968, the Beatles journeyed to the International Academy of Meditation in Rishikesh, India. Although their association with TM ended in a controversy—the group left Rishikesh after hearing rumors that Maharishi made sexual advances toward Mia Farrow—their practice of TM has been credited with their move away from psychedelic drug use and the inspiration for many of their more popular songs, including much of the *White Album*. The Beatles' endorsement of TM grafted it into the American counterculture of the 1960s and early 1970s. American youth were drawn to the promise of mental freedom and peace from sources outside of established religious traditions. TM's proestablishment and antidrug stances sometimes clashed with other aspects of the counterculture, and, as a result, TM was seen as more of an oddity than a threat by the more conservative elements of American society. As its popularity waned in the 1980s, Transcendental Meditation became more recognized as an alternative form of religiosity, and many of the same youth who earlier embraced the practice as a form of rebellion began using it as a modern form of spirituality more closely aligned to capitalistic conservatism than the ideals of the counterculture.

See also Beatles, The (1959–1970); Youth Culture.

Bibliography

Gilpin, Geoff. *The Maharishi Effect: A Personal Journey through the Movement That Transformed American Spirituality*. New York: Penguin, 2006.

Mason, Paul. *The Maharishi: The Biography of the Man Who Gave Transcendental Meditation to the World*. Bramshaw, England: Evolution Publishing, 2005.

Yogi, Maharishi Mahesh. *Science of Being and Art of Living: Transcendental Meditation*. New York: Meridian, 1995.

ANDREW POLK

TRUE GRIT (1969). *True Grit*, which won John Wayne his only Oscar, as Best Actor, was also one of the last important films of the 1960s. The film featured one of the strangest trios ever to track a killer. There was drunken, hard-nosed U.S. Marshal Reuben "Rooster" Cogburn (John Wayne); Texas Ranger La Boeuf (Glen Campbell); and the stubborn young Mattie Ross (Kim Darby), whose father's murderer they help to track down in Indian territory. The teenager, on a mission of "justice," recruits Cogburn because he has "grit" and a reputation of getting the job done. The two are joined by La Boeuf, who is looking for the same man (Jeff Corey) for a separate murder in Texas. Their odyssey takes them from Fort Smith, Arkansas, deep into Indian Territory (present-day Oklahoma).

Besides Wayne, Darby, and Campbell, the cast included Jeremy Slate, Robert Duvall, Dennis Hopper, Alfred Ryder, Strother Martin, Jeff Corey, Ron Soble, John Fiedler, James Westerfield, John Doucette, Donald Woods, Edith Atwater. It was directed by Henry Hathaway (1898–1985) with a screenplay by Marguerite Roberts (1905?–1989), based on the book by Charles Portis.

Copies of Portis's book, with its special form of Arkansas speech, were sent by his agents, while still in galleys, to all the major studios. Hal Wallis, an independent producer at Paramount, won the contract with his bid of $300,000. Another bidder was John Wayne. When Wayne congratulated Wallis and told him how much he wanted to play the role of Rooster Cogburn, Wallis offered him the part.

Shot in Colorado, one of the highlights of *True Grit* is the beautiful location photography. Much of the film was shot against a background of fall foliage, with its autumn colors of red and gold. The scene near the end where Rooster Cogburn and Ned Pepper's gang meet in a field and Pepper (Robert Duvall) is shot was filmed in a clearing near the top of Owl Creek Pass outside Ridgway, Colorado. The field is off the road to the left and is very easy to find. The closing scene was shot in winter, in a snow-covered graveyard where Rooster jumps the fence on his horse, telling Mattie to "Come see a fat old man sometime."

In a sense, *True Grit* was a swan song to the classical Western film genre, represented by John Wayne and Henry Hathaway. They were being replaced by rising young actors, such as Duvall and Hopper, and this film was testament to that. By 1969, the Western entered a period of revisionism in which its myths and archetypes were treated either satirically (*Little Big Man*, 1970) or with contempt (Robert Altman's *McCabe and Mrs. Miller*, 1971). *True Grit* was actually one of the last of this genre to tell a rollicking good story concerned with positive values, especially the moving relationship between the overweight, heavy-drinking sheriff and the young girl. Roberts used many of the scenes in the novel and kept whole sections intact. The final scene in the cemetery, between Rooster and Mattie, was the screenwriter's own invention and is quite effective.

The Western of the 1970s also introduced a new type of Western hero typified by Clint Eastwood who were a change from the stereotype of the cowboy that Wayne and others represented for so long and that symbolized the Old West. In *True Grit*, Wayne plays with his image while he also honors the integrity of the character, a frontier marshal.

The character of Mattie, both on screen in Darby's portrayal and in the Portis novel, is a definite break from another old stereotype, that of the passive frontier maiden. In the film, Mattie is seeking revenge for her father's murder.

True Grit became a classic Western, one of the best in the 1960s, and a big success at the box office. It took in $15 million and became one of the highest-grossing Westerns of all time. It was helped by Elmer Bernstein's score. Its popular title song sung by Campbell became a hit on radio and on records.

See also Wayne, John (1907–1979).

Bibliography

Davis, Ronald L. *Duke: The Life and Image of John Wayne*. Norman: University of Oklahoma Press, 1998.

Magill, Frank N., ed. *Magill's Survey of Cinema: English Language Films; First Series, Volume. 4: SCA-Z*. Englewood Cliffs, NJ: Salem Press, 1980.

Shepherd, Donald, and Robert Slatzer. *Duke: The Life and Times of John Wayne.* New York: Zebra Books and Kensington, 1985.

Slotkin, Richard. *Gunfighter Nation: The Myth of the Frontier in Twentieth-Century America.* New York: Macmillan International, 1992.

Wallis, Hal, and Charles Higham. *Starmaker: The Autobiography of Hal Wallis.* New York: Berkley Books, 1980.

MARTIN J. MANNING

TRUFFAUT, FRANÇOIS (1932–1984). François Truffaut is an icon of French cinema, film theory, and criticism. He is one of the originators of the French New Wave and the *auteur* theory as well as a contemporary of Jean-Luc Godard, Eric Rohmer, Claude Chabrol, and Jacques Rivette, all of whom began their careers with the film magazine *Cahiers du cinéma.* In a directorial career that spanned 29 years, Truffaut made 24 films, including three shorts and 21 features.

François Roland de Montferrand was born out of wedlock on February 6, 1932, to Janine de Montferrand in Paris. He was adopted by his mother's husband, Roland Truffaut, in 1933 but did not live with the couple until the death of his maternal grandmother in 1942. A tumultuous relationship with his mother and stepfather marked his adolescence and led to his parents' decision to place him in a center for juvenile delinquents when he was a teenager. These experiences informed some of his most celebrated films such as the *Les Quatre cents coups (The 400 Blows)* (1959).

The performing and literary arts played an essential role in Truffaut's formative years. His goal as an adolescent was to see three films a day and to read three books a week. With his best friend, Robert Lachenay, Truffaut founded a film club, the Cercle Cinémane, in 1948. During the club's brief existence, Truffaut met the critic André Bazin and formed a friendship that lasted until the latter's death in 1958. In 1951, Truffaut enlisted in the military but deserted his post on the eve of his departure for Indochina. He was subsequently arrested and spent time in military prison. Bazin gave Truffaut his first film-related job at *Cahiers du cinéma* upon his release in 1952. He recognized the young man's passion for the cinema and, significantly, approached film with a similar appreciation for its aesthetics of reality. As a new critic Truffaut published his first article, "A Certain Tendency of the French Cinema," in 1954. The article targeted the tendency of postwar French films to depend too much on plot and dialogue and proposed a cinema of *auteurs.* The article caused intense debate in the French film community. Once he became a director himself, Truffaut revised some of his

French film director François Truffaut, in France, May 22, 1969. (AP/Wide World Photos)

harsh criticisms. He eventually declared that his filmmaking was a combination of the literary, the musical, and the visual.

Truffaut made his first short, the 16mm film *Une Visite*, in 1955. From 1954 to 1956, he worked for Roberto Rossellini, assisting him with three unreleased films. In 1957, Truffaut was in a position to make *Les Mistons* (*The Mischief Makers*), based on a short story by Maurice Pons. His friend Lachenay had come into a small inheritance and used the money to help him. Truffaut was also romantically involved with Madeleine Morgenstern, the daughter of film producer and distributor Ignace Morgenstern, and she convinced her father to finance the film. Truffaut thus started les Films du Carrosse. *Les Mistons* starred Gérard Blain and Bernadette Lafont. When the film was complete, Truffaut and Madeleine married on October 29, 1957.

Following *Les Mistons*, Truffaut devoted his energy to developing other films. He worked on a series of small projects, including a short film with Godard, *Histoire d'eau*. With the backing of his father-in-law, Truffaut developed his first feature-length film, *Les Quatre cents coups*. The screenplay was autobiographical, based on his and Lachenay's collective experiences as adolescents during the 1940s and '50s. The title was based on the French expression *faire les quatre cents coups*, meaning "to be up to no good." Unfortunately, that meaning is lost in the English translation, *The 400 Blows*. Truffaut chose Jean-Pierre Léaud to play the leading role of Antoine Doinel and Patrick Auffay as his friend, René. The filming was marked by bad luck, including the death of Truffaut's mentor and friend André Bazin in October 1958 from leukemia. Despite Truffaut's misgivings about the film, *Les Quatre cents coups* was well received upon its debut at the Cannes Film Festival in 1959, winning the prestigious Grand Prix.

Les Quatre cents coups changed Truffaut's life. He wrote the script for Godard's *Breathless* in 1959 and directed *Tirez sur le pianiste* (*Shoot the Piano Player*) in 1960. In 1961, his film *Jules et Jim* was released. He produced, supervised, and helped to write the script for Claude de Givray's *Tire au flanc* (1961). Other films Truffaut completed in the 1960s include *Antoine et Colette* (1961), *La Peau douce* (*The Soft Skin*) (1964), *Fahrenheit 451* (1966), *La Mariée était en noir* (*The Bride Wore Black*) (1967), *Baisers volés* (*Stolen Kisses*) (1968), and *L'Enfant sauvage* (*The Wild Child*) (1969), and *La Sirène du Mississippi* (*Mississippi Mermaid*) (1969). He also published a book on Alfred Hitchcock's films, *Le Cinéma selon Hitchcock* (1966), and was instrumental in the Langlois Affair in 1968, during which the French government dismissed Henri Langlois, the head of the Cinémathèque Française. Truffaut organized protests until the government reinstated Langlois. He also participated in the cancellation of the Cannes Film Festival in 1968 in response to the May 1968 uprisings.

In the 1970s and '80s, Truffaut directed *Domicile conjugal* (Bed and Board) (1970), *Les Deux anglaises et le continent* (*Two English Girls*) (1971), *Une Belle fille comme moi* (*Such a Gorgeous Kid as Me*) (1972), *La Nuit américaine* (*Day for Night*) (1973), *L'Histoire d'Adèle H.* (*The Story of Adele H.*) (1975), *L'Argent de poche* (*Small Change*) (1976), *L'Homme qui aimait les femmes* (*The Man Who Loved Women*) (1977), *La Chambre verte* (*The Green Room*) (1978), *L'Amour en fuite* (*Love on the Run*) (1979), *Le Dernier métro* (*The Last Metro*) (1980), *La Femme d'à côté* (*The Woman Next Door*) (1981), and *Vivement dimanche!* (*Confidentially Yours*) (1983). Truffaut won the Best Foreign Film Academy Award for *La Nuit américaine*. In 1977, he starred in Steven Spielberg's *Close Encounters of the Third Kind* as the character Claude Lacomb.

Truffaut's films inform one another structurally, thematically, and formally, forming a discursive whole. A number of his films deal with the theme of adolescence and young adulthood, while others might be called genre films. Jean Renoir and Alfred Hitchcock as well as Rossellini, Ernst Lubitsch, and Howard Hawks inspired Truffaut's work. He was a great enthusiast of literature. His film *L'Histoire d'Adèle H.* is a tribute to Victor Hugo's daughter, while *Fahrenheit 451* conveys his love of books. At the heart of all of these films are an interest in people, the characters, their emotions, conflicts, and relationships. Truffaut's films share a common tension between form and visual aesthetic. They also reflect his lifelong attraction to women. His many lovers included Liliane Litvin, Jeanne Moreau, Claude Jade, Françoise Dorléac, Jacqueline Bisset, Leslie Caron, Catherine Deneuve, Fanny Ardant, and his wife, Madeleine Morgenstern.

Truffaut died on October 21, 1984, from a brain tumor. He is survived by his daughters Laura (b. 1959) and Eva (b. 1961) from his marriage to Madeleine Morgenstern and Joséphine (b. 1983) from his relationship with Fanny Ardant.

Bibliography

Baecque, Antoine de, and Serge Toubiana. *Truffaut: A Biography*. Translated by Catherine Temerson. New York: Alfred A. Knopf, 1999.

Crisp, C. G. *François Truffaut*. New York: Praeger, 1972.

Ingram, Robert, and Paul Duncan. *François Truffaut: Film Author 1932–1984*. New York: Taschen, 2004.

Insdorf, Annette. *François Truffaut*. Boston: Twayne, 1978.

Truffaut, François. *The Films in My Life*. Translated by Leonard Mayhew. New York: Simon & Schuster, 1978.

CAROLINE E. KELLEY

TWIGGY (1949–). As one of the first celebrity supermodels, the teenage Twiggy was an iconic face for the fashion-conscious 1960s. Her ultra-slim figure, doe-like eyes, and cropped hair offered an instant image for the era as she became a frequent cover star for fashion magazines across the globe. While her later career has garnered her a number of acting plaudits, she continues to wield enduring influence upon contemporary fashion.

Born to a working-class family in the East End of London in 1949, Leslie Hornby was only 16 years old when she was declared the "Face of 1966" by the British newspaper the *Daily Express*. Given the immortal nickname "Twiggy" by the brother of her boyfriend and agent, Justin de Villeneuve, on account of her slightness, her strikingly slender frame and stylishly cropped hair offered a modern, androgynous image for the period. Soon young women across Britain were sporting Twiggy-inspired haircuts and dresses, while "Twiggies"—the false eyelashes worn by Twiggy herself to emphasize her striking eyes—also became extremely popular.

Initially some deemed Twiggy "The Paper Girl," anticipating that her fame would be short-lived amidst the constant innovations of '60s fashions. Instead, just like the Beatles before her, Twiggy's fame entered the stratosphere following a U.S. visit in 1967. Seized upon as the face of "Swinging London," Twiggy became a regular feature of fashion magazines from French *Elle* to American *Vogue*. However, her stardom did encounter something of a backlash. Her discovery by a newspaper rather than a photographer provoked long-standing resentment within the industry to the extent that the agent of four seminal British male photographers, including

David Bailey, declared that his men would never work with her. Moreover, although models like Jean Shrimpton and Jane Birkin had already instigated a move away from the curvier female figures celebrated throughout the 1950s, Twiggy is often unfairly held responsible for introducing the "skinny" aesthetic, a cultural valuation of female thinness that is both vaunted and criticized to this day.

Toward the end of the decade, Twiggy's relationship with de Villeneuve grew increasingly strained, with his influence being depicted as Svengali-like in the British media. As the pair parted ways, Twiggy made a concerted attempt to move beyond the confines of the modeling world. She made a notable acting debut by winning two Golden Globes for her performance in *The Boyfriend* (1970) under director Ken Russell. She subsequently pursued a successful career on Broadway in the 1980s, garnering a number of Tony awards.

Despite these respectable forays into the acting world, Twiggy nonetheless remains a legendary figure within the fashion industry; after all, the emergence of the slender Kate Moss and the "heroin chic" of the 1990s became typically regarded as a revival of the Twiggy look of the "Swinging '60s." Having recently returned to modeling for a successful British clothing chain, Twiggy's current position as an elder states-woman of the fashion world only serves to complement a legacy that will always be intertwined with the cultural history of twentieth-century style.

Bibliography

"The Arrival of Twiggy." *Life* 3 62, no. 5 (February 3, 1967): 33–40.
Dening, Penelope, and Twiggy. *Twiggy in Black and White*. London: Pocket Books, 1998.

ROSEMARY DELLER

2001: A SPACE ODYSSEY (1968). Premiering only months before man first set foot on the moon, *2001: A Space Odyssey* explores humanity's quest for the stars. Using a classical score and an open-ended narrative, director Stanley Kubrick and cowriter Arthur C. Clarke ask whether mankind's potential for knowledge or propensity for violence would define the future.

The film begins at the dawn of man. One morning a group of apelike creatures encounter a huge, black monolith. Thereafter one of the creatures has an epiphany. No longer would his tribe bend to their environment; they would use tools to shape it. After unleashing their new, murderous power upon a rival tribe, the movie shifts to the end of the twentieth century.

Here the audience meets Dr. Heywood Floyd (William Sylvester) on his way to investigate the discovery of a black monolith on the moon. His visit is interrupted by the sudden transmission of a single, high-pitched communication from the object toward Jupiter. The film then jumps 18 months into the future to the spaceship *Discovery*. The crew consists of Dr. Frank Poole (Gary Lockwood), Dr. Dave Bowman (Keir Dullea), and HAL (voiced by Douglas Rain), a sentient computer whose ever-present glowing red eye watches over *Discovery* and the crew. Only HAL knows they have been sent to find the destination of the monolith's broadcast.

The trio's strange familial relationship takes a turn for the worse when HAL asks Bowman if he has misgivings about the mission. Mid-conversation a communications unit fails. *Discovery* will shortly lose contact with earth. Worried that HAL is malfunctioning, Poole and Bowman discuss whether the computer will need to be

battalions totaling 3,500 men arrived in South Vietnam to take up defensive positions around Danang.

However, within a few weeks, several officials began to suggest that more American troops may be needed. The instability of the Saigon government along with the dismal performance of ARVN troops, led many U.S. political and military leaders to conclude that the only way to stave off defeat was to dispatch at least two U.S. Army divisions. After returning from a weeklong trip to South Vietnam in early March, U.S. Army Chief of Staff General Harold Johnson suggested deploying additional American ground troops in order to help create a stable government in South Vietnam, crush the insurgency, and ultimately persuade North Vietnam to abandon their support of the Viet Cong. Likewise, General Westmoreland made a similar proposal later that month, arguing that the air war against North Vietnam was not enough to save South Vietnam.

By early April, a consensus had developed among administration officials on the need for more American military involvement. After meeting with his top advisors, President Johnson approved NSAM 328 on April 6, which not only called for the deployment of an additional 18,000–20,000 American troops, but also authorized the administration to explore the possibility of acquiring combat forces from Australia, New Zealand, and South Korea for use in Vietnam. Two weeks later, the president directed his top military and civilian officials to discuss the matter further at a conference in Honolulu. At that meeting, U.S. policy makers supported the continuation of the air campaign, but recognizing its limitations, they approved a plan to deploy 40,000 additional U.S. ground forces to conduct military operations in South Vietnam in areas around American military bases. They also approved the idea of utilizing third-country combat troops for operations in South Vietnam. Several days later, President Johnson authorized the plan. The decisions of April 1965 proved crucial in the evolution of U.S. military involvement in Southeast Asia. No longer operating in a defensive capacity, U.S. troops received authorization to engage in offensive ground operations against Viet Cong and North Vietnamese forces throughout South Vietnam. This important change in U.S. military operations quietly went unnoticed by the American public until the summer of 1965, by which time the U.S. military presence on the ground in Vietnam was an accepted fact.

By the spring of 1965, the merry-go-round of governments that had followed Diem's assassination finally came to an end as a new regime led by Generals Nguyen Cao Ky and Nguyen Van Thieu came to power. Both men would serve as leaders of South Vietnam until the end of the war in 1975, thereby instilling a sense of stability and continuity that thus far had been lacking in Saigon. Unfortunately, little else changed. For the next decade, the South Vietnamese government's reputation for dishonesty persisted. Allegations of corruption, bribes, and kickbacks among officials were rampant, and the influx of American dollars, military equipment and goods led to a thriving black market. Fraudulent elections and political intrigue undermined any hope of creating a legitimate government backed by popular support. Furthermore, in spite of massive amounts of U.S. financial assistance and military training, the ARVN never came close to becoming a reliable fighting force. For the remainder of the war it suffered from desertion, absenteeism, cronyism, and nepotism. Barely 10 percent of young men drafted ever reported for military service, and the desertion rate of 6,000 a month in 1964 increased to 11,000 a month by 1965. Many officers received promotions due to political connections rather than their tactical abilities. This, in combination with involuntary enlistments and indefinite tours of duty, led to poor morale throughout the ARVN. As more American troops arrived, the United States assumed more of the fighting burden, and these systemic problems within the South Vietnamese army became endemic.

American Military Strategy in Vietnam.

U.S. commanders in Vietnam, beginning with Harkins and continuing with Westmoreland, pursued a military policy of attrition. The idea behind this strategy was to use the U.S.'s huge advantage in weaponry, technology, and mobile forces to wear down the Viet Cong to the point where they could no longer make up their losses through southern recruiting and northern replacement. According to the theory, once the enemy reached that crossover point, the United States would crush the insurgency. In an attempt to gauge success, U.S. military leaders began to add up the numbers of combat operations, tactical air sorties, bombing tonnages, weapons captured, and the most important statistic of all, the "body count," a reference to the number of Viet Cong killed. Unfortunately, as Americans would gradually discover, attrition actually favored the enemy. The Viet Cong in the south and Hanoi's conventional forces up north were far more capable of suffering huge losses in manpower and replacing them than were U.S. troops.

One thing the Johnson administration did understand very well was the notion that the American public would not tolerate a long-term military commitment with mounting casualties. Under those circumstances, the war would rapidly lose political support at home. In an attempt to keep casualties to a minimum, President Johnson initially adopted the enclave strategy. Under this approach, American combat troops would concentrate their operations along the populated coastal zone in order to protect the larger urban areas and deny the resources of those regions to the enemy. By controlling the large cities, communication routes, and commercial areas, the United States hoped to isolate the guerrillas in the countryside. The hope was that this strategy would not only prevent the United States from engaging in a large-scale ground war, but would also buy time for the South Vietnamese government to stabilize. In concert with bombing raids against insurgent targets in the south and military and industrial targets up north, the administration hoped to force North Vietnam and the Viet Cong to the negotiating table. Once again, however, the American strategy was badly flawed. Typically, insurgents and guerrillas are most comfortable in rural areas, where they can intermingle with the peasant population. Their very survival is predicated upon contact and support from the people who provide them with shelter, food, clothing, information, and, most importantly, new recruits.

After recognizing the problems inherent in this strategy, and with the South Vietnamese government's ongoing struggles, the Johnson administration decided to move from the defensive to the offensive by authorizing "search and destroy" operations in the latter half of 1965. Rather than simply trying to deny the enemy victory and buying time for the buildup of the ARVN, the United States would now actively seek to flush out the enemy and defeat him militarily. U.S. forces would now venture out into the countryside using their mobile forces and superior firepower to annihilate the enemy. These operations led to the widespread use of herbicides and chemical defoliants such as Agent Orange, designed to deny the enemy cover and expose them to U.S. air and ground attack. In a campaign dubbed Operation Ranch Hand, American pilots during the course of the war dumped 19 million gallons of chemical poison across 20 percent of the entire land mass of South Vietnam, turning millions of acres of jungle and rice paddies into mud. In an attempt to isolate the guerrillas and deny them assistance from villagers, American and South Vietnamese forces attempted to resettle some of the rural population. While these policies did in fact result in the discovery and death of many Viet Cong troops, they also caused many innocent deaths and angered villagers who were forced off ancestral lands, which in some cases, they had farmed for centuries.

This new strategy would also require substantial increases in U.S. forces. In June, President Johnson had approved U.S. troop levels to 95,000 men. Within weeks, Westmoreland and General Earle G. Wheeler, chairman of the Joint Chiefs of Staff, requested another 150,000 troops. The president decided on a middle course. At the end of July, he approved the deployment of another 50,000 troops and increased the number of bombing sorties over North Vietnam. However, fearful of a repeat of the Korean War when communist Chinese forces joined the conflict following the U.S. invasion of North Korea, Johnson was careful not to provoke a wider war. As a result, he instituted strict restrictions on bombing missions over North Vietnam and never considered sending American troops north of the 17th parallel. However, the administration did secretly approve small,

U.S. Air Force UC-123 Providers spray the defoliant chemical Agent Orange over dense vegetation in South Vietnam in 1966. (AP/Wide World Photos)

covert operations into neighboring Laos and Cambodia in order to interdict supplies and men along the Ho Chi Minh Trail. Furthermore, the administration also authorized selective bombing missions over Laos and Cambodia for the same purpose, although this too remained hidden from the American public until the next decade. While these bombing missions over the Ho Chi Minh Trail made infiltration more difficult, it did not stop it. Tons of food, weapons, and ammunition continued to pour into South Vietnam from the north. By the middle of 1966, nearly 8,000 North Vietnamese Army (NVA) troops were coming into South Vietnam each month.

Third-Country Participation in the Vietnam War. In an attempt to lessen the burden facing American troops and convince the public that the administration's policies had the support of the international community, President Johnson actively urged America's allies to support the war effort in Vietnam. Organized under the title of Free World Military Assistance, the United States encouraged nations to provide economic, humanitarian, and military assistance to the government of South Vietnam. While dozens of nations provided various types of aid, besides the United States, only Australia, New Zealand, Thailand, and South Korea deployed combat troops to Vietnam. Throughout the entire course of the war, well over 375,000 soldiers from these nations served in South Vietnam. However, this represented only about 15 percent of the overall U.S. commitment during the duration of the conflict. Despite Johnson's best efforts, Vietnam essentially remained an American war.

Early Engagements and Deepening U.S. Involvement. The first major engagement between U.S. and enemy forces occurred in November 1965 in the Ia Drang Valley in the Central Highlands near the Cambodian border. There U.S. troops with the First Air Cavalry Division engaged North Vietnamese soldiers (known officially as the People's Army of Vietnam, or PAVN). The U.S. air cavalry was a new concept that utilized the helicopter to provide mobility and firepower to U.S. troops. Helicopters were used to quickly insert forces into an area, provide support, and then extract them once the mission was complete. The battle began when about 400 American soldiers were surprised by approximately 3,000 troops from the PAVN Sixty-sixth Regiment while on patrol through what they believed was an unoccupied valley. After four days of intense fighting where the United States deployed B-52 bombers and fired thousands of artillery rounds and aerial rockets, U.S. forces killed perhaps 2,000 to 2,500 enemy soldiers while losing only about 250 men. Both sides drew important lessons from the engagement. For U.S. military commanders and political leaders wedded to the statistical body count, it appeared that American tactics and firepower had won the day and that the strategy of attrition was working. However, the North Vietnamese realized that in the future they must avoid big-unit engagements and instead focus on guerrilla warfare and hit-and-run tactics. Ho Chi Minh and General Vo Nguyen Giap, the Commander of the PAVN, came to understand that time was on their side. Rather than face U.S. forces in large, conventional battles, the communists avoided big-unit engagements and instead slowly bled the Americans through unconventional warfare. They reasoned that eventually the American public would grow weary and demand an end to the conflict.

General Westmoreland used the battle of the Ia Drang Valley to justify further increases in U.S. troop levels, which would reach about 184,000 by the end of the year. The U.S. MACV commander now asked President Johnson for 200,000 more men. Before approving such a huge increase, Johnson decided to attempt a peace initiative. On Christmas Eve 1965, the president ordered a bombing pause. However, Ho Chi Minh insisted that the United States unconditionally withdraw all of its troops and allow the NLF to participate in the South Vietnamese government. Frustrated, Johnson resumed the bombing raids on January 31, 1966, and approved Westmoreland's request for more soldiers. That same month, the Joint Chiefs urged the president to intensify the bombing of North Vietnam and remove the self-imposed restrictions on U.S. air operations. The chiefs believed that by increasing direct pressure against Hanoi, they could convince North Vietnam to cease directing and supporting the southern insurgency. They advised the president to authorize air attacks against industrial, military, and petroleum storage facilities in and around Hanoi and the coastal town of Haiphong. By the early summer of 1966, Johnson agreed to permit selective strikes against targets in these areas. However, similar to U.S. air operations against the Ho Chi Minh Trail, the strategic bombing of North Vietnam was ineffective. The attacks had a minor effect on Hanoi's ability to mount and support military operations in the south. There was relatively little domestic industry to target since the vast majority of North Vietnamese war material originated in Russia and China. Furthermore, the air campaign did not break the will of the people, but rather hardened their attitude and led them to rally behind their government's war effort. This was truly remarkable in light of the fact that in Vietnam between 1964 and 1968, the United States dropped three times as much ordinance as it had over Germany and Japan combined during the entire course of World War II.

Domestic Opposition to the War. As the war in Southeast Asia intensified in 1966 and U.S. casualties began to mount, many Americans began to question the nation's involvement in the conflict. More than 1,700 U.S. soldiers lost their lives in the first three months of the year. To meet the growing manpower demand, draft calls intensified. On college campuses across the country, student organizations, many of which had been active in the civil rights movement and had participated in nonviolent civil disobedience, began to channel their energy into criticizing the war. Organizations such as Students for a Democratic Society (SDS) and the Student Nonviolent Coordinating Committee (SNCC) began to lead antiwar marches in Washington as early as mid-1965. Over the next 12 months, the ranks of SDS swelled, and many students turned in their daft cards or publicly burned them. Criticism in Congress also intensified. Senator J. William Fulbright of Arkansas emerged as the leading critic on Capitol Hill. As chairman of the powerful Senate Foreign Relations Committee, Fulbright convened special hearings on the war in February 1966. A onetime friend and political ally of Johnson, Fulbright had become disillusioned by the war and decided to expose it to public scrutiny. Even within Johnson's own administration, the stress of the war began to take its toll. In the second half of 1966, longtime critic of the war George Ball resigned as under secretary of state. Johnson would later appoint him as U.S. ambassador to the United Nations two years later. National Security Advisor McGeorge Bundy, who had also questioned the huge military buildup in Vietnam, stepped down and was replaced by the more hawkish Walt Rostow.

Problems and Consequences of American Military Strategy. The manpower increases authorized in 1966 brought U.S. troop totals up to 385,000 by the end of the year. However, even with these massive numbers, U.S. commanders were finding it no easier to locate communist guerrillas, who refused to come out of hiding except when conditions were favorable for their success. Even when U.S. forces did directly engage the enemy in combat, the long-term results were often counterproductive. For example, in January 1967, U.S. soldiers attempted to clear an area known as the "Iron Triangle" just north of the capital of Saigon. The region had become a major stronghold for the Viet Cong, and the objective was to use a hammer and anvil strategy where U.S. units at one end of the war zone would drive the enemy into the other units deployed on the opposing edge of the battlefield. Prior to the mission, known as Operation Cedar Falls, U.S. forces had to clear the area of civilians so they could establish a "free-fire zone" in which all remaining Vietnamese were considered VC and therefore legitimate military targets. In the ensuing campaign, approximately 35,000 U.S. and ARVN troops laid waste to the whole region, including a number of small villages. Although they destroyed a huge complex of underground tunnels and killed about 750 Viet Cong guerrillas, many more escaped and simply returned to the area following the battle. After the displacing and destroying of rural communities by U.S. forces, the returning communists received even more support from the local population, who were angered by U.S. actions. Within six months, the Viet Cong had returned to full strength in the region.

Military operations through rural villages, combined with the use of chemical defoliants, took a heavy toll on the civilian population. So too did American B-52 raids inside South Vietnam. Designed in the mid-1950s, the B-52 was capable of unleashing a level of destruction similar to that of a tactical nuclear weapon. From 30,000 feet, six B-52s could release a bomb load that would pulverize practically everything within a 1.5-square-mile area. At the height of the war in 1968, U.S. B-52s, along with smaller bombers, helicopter gunships, and artillery, detonated about 3.5 million pounds of explosives every day in South Vietnam alone. This level of destruction had a chilling effect on the civilian population. In 1967, 3 million South Vietnamese peasants lost their homes. One year later, the number of homeless had reached almost 4 million. Additionally, between 1965 and 1972, more than 400,000 civilians died in South Vietnam and another one million were wounded as a result of friendly fire.

Although the United States never intentionally targeted innocent civilians, as communist insurgents sometimes did, there were a few high-profile cases where American troops committed atrocities, and these incidents added tremendous fuel to the antiwar movement. The most infamous case during the war occurred in the village of My Lai in central Vietnam in March 1968. Lieutenant William Calley led an infantry platoon into the rural hamlet of approximately 700 people searching for Viet Cong guerrillas. Shortly after arriving, Calley ordered his men to round up all of the civilians. With tensions running high and frustrated by their inability to distinguish civilians from VC, the soldiers quickly lost their patience. Suddenly Calley began to open fire on the villagers, and he ordered his men to do the same. After the smoke cleared, over 400 Vietnamese men, women, and children were dead. Even though several high-ranking officers were aware of the killings, there was no official report or investigation. The story eventually broke a year-and-a-half later when accounts appeared in the press along with color photographs taken at the site. After a long and highly publicized trial, a military court found Calley guilty of the premeditated murder of at least 22 civilians and sentenced him to life in prison. There were no other convictions in the case, and Calley received his release after serving only three years.

By 1967, it was spending nearly $2 billion per month on the war, and although the communists had sustained tremendous casualties, the United States was no closer to victory. U.S. troop levels continued to climb and ultimately reached more than 480,000 by the end of the year. With U.S. casualties mounting and the war appearing to become more of a stalemate, the American public began to lose confidence in its political and military leaders and to question their rosy assessments of the war. Eventually a "credibility gap" emerged, which referred to the belief among many Americans that they were being misled by their elected officials regarding the true nature of the war and the chances for success. While General Westmoreland continued to quote the body count along with other statistical evidence to demonstrate tactical success against the VC, support for the war began to decline. Throughout 1967, students across the country and on college campuses held rallies and protests against the war. They hounded government officials, obstructed their movements, and interrupted their speeches. They campaigned to abolish Reserve Officer Training Corps (ROTC) programs on campus and chased military recruiters off university grounds. In October 1967, more than 100,000 people gathered in Washington to protest the war. For the first time ever, public support for the war dropped below 50 percent, and the president's approval numbers dipped to about 28 percent.

That same year witnessed a shake-up within the Johnson administration as a result of conflicting views regarding the war's prosecution. In April, Henry Cabot Lodge Jr., U.S. ambassador to South Vietnam since 1965, resigned after becoming disgruntled with Westmoreland's handling of the war. Lodge and Westmoreland had clashed for some time, and Lodge's replacement, Ellsworth Bunker, vowed to give his full support to the general and the war effort. The president also lost the support of Secretary of Defense Robert McNamara, one of the chief architects of Johnson's Vietnam policy. During the last 12 months, McNamara had become disillusioned with Westmoreland's attrition strategy, and he began to privately question whether victory was possible. In the spring of 1967, he urged Johnson to halt the air war over North Vietnam, cap troop levels, and seek a diplomatic settlement with Hanoi.

Having lost confidence in McNamara, Johnson replaced him with Clark Clifford at the end of February 1968.

1968—*The Beginning of the End.* As difficult as 1967 was for President Johnson, things were about to get even worse. Although the United States had lost 16,021 soldiers in the war by the end of the year, the enemy death toll was more than 15 times that number. Westmoreland used these figures to assert that nearly half of all enemy battalions were no longer combat effective. As a result, the MACV commander believed that the communists were no longer capable of threatening the heart of South Vietnam and were largely confined to the periphery of the state. Westmoreland felt that North Vietnam was now planning for a conventional invasion with its focal point being the U.S. military base at Khe Sanh, located in the northwest corner of South Vietnam, about 18 miles south of the 17th parallel and 8 miles east of Laos. Military intelligence indicated that in the closing months of 1967, the NVA had massed nearly 40,000 troops in the hills surrounding the base. On January 21, 1968, the North Vietnamese launched a massive artillery bombardment against the outpost. While U.S. military leaders prepared for a major communist thrust across the 17th parallel, tens of thousands of Viet Cong guerrillas were sneaking into the cities and population centers of South Vietnam in preparation for a surprise, coordinated assault.

Republic of Vietnam soldiers inspect the extensive damage in Saigon's Cholon district, the Chinese quarter of the city, following the communist Mini-Tet Offensive of May 1968. (AP/Wide World Photos)

On the morning of January 31, 1968, the beginning of the Vietnamese Lunar New Year known as Tet, the Viet Cong came out of hiding and attacked South Vietnamese provincial and district capitals, government installations, and buildings as well as U.S. civil and military targets. While the United States was preparing for a northern invasion that never materialized, the communist insurgents launched a strike against the heart of the Saigon regime. NVA units in the north created diversions and attempted to draw American troops out of the cities, while in the south over 100,000 Viet Cong soldiers and NVA support personnel abandoned their guerrilla tactics and launched coordinated strikes aimed at sparking a general uprising among the civilian population and undermining the credibility of the South Vietnamese government. The communists hoped that this show of strength would weaken the faith of southern citizens in the ability of the United States and the Saigon government to protect them, and impress upon everyone the strength and popular support of the Viet Cong, and hopefully lead to the collapse of the Thieu regime. During the Tet Offensive, which lasted for approximately two months with a series of smaller offensives continuing into the spring and summer of 1968, nearly all of the major cities in South Vietnam suffered attack, including the capital of Saigon. There, Viet Cong troops even led a spectacular attack against the American Embassy, which lasted for several hours and left the grounds littered with bodies from both sides. Some of the heaviest fighting during the offensive took place in the ancient city of Hue, where NVA troops succeeded in temporarily capturing the city. Before an American counteroffensive regained control of the town, the communists rounded up and executed thousands of civilians, government officials, and intellectuals. When the Tet Offensive finally ended, over 40,000 Viet Cong troops had been killed along with 1,100 Americans and 2,300 South Vietnamese soldiers. About 45,000 civilians were dead or wounded and more than 1 million people became homeless.

The Tet Offensive was a major turning point in the war. Although it was a tactical defeat for the communists, who were routed by American troops when they came out of hiding, the operation proved to be a strategic victory for North Vietnam. During the peak of the fighting, the United States was suffering 300 combat deaths a week, and the daily carnage and devastation witnessed by millions of Americans back home thanks to nightly television news broadcasts weakened American resolve. The Vietnam War was the first U.S. conflict to receive widespread video coverage. Unlike any other conflict in the past, Americans were able to witness this war first-hand and in color. What they saw clearly contradicted everything their political and military leaders argued in defense of continuing the struggle. The sight of U.S. troops fighting and dying on the streets of Saigon and Hue and dozens of smaller towns in between demonstrated the weakness of the South Vietnamese government. It also proved that the war was not winding down after all and that the Viet Cong were not on the verge of collapse. Suddenly the American people recognized that military victory was a long way off and the cost had become too high in political, economic, and military terms. The American public had had enough. Walter Cronkite, one of the most prominent broadcast journalists in the country and anchor of the *CBS Evening News*, announced in late February that in his opinion the Vietnam War could only end in a stalemate. The significance of Cronkite's statement was not lost on President Johnson, who privately noted that if he lost the support of Walter Cronkite, he has lost the average American citizen.

General Westmoreland's response to the Tet Offensive was to request an expansion of the air war as well as an additional 206,000 troops. He also suggested invading Laos, Cambodia, and North Vietnam to destroy enemy sanctuaries. Such a move was totally out of the question for Johnson, who was losing political support by the minute back home. In early March 1968, Senator Eugene McCarthy of Minnesota, an outspoken opponent of the war, challenged Johnson in the Democratic presidential primary in New Hampshire. The results were shocking. Although Johnson won the primary with 48 percent of the vote, McCarthy received 42 percent. The outcome showed that Johnson was very vulnerable in the upcoming November 1968 presidential election. Public opinion polls at the time indicated that only about 25 percent of the American public supported Johnson's conduct of the war. The best the president could do for Westmoreland was to approve the deployment of another 12,000 troops. There would be no further major escalations. American troop levels in Vietnam would peak at 536,000 soldiers by the end of 1968.

For President Johnson, the handwriting was on the wall. After meeting with his top advisors in late March, he made a televised speech to the nation from the Oval Office on the evening of March 31, 1968. He informed the American people that the time had come to begin to reduce the level of hostilities in Vietnam. Johnson closed his speech with the stunning announcement that he had decided not to seek reelection in November. The very next day, the president suspended all Rolling Thunder raids north of the 19th parallel and offered to open peace negotiations with North Vietnam. Two days later, Hanoi accepted the invitation, and talks began in Paris on May 13, 1968. Along with President Johnson, General Westmoreland was another casualty of Tet. The president removed Westmoreland by naming him army chief of staff in April 1968. Johnson replaced him as MACV commander with General Creighton Abrams. Although the war would drag on for almost five more years with tens of thousands of U.S. casualties, the United States had finally begun the slow and painful process of disengaging from Vietnam.

President Richard Nixon and American Withdrawal. In the 1968 presidential race the Democrats nominated Vice President Hubert Humphrey. Humphrey had faced a tough challenge in the primaries from Senator Robert F. Kennedy of New York and Senator Eugene McCarthy. Both McCarthy and Kennedy, the brother of the former president, had strong support from the antiwar movement. However, following Kennedy's assassination in June 1968, Humphrey was able to pull ahead in the primaries and secure the nomination. The Democratic Convention in Chicago was marked by demonstrations and protests outside the convention hall by antiwar activists and various student and New Left organizations who opposed Humphrey due to his affiliation with the current administration. Meanwhile, the Republicans nominated former Vice President Richard Nixon, who pledged to end the war and win the peace. Without offering any specifics, he stated he had a formula for success that would end the war but preserve America's strategic goals in Vietnam. The presence of third-party candidate George C. Wallace, segregationist candidate from Alabama, ensured a very close election. In the end, Richard Nixon edged out Humphrey to become the 37th president.

Shortly after coming into office, Nixon and his national security advisor, Henry Kissinger, unveiled their plan for extricating American troops from Vietnam. The plan, known as Vietnamization, involved slowly withdrawing U.S. combat soldiers from Vietnam, while at the same time building up the ARVN so that they could continue the war against the communists on their own. The policy fit well with General Abrams's new tactical approach, which utilized smaller unit action as opposed to Westmoreland's broad search and destroy missions. The problem with the strategy was that this was precisely what the United States had tried to do starting with President Eisenhower and continuing through the Kennedy and Johnson years. The reason U.S. troops were originally deployed in 1965 was because after years of U.S. training and financial and material support, the ARVN was totally ineffective and incapable of defending South Vietnam.

In late February 1969, the North Vietnamese launched another offensive. Three weeks of bitter fighting cost 1,100 American lives, and antiwar activists resumed their calls for peace. Discussions continued at the Paris Peace Talks, but with no real progress. The North Vietnamese continued to insist that there could be no peace until all U.S. troops had been completely withdrawn and the NLF allowed to participate in a new coalition government, something neither Nixon nor Thieu and Ky could accept. Throughout 1969, Vietnamization progressed as the ARVN assumed more responsibility for offensive operations and U.S. troops began to withdraw. By the end of the year, U.S. troop levels dropped to 475,200 people, but the fighting remained intense as another 9,415 Americans died in the war. After decades of American military assistance and training, ARVN troops showed very little improvement. As a result, the only way the United States could keep enemy troops from overrunning the country while they were pulling out was to increase aerial bombardment. Tactical and strategic airstrikes by B-52 bombers increased dramatically as the Nixon administration relaxed targeting constraints. In the spring and summer of 1969, the president authorized the secret bombing of Cambodia and Laos in order to take out VC supply dumps and staging areas just over the border. Although the administration denied reports, the press learned of the bombing raids. The news stories breathed new life into the antiwar campaign as many protesters saw this action as an expansion of the war. Across the country mass demonstrations followed, and on November 15, 1969, 500,000 people marched in Washington, D.C., marking the largest demonstration in U.S. history.

The passing of Ho Chi Minh in early September 1969 had little impact on the war. The collective leadership in Hanoi vowed to continue fighting until all Americans left from Indochina. Nixon gradually withdrew U.S. troops down to about 24,000 troops in-country by the time he was reelected in November 1972. Negotiations dragged on in Paris until the signing of the peace agreement on January 27, 1973. According to the terms of the Paris Peace Accords, the communists were permitted to retain control of large sections of South Vietnam, and the Saigon regime had to recognize the Provisional Revolutionary Government (PRG), which had superseded the NLF in the summer of 1969. North Vietnam agreed to release all U.S. prisoners of war within 60 days, at which time the United States would then remove all of its remaining troops from South Vietnam. Unhappy with the terms of the agreement, President Thieu nonetheless signed off on the treaty after Nixon reassured him that the United States would continue to support his government. That proved to be an empty promise. Within a year and a half, Nixon was out of office, a victim of the Watergate scandal, and his successor, Gerald Ford, was constrained by Congress and a weary American public. By the time North Vietnam invaded the south in December 1974, U.S. domestic and political support for Saigon had completely evaporated. The ARVN quickly retreated, and within four months, the nation collapsed. On April 30, 1975, South Vietnam officially ceased to exist, and the Vietnam War finally came to end.

See also 17th Parallel; Antiwar Movement, United States; Ball, George Wildman (1909–1994); Bundy Brothers: McGeorge Bundy (1919–1996) and William Bundy (1917–2000); Calley, Lt. William L. Jr. (1943–); Civil Disobedience; Clifford, Clark (1960–1998); Democratic Party (1960–1969); Diem, Ngo Dinh (1901–1963); Fulbright, James William (1905–1995); Giap, Vo Nguyen (1911–); Goldwater, Barry (1909–1998); Humphrey, Hubert (1911–1978); Johnson, Lyndon Baines (1908–1973); Kennedy, John F. (1917–1963); Kennedy, Robert F. (1925–1968); Ky, Nguyen Cao (1930–2011); McCarthy, Eugene Joseph (1916–2005); Minh, Ho Chi (1890–1969); My Lai (1968); Napalm; Nixon, Richard Milhous (1913–1994); Operation Rolling Thunder (1965–1968); Paris Peace Talks (1968–1973); Pleiku; Presidential Election of 1964; Presidential Election of 1968; Republican Party (1960–1969); Rostow, Walt Whitman (1916–2003); Rusk, Dean (1909–1994); Student Nonviolent Coordinating Committee (SNCC); Students for a Democratic Society (SDS); Taylor, Maxwell (1901–1987); Tet Offensive (1968); Thieu, Nguyen Van (1924–2001); Viet Cong; Viet Minh; Vietnamization.

Bibliography

Anderson, David L., ed. *Shadow on the White House: Presidents and the Vietnam War, 1945–1975.* Lawrence: University Press of Kansas, 1993.

Belknap, Michal R. *The Vietnam War on Trial: The My Lai Massacre and the Court-Martial of Lieutenant Calley.* Lawrence: University Press of Kansas, 2002.

Blackburn, Robert M. *Mercenaries and Lyndon Johnson's "More Flags": The Hiring of Korean, Filipino and Thai Soldiers in the Vietnam War.* Jefferson, NC: McFarland, 1994.

Bradley, Mark Philip. *Vietnam at War.* Oxford: Oxford University Press, 2009.

Bradley, Mark Philip and Marilyn B. Young, eds. *Making Sense of the Vietnam Wars: Local, National and Transnational Perspectives.* Oxford: Oxford University Press, 2008.

Buzzanco, Robert. *Masters of War: Military Dissent and Politics in the Vietnam Era.* Cambridge: Cambridge University Press, 1996.

Buzzanco, Robert. *Vietnam and the Transformation of American Life.* Malden, MA: Blackwell, 1999.

Carter, James M. *Inventing Vietnam: The United States and State Building, 1954–1968.* Cambridge: Cambridge University Press, 2008.

Clarke, Jeffrey J. *Advice and Support: The Final Years—The United States Army in Vietnam.* Washington, DC: Center of Military History, United States Army, 1988.

Duiker, William J. *U.S. Containment Policy and the Conflict in Indochina.* Stanford, CA: Stanford University Press, 1994.

Elliot, David. *The Vietnamese War: Revolution and Social Change in the Mekong Delta, 1930–1975.* Armonk, NY: M. E. Sharpe, 2003.

Ellsberg, Daniel. *Secrets: A Memoir of Vietnam and the Pentagon Papers.* New York: Viking, 2002.

Gardner, Lloyd C. *Approaching Vietnam: From World War II Through Dienbienphu.* New York: W. W. Norton, 1988.

Gardner, Lloyd C. *Pay Any Price: Lyndon Johnson and the Wars for Vietnam.* Chicago: I. R. Dee, 1995.

Gibbons, William Conrad. *The U.S. Government and the Vietnam War: Executive and Legislative Roles and Relationships, Part III: January–July 1965.* Princeton, NJ: Princeton University Press, 1986.

Gibbons, William Conrad. *The U.S. Government and the Vietnam War: Executive and Legislative Roles and Relationships, Part II: 1961–1964.* Princeton, NJ: Princeton University Press, 1986.

Gibbons, William Conrad. *The U.S. Government and the Vietnam War: Executive and Legislative Roles and Relationships, Part I: 1945–1960.* Princeton, NJ: Princeton University Press, 1986.

Halberstam, David. *The Best and the Brightest.* New York: Random House, 1972.

Herring, George C. *America's Longest War: The United States and Vietnam, 1950–1975.* 2nd ed. New York: Alfred A. Knopf, 1986.

Herring, George C. *LBJ and Vietnam: A Different Kind of War.* Austin: University of Texas Press, 1994.

Hunt, Michael H. *Lyndon Johnson's War: America's Cold War Crusade in Vietnam: 1945–1968.* New York: Hill and Wang, 1996.

Joint Chiefs of Staff. Historical Division, Joint Secretariat. *The History of the Joint Chiefs of Staff, The Joint Chiefs of Staff and the War in Vietnam: 1960–1968, Part I & II.* Washington, DC: July 1970.

Kahin, George McT. *Intervention, How America Became Involved in Vietnam.* New York: Alfred A. Knopf, 1986.

Kaiser, David. *American Tragedy: Kennedy, Johnson, and the Origins of the Vietnam War.* Cambridge, MA: Harvard University Press, 2000.

Karnow, Stanley. *Vietnam: A History.* New York: Viking, 1983.

Kolko, Gabriel. *Anatomy of a War: Vietnam, the United States, and the Modern Historical Experience.* New York: Pantheon, 1985.

Krepinevich, Andrew F. *The Army in Vietnam.* Baltimore: Johns Hopkins University Press, 1986.

LaFeber, Walter. *The Deadly Bet: LBJ, Vietnam, and the 1968 Election.* Lanham, MD: Rowman & Littlefield, 2005.

Lawrence, Mark Atwood. *The Vietnam War: A Concise International History*. New York: Oxford University Press, 2008.

Lomperis, Timothy J. *From People's War to People's Rule: Insurgency, Intervention, and the Lessons of Vietnam*. Chapel Hill: University of North Carolina Press, 1996.

McMaster, H. R. *Dereliction of Duty: Lyndon Johnson, Robert McNamara, the Joint Chiefs of Staff, and the Lies That Led to Vietnam*. New York: HarperCollins, 1997.

McNamara, Robert S. *In Retrospect: The Tragedy and Lesson of Vietnam*. New York: Times Books, 1995.

Military History Institute of Vietnam. *Victory in Vietnam: The Official History of the People's Army of Vietnam, 1954–1975*. Lawrence: University Press of Kansas, 2002.

Moise, Edwin E. *Tonkin Gulf and the Escalation of the Vietnam War*. Chapel Hill: University of North Carolina Press, 1996.

Moyar, Mark. *Triumph Forsaken: The Vietnam War, 1954–1965*. New York: Cambridge University Press, 2006.

Nagl, John A. *Learning to Eat Soup with a Knife: Counterinsurgency Lessons from Malaya and Vietnam*. Chicago: University of Chicago Press, 2002.

Olson, James S., and Randy Roberts. *Where the Domino Fell: America and Vietnam, 1945–1990*. New York: St. Martin's, 1991.

Palmer, Bruce Jr. *The 25-Year War: America's Military Role in Vietnam*. New York: Simon & Schuster, 1984.

Prados, John. *The Hidden History of the Vietnam War*. Chicago: Ivan R. Dee, 1995.

Prados, John. *Vietnam: The History of an Unwinnable War, 1945–1975*. Lawrence: University Press of Kansas, 2009.

Rotter, Andrew J. *The Path to Vietnam: Origins of the American Commitment to Southeast Asia*. Ithaca, NY: Cornell University Press, 1987.

Rusk, Dean, and Richard Rusk. *As I Saw It*. New York: W.W. Norton, 1991.

Schandler, Herbert Y. *America in Vietnam: The War That Couldn't Be Won*. Lanham, MD: Rowman & Littlefield, 2009.

Sheehan, Neil. *A Bright Shining Lie: John Paul Vann and America in Vietnam*. New York: Random House, 1988.

Sigler, David B. *Vietnam Battle Chronology: U.S. Army and Marine Corps Combat Operations, 1965–1973*. Jefferson, NC: McFarland, 1992.

Spector, Ronald H. *Advice and Support: The Early Years of the United States Army in Vietnam 1941–1960*. New York: Free Press, 1985.

Stanton, Shelby. *The Rise and Fall of an American Army: U.S. Ground Forces in Vietnam, 1965–1973*. Novato, CA: Presidio, 1985.

Stanton, Shelby. *Vietnam Order of Battle*. New York: Galahad Books, 1986.

Tucker, Spencer. *Vietnam*. Lexington: University Press of Kentucky, 1999.

U.S. Department of Defense. *Pentagon Papers: The Defense Department History of United States Decision-Making on Vietnam, the Senator Gravel ed.* Vols. 1–5, Boston: Beacon Press, 1971.

VanDeMark, Brian. *Into the Quagmire: Lyndon Johnson and the Escalation of the Vietnam War*. New York: Oxford University Press, 1991.

Wirtz, James J. *The Tet Offensive: Intelligence Failure in War*. Ithaca, NY: Cornell University Press, 1991.

Young, Marilyn B. *The Vietnam Wars, 1945–1990*. New York: HarperCollins, 1991.

CHRISTOS G. FRENTZOS

VIETNAMIZATION. By the time Richard Nixon ran as the Republican nominee for president in 1968, the U.S. commitment to fighting communism in Vietnam had grown far beyond the level of involvement that initial policy makers had envisioned.

Recognizing the failure to achieve a noncommunist victory and the growing public frustration with the war at home, Nixon promised that if elected he would pursue a policy that would ensure "peace with honor." To live up to his commitment, the president and his foreign policy team used a multifaceted approach to ending American involvement in Southeast Asia including the implementation of Vietnamization. As a major component of Nixon's exit strategy, the program provided for the de-Americanization of the war by providing better training to the South Vietnamese Army (the noncommunist forces) and by accelerating U.S. troop withdrawals.

The Americanization of the Vietnam War began in 1965, when President Lyndon B. Johnson concluded that without further U.S. assistance, South Vietnam would fall to communism. In the early 1960s, the noncommunist government in South Vietnam underwent a series of leadership changes and its control over the country was shaky at best. Meanwhile, the North Vietnamese-backed communist movement had stepped up efforts to topple the South Vietnamese government. Johnson expanded the air war in March, which in turn provided a justification for introducing 50,000 ground troops in July. U.S. leaders thought mistakenly that once their forces took on the communists directly, victory would be quick and easy. With over 500,000 troops in Vietnam by 1968, the United States had come no closer to defeating the communists or stabilizing the noncommunist government. Meanwhile, in the United States, public frustration with the war grew and protests were common.

In many ways, the presidential election in 1968 was a referendum on Lyndon Johnson's handling of the war. Since he chose not to run again, his vice president, Hubert Humphrey, eventually won the Democratic nomination. However, divisions within the party hurt Humphrey's chances for election in November. Thus, the American failure in Vietnam paved the way for Republican Richard Nixon to make a strong showing. During the campaign, he indicated that new leadership would end the war and win the peace. Then again, Nixon kept his statements vague about what policies he would enact to achieve those objectives. Once in office, Vietnamization became a way for him to pull out American forces and to appease public outrage with the war.

Richard Nixon began discussing the possibility of withdrawing troops with Henry Kissinger (his national security advisor) and Melvin Laird (the secretary of defense) early in his presidency. The Nixon team favored removing troops, so long as the military could do so in a way that did not suggest an American defeat. The major point of debate during a series of meetings in March 1969 was whether withdrawal would be one sided or the Americans expected the North Vietnamese to pull troops from the South as well. In April 1969, Nixon asked Kissinger to prepare a National Security Council study (NSSM 36) directing Laird to recommend a timetable for unilateral withdrawal. In the end, the administration did not set a fixed timetable. Instead, based on Laird's suggestion, the United States would withdrawal forces based on conditions in South Vietnam. The secretary of defense also advocated calling the program "Vietnamization" instead of de-Americanization. He hoped to put a positive spin on the decision to pull out troops regardless of the progress made during the ongoing peace negotiations with North Vietnam. Nixon and his advisors maintained that Vietnamization would help condition the South Vietnamese Army to fight without U.S. assistance. As that happened, the U.S. military could remove troops from Vietnam. Nixon announced the program on June 8, 1969, and the withdrawals began in August. The president then announced periodic reductions throughout the remainder of the war.

In 1971, Richard Nixon and his advisors decided to test the effectiveness of Vietnamization in order to justify continued troop withdrawals. In conjunction with South Vietnamese military leaders, the administration planned an attack against North Vietnamese supply lines along the Ho Chi Minh Trail in neighboring Laos. The operation had two goals. First, it would make a major dent in the North Vietnamese ability to wage war in the South. Second, it would demonstrate the ability of the South Vietnamese Army to carry out an offensive operation on its own. According to the plan of action, only South Vietnamese forces would cross into Laos. U.S. forces would remain in Vietnam to provide logistical support and air cover. When the Laotian invasion began in February, the South Vietnamese seemed to do well on their own. However, by March the North Vietnamese counterattack forced the South Vietnamese to scurry back across the border as quickly as possible. When Nixon addressed the nation in April about the operation, he made every effort to suggest that it had met both of its objectives. In spite of what the president said publicly, Vietnamization did not prepare the noncommunists for complete U.S. withdrawal.

In the end, Vietnamization did reduce the number of U.S. ground troops in Vietnam; gradually forces dropped from over 500,000 in August 1969 to just below 40,000 in August 1972. When Richard Nixon and his advisors decided to include Vietnamization in their efforts to end the war, they hoped troop removal would buy the president political capital with the American people. Given the rate of withdrawal, Nixon could in fact profess that his policy was ending U.S. involvement. At the same time, the South Vietnamese Army had clearly not gained the capability to defend itself or win a war against the north. Less than two years after the Paris Peace Accords of 1973 ended American involvement in Vietnam, North Vietnam overthrew the South Vietnamese government.

See also Nixon, Richard Milhous (1913–1994); Vietnam War.

Bibliography

Bundy, William. *A Tangled Web: The Making of Foreign Policy in the Nixon Years.* New York: Hill and Wang, 1998.

Herring, George. *America's Longest War: The United States and Vietnam, 1950–1975.* 3rd ed. New York: McGraw-Hill, 1996.

Kimball, Jeffrey. *Nixon's Vietnam War.* Lawrence: University Press of Kansas, 1998.

Kissinger, Henry A. *White House Years.* Boston: Little, Brown, 1979.

Nixon, Richard M. *RN: The Memoirs of Richard Nixon.* New York: Grosset and Dunlap, 1979.

Szulc, Tad. *The Illusion of Peace: Foreign Policy in the Nixon Years.* New York: Viking, 1978.

SARAH KATHERINE MERGEL

VOTING RIGHTS ACT OF 1965. President Lyndon B. Johnson signed the Voting Rights Act of 1965 into law on August 6, 1965. This act was designed to reiterate the Fifteenth Amendment, passed in 1870, which allowed all citizens of the United States the right to vote regardless of race, color, or previous condition of servitude. However, in the years following Reconstruction, Southerners had come up with a variety of methods to keep African Americans from voting, including the poll tax, Grandfather Clause, and literacy tests. The Voting Rights Act of 1965 outlawed literacy tests and poll taxes, which the government had ended in federal elections with the passage of the Twenty-fourth Amendment on January 23, 1964, but now were illegal in state and local elections as well. The act also provided the federal government with the power to send in inspectors to register people to vote in areas where African Americans were significantly underrepresented. The act also stated that regardless of race or color, all citizens of the United States had the right to vote.

The Voting Rights Act of 1965 was passed during the height of the civil rights movement. Though the Civil Rights Act of 1957, Civil Rights Act of 1960, Civil Rights Act of 1964, and the Twenty-fourth Amendment had all been passed, none was strong enough to overturn the Jim Crow laws in the South that had prevented African Americans from voting. In particular, the ineffectiveness of the Civil Rights Act of 1960, combined with 1964's Freedom Summer in Mississippi—which resulted in the deaths of four civil rights workers—and the attack by police on peaceful demonstrators in Selma, Alabama, convinced President Johnson that strong action had to be taken so that African Americans would have not only the right but the ability to vote.

Though some sections of the Voting Rights Act are permanent, such as making poll taxes and literacy tests illegal, other sections are more temporary and have come up for renewal in 1970, 1975, 1982, and 2006. On July 27, 2006, President George W Bush re-signed the Voting Rights Act into law for an additional 25 years, even though he faced tremendous criticism from southern states that claimed that they were being unjustly targeted. There is also criticism from those who say that ballots in languages other than English should not be offered because they discourage those living in the United States from learning English. Even with these criticisms, Congress overwhelming supported the re-signing of this bill, acknowledging that even though much had been accomplished, there was still more that could be done.

For African Americans living in the South, the Voting Rights Act of 1965 had an immediate impact. By the end of 1965, federal examiners had registered over 250,000 African Americans to vote. By the end of the following year, only 4 of 13 southern states had less than 50 percent of African Americans in their states registered to vote.

See also Civil Rights Act of 1960; Civil Rights Act of 1964; Freedom Rides.

Bibliography

Garrow, David. *Protest at Selma: Martin Luther King Jr. and the Voting Rights Act of 1965.* New Haven, CT: Yale University Press, 1980.

Our Documents. "Our Documents—Voting Rights Act of 1965." Available at http://www .ourdocuments.gov/doc.php?flash=old&doc=100 (accessed January 11, 2010).

U.S. News and World Report. "The People's Vote: Voting Rights Act (1965)." Available at http://www.usnews.com/usnews/documents/docpages/document_page100.htm (accessed January 11, 2010).

ELIZABETH BRYANT MORGENSTERN

VREELAND, DIANA (1906–1989). Diana Vreeland was a fashion editor, writer, and columnist. As an arbiter of taste, her writing and sensibilities influenced American women's fashions for most of the twentieth century. First as an associate editor of *Harper's Bazaar*, and then as editor of *Vogue*, Vreeland's life's work culminated as a special consultant to the Costume Institute at the Metropolitan Museum of Art in New York City.

Born on July 29, 1906, to Frederick Y. Dalzeil and Emily Key Hoffman in Paris, France, Vreeland grew up in opulence and regularly traveled between European countries. Her early experiences in Paris helped her cultivate an eye for personal style and fashion. Her family relocated to the United States because of World War I in 1914. A Manhattan adolescence immersed her in the world of private schools, equestrian and ballet lessons, and exclusive events, all which cultivated her proclivity for audacity.

Vreeland honed her eye and helped guide *Harper's Bazaar*, where she had started as a freelance columnist. After 26 years at that magazine, Vreeland left in 1962 for an associate editor position of *Vogue*, which offered a very large salary and generous expense account as well as regular trips to Paris. She applied her decades of experience in the industry and her distinctive writing style—known for its wit, whimsy, and wicked qualities—to *Vogue*, where she advanced to editor within two years.

She immediately steered *Vogue* away from its focus on haute couture and expanded its scope to embrace the pop art and youth-inspired fashions of the decade. Several trends associated with the decade were pet projects of Vreeland's: costume jewelry, boots, peasant blouses, thong sandals, and pants for women. Likewise, Vreeland sought out inventive photographers with whom she collaborated by creating an untried tone and style for layouts for *Vogue* rather than continue with the elaborately staged backdrops associated with the magazine. Her penchant for change expressed itself in the type of models she promoted within *Vogue*'s pages.

Vreeland favored unusual models like Lauren Hutton, whose gap-toothed smile was considered unappealing by traditional beauty standards. Similarly she brought Twiggy to the United States and introduced American women to Cher's arresting beauty. She featured Baby Jane Holzer, a blonde model of Jewish descent, despite being cautioned against it. *Vogue*'s circulation soared by 500,000 the first three years that she edited it because her vision for the magazine appealed to a wide audience.

During the 1960s, Vreeland's taste ruled the world of fashion journalism. She was the most influential woman of the decade in terms of style, taking credit for influencing Jacqueline Kennedy's redecoration of the White House as well as Kennedy's personal style. Her association with Andy Warhol and his Factory no doubt influenced her avant-garde choice of experimental photography and backdrops for fashion layouts. Her power and voice as a bellwether allowed her to push trends until they were accepted by popular culture. Vreeland influenced the direction of journalism for women's magazines by imposing her personal beliefs about fitness onto the pages of *Vogue*, which reflected her personality in the decade that she steered it.

Bibliography

Vreeland, Diana. *D. V.* New York: Alfred A. Knopf, 1984.

REBECCA TOLLEY-STOKES

W

WAR ON POVERTY. A major feature of President Lyndon B. Johnson's Great Society initiatives, the War on Poverty was a series of federal programs designed to combat the effects and solve the root causes of poverty in the United States. Michael Harrington's pathbreaking book *The Other America: Poverty in the United States* (1962) painted a devastating portrait of poverty in American cities and towns. Americans soon paid greater attention to the massive poverty then affecting nearly a fifth of the country's population—most unnoticed and ignored by the majority of Americans enjoying the affluence of Cold War economic prosperity. In Johnson's first state of the union address following the assassination of John F. Kennedy in November 1963, the president declared an unconditional War on Poverty in America.

The passage of the Economic Opportunity Act in 1964 facilitated the creation of hundreds of Community Action Agencies (also known as Community Action Programs, or CAP) to fight poverty in urban and rural communities throughout the United States. The most controversial aspect of the Economic Opportunity Act in the 1960s was the legal mandate for "maximum feasible participation" of the poor in solving the root causes of poverty and in establishing self-help poverty programs. War on poverty programs soon became a vehicle for civil rights activism, much to the consternation of both conservatives and local governments wishing to control how poverty programs were implemented. Nevertheless, through a series of bills and acts such as Head Start, food stamps, Volunteers in Service to America (VISTA), work study, Medicare and Medicaid, the War on Poverty's institutional legacy has endured into the twenty-first century despite chronic underfunding. By expanding the American welfare state and entitlement system, the War on Poverty reduced real rates of poverty, and hunger, and improved living standards and education for America's poorest citizens.

Four decades after the War on Poverty began, scholarly interpretations dismissing the federal effort as a failure have undergone significant revision. Recent studies have explored the intricate connections between Community Action Agencies and broader movements for cultural, economic, political, and gendered empowerment.

President Lyndon B. Johnson and his wife, Claudia Alta "Lady Bird," leaving the Inez, Kentucky, home of Tom Fletcher, a father of eight who had been unemployed for nearly two years when the Johnsons visited on April 24, 1964. After touring the Appalachian area of eastern Kentucky, Johnson declared the nation's War on Poverty from the front porch of Fletcher's home. (AP/Wide World Photos)

The Great Society and War on Poverty by extension increased faith in liberal government at the federal level among America's racial minorities, especially considering that state and municipal governments were long the architects of Jim Crow–style racial discrimination. The grassroots aspect of the War on Poverty was however short-lived. By 1966, the program came under siege by conservatives, especially the idea of "maximum feasible participation" of the poor. This language itself, enshrined in the Economic Opportunity Act, became the "red herring" for opponents of federal programs for the poor.

Relationships between Community Action Agencies and city governments proved especially controversial, subject to partisan fights among Democrats, Republicans, and civil rights activists. Many local War on Poverty officials complained to Washington that so-called Marxists used CAP to promote class struggle. Republicans across the United States exploited deep-rooted, antiwelfare sentiments held by white citizens. Critics of the War on Poverty argued that the federal government subsidized nationalism, separatism, and antiwhite politics through funding antipoverty programs. Ignoring the structural inequalities caused by deindustrialization and capital flight, conservatives focused politically on the moral deficiencies of the poor as the root cause of poverty. Conservatives mobilized to preserve "law and order" in the public sphere, arguing that the War on Poverty rewarded bad behavior, evidenced by the fact that cities that experienced destructive riots received the largest antipoverty grants. To temper the political fallout and preserve the Democratic political coalition, Johnson attempted to neutralize

OEO. Johnson often clashed politically with OEO director Sargent Shriver as a result of political intrigue.

The War on Poverty began to falter by 1966, a casualty of fiscal expenditures on the Vietnam War, threatened inflation, economic disarray, and internal contradictions. The participation of the poor in Community Action Agencies weakened over time and was replaced by a more top-down governing style as the '60s came to a close. The election of Ronald Reagan to the California governor's office was a major boost and tool for the conservative right to dismantle and disrupt grassroots coalitions, first throughout California and later at the federal level when Richard Nixon won the presidency in 1968. Although the Community Action Program never drew more than 1.5 percent of the entire federal budgets between 1965 and 1970, the War on Poverty's significance to the political fortunes of both the political left and right proved far beyond its monetary cost.

See also Great Society, The; Johnson, Lyndon Baines (1908–1973).

Bibliography

Clayson, William S. *Freedom Is Not Enough: The War on Poverty and the Civil Rights Movement in Texas.* Austin: University of Texas Press, 2010.

Dallek, Robert. *Flawed Giant: Lyndon Johnson and His Times, 1961–1973.* New York: Oxford University Press, 1998.

Flamm, Michael. *Law and Order: Street Crime, Civil Unrest, and the Crisis of Liberalism in the 1960s.* New York: Columbia University Press, 2005.

Matusow, Allen. *The Unraveling of America: A History of Liberalism in the 1960s.* Athens: University of Georgia Press, 2009.

Orleck, Annelise. *Storming Caesar's Palace: How Black Mothers Fought Their Own War on Poverty.* Boston: Beacon Press, 2005.

Sugrue, Thomas J. *Sweet Land of Liberty: The Forgotten Struggle for Civil Rights in the North.* New York: Random House, 2009.

OLIVER A. ROSALES

WARHOL, ANDY (1928–1987). As the somewhat infamous figure at the heart of the 1960s New York art scene, Andy Warhol became one of the most iconic artists of the twentieth century. Installed as the figurehead of the pop art movement and overseer of avant-garde excess at his studio, the Factory, Warhol's world is an enduring reference point for contemporary visual culture.

Born in Pittsburgh on August 6, 1928, to a family of Czech immigrants, Andy Warhola was confined by frequent bouts of illness to his sickbed throughout much of his childhood. Having nonetheless demonstrated considerable artistic talent, Warhol attended the Carnegie Institute of Technology in Pittsburgh, graduating in 1948.

After shedding the last letter of his surname upon his 1948 relocation to New York, Warhol initially pursued freelance work for magazines. Yet, despite this mainstream commercial success, Warhol was attentive to the pop art movement associated with artists such as Jasper Johns. Inspired, he spectacularly announced his own "pop" intentions in 1962 with a series of paintings of Campbell soup cans. The outrage of critics riled by the apparent banality of his art helped establish Warhol as the media face of pop art; a position only bolstered by his now legendary silk-screen paintings of the recently deceased Marilyn Monroe and a grief-stricken Jackie Kennedy.

As pop art reworked American iconography in a gesture that merged the mundane and the magical, Warhol's image transformed accordingly. Always self-conscious of his appearance, his uniform of leather jacket, sunglasses, and silver wig made the artist as instantly recognizable as his artistic productions.

As Warhol turned to the medium of film in 1964, he rented a new studio, subsequently dubbed the Factory. Although Warhol worked in the studio by morning, at night the boy who had courted celebrity autographs from his sickbed became the heart of an almost continuous party enjoyed by an entourage of self-willed starlets, rock stars, models, and drag queens. While influential rock band the Velvet Underground forged a career independent from Warhol after sacking him as manager, Warhol gained a reputation for making—and subsequently breaking—a number of associates, including model Edie Sedgwick. As the media propagated an image of Warhol as a cold-hearted Svengali, the situation came to a shocking head after rejected acolyte Valerie Solanas shot Warhol in 1968.

Although this incident nearly killed Warhol, he seemed to have lost none of his taste for publicity following his recovery. While his attempt to launch a television show in 1978 may have somewhat stretched his credibility, he nonetheless remained a prominent force in the New York art scene. Not only was Warhol an early supporter of graffiti, but he was also mentor to the young Jean-Michel Basquiat, even if this relationship would come to a stormy end by 1985.

In February 1987, Warhol was admitted to hospital following a short period of ill health. Diagnosed with a gall bladder infection, he died alone on February 22, 1987, in the hospital following complications from an otherwise routine operation. Although his solitary death brought to a close a career shrouded in myth, rumor, and notoriety, Warhol remains one of the most prominent figures in the history of twentieth-century art.

See also Pop Art.

Bibliography

Bockris, Victor. *The Life and Death of Andy Warhol*. New York: Bantam, 1989.
Koestenbaum, Wayne. *Andy Warhol*. London: Weidenfeld and Nicolson, 2001.

ROSEMARY DELLER

WARREN COMMISSION (1962–1964). The assassination of President John F. Kennedy on November 22, 1963, in Dallas sparked confusion and controversy from the start. While the FBI was running a massive investigation and had arrested a suspect, Lee Harvey Oswald, the murder of Oswald on November 24 by nightclub owner Jack Ruby indicated a possible conspiracy. The next day, Texas attorney general Waggoner Carr announced that the state would conduct its own investigation, separate from that of the FBI. Because the Senate Judiciary Committee was also considering its own investigation, newly sworn-in President Lyndon Baines Johnson created the President's Commission on the Assassination of President Kennedy with Executive Order 11130 to forestall other inquiries and consolidate information.

The committee became popularly known as the Warren Commission after its head, Supreme Court Chief Justice Earl Warren. The other members of the commission included Senators John Sherman Cooper (R-KY), and Richard Russell (D-FA);

Congressmen Hale Boggs (D-LA) and Gerald R. Ford (R-MI), as well as World Bank president John J. McCloy and former CIA chief Allen Dulles. The commission also included over two dozen additional lawyers and investigators. Johnson wanted to have the commission's report by the end of June to avoid the election and campaigning season of November. But in fact, the report, weighing in at 888 pages, appeared September 24, 1964.

The Warren Commission had parsed the 25,000-page report submitted by the FBI. It also interviewed 554 assassination witnesses, 94 of whom testified before the Commission itself. It was somewhat hampered in its investigation, however, by the short timetable mandated by President Johnson, as well as the withholding of evidence and information by the CIA and FBI. The commission was also unable to obtain the autopsy photos and X-rays from the Kennedy family. Nevertheless, the commission concluded that Oswald had acted alone, as had Jack Ruby in the murder of Oswald. They also posited the now-famous "single bullet theory," which held that of the three shots Oswald had time to fire from the sixth floor of the Texas Book Depository (in the five seconds of the crime's timeline), a single bullet had passed through Kennedy's neck and into the body of Texas governor John Connally, traveling through his back and into his thigh. An additional bullet struck Kennedy in the head. The third bullet struck the windshield. Moreover, the commission stated unequivocally that no conspiracy was involved in the assassination. The commission followed up its initial report with 26 volumes of material. Its papers were transferred to the National Archives and sealed for 75 years, until the Freedom of Information Act made most of the commission's documents available to public scrutiny.

Criticism of the Warren Report began almost immediately upon its publication in 1964, and a network of assassination buffs rose up, determined to conduct their own investigations and root out the conspiracy to which many believed the evidence clearly pointed. The most conspicuous of these investigators was New Orleans district attorney Jim Garrison, who dedicated the rest of his life to unearthing conspirators in the assassination, even going so far as to charge Louisiana businessman Clay Shaw in 1967—Shaw was acquitted in 1969.

The assassination was officially investigated again three times: in 1968, the Clark Commission backed up the Warren findings as to the autopsy and direction of bullets; in 1975, the Rockefeller Commission concurred; and in 1978, the House Select Committee on Assassinations (reviewing both the JFK and Martin Luther King assassinations) determined that while Oswald was the lone shooter, he had indeed been involved in a conspiracy to kill the president. The committee then reversed itself and concluded there was a second gunman, based on acoustic evidence later deemed suspect.

President Gerald R. Ford, the last remaining member of the Warren Commission, passed away on December 26, 2006. The findings of the Warren Commission continue to generate controversy, and interest in both the assassination of President Kennedy and in the investigation have not waned. The Warren Commission has entered posterity simultaneously as (1) a body of wise and thorough men, and (2) a group that allowed itself to be cowed by the FBI and the CIA, effectively rubber-stamping an official version of events that, while designed to let the nation heal, instead created even more doubt. The truth lies somewhere in between.

See also Kennedy, John F. (1917–1963); Oswald, Lee Harvey (1939–1963); Ruby, Jack (1911–1967); Single Bullet Theory.

Bibliography

Epstein, Edward Jay. *Inquest: The Warren Commission and the Establishment of Truth.* New York: Viking, 1966.

McAdams, John. *JFK Assassination Logic: How to Think About Claims of Conspiracy.* Washington, DC: Potomac Books, Inc., 2011.

McKnight, Gerald D. *Breach of Trust: How the Warren Commission Failed the Nation and Why.* Lawrence: University Press of Kansas, 2005.

Meagher, Sylvia. *Accessories After the Fact: The Warren Commission, the Authorities, and the Report.* New York: Vintage, 1992.

Posner, Gerald. *Case Closed: Lee Harvey Oswald and the Assassination of JFK.* New York: Doubleday, 1993.

Report of the President's Commission on the Assassination of President Kennedy. Available at http://www.archives.gov/research/jfk/warren-commission-report/.

ELIZABETH DEMERS

WATTS RIOTS (1965). The Watts Riots began on the evening of Wednesday, August 11, 1965, and lasted for six days in the Watts section of Los Angeles, California. An estimated 10,000 African Americans surged through the streets, setting fires, looting stores, shouting epithets, and attacking innocent people who got in the way. Over 1,000 people were injured, 34 fatally. Nearly 1,000 businesses and private buildings were damaged, burned, or looted; of these, 207 were completely destroyed.

The incident that sparked the riot occurred when a motorist hailed California Highway Patrolman Lee Minikus on motorcycle to let him know of an automobile being driven recklessly. Officer Minikus then sped after the car and overtook the alleged offender and motioned the driver to the curb. Residents seeking relief from the heat on their porches and lawns watched the commotion with interest. The driver of the car was an African American, Marquette Frye, 21.

When Frye failed the sobriety test, Minikus informed him that he was under arrest on a charge of drunk driving. By the time Frye was placed in a police car for transport to jail, a crowd of nearly 300 persons was clamoring for vantage points to see what was happening.

Officers were beginning to leave the arrest site when someone in the assembled crowd spat on one of them. This led to highway patrolmen arresting two blacks who were witnessing the scene: a young woman suspected of having spat on the officer and a man the officers believed was inciting the crowd to violence as they took the woman into custody.

Rumors began to fly regarding the incidents of that evening. There were reports that Frye was beaten once inside the patrol car. There were reports that the young woman arrested was pregnant and that the officers had handled her roughly. Whether true or not, these rumors were the basis for the subsequent early violence in the Watts Riots that occurred later that evening.

The ugliest portion of the rioting lasted from Thursday, August 12, through Saturday, August 14. During this period the disorder spread to adjoining areas, and ultimately an area covering 46.5 square miles had to be controlled with the aid of military authority before public order was restored.

In retrospect, a number of factors were suggested as possible reasons for the violence: (1) lack of jobs; (2) lack of skilled training for area residents; (3) a resentment of the local police; (4) the failure of the federal antipoverty program to live up its advance billing; (5) a willingness of locals to be influenced by well-publicized episodes of urban violence elsewhere in the country; and (6) dismay over a Fair Housing Act in the city that had recently been repealed.

See also McCone, John Alexander (1902–1991).

Bibliography

Abu-Lughod, Janet. *Race, Space, and Riots in Chicago, New York, and Los Angeles.* Oxford: Oxford University Press, 2007.

Crump, Spencer. *Black Riot in Los Angeles; The Story of the Watts Tragedy.* Los Angeles: Trans-Anglo Books, 1966.

STAN C. WEEBER

WAYNE, JOHN (1907–1979). John Wayne, born Marion Morrison on May 26, 1907, in Winterset, Iowa, was an American screen actor who played in Westerns and military films. Known as Duke, Morrison grew up in Glendale, California. He attended the University of Southern California for two years on a football scholarship. After losing the scholarship, he worked for Fox Studio as a prop man and extra.

Fox director Raoul Walsh, who had noticed Morrison's height and good looks, cast him in the leading role for *The Big Trail* (1930), billing him as John Wayne. The film was intended to be an epic of the West, but it flopped. Wayne spent the rest of the decade playing in B-movies, mostly Westerns. His major break came when John Ford cast him as the Ringo Kid in *Stagecoach* (1939), a box-office success that became a classic Western. Wayne made his best pictures under Ford's direction, most notably the cavalry trilogy of *Fort Apache* (1948), *She Wore a Yellow Ribbon* (1949), and *Rio Grande* (1950). Wayne also made many commercially successful, if less artistic, pictures with director Howard Hawks, and he produced films with his own company named Batjac.

In the late 1940s and 1950s, Wayne was one of Hollywood's leading men, and he remained widely popular through the 1960s as well. Wayne turned in remarkable performances in the Cavalry trilogy, *The Searchers* (1956), *The Man Who Shot Liberty Valence* (1962), and *True Grit* (1969). In most of his over 150 films, though, he was not a great actor. But Wayne was a star. His screen persona captured audiences as the essence of the American hero. He typically played two characters. One was the western hero. Wearing a cavalry bib shirt, vest, boots, stetson, and, of course, a gun belt, Wayne played cowboys and cattle barons, lawmen and hired guns, but never the scoundrel. (Ironically, though, his strongest roles were those that came closest to being antiheroes, such as Ethan Edwards in *The Searchers*.) Wayne's second character, which was virtually a reprisal of the first, was the military leader in films like *The Sands of Iwo Jima* (1949) and *The Longest Day* (1962). As any character, Wayne was a believable hero, one who might have a shady past but who invariably fought for right. Wayne was a success not because he delivered great performances in any particular roles, but because he played the same role in all of his films: the role of John Wayne.

Wayne threw his weight as American icon on the side of political conservatism. Wayne strongly opposed communism, so he turned down the leading role in *High Noon* (1952) on the grounds that the film opposed blacklisting and McCarthyism. He later called the film "the most un-American thing I've ever seen." Wayne strongly supported the Vietnam War, though he never served in the military himself. In *The Green Berets* (1968), a film produced by Batjac and directed by Wayne himself, Wayne played a Special Forces colonel. His character fights the Viet Cong with courage and humanity, rescues a Vietnamese orphan, and walks off-screen into the sunset in a film that is a Western set in Vietnam. Wayne's cop films *McQ* (1974) and *Brannigan* (1975) were both an attempt to capitalize on the success of Clint Eastwood's *Dirty Harry* pictures and to counter their message that government was corrupt.

Though aging, Wayne maintained his role as symbol of America to the end of his career. In his final film, *The Shootist* (1976), Wayne played a retired gunfighter dying of cancer, the disease from which he died on June 11, 1979.

See also True Grit (1969).

Bibliography

Levy, Emanuel. *John Wayne: Prophet of the American Way of Life*. Metuchen, NJ: Scarecrow, 1988.
Roberts, Randy, and James Stuart Olson. *John Wayne: American*. New York: Free Press, 1995.
Wills, Garry. *John Wayne's America: The Politics of Celebrity*. New York: Simon & Schuster, 1997.

LINCOLN MULLEN

WEST SIDE STORY (1957–1961). Having made its Broadway debut in 1957, *West Side Story's* translation to the big screen was a worldwide success and winner of 10 Oscars in 1962. Its combination of striking choreography and social commentary made the musical a mammoth '60s hit.

West Side Story was initially conceived by director and choreographer Jerome Robbins in 1948. His wish to create a musical version of *Romeo and Juliet* led Robbins to transport this most quintessential of tragic love stories to a contemporary setting. Set in a New York slum, the film's central conflict concerned love across the borders of warring Polish American and Puerto Rican gangs, the Jets and the Sharks respectively. With the esteemed Leonard Bernstein writing the music and a young Stephen Sondheim providing lyrics, *West Side Story* hit Broadway at the tail-end of the classic decade of musical theatre in 1957.

The thwarted romance between a Polish American Romeo, Tony, and Puerto-Rican Juliet, Maria, enjoyed success on the stage, in part due to its choreography and blend of musical styles. However, while this vibrant mix of music, story, and dance was considered to have tested musical theatre to its limits, it was the move to the big screen in 1961 that secured *West Side Story's* iconic status. Although most of the original choreography was retained for the adaptation, its production took a number of creative risks. Despite Robbins being originally hired to direct the film, United Artists demanded that Robert Wise replace him at the helm. Wise's casting is to this day believed to represent the film's weakest element; not only did he pick a trio of unknowns for the three male leads, but the decision to cast Natalie Wood in the role of Maria was also criticized due to her weak voice, which famously required dubbing. In addition, studio executives remained unconvinced of the show's commercial appeal, particularly for the worldwide market.

These gambles nonetheless paid off as *West Side Story* became a notable popular and critical success. Although it was believed that a musical could never secure true

Rita Moreno plays Anita in a scene from United Artists' *West Side Story*, 1961. Moreno was one of the most recognized entertainers of all time and the only performer ever to win at least one Emmy, Oscar, Tony, Golden Globe, and Grammy. (AP/Wide World Photos)

international popularity—particularly one with a running time of over two-and-a-half hours—the musical was a worldwide hit at the box office and was awarded 10 Oscars in 1962, including Best Picture, making it the most successful musical in the history of the Academy Awards. Its success can partly be attributed to its contemporary resonance; while the film concerns interracial conflict among urban youth, the characters revolt as much against the authority of the adult world as against each other, enabling *West Side Story* to capture the mood of a generation. That Robert Wise's numerous risks paid off would furthermore mark *West Side Story* as a prime exemplar of the growing authority afforded to Hollywood directors.

Combining musical and choreographical panache with pertinent social commentary, the 1961 film adaptation of *West Side Story* is a stunning example of '60s cinema that remains popular with both the viewing public and critics alike.

Bibliography

Citron, Stephen. *Sondheim and Lloyd Webber: The New Musical.* New York: Oxford University Press, 2001.
Monaco, Paul. *History of the American Cinema, Vol. 8, 1960–69.* Berkeley: University of California Press, 2001.

ROSEMARY DELLER

WHITE CITIZENS' COUNCILS. Amidst the racial turbulence that transpired within the U.S. South during the 1950s and 1960s emerged White Citizens' Councils (later christened Citizens' Councils of America and forerunner to the modern Council of Conservative Citizens). These racist, grassroots-based organization chapters were established in states such as Mississippi, Alabama, Tennessee, and Texas to express opposition to school desegregation and interracial marriage, to maintain racial segregation between whites and blacks under Jim Crow laws, and to preserve the "Southern way of life." Although not nearly as well known or as visible as the Ku Klux Klan, the White Citizens' Councils were arguably far more socially and politically influential than their hooded counterparts due to the fact that they often attracted members from relatively higher educational and socioeconomic backgrounds, such as doctors, attorneys, clergymen, and businessmen.

The first White Citizens' Council was established by Robert Patterson in Indianola, Mississippi on July 11, 1954, less than two months after the U.S. Supreme Court's ruling in the landmark *Brown v. Board of Education* case that struck down racial segregation in public schools. Nevertheless, the White Citizens' Council's political and economic clout proved partially responsible for the prevention of any major public school integration in the state of Mississippi within the first decade after the Court's ruling. From its Indianola origins, additional chapters of the White Citizens' Councils cropped up exponentially in other parts of Mississippi and in other southern states. By 1955, more than 250 councils had been established, with a total membership that exceeded 60 thousand.

Although White Citizens' Councils officially disavowed violent tactics, the use of violence among its members was not unheard of. Byron De La Beckwith, a Ku Klux Klansman and one of the founding members of Mississippi's White Citizens' Council, was eventually charged and convicted with the murder of Medgar Evers, NAACP field secretary, during the early morning of June 12, 1963, in Jackson, Mississippi. The councils' nonviolent tactics included using its published literature to proclaim the alleged mental and moral inferiority of blacks and to advocate the maintenance of antimiscegenation laws. The White Citizens' Councils also endorsed Arizona Republican senator Barry Goldwater's unsuccessful campaign against incumbent President Lyndon B. Johnson in the 1964 election.

The Rev. Dr. Martin Luther King Jr. and his supporters encountered fierce resistance from White Citizens' Councils during the late 1950s and the 1960s. For example, throughout the 1960s, These councils collaborated with the far right-wing John Birch Society, an anticommunist organization, to lobby for a federal investigation of King and other civil rights activists, under the allegation that these activists were either communists themselves or had ties to the Communist Party. King himself expressed concern that the relentless efforts of these councils would undermine his attempts to attract the support of open-minded whites to his civil rights cause. As early as 1956, King had declared of White Citizens' Councils, "They must be held responsible for all of the terror, the mob rule, and brutal murders that have encompassed the South over the last several years."

See also Evers, Medgar (1925–1963); King, Martin Luther, Jr. (1929–1968).

Bibliography

Anti-Defamation League. "Council of Conservative Citizens." Available at http://www.adl .org/learn/ext_us/CCCitizens.asp (accessed July 3, 2010).

Dobratz, Betty A., and Stephanie L. Shanks-Meile. *The White Separatist Movement in the United States Today.* Baltimore: Johns Hopkins University Press, 2000.

Southern Poverty Law Center. "Council of Conservative Citizens." Available at http://www .splcenter.org/get-informed/intelligence-files/groups/council-of-conservative-citizens (accessed July 3, 2010).

Zeskin, Leonard. *Blood and Politics: The History of the White Nationalist Movement from the Margins to the Mainstream.* New York: Farrar, Straus, and Giroux, 2009.

JUSTIN D. GARCIA

WHO, THE (1964–1978). The Who was one of the most popular and successful British rock bands of the 1960s. The band's lineup included lead singer Roger Daltrey, guitarist and principal songwriter Pete Townshend, bass guitarist John Entwistle, and drummer Keith Moon. The band enjoyed its greatest success from the mid-1960s to the late 1970s, although surviving members were still performing in 2011.

In 1959, Townshend and Entwistle began playing together in a variety of bands in London. Later, Daltrey invited them to join his band the Detours. In 1964, the band adopted the name the Who (although they briefly changed it to the High Numbers), and Keith Moon joined the group. Soon, the Who became the focal point of Britain's mod youth subculture. The band also developed a reputation as being loud, energetic, and nonconformist, contributing to its rising popularity. The Who also drew on the visual aspects of pop art to complement their music, as seen in their smashing of instruments at the end of shows and Townshend's jackets made from the Union Jack.

In 1965, the Who released three successful singles that helped establish it as one of Britain's key rock groups, along with the Beatles and the Rolling Stones. "I Can't Explain" and "Anyway, Anyhow, Anywhere" both became top ten hits in Britain. In October, they released "My Generation," which became one of the band's signature songs, as it appealed to the rebellious nature of the youth of the 1960s.

After releasing the top five hit single "Substitute" in early 1966, legal troubles with its record company prevented the band from recording for much of the year. Nevertheless, numerous live shows maintained the group's popularity and finances. At the same time, personality clashes sometimes threatened to break up the Who. Also, unlike the Beatles and the Rolling Stones, the Who had yet to gain a following in the United States.

In 1967, the band made several trips to the United States. In June, a performance at the Monterey International Pop Festival finally established the Who as major presence in the United States. Later that year, the single "I Can See for Miles" reached number nine on the *Billboard* charts, the highest the band would ever achieve in the United States.

In 1969, the Who released the album *Tommy*, a so-called rock opera. Developed by Townshend, the album traces the path of a deaf, dumb, and blind boy named Tommy on his quest for spiritual enlightenment. The album was well received, especially in the United States, where it garnered the Who its first gold record in that country. The live performance of *Tommy* was also a resounding success, including shows at Woodstock and a tour of European opera houses. Later, in 1975, a film version of *Tommy* contributed to its continued importance.

The Who continued to enjoy success beyond the 1960s. Indeed, by 1970, many critics and fans called the Who the greatest rock-and-roll band in the world. One of the quintessential hard rock acts of the 1970s, they produced such classic rock hits as "Baba O'Riley" and "Won't Get Fooled Again."

The original band came to an end in 1978 when Keith Moon died from an overdose of medication he took for alcoholism. The surviving members decided to continue, hiring new drummer Kenny Jones. The band produced two more studio albums after Moon's death and has toured on and off since then. Entwistle died in 2002, with Daltrey and Townshend continuing to perform as the Who, including a well-publicized performance at the halftime show of the 2010 Super Bowl.

Bibliography

Barnes, Richard. *The Who: Maximum R&B*. London: Plexus, 2000.
Marsh, Dave. *Before I Get Old: The Story of the Who*. London: Plexus, 2003.
Neil, Andy. *Anyway, Anyhow, Anywhere: The Complete Chronicle of the Who, 1958–1978*. London: Virgin Books, 2007.

RONALD E. YOUNG JR.

WILD BUNCH, THE (1969). Directed and cowritten by iconoclast Sam Peckinpah, *The Wild Bunch* tells the tale of the passing of an era, and with it, the loss of meaning and identity for those who belonged to it. Set in 1913, on the eve of World War I, the film focuses on a gang of aging, world-worn outlaws, bound together by a code of honor and camaraderie. The gang, led by Pike Bishop (William Holden), has set its sights on one final job before they retire from outlaw life in a rapidly changing West that they no longer understand, where automobiles and machine guns are being introduced to a social landscape not yet ready to receive them. The film's extreme violence, unparalleled in the genre to that time, was further accentuated by its juxtaposition with a questioning of purpose so characteristic of the 1960s youth culture.

Unaware that the railroad has hired bounty hunters—led by Pike's nemesis, Pat Harrigan (Albert Dekker), and his former partner, Deke Thornton (Robert Ryan)—to ambush them, the gang boldly seizes the railroad office bank. As the action unfolds, the ensuing bloodbath fills the town's streets with human carnage, as outlaws, bounty hunters, and townspeople alike are torn apart by bullets, trampled, and left writhing in the streets. Only Pike and four of the gang survive: Dutch Engstrom (Ernest Borgnine), Angel (Jaime Sanchez), and brothers Lyle and Tector Gorch (Warren Oates and Ben Johnson), their comrades sacrificed, not for the cache of silver they sought but for a load of steel washers. Their failure underscores the increasing meaninglessness of the characters and life ways of the Old West in the face of progress.

The remainder of the film follows the outlaws as they make their escape to Mexico, still pursued by Deke and his posse, relocating the action in the war-torn aftermath of the Mexican Revolution. The gang enters into a complex and fragile alliance with the ruthless Federale, Mapache (Emilio Fernandez), whose troops have been victimizing the rural townspeople. Pike's deal with Mapache is doomed from the start, and the film's sense of desperation grows as the gang begins a series of heists, close-calls, double-crosses, and intrigues that ultimately achieve nothing but death for this gathering of icons of the West—Mapache and the Federales, the posse, and finally, the Wild Bunch themselves. The final suicidal showdown is as bloody and cataclysmic as its predecessor on the other side of the border, making it clear that the Old West will not vanish quietly.

The original release of *The Wild Bunch* was 144 minutes in length, but the film was cut and re-released almost immediately, this time running 134 minutes, to allow theaters greater screening flexibility. The deleted scenes contained much of the narrative background—including Pike's earlier life and his lingering guilt about the betrayal of his former compadre, Thornton—leaving the film vulnerable to critical condemnations for its seemingly senseless violence and disjointed plot. In 1995, the film was restored and re-released to critical acclaim.

Despite the controversy that surrounded it, *The Wild Bunch* was ranked in the American Film Institute's Top Ten Western Films. The film received two Academy Award nominations, while Peckinpah received a nomination for the Directors Guild of America Award for Outstanding Director, Feature Film. In 1999, *The Wild Bunch* was selected for inclusion in the National Film Registry of the Library of Congress, recognition reserved for films deemed "culturally, historically, and aesthetically significant."

Bibliography

Seydor, Paul. *Peckinpah: The Western Films—A Reconsideration*. Urbana and Chicago: University of Illinois Press, 1999.
Simmons, Garner. *Peckinpah: A Portrait in Montage*. New York: Limelight, 2004.

CYNTHIA J. MILLER

WOMEN'S INTERNATIONAL TERRORIST CONSPIRACY FROM HELL (WITCH).

The Women's International Terrorist Conspiracy from Hell (WITCH) was founded in 1969 after the dissolution of the New York Radical Women, a feminist group formed by Shulamith Firestone, the author of *The Dialectic of Sex* (1971). Other radical women's groups that appeared around this time include the Redstockings, BITCH, and SCUM (Society for Cutting Up Men). At a November 1968 conference on women's rights in Chicago, members of New York Radical Women split into three discussion groups. One of these groups held together and became the WITCH organization.

WITCH members represented a younger group of radical feminists who came to the women's movement out of their experiences in the civil rights and anti-Vietnam War movements. These women activists viewed sexism as the root of oppression after being influenced by the New Left's ideology of liberation and experiencing the realities of sex discrimination within these movements. They were thus encouraged to call for women's liberation. WITCH was anticapitalist and viewed American consumerist society, advertising, and the media as harmful to women. They disagreed with the tendency of other radical women's groups to vilify men as the sole enemy of women's liberation. Unlike the National Organization of Women (NOW), WITCH had no national association. Instead, its adherents derided bureaucratic, hierarchical structures. Robin Morgan, Florika, Peggy Dobbins, Judy Duffett, Cynthia Funk, and Naomi Jaffe were among the approximately 13 "heretical" women who comprised WITCH.

WITCH was action oriented and excelled at gaining media attention. Its members once dressed up as witches on Halloween and hexed the New York Stock Exchange from the trading floor. The market stumbled that day. On another occasion, WITCH stormed a Madison Square Garden bridal fair. Their members circulated among the flowers, decorations, and bridesmaid dresses and hexed the vendors as they advanced. WITCH members had a great deal of experience as university campus activists and knew how to manipulate the media with protests; however, as feminists they were often unable to get journalists to report seriously on their antics. WITCH survived until 1970, dissolving into and forming other radical feminist groups. Some of its members joined the Weather Underground, a radical arm of the Students for a Democratic Society (SDS).

Bibliography

Echols, Alice. *Daring to Be Bad: Radical Feminism in America, 1967–1975*. Minneapolis: University of Minnesota Press, 1989.

Rodnitzky, Jerome L. *Feminist Phoenix: The Rise and Fall of a Feminist Counterculture*. Westport, CT: Greenwood Publishing Group, 1999.

Siegel, Deborah. *Sisterhood, Interrupted: From Radical Women to Girls Gone Wild*. New York: Macmillan, 2007.

Tong, Rosemarie. *Feminist Thought: A More Comprehensive Introduction*. 3rd ed. New York: Westview Press, 2008.

CAROLINE E. KELLEY

WOODSTOCK (1969). Woodstock was the most famous rock festival of the twentieth century. Officially named the Woodstock Music & Art Fair: An Aquarian Exposition, it was held August 15–18, 1969 in Bethel, New York, with the slogan "Three Days of Peace and Music . . . An Aquarian Exposition." The three-day rock concert brought in 400,000 people and 34 bands. Other cities, such as Altamont, Atlanta, Denver, Miami, Newport, New Orleans, and Sky River, attempted to create the large crowds of Woodstock, but none came close to establishing the same mythology of Woodstock.

Rock and roll, because of its ability to reduce inhibitions as well as carry a distinct message, proved vitally important to the counterculture of the '60s. Youths of that generation craved different styles of rock, from folk rock, garage rock, and progressive rock, psychedelic rock, blues rock, and roots rock, and Woodstock offered them all. Rock and roll offered an inspiration and background music for other activities, such as doing recreational drugs and having sex. Besides the musicians, others tried to capitalize on the profitability of concerts by assembling multiple bands for a festival.

Woodstock began as a commercial endeavor. The four producers, Michael Lang, John Roberts, Joel Rosenman, and Artie Kornfeld, found an appropriate location at Max Yasgur's thousand-acre dairy farm in Bethel, south of Woodstock, New York. In anticipation of 200,000 people (although they reassured the Bethel authorities no more than 50,000 would show), they offered Yasgur $50,000 to use his land, hoping local musicians like Bob Dylan would agree to perform. Creedence Clearwater Revival was the first to sign a contract for $10,000, reassuring other big acts to participate. The producers charged $18 per advance ticket that allowed entrance for three days and planned to sell tickets at the gate for $24 each; 186,000 tickets were sold before the festival.

However, due to fence inadequacies and many more people than anticipated, they decided to cut the fences the night before the concert to allow free entry to the festival. Unprecedented numbers streamed into the area, clogging roads for miles and

Brashler, William. *The Don: The Life and Death of Sam Giancana.* New York: Harper & Row, 1977. This biography details the life and times of Chicago's well-known mobster and chronicles the city's criminal history.

Brauch, Hans, and Rip Bulkeley. *The Anti-Ballistic Missile Treaty and World Security.* Mosbach, Germany: AFES Press, 1988. This report from the International Group of Researchers on the ABM Treaty outlines the ABM and its goals and objectives toward world security.

Bregman, Ahron. *Israel's Wars, 1947–93.* New York: Routledge, 2000. This book chronicles the major wars the country has engaged in with its Arab neighbors and relies on military and civilian reminiscences.

Breitman, George. *The Last Year of Malcolm X: The Evolution of a Revolutionary.* New York: Grove Press, 1965. This book studies the revolutionary's last year after his expulsion from the Nation of Islam.

Brill, Lesley. *John Huston's Filmmaking.* New York: Cambridge University Press, 1997. This volume analyzes the filmmaker's life and work.

Britton, Wesley. "Bond, Beatles, and Camp: The Men from U.N.C.L.E." Chapter 3 (pp. 35–56) of *Spy Television.* Westport, CT: Praeger, 2004. This chapter focuses on the genesis of the television series and describes the extent to which the Beatles were fans of the show.

Britton, Wesley. *Spy Television.* Santa Barbara, CA: Praeger, 2004. This entertaining book delves into the subject of fictional spies and their depiction on television.

Britton, Wesley. "From Tongues in Cheek to Tongues Sticking Out: *Get Smart* and the Spoofing of a Genre." Chapter 10 (pp.163–78) of *Spy Television.* Westport, CT: Praeger, 2004. This chapter describes the conception of *Get Smart*, a spoof of the spy genre so popular in the media in the 1960s.

Broderick, Walter J. *Camilo Torres: A Biography of the Priest-Guerrillero.* New York: Doubleday, 1975. This biography of the popular Colombian leader also chronicles the range of Colombian politics in the 1950s and 1960s.

Brody, Richard. *Everything Is Cinema: The Working Life of Jean-Luc Godard.* New York: Metropolitan Books, 2008. This critical biography of one of the leaders of the French New Wave reveals the subject's life and influences on intellectual history.

Bromell, Nick. *Tomorrow Never Knows: Rock and Psychedelics in the 1960s.* Chicago: University of Chicago Press, 2000. This history deconstructs the era's rock music by focusing on the lives and work of the Beatles, Bob Dylan, and Jimi Hendrix.

Brooks, Gwendolyn. *Report from Part One.* Detroit: Broadside, 1972. The first volume of the poet's autobiography documents her growth as a person and a poet and explains her attitude toward her racial heritage.

Brown, H. Rap. *Die Nigger Die!* New York: Dial, 1969. This political autobiography tells the author's life story and his role as the chairperson of the radical black power organization SNCC.

Brown, Jared. *Moss Hart: A Prince of the Theatre: A Biography in Three Acts.* New York: Back Stage Books, 2006. This traditional biography examines its subject's life in great detail and is based in part on Hart's diary and letters.

Brown, Jim, and Steve Delsohn. *Out of Bounds.* New York: Kensington, 1989. This biography of the Cleveland Browns player covers his career at Syracuse University through the Browns within the context of race relations and gangs.

Brown, Robert McAfee. *Liberation Theology: An Introductory Guide.* Louisville, KY: Westminster John Knox, 1993. This introduction to the philosophy/theology details the author's experiences while providing Christian witness and risk taking in Central America.

Brownmiller, Susan. *Shirley Chisholm.* Garden City, NJ: Doubleday, 1970. This short biography for children details the life of the first black woman elected to Congress.

Brunette, Peter. *The Films of Michelangelo Antonioni*. Cambridge: Cambridge University Press, 1998. This overview of the filmmaker's life and career examines six of his films including three from the 1960s: *L'Avventura, La Notte, and L'Eclisse.*

Bryant, Nick. *The Bystander: John F. Kennedy and the Struggle for Black Equality*. NY: Basic Books. 2006. This critical analysis of Kennedy's manipulation of black opinion argues that his tepid handling of civil rights incited violent outbreaks of the early 1960s.

Bufwack, Mary A., and Robert K. Oermann. *Finding Her Voice: Women in Country Music, 1800–2000*. Nashville: Country Music Foundation Press, 2003. This classic history chronicles the changing roles of women in country music.

Bugliosi, Vincent. *Helter Skelter: The True Story of the Manson Murders*. New York: W. W. Norton, 1994. Written by the prosecuting attorney of the infamous Charles Manson trial, this book reveals insider information about the Tate-LaBianca murders of 1969 that shocked the country.

Bugliosi, Vincent. *Reclaiming History: The Assassination of President John F. Kennedy*. New York: W. W. Norton, 2007. The author defends the Warren Commission's conclusion that Lee Harvey Oswald acted alone in his assassination of President John F. Kennedy.

"Bullitt," http://www.filminamerica.com/Movies/Bullitt/ (accessed January 28, 2010). This website identifies shooting locations for the 1968 thriller starring Steve McQueen.

Bullock, Charles S. III, and Charles L. Lamb, eds. *Implementation of Civil Rights Policy*. Monterey, CA: Brooks/Cole, 1984. This book chronicles the execution of the political structures and processes at the heart of the civil rights policy.

Bundy, William. *A Tangled Web: The Making of Foreign Policy in the Nixon Years*. New York: Hill and Wang, 1998. This history details multiple intricacies of Richard Nixon's international dealings with other countries.

Bunn, Matthew. *Foundation for the Future: The ABM Treaty and National Security*. Washington, DC: Arms Control Association, 1990. This book outlines an exhaustive history of the ABM Treaty and its effect on national security while serving as a resource for understanding issues of national defense.

Bunzel, Peter. "Music Biz Goes Round and Round: It Comes Out Clarkola." *Life*, May 16, 1960. This article reports on Dick Clark's testimony to the Harris Committee, which investigated payola in the music and broadcasting industry.

Burgess, Colin, and Rex Hall. *The First Soviet Cosmonaut Team: Their Lives and Legacies*. Chichester, UK: Praxis, 2008. This book includes photographs and biographical sketches of the first group of 20 Soviet cosmonauts.

Burgess, Colin, ed. *Footprints in the Dust: The Epic Voyages of Apollo, 1969–1975*. Lincoln: University of Nebraska Press, 2010. This book situates American spaceflight into historical context, chronicles Apollo 11 through Apollo 13, and concludes with events after the 1960s.

Burr, William. "Avoiding the Slippery Slope: Eisenhower and the Berlin Crisis, November 1958–January 1959." *Diplomatic History* 18 (Spring 1994): 177–206. This scholarly article chronicles the development of the Berlin Crisis.

Burrell, Barbara C. *A Woman's Place is in the House: Campaigning for Congress in the Feminist Era*. Ann Arbor: University of Michigan Press, 1994. This comprehensive examination of women candidates for the U.S. House of Representatives spanning 1968–1992 argues that women are as successful at winning seats as men.

Bush-Brown, Albert. *Skidmore, Owings & Merrill: Architecture and Urbanism, 1973–1983*. New York: Van Nostrand Reinhold, 1984. A survey of the architecture firm's work in the 1970s and 1980s.

Buzzanco, Robert. *Vietnam and the Transformation of American Life*. Malden, MA: Blackwell, 1999. This book focuses on the Vietnam War and movements of the 1960s with a major emphasis on the New Left, including treatment of the civil rights and women's movements.

Buzzanco, Robert. *Masters of War: Military Dissent and Politics in the Vietnam Era.* Cambridge: Cambridge University Press, 1996. This volume explores the internal schisms at the top of the U.S. defense hierarchy in the opposition and support of the Vietnam War.

Byrd, Ayana, and Lori L. Tharps. *Hair Story: Untangling the Roots of Black Hair in America.* New York: St. Martin's, 2002. This book covers the social, cultural, and economic significance of African American hair from 1400 to the present, but its relevance to the 1960s provides context for Angela Davis's Afro.

Campbell, W. Joseph. *Getting It Wrong: Ten of the Greatest Misreported Stories in American Journalism.* Berkeley: University of California Press, 2010. The author examines journalism myths including answering whether the *Washington Post* brought down President Nixon by reporting the Watergate scandal and whether remarks by Walter Cronkite helped end the Vietnam War.

Cannell, Michael. *I. M. Pei: Mandarin of Modernism.* New York: Carol Southern Books, 1995.This book profiles the architect who designed the John F. Kennedy Library after the president's assassination.

Carawan, Guy and Candie Carawan, eds. *Sing for Freedom: The Story of the Civil Rights Movement Through Its Songs.* Montgomery: New South Books, 2007. This audio CD contains a collection of 26 hymns, speeches, spirituals, gospel songs, and prayers recorded in Alabama, Georgia, Mississippi, and Tennessee in the 1960s.

Cardullo, Bert, ed. *Michelangelo Antonioni: Interviews.* Jackson: University Press of Mississippi, 2008. This book contains 14 interviews with the filmmaker over a time span of 23 years beginning in 1960.

Carey, Elaine. *Plaza of Sacrifices: Gender, Power, and Terror in 1968 Mexico.* Albuquerque: University of New Mexico Press, 2005. In the first English-language study of student protesters killed in Mexico City in 1968, the author gives a gendered analysis of the protest movement in which 700 students were killed by the government.

Carmichael, Stokely. *Ready for Revolution: The Life and Struggles of Stokely Carmichael (Kwame Ture).* New York: Scribners, 2003. The civil rights leader's autobiography, pieced together after his death, charts his path from immigrant child of Trinidad to magnetic U.S. student activist and SNCC visionary.

Carney, George O. "Cowabunga! Surfer Rock and the Five Themes of Geography." *Popular Music and Society* 23 (1999): 3–29. This scholarly article examines the genesis of surf rock and how five "themes of geography" inform the genre's lyrics, styling, and performance.

Caro, Robert A. *Master of the Senate: The Years of Lyndon Johnson, Vol. 3.* New York: Vintage, 2003. This study covers Johnson's Senate career beginning in 1950 and straddling the next decade before he was elected vice president in 1960.

Caro, Robert A. *The Power Broker: Robert Moses and the Fall of New York.* New York, Alfred A. Knopf, 1974. This biography describes Moses's life and career as he affected politics, the physical structures, and problems of urban renewal in New York City.

Carpenter, M. Scott, et. al. *We Seven.* New York: Simon & Schuster, 1962. This book's descriptions of training, technology, and teamwork evinced and written by the original Mercury Seven astronauts takes readers behind the scenes on individual missions.

Carr, Jay, ed. *The A List; The National Society of Film Critics' 100 Essential Films.* Cambridge, MA: Da Capo, 2002. Entries compiled in this book are international in scope, provide historical context, and include films such as *2001: A Space Odyssey* (1968), *Blow-Up* (1966), *Bonnie and Clyde* (1967), *Breathless* (1960), *Closely Watched Trains* (1967), *Easy Rider* (1969), *The Entertainer* (1960), and others.

Carraze, A. and Putheaud, J. *The Avengers Companion.* London: Titan, 1997. Covering all six seasons the show aired, including the 1960s, this guide includes photographs, interviews, essays, and an episode guide.

Carson, Clayborne. *The Autobiography of Martin Luther King, Jr.* New York: Grand Central Publishing, 2001. The author has organized King's papers, essays, notes, lectures, and sermons into a posthumous autobiography.

Carson, Clayborne. *In Struggle: SNCC and the Black Awakening of the 1960's.* Cambridge, MA: Harvard University Press, 1981. Inside lies the story of SNCC's evolution as well as its contributions to the political awakening of blacks and allied individuals.

Carson, Rachel. *Silent Spring.* Boston: Mariner Books, 2002. Carson's book inspired environmental awareness in the American mind with her look at the poisons from insecticides, weed killers, and other common products as well as the use of sprays in agriculture.

Carter, David. *Stonewall: The Riots That Sparked the Gay Revolution.* New York: St. Martin's, 2004. Carter's book traces the events of seven days of riots in Greenwich Village, New York, which became the basis of the American gay rights movement.

Carter, James M. *Inventing Vietnam: The United States and State Building, 1954–1968.* Cambridge: Cambridge University Press, 2008. Carter argues that the plan to build a nation in Vietnam was doomed from its inception.

Cash, Johnny, with Patrick Carr. *Cash: The Autobiography.* New York: HarperCollins, 1997. Cash's autobiography covers his life, career, and addictions and includes mention of his performance at the Newport Folk Festival in 1964, his series of prison concerts during the decade, and his visit to wounded American soldiers in Vietnam in 1969.

Cassell, Christine K. *Medicare Matters: What Geriatric Medicine Can Teach American Health Care.* New York: Milbank Memorial Fund, 2005. This comprehensive study of Medicare analyzes the program's social, demographic, institutional, political, and policy contexts.

Castaneda, Jorge. *Compañero: The Life and Death of Che Guevara.* New York: Vintage, 1998. This reconstruction of the revolutionary's life draws from CIA records and recollections from his closest friends.

Castleman, Riva. *Jasper Johns: A Print Retrospective.* New York: Museum of Modern Art, 1986. This retrospective is an exhibition catalog of the painter's oeuvre beginning in 1960.

Casty, Alan. *The Films of Robert Rossen.* New York: Museum of Modern Art, 1969. Casty covers Rossen's films *The Hustler* (1961), and *Lilith* (1964) as well as plays and films attributed to him beginning in the 1930s.

Catsam, Derek. *Freedom's Main Line: The Journey of Reconciliation and the Freedom Rides.* Lexington: University Press of Kentucky, 2009. This book catalogs the civil rights movement's long journey to dismantle institutional discrimination and increase support for passage of the Civil Rights Act of 1964.

Catton, Philip E. *Diem's Final Failure: Prelude to America's War in Vietnam.* Lawrence: University Press of Kansas, 2002. Catton's treatment of the Vietnamese leader provides insight into Diem's no-win position between communists and the United States.

Center for the Study of Democratic Institutions. *Anti-Ballistic Missile: Yes or No?* New York: Hill and Wang, 1968. This book condenses the discussion and position papers presented at two meetings at the Center for the Study of Democratic Institutions in New York, NY.

Chafe, William H. *Civilities and Civil Rights: Greensboro, North Carolina and the Black Struggle for Freedom.* Oxford: Oxford University Press, 1980. This study reveals the interplay between whites and blacks during the civil rights movement in the southern city where the sit-ins began.

Chafe, William H. *Never Stop Running: Allard Lowenstein and the Struggle to SaveAmerican Liberalism.* New York: Basic Books, 1993. This biography of Lowenstein highlights his activities in the 1960s civil rights movement and the campaign to end the war in Vietnam.

Chaikin, Andrew. *A Man on the Moon: The Voyages of the Apollo Astronauts.* New York: Penguin, 1994. The 24 astronauts interviewed for this book share their accounts of the space progam, from its launch in 1961 through the next decade.

Champlin, Charles. *The Movies Grow Up: 1940–1980*. Athens, OH: Swallow Books, 1981. The author's survey of movies is informed by his coverage of art and entertainment for magazines and newspapers like *Time* and the *Los Angeles Times* since 1959.

Chang, Jung, and Jon Halliday. *Mao: The Unknown Story*. New York: Alfred A. Knopf, 2005. This biography draws from archival resources and places Mao's policies within the context of global events.

Chapman, C. Stuart. *Shelby Foote: A Writer's Life*. Jackson: University Press of Mississippi, 2003. Foote's three-volume work on the American Civil War was published during the 1960s; Chapman highlights Foote's private opposition to segregation.

Chapman, James, and Nicholas J. Cull. *Projecting Empire: Imperialism and Popular Cinema*. London: I. B. Tauris, 2009. The authors examine imperialism and the cinema; six films from the 1960s appear in three separate chapters.

Chapman, James. *License to Thrill: A Cultural History of the James Bond Films*. London: I. B. Tauris, 1999. Chapman covers the Bond films beginning with *Dr. No* (1962) through *Casino Royale* (2006) and examines the context of culture and politics depicted in each film.

Chapman, James. *Saints and Avengers: British Adventure Series of the 1960s*. London: I. B. Tauris, 2002. The author uses case studies to interpret national identity and world politics of the 1960s and 1970s.

Charney, Marc D. "Rev. William Sloane Coffin Dies at 81; Fought for Civil Rights And Against a War." *New York Times*, April 13, 2006. This article reports the death of Coffin and serves as an obituary.

Chase, Robert T. "Class Resurrection: The Poor People's Campaign of 1968 and Resurrection City." *Essays in History* 40 (1998): http://etext.virginia.edu/journals/EH/EH40/chase40.html (accessed January 18, 2011). This article examines the peaceful gathering of people on May 12, 1968, supporting Martin Luther King Jr.'s initiative to get Congress to pass antipoverty legislation.

Chedd, G. "Theodore Roszak: Romantic in Reason's Court." *New Scientist* 49, no. 741 (March 4, 1971): 484–86. This article profiles the author and elaborates on his pacifist leanings, involvement in the peace movement, and creation of *Making of a Counter Culture* (1969).

Cherry, Robert. *Wilt: Larger Than Life*. Chicago: Triumph Books, 2004. In this biography of the controversial athlete, Cherry covers the career highlights of Chamberlain including his record-making third NBA season (1961–1962).

Chesler, Ellen. *Woman of Valor: Margaret Sanger and the Birth Control Movement in America*. New York: Simon & Schuster, 2007. Ostensibly a biography of Sanger, this history of the birth control movement in the United States culminates with the production and mass availability of the birth control pill, which had a significant effect on women's rights in the 1960s.

Child, Lauren. "Voodoo Child: Jimi Hendrix and the Politics of Race in the Sixties." In *Imagine Nation: The American Counterculture of the 1960s & 1970s*. Peter Braunstein and Michael William Doyle, eds. New York: Routledge, 2002. This chapter examines Hendrix's race, a mixture of African American and Cherokee, and how that limited his success in the United States but was an asset in Great Britain, where his career took off.

Chisholm '72: Unbought and Unbossed. DVD. Dir. by Shola Lynch. Twentieth Century-Fox, 2004. This documentary follows Chisholm's campaign to become the Democratic Party's presidential nominee in 1972.

Chisholm, Shirley. *The Good Fight*. New York: Harper & Row, 1973. This autobiography focuses on the opposition she fought as she campaigned across the United States to become the Democratic Party's presidential nominee in 1972.

Chisholm, Shirley. *Unbought and Unbossed*. Boston: Houghton Mifflin, 1970. This autobiography captures the author's early years as a girl growing up in Brooklyn, New York through her achievement as America's first African American congresswoman.

Chomsky, Noam. "Dow Shalt Not Kill." In *The Zinn Reader: Writings on Disobedience and Democracy*, by Howard Zinn, pp. 314–21. New York: Seven Stories, 1997. This essay persuades readers to oppose the U.S. government's use of napalm, a Dow Chemical product, in Vietnam.

Chong, Denise. *The Girl in the Picture: The Story of Kim Phuc, the Photograph, and the Vietnam War.* New York: Viking, 2000. Chong's biography of Phuc traces the girl's life and the effect that being a living symbol of the horrors of the Vietnam War had on her adulthood.

Chun, Clayton. "Winged Interceptor: Politics and Strategy in the Development of the Bomarc Missile." *Air Power History* 45, no. 4 (Winter 1998): 44–59. This scholarly article outlines the history of the Bomarc Missile and its role in national security.

Churchill, Ward, and Jim Vander Wall. *Agents of Repression: The FBI's Secret Wars Against the Black Panther Party & the American Indian Movement.* Detroit: South End Press, 2002. This study surveys the FBI's counterintelligence program against the Black Panthers and the American Indian Movement.

Citron, Stephen. *Jerry Herman: Poet of the Showtune.* New Haven, CT: Yale University Press, 2004. In this laudatory biography and comprehensive overview of Herman's work, Citron draws from extensive interviews.

Citron, Stephen. *Stephen Sondheim and Andrew Lloyd Webber: The New Musical.* New York: Oxford University Press, 2001. This comparative biography traces the childhoods and careers of these two musical theater composers.

Clancy, John G. *Apostle for Our Time: Pope Paul VI.* New York: P. J. Kennedy and Sons, 1963. This portrait of the subject focuses on his interest in labor causes and years in Milan.

Clark, Dick, and Richard Robinson. *Rock, Roll & Remember.* New York: Thomas Y. Crowell, 1976. Clark's memoir describes the creation of *American Bandstand* and its influence on popular culture and popular music.

Clark, Judith, and Amy de la Haye. *Carnaby Street 1960–2010,* London: London College of Fashion, 2010. This exhibition catalog includes original clothing from the 1960s.

Clarke, Gerald. *Capote: A Biography.* Cambridge and New York: Da Capo, 2005. While not the most comprehensive biography of the writer, this book features sections describing Capote's January 1960 meetings with the subjects of his narrative *In Cold Blood* (1966).

Clarke, Jeffrey J. *Advice and Support: The Final Years 1965–1973—The United States Army in Vietnam.* Washington, DC: Center of Military History, United States Army, 1988. This book describes the U.S. Army's final military activities in Vietnam.

Clayson, William S. *Freedom Is Not Enough: The War on Poverty and the Civil Rights Movement in Texas.* Austin: University of Texas Press, 2010. This in-depth study focuses on the problem Texas presented in fighting the War on Poverty.

Cleaver, Eldridge. *Soul on Ice.* Surrey, UK: Delta, 1999. A collection of essays comprising a spiritual memoir covering the author's identity as a felon, Negro, rapist, and uneducated man.

Cleaver, Eldridge. *Target Zero: A Life in Writing.* New York: Palgrave MacMillan, 2006. In four parts this volume traces the civil rights leader's work and life via essays, poems, autobiographical excerpts, and interviews.

Cleaver, Kathleen, and George Katsiaficas. *Liberation, Imagination, and the Black Panther Party: A New Look at the Panthers and Their Legacy.* New York: Routledge, 2001. These essays feature a range of voices including scholars, activists, contemporary political prisoners, and original members of the Black Panther Party that bring uncommon diversity to the topic.

Clifford, Clark. *Counsel to the President.* New York: Random House, 1991. This memoir covers Clifford's lengthy political career, which includes serving Presidents Kennedy and Johnson as special counsel.

Clinton, Bill. "Statement on the Death of Willie Morris." *Weekly Compilation of Presidential Documents* 35, no. 31 (August 9, 1999): 1552. (Accessed November 7, 2010). This statement on the death of Morris by President Clinton mentions his pleasure at meeting Morris and reading his memoir.

Clout, Robert E. *Rivers of Blood, Years of Darkness: The Unforgettable Account of the Watts Riot*. New York: William Morrow, 1968. Clout's narrative is unparalleled due to his interviewing of 1,000 people and statements from 500 others about the violence of the Watts Riots.

Clymer, Adam. *Edward M. Kennedy: A Biography*. New York: HarperCollins, 1999. This biography follows Kennedy's career as a senator with special emphasis on his family identity as a brother to John and Robert.

Coffin, William Sloane. *Credo*. Louisville, KY: Westminster John Knox Press, 2005. The author, who became famous while chaplain at Yale in the 1960s for his active opposition to the Vietnam War, shares his beliefs that promote social justice within the context of the Christian spirit.

Coffin, William Sloane. *The Heart Is a Little to the Left: Essays on Public Morality*. Dartmouth, NH: Dartmouth College Press, 2011. This work includes seven sermons and speeches delivered primarily to university audiences by the famous antiwar chaplain.

Coffin, William Sloane. *Letters to a Young Doubter*. Louisville, KY: Westminster John Knox Press, 2005. The author writes letters to a theology student as a means to address matters of sexuality, grades, grief, narcissism and humility, war and the draft, and prayer.

Coffin, William Sloane. *Living the Truth in a World of Illusions*. San Francisco: Harper & Row, 1985. This is a collection of the author's sermons.

Coffin, William Sloane. *Once to Every Man: A Memoir*. New York: Atheneum, 1978. This autobiography chronicles the peace activist's life and covers his early aspirations as a pianist to his ordainment and works in social justice by opposing military intervention in Vietnam and Iraq, as well as supporting gay rights.

Cohen, Adam, and Elizabeth Taylor. *American Pharaoh: Mayor Richard J. Daley—His Battle for Chicago and the Nation*. Boston: Little, Brown, 2001. This account of Daley's life chronicles his boyhood and career, but especially the most famous crisis during his tenure as Chicago's mayor, the 1968 Democratic convention.

Cohen, Cynthia et al. *Music and Conflict Transformation: Harmonies and Dissonance in Geopolitics*. London: I. B. Tauris, 2008. This book combines stories from musicians, theory from scholars, and an interview with Pete Seeger in the interest of answering the question, How can music and politics collaborate to promote world peace?

Cohen, Lizabeth. *A Consumers' Republic: The Politics of Mass Consumption in Postwar America*. New York: Alfred A. Knopf, 2003. This study illustrates the failure of consumer culture in the aim for egalitarianism during the postwar era.

Cohen, Michael P. *The History of the Sierra Club, 1892–1970*. San Francisco: Sierra Club Books, 1988. This history examines the organization's growth and leadership over the course of two centuries and int influence on ecological philosophy that spurred environmental movements of the 1950s, 1960s, and 1970s.

Cohen, Robert, and Reginald E. Zelnick, eds. *Free Speech Movement: Reflections on Berkeley in the 1960s*. Berkeley: University of California Press, 2002. In this collection of essays, veterans of the Free Speech Movement recall the turbulent intellectual atmosphere of the 1960s.

Cohen, Robert. *Freedom's Orator: Mario Savio and the Radical Legacy of the 1960s*. Oxford; New York: Oxford University Press, 2009. This biography describes Savio's life and role in the Berkeley Free Speech Movement, as well as his experience registering black voters during the Freedom Summer of 1964.

Cohen, Ronald D. *Folk Music: The Basics*. New York: Routledge, 2006. Giving an introduction to the birth of the American folk music scene, Cohen examines both popular and commercial expressions.

Cohen, Warren I. and Nancy Bernkopf Tucker, eds. *Lyndon Johnson Confronts the World: American Foreign Policy, 1969–1977*. New York: Cambridge University Press, 1994. This collection of essays presents work by scholars who analyze various aspects of Johnson's foreing policy.

Cohodas, Nadine. *The Band Played Dixie: Race and the Liberal Conscience at Ole Miss*. New York: Free Press, 1997. This review of the post-civil rights era demonstrates that the struggle for racial equality continued on the campus of Ole Miss with James H. Meredith's Supreme Court-ruled enrollment there as the first black student.

Cole, Bill. *John Coltrane*. New York: Schirmer Books, 1976. This biography of the saxophonist focuses on Coltrane's spirituality and its effect on his life and work.

Coleman, J. D. *Pleiku: The Dawn of Helicopter Warfare in Vietnam*. New York: St. Martin's, 1988. This history covers the development of the U.S. military's first air assault division and covers the testing of the program in South Vietnam in the fall of 1965.

Collier-Thomas, Bettye and V. P. Franklin. *Sisters in the Struggle: African American Women in the Civil Rights-Black Power Movement*. New York: New York University Press, 2001. This collection of essays, including writings by Mary McLeod Bethune, Ella Baker, and Rosa Parks, covers African American women's activism in social and political movements such as the Mississippi Freedom Democratic Party, the Black Panther Party, and SNCC.

Collins, Bud. *Total Tennis: The Ultimate Tennis Encyclopedia*. Toronto: Sports Classic, 2003. This reference work on the sport provides a year-by-year chronology noting the highlights for each year; statistics for championship singles, doubles, and mixed-doubles winners in the major events; and profiles of players reprinted from magazines.

Collins, Michael. *Carrying the Fire: An Astronaut's Journeys*. 1974. New York: Farrar, Straus, and Giroux, 2009. Collins's memoir captures the experience of journeying through space.

Commoner, Barry. *The Closing Circle: Nature, Man and Technology*. New York: Alfred A. Knopf, 1971. This early book on the looming environmental crisis repots on the state of the natural world.

Congress of Racial Equality, "The History of Core," http://www.core-online.org/History/history.htm (accessed November 11, 2010). This website outlines the history of CORE, a part of the larger civil rights movement.

Connery, Robert H., and Gerald Benjamin. *Rockefeller of New York: Executive Power in the Statehouse*. Ithaca, NY: Cornell University Press, 1979. The authors present Rockefeller as a pragmatist whose problem solving did not fall neatly into conservative or liberal ideology.

Conway, Jill Ker, ed. *Written by Herself: Autobiographies of American Women: An Anthology*. New York: Vintage, 1992. This collection includes primary autobiographical writing by women such as Maya Angelou, Marian Anderson, and Gloria Steinem.

Conway-Lanz, Sahr. *Collateral Damage: Americans, Noncombat Immunity, and Atrocity After World War II*. New York: Routledge, 2006. Drawing on policy makers' responses to the atomic bomb, the author examines modern American discourse on the topic of civilian casualties.

Cook, John W., and Heinrich Klotz. *Conversations with Architects*. New York: Praeger, 1973. This collection of interviews reveal ideas and intentions of architects working in the International Style.

Corliss, Richard. *Lolita*. London: British Film Institute, 1994. This summation of Stanley Kubrick's film based on the eponymous book covers the novel's trajectory into a screenplay as well as insider quotes, notes on casting, and other items.

Corrin, Lisa G., Robert Kudelka, and Frances Spalding, eds. *Bridget Riley: Paintings from the 1960s and 70s*. London: Serpentine Gallery, 1999. Five dialogues between the artist and a well-known art figure broadcast by the BBC are presented in this volume that discusses her oeuvre that includes celebrated black-and-white op art works conceived in the 1960s.

Cortright, David. *Soldiers In Revolt: GI Resistance During the Vietnam War*, 2nd ed. Chicago: Haymarket Books, 2005. This account documents the common soldier's resistence to the Vietnam War.

"Council of Federated Organizations." In *Organizing Black America: An Encyclopedia of African American Associations*. New York: Routledge, 2001.

"Country Joe McDonald." In *Leaders from the 1960s: A Biographical Sourcebook of American Activism*, ed. David DeLeon. (Westport, CT: Greenwood, 1994): 411–16

Coyote, Peter. *Sleeping Where I Fall: A Chronicle*. Washington, DC: Counterpoint, 1998. Coyote reexamines his life with the San Francisco Mime Troupe, the Diggers, and his navigation of the 1960s counterculture.

Craik, Jennifer. *The Face of Fashion: Cultural Studies in Fashion*. London: Routledge, 1994. This volume covers a multitude of issues such as the interest in the ethnic look of the 1960s, the limitations of women's roles in the 1960s, Twiggy, the way the 1960s affected fashion photography, the dwindling use of foundation garments in that decade, and others.

Crick, Alan Robert. *The Big Screen Comedies of Mel Brooks*. Jefferson, NC, and London: McFarland, 2002. This book covers Brooks's films and includes an analysis of *The Producers* (1968).

Crighton, Kathleen. "The Girl from U.N.C.L.E." *Epi-Log Journal*, issue 13 (February 1994). Online at: http://www.manfromuncle.org/kcgfu.htm (accessed January 18, 2011). This article discusses the history and exection of *The Girl from U.N.C.L.E.*, a spin-off series from *The Man from U.N.C.L.E.*

Crisp, C. G. *François Truffaut*. New York: Praeger, 1972. This study includes all of the French New Wave filmmaker's work up to *The Wild Child* (1970).

Cristol, A. Jay. *The Liberty Incident: The 1967 Attack on the U.S. Navy Spy Ship*. Dulles, VA: Brassey's, 2002. The author's use of documents retrieved via the Freedom of Information Act as well as extensive oral interviews provide a comprehensive volume about the attack on the USS *Liberty*.

Critchlow, Donald T. *The Conservative Ascendancy: How the GOP Right Made Political History*. Cambridge, Mass.: Harvard University Press, 2007. This history of American conservatism begins with the postwar right and concludes with the 2006 presidential election.

Critchlow, Donald T. *Phyllis Schlafly and Grassroots Conservatism: A Woman's Crusade*. Princeton, N.J.: Princeton University Press, 2005. The author's unrestricted access to Schlafly's personal papers provide ample documentation for this combined biography and history of American conservatism.

Cronin, Paul. *Roman Polanski: Interviews*. Jackson: University Press of Mississippi, 2005. This volume collects 28 interviews with the director published in international film journals that span 40 years and includes his mainstream *Rosemary's Baby* (1968).

Crosse, Jesse. *The Greatest Movie Car Chases of All Time*. St. Paul, MN: Motorbooks, 2006. This book provides insight into the filmmaking of car chases, with the majority of commentary coming from Peter Yates, director of *Bullitt* (1968).

Crowther, Bosley. "Bonnie and Clyde." *New York Times*, April 14, 1967. Available online from http://movies.nytimes.com/movie/review?res=EE05E7DF173CE361BC4C52 DFB266838C679EDE (accessed January 30, 2010). This article is a review of the film *Bonnie and Clyde*.

Crowther, Bosley. "Fellini Film Lives Up to Foreign Hurrahs." *New York Times*, April 20, 1961. http://movies.nytimes.com/movie/review?res=9D04EFD9153BE13ABC4851DF B266838A679EDE (accessed February 2, 2010). This article reviews the critical reception of Fellini's *La Dolce Vita* (1960).

Crump, Spencer. *Black Riot in Los Angeles the Story of the Watts Tragedy*. Los Angeles: Trans-Anglo Books, 1966. This day-to-day account of the riots lends a journalistic perspective to the events.

Cummings, Richard. *Pied Piper: Allard K. Lowenstein and the American Dream*. New York: Grove Press, 1985. This biography of Lowenstein follows his activities as founder of the Dump Johnson Movement, his election to Congress, and his criticism of federal and local authorities' unwillingness to reopen the investigation of the assassination of Senator Robert F. Kennedy.

Cunningham, Frank R. *Sidney Lumet: Film and Literary Vision*. Lexington: University Press of Kentucky, 2001. This book offers an expanded analysis of Lumet's earlier films as well as his most recent works, all within the context of his dedication to social justice.

Currey, Cecil. *Edward Lansdale: The Unquiet American*. Boston: Houghton Mifflin, 1988. This second half of his biography describes Lansdale's struggles in Saigon to prevent the collapse of the tenuous nation he fostered.

Currey, Cecil B. *Victory at Any Cost: The Genius of Viet Nam's Gen. Vo Nguyen Giap*. Dulles, VA: Potomac Books, 2005. This book is a comprehensive biography of the leader of the Vietnamese Communist forces against the Japanese, French, and Americans.

Curry, G. David. *Sunshine Patriots: Punishment and the Vietnam Offender*. Notre Dame, IN: University of Notre Dame Press, 1985. This book includes research data supporting the author's thesis that the Vietnam deserter was usually a by-product of instutionalized discrimination.

Curtis, Daniel. *The Berrigan Brothers: The Story of Daniel and Philip Berrigan*. New York: Hawthorn Books, 1972. This book covers the antiwar activities of the Berrigan brothers, two priests who burned Maryland draft board records with homemade napalm.

D'Antonio, Michael. *A Ball, a Dog, and a Monkey: 1957—The Space Race Begins*. New York: Simon & Schuster, 2007. This technology-focused history of the space race recounts orbital objects such as canines and squirrel monkeys.

D'Emilio, John. *World Turned: Essays on Gay History, Politics, and Culture*. Durham, NC: Duke University Press, 2002. The author's previously published personal essays, speeches, reviews, and biographical sketches cover the burgeoning of gay rights and gay acceptance in American culture.

Dallek, Robert. *An Unfinished Life: John F. Kennedy, 1917–1963*. New York: Back Bay Books, 2003. This biography is drawn from unrestricted access to key Kennedy family papers, as well as papers from family friends and colleagues, which result in an expansive treatment of Kennedy's life and legacy.

Dallek, Robert. *Flawed Giant: Lyndon Johnson and His Times, 1961–1973*. New York: Oxford University Press, 1998. This objective biography draws from recently released presidential papers and transcripts and covers Johnson's White House years.

Dallek, Robert. *Nixon and Kissinger: Partners in Power*. New York: HarperCollins, 2007. This comprehensive biography of Nixon and Kissinger examines the personal motivations behind the men's public and private intrigues.

Dass, Ram, Ralph Metzner, and Gary Bravo. *Birth of a Psychedelic Culture: Conversations about Leary, the Harvard Experiments, Milbrook and the Sixties*. Santa Fe, NM: Synergetic Press, 2010. Interviews and firsthand accounts reveal the lives and legacies of the leaders of the psychedelic movement.

Daum, Andreas. *Kennedy in Berlin*. Cambridge: Cambridge University Press, 2007. This book traces the changes in German-American relations and details President Kennedy's historic 1963 visit to Berlin.

Davies, Dave. *Kink: An Autobiography*. New York: Hyperion, 1997. Davies's autobiography details the shenanigans, substance abuse, and hanging out with other rock musicians that comprise the lifestyle of rock-and-roll musicians.

Davis, Flora. *Moving the Mountain: The Women's Movement in America Since 1960.* Chicago: University of Illinois Press, 1999. This chronicle of the twentieth-century U.S. women's movement begins in 1960 and illustrates the reinvention of feminism after mid-century and how social movements provided a groundswell of women activists who later worked on the Equal Rights Amendment.

Davis, Harold Eugene. *Latin American Thought: A Historical Introduction.* New York: Free Press, 1972. This is a basic introduction to the history of Latin American thought.

Davis, Michael D., and Hunter R. Clark. *Thurgood Marshall: Warrior at the Bar, Rebel on the Bench.* New York: Carol Publishing, 1992. This book surveys the subject's life and delves into his private life more than any other biography to that date.

Davis, Michael. *Street Gang: The Complete History of Sesame Street.* New York: Viking, 2008. The history of the popular children's television show begins with its 1969 debut and how it addressed the inequities of lower-class children's preschool educational preparation.

Davis, Ronald L. *Duke: The Life and Image of John Wayne.* Norman: University of Oklahoma Press, 1998. This exhaustive biography of Wayne is drawn from 65 interviews, clipping files, printed interviews, film reviews, and magazine articles, in addition to major studio production files, Indiana University's John Ford Collection, and the papers of Wayne's agent, Charles K. Feldman.

Davis, Vernon. *The Long Road Home: U.S. Prisoner of War Policy and Planning in Southeast Asia.* Washington, DC: Historical Office, Office of the Secretary of Defense, 2000. This history examines the U.S. role in developing prisoner-of-war policy during the Vietnam War.

Dawidoff, Nicholas. *In the Country of Country: A Journey to the Roots of American Music.* New York: Vintage, 1998. This book documents the origins of country music's performers and features 40 photographs.

De Fornari, Oreste. *Sergio Leone: The Great Italian Dream of Legendary America.* Rome: Gremese, 1997. This book collects interviews and behind-the-scenes anecdotes from cast, crew, and Leone himself.

De la Durantaye, Leland. *Style Is Matter: The Moral Art of Vladimir Nabokov.* Ithaca, NY: Cornell University Press, 2007. This criticism of the writer's work offers a fresh reinterpretation of the "old poet's" lines in *Lolita* (1967).

De Leon, David. *Leaders from the 60s: A Biographical Sourcebook of American Activism.* Westport, CT: Greenwood, 1994. Photographs and bibliographies accompany entries in this reference work that collects biographical information about American activists of the 1960s.

DeBenedetti, Charles, and Charles Chatfield. *An American Ordeal: The Antiwar Movement of the Vietnam Era.* New York: Syracuse University Press, 1990. This book examines the political attitudes of leaders and the American people during the 1960s.

Debusscher, Gilbert. *Edward Albee: Tradition and Renewal.* Brussels: Center for American Studies: 1969. This book provides biographical information in the introduction but is focused on literary criticism of Albee's work.

Deford, Frank. *There She Is: The Life and Times of Miss America.* New York: Viking, 1971. This laudatory history of the Miss America pageant follows its establishment in 1921 through its first color broadcast on television in 1966, the women's liberationist protests against it in 1968 and 1969, and the crowning of Miss American 1970.

Del Castillo, Richard Griswold, and Richard A. Garcia. *César Chávez: A Triumph of Spirit.* Norman: University of Oklahoma Press, 1995. This biography focuses on Chávez's formation, growth, and development as a leader in social justice and rights for agricultural workers.

DeLaughter, Bobby. *Never Too Late: The Prosecutor's Story of Justice in the Medgar Evers Case.* New York: Scribners, 2001. The author draws from his journals and the legal transcriptions to recreate the research and interviews he did while prosecuting Byron De La Beckwith for the 1963 murder of NAACP leader Medgar Evers.

Deloria, Vine. *Custer Died for Your Sins: An Indian Manifesto*. New York: Macmillan, 1969. This is the seminal work for understanding the American Indian perspective on U.S. race relations, federal bureaucracies, Christian churches, and social scientists.

Deloria, Vine. *God Is Red*. New York: Grosset and Dunlap, 1973. This is the seminal work for understanding the American Indian experience and expression of spirituality.

Deloria, Vine. *We Talk, You Listen: New Tribes, New Turf*. New York: Macmillan, 1970. In this book the author enumerates his ideas about a variety of topics including black power, American Indian stereotyping, liberal politics, and others.

Demallie, Raymond J. "Vine Deloria Jr. (1933–2005)." *American Anthropologist* 108 no. 4 (December 2006): 932–35. This obituary pays homage to the leading American Indian academic and the most respected and well-known national speaker on Indian issues of his generation.

Dening, Penelope, and Twiggy. *Twiggy in Black and White*. London: Pocket Books, 1998. This autobiography covers the model's life and career as an actor and singer.

Densmore, John. *Riders on the Storm: My Life with Jim Morrison and the Doors*. New York: Delacorte, 1990. This account of the Doors' drummer's life focuses on his relationship with Morrison and includes italicized text written directly to the deceased Morrison.

DeRoche, Andrew. *Andrew Young: Civil Rights Ambassador*. Wilmington, DE: Scholarly Resources, 2003. This book bases its study of Young's life on his formative years as a top assistant to Martin Luther King in the 1960s and how those experiences influenced Young's contributions as an African American activist, politician, and diplomat to U.S. foreign policy.

DeRogatis, Jim. *Turn on Your Mind: Four Decades of Great Psychedelic Rock*. Milwaukee, WI: Hal Leonard, 2003. This is the definitive history of psychedelic rock, chronicling the Summer of Love, Haight-Ashbury, the Velvet Underground, the Beatles, and more.

Desser, David, and Lester D. Friedman. *American Jewish Filmmakers*. Urbana: University of Illinois Press, 2004. This book discusses the careers of many Jewish filmmakers including Mel Brooks, Woody Allen, and Sidney Lumet.

Diem, Bui, and David Chanoff. *In the Jaws of History*. Bloomington: Indiana University Press, 1987. This book chronicles the leader's life and political career covering the period after World War II to the end of the Vietnam War.

Dierenfield, Bruce J. *The Battle over School Prayer: How Engel v. Vitale Changed America*. Lawrence: University Press of Kansas, 2007. This book describes the political issue of school prayer and chronicles the Engel decision and its effect on the school systems in the United States.

Dietsch, Deborah K. *Architecture for Dummies*. Indianapolis, IN: Wiley, 2002. This book provides an introduction to architecture that explains its essentials to the layperson or novice.

DiLeo, David L. *George Ball, Vietnam, and the Rethinking of Containment*. Chapel Hill: University of North Carolina Press, 1991. This comprehensive study of Ball's tenure as under secretary of state from 1961 to 1966 chronicles his opposition to American military intervention in Southeast Asia.

Dirda, Michael. "James Bond as Archetype (and Incredibly Cool Dude)." *Chronicle of Higher Education* June 20, 2008. B20–B22. This analysis of Ian Fleming's James Bond and Sebastian Faulks's continuation of the series characterizes the writing as undistinguished but Bond as archetypal.

Dirks, Tim. "Butch Cassidy and the Sundance Kid (1969)." http://www.filmsite.org/butc.html (accessed February 2, 2010). This review of the film includes dialogue, plot summary, and information about the film, such as how many Oscars it was nominated for.

Dirks, Tim. "Cool Hand Luke (1967)." http://www.filmsite.org/cool.html (accessed February 2, 2010). This review of the film includes a lengthy plot summary and description of scenes from the movie, as well as minimal mention of prominent themes and symbols in it.

Dirks, Tim. "Easy Rider (1969)." http://www.filmsite.org/easy.html (accessed February 2, 2010). This review of the film includes a summary of the context in which it was released, its iconography, plot summary, and lyrics from a Steppenwolf song.

Dirks, Tim. "Midnight Cowboy (1969)." http://www.filmsite.org/midn.html (accessed February 2, 2010). This review of the film includes a synopsis, song lyrics from the soundtrack, description of scenes, and dialogue.

Dirksen, Everett. *The Education of a Senator*. Champaign: University of Illinois Press. 1998. Written at the time of his death in 1969, this memoir covers his boyhood through his election to the Senate in 1950 and his role as a leader of civil rights legislation.

Di Sabatino, David. *The Jesus People Movement: An Annotated Bibliography and General Resource*. Westport, CT: Greenwood, 1999. This resource provides an overview of the Jesus People and examines its participants, their beliefs, and their activities within the bibliographical format.

Dittmer, John. *Local People: The Struggle for Civil Rights in Mississippi*. Urbana: University of Illinois Press, 1994. This history of the civil rights struggle in Mississippi in the 1960s covers postwar voting registration efforts and the murders of James Chaney, Michael Schwerner, and Andrew Goodman.

Dobratz, Betty A., and Stephanie L. Shanks-Meile. *The White Separatist Movement in the United States Today: "White Power, White Pride!"* Baltimore, MD: Johns Hopkins University Press, 2000. The authors document the history of the Ku Klux Klan and other white separatist groups in the United States.

Doggett, Peter. *Are You Ready for the Country: Elvis, Dylan, Parsons and the Roots of Country Rock*. New York: Penguin, 2000. This exhaustive work chronicles the interplay between country music and rock music beginning with the late 1960s with the advent of country rock.

Dolenz, Mickey, and Bego, Mark. *I'm a Believer: My Life of Monkees, Music, and Madness*. New York: Hyperion, 1993. This memoir chronicles the author's experience of what life was like as a member of an Anglo-American pop band in the 1960s.

Dommen, Arthur J. *The Indochinese Experience of the French and the Americans: Nationalism and Communism in Cambodia, Laos, and Vietnam*. Bloomington: Indiana University Press, 2001. This work studies the complex history of the people who fought against the United States and won.

Doonan, Simon. "Five Best: Books About Fashion." *Wall Street Journal*, September 17 2005, Eastern Edition. This newspaper story reports a list of five favorite books of Simon Doonan, one being Muriel Spark's *The Girls of Slender Means* (1963).

Doris, Sara. *Pop Art and the Contest over American Culture*. New York: Cambridge University Press, 2007. This work demonstrates how the artists working within the pop art movement challenged and discarded established hierarchies and replaced them with mass-produced processes, images, and objects.

Doss, Erika, ed. *Looking at Life Magazine*. Washington, DC: Smithsonian Institution Press, 2001. This collection of chapters written by 13 authors examines how the magazine's stories and news coverage shaped national identity up to the 1960s.

Doyle, Michael William, and Peter Braunstein, eds. *Imagine Nation: The American Counterculture of the 1960s and 1970s*. New York; Routledge, 2002. This work studies the counterculture of the 1960s and 1970s in 14 essays written by academics and scholars covering topics such as politics, sexual and racial identity, and communal living, to name a few.

Doyle, Robert. *A Prisoner's Duty: Great Escapes in U.S. Military History*. Annapolis, MD: Naval Institute Press, 1997. True stories gathered from American soldiers held as prisoners of war from the Colonial period up to the 1980s are compiled in this book, which includes some stories from the Vietnam War.

Doyle, Robert. *Voices from Captivity: Interpreting the American POW Narrative.* Lawrence: University Press of Kansas, 1994. In this comprehensive listing of American POW narratives from seventeenth-century America up to the present, the author briefly analyzes the psychological aspects of captivity, with a primary focus on excerpting the works themselves.

Doyle, William. *An American Insurrection: James Meredith and the Battle of Oxford.* New York: Anchor, 2003. In this micro-history of a segregation crisis at the University of Mississippi on September 30, 1962, the author minutely documents a turning point in the civil rights movement based on years of intensive research, including over 500 interviews, JFK's White House tapes, and 9,000 pages of FBI files

Drukman, Steven. "Oh, You Beautiful Dolls." *American Theatre* (December 1, 2001): 7. This article reviews the play based on Jacqueline Susann's book *Valley of the Dolls.*

Duberman, Martin B. *Stonewall.* New York: Plume, 1994. This chronicle of the summer of 1969 Stonewall riots, which marked the birth of the modern gay and lesbian movement.

Dudziak, Mary L. *Cold War Civil Rights: Race and the Image of American Democracy.* Princeton, NJ: Princeton University Press, 2000. This study of the reframing of the "new Negro Problem" directly connects civil rights and the Cold War.

Duiker, William J. *Ho Chi Minh: A Life.* New York: Hyperion, 2000. In this detailed biography, the author presents a thoroughly researched chronicle of Ho Chi Minh's personal and public life.

Duiker, William J. *The Rise of Nationalism in Vietnam, 1900–1941.* Ithaca, NY: Cornell University Press, 1976. This study broadens and expands studies in the area of rising nationalism in Vietnam prior to the U.S.'s Vietnam policy.

Duiker, William J. *U.S. Containment Policy and the Conflict in Indochina.* Stanford, CA: Stanford University Press, 1994. This book presents an overview of the U.S. experience in Vietnam and includes a discussion of feasible alternatives strategies that were employed.

Dunaway, David King. *How Can I Keep from Singing? The Ballad of Pete Seeger.* New York: Villard, 2008. This biography includes photographs, interviews as it traces the subject's life as a musical performer and target of the CIA and FBI.

Dunaway, David King, and Molly Beer. *Singing Out: An Oral History of America's Folk Music Revivals.* New York: Oxford University Press, 2010. This introduction to folk music revivals interviews singers, songwriters, promoters, and activists from three separate revivals of the twentieth century, including the one of the 1960s.

Duriez, Colin. *Francis Schaeffer: An Authentic Life.* Wheaton, IL: Crossway Books, 2008. This biography of the theologian and Christian apologist whose ideas helped spark the rise of the Christian Right in the United States with the publication of Schaeffer's first book in 1968.

Dussel, Enrique. *Teología de la Liberación: Un Panorama de su Desarollo.* Mexico: Potrerillos Editores, 1995. This collection offers a selection of contributions to the first World Forum on Theology and Liberation held in the late 1970s and includes chapters giving European, African, Indian, and American perspectives on liberation theology.

Eagles, Charles W. *The Price of Defiance: James Meredith and the Integration of Ole Miss.* Chapel Hill: University of North Carolina Press, 2009. This history of integration at Ole Miss examines the opposition to black students at the university from its founding in 1848 until James Meredith's enrollment in 1962.

Ebert, Roger. "La Dolce Vita (1960)." *Chicago Sun-Times,* January 5, 1997. Available online at http://rogerebert.suntimes.com/apps/pbcs.dll/article?AID=/19970105/REVIEWS08/401010336/1023 (accessed February 2, 2010). This review describes Fellini's shooting of the film on Roman streets; provides cinematic insight, plot, and scene summary; and offers lively commentary by Roger Ebert.

Echols, Alice. *Daring to be Bad: Radical Feminism in America, 1967–1975.* Minneapolis: University of Minneapolis Press, 1989. This study shows how various feminist groups formed and merged and splintered during the postwar era due to controversies over philosophies, objectives, and practices.

Echols, Alice. *Scars of Sweet Paradise: The Life and Times of Janis Joplin*. New York: Henry Holt, 1999. This feminist-focused biography of Joplin weaves sex, drugs, and rock and roll with insights from over 150 interviews to paint a picture of the artist as someone constrained by gender roles and smalltown thinking who escaped to the broad world and claimed the fame that awaited her.

Edgren, Gretchen. *Inside the Playboy Mansion: If You Don't Swing, Don't Ring*. Los Angeles: Playboy Enterprises, 1998.

Edmunds, R. David. *The New Warriors: Native American Leaders Since 1900*. Lincoln: University of Nebraska Press, 2001. This collection profiles 14 Native American leaders who have changed their communities and the larger world, including American Indian Movement (AIM) founder Russell Means.

Edwards, John. *The Geeks of War: The Secretive Labs and Brilliant Minds Behind Tomorrow's Warfare*. New York: AMACOM, 2005. This book describes developments in technology and their implications for warfare as well as providing a history of past technology and their applications to war.

Edwardson, Ryan. *Canuck Rock: A History of Canadian Popular Music*. Toronto: University of Toronto Press, 2009. This compendium of Canadian rock-and-roll musicians begins in 1950 and covers the Guess Who, Gordon Lightfoot, Joni Mitchell, Neil Young, and others.

Egan, Michael. *Barry Commoner and the Science of Survival: The Remaking of American Environmentalism*. Cambridge: MIT Press, 2007. This biography of examines the life and career of Commoner, a biologist and environmentalist, whose work in social justice linked socioeconomic standing to exposure to environmental hazards.

Egan, Sean. *The Mammoth Book of the Beatles*. London: Constable and Robinson, 2009. This comprehensive volume offers memoirs, interviews, musical critiques, and magazine and newspaper articles about the musical group, most of which were written by the author.

Eisenberg, John. *The First Season: How Vince Lombardi Took the Worst Team in the NFL and Set It on the Path to Glory*. New York: Houghton Mifflin Harcourt, 2009. This study chronicles Lombardi's early days in Green Bay, Wisconsin, and provides detailed game recaps along with information from players about the coach's unforgiving approach to whipping them into shape.

Elder, Rob. "Down on the Peacock Farm," November 16, 2001, http://www.salon.com/people/feature/2001/11/16/kesey99 (accessed June 27, 2010). This previously unpublished interview with Ken Kesey provides insight into his life and how his experiences inspired others.

Eliot, Marc. *Death of a Rebel: A Biography of Phl Ochs*. Garden City, NY: Anchor, 1979. This biography reflects on folksinger Phil Ochs's influence on his genre, as well as his rise to fame and his downfall.

Elliot, David. *The Vietnamese War: Revolution and Social Change in the Mekong Delta, 1930–1975*. Armonk, NY: M. E. Sharpe, 2003. This micro-study of Dinh Tuong/My Tho Province, Vietnam, examines the local revolutionary developments, drawing from 415 in-depth interviews of prisoners and defectors and about 100 Vietnamese-language postwar histories.

Elliot, Jeffrey M., ed. *Conversations with Maya Angelou*. Jackson: University Press of Mississippi, 1989. This volume gathers interviews from American and British magazines with the poet spanning the 1970s and 1980s in which she speaks about her growth as an artist, her work as an activist, and her struggles against racism.

Ellsberg, Daniel. *Secrets: A Memoir of Vietnam and the Pentagon Papers*. New York: Penguin, 2002. This memoir chronicles the author's change of mindset from government insider to antiwar crusader who leaked the *Pentagon Papers* to the *New York Times* in 1971.

Engel, Joel. *Gene Roddenberry: The Myth and the Man Behind Star Trek*. New York: Hyperion, 2004. This biography presents a balanced view of the subject's life and recounts his substance abuse and downward spiral into erratic behavior.

Engerman, David C., Nils Gilman, Mark H. Haefele, and Michael E. Latham. *Staging Growth: Modernization, Development and the Global Cold War*. Amherst: University of Massachusetts Press, 2003. Essays in this volume expound on the theory of modernization as it relates to U.S. foreign policy in South Asia and East Asia as well as other countries.

Environmental Protection Agency. "Clean Water Act." Available at http://cfpub.epa.gov/ npdes/cwa.cfm?program_id=45 (accessed August 10, 2010). This website provides amendments and working to the Clean Water Act.

Environmental Protection Agency. "The Clean Air Act." Available at http://www.epa.gov/air/ caa/ (accessed August 10, 2010). This website provides information about the Clean Air Act such as links to sections of the US Code, and 1990 amendments to the Clean Air Act.

Epstein, Edward Jay. *Inquest: The Warren Commission and the Establishment of Truth*. New York: Viking, 1966. This book expands on the author's Cornell master's thesis that the Warren Commission was extremely superficial and that it acted hastily in agreeing that Oswald was the sole assassin of President Kennedy.

Eskew, Glenn. *But for Birmingham: The Local and National Movements in the Civil Rights Struggle*. Chapel Hill: University of North Carolina Press, 1997. This prize-winning history of the civil rights movement in Birmingham, Alabama, focuses on the late 1950s and early 1960s.

Evans, Sara M. *Born For Liberty: A History of Women in America*. New York: Free Press, 1997. In this history of women's roles in U.S. history from the seventeenth century to modern day, Evans offers perspectives from well-known and lesser-known women within the country's large social and political movements.

Evans, Sara M. *Tidal Wave: How Women Changed America at Century's End*. New York: Free Press, 2003. Covering modern feminism in the United States in this nonpartisan and comprehensive account, Evans documents the movement's swelling tide in the 1960s.

"Ex-Boston Teacher Tells Of Whippings Given Pupils." *New York Times*, October 26, 1967, p. 19. This newspaper article reports that Jonathan Kozol, a white former teacher in a Boston black ghetto, describes how white teachers there beat the pupils with a rattan stick.

Exner, Judith. *My Story*. New York: Grove, 1977. While offering no new information on her role as a messenger between President Kennedy and mobster Sam Giancana, this book follows her life and allows glimpses of lifestyles of the rich and famous.

Ezra, Michael. *Muhammad Ali: The Making of an Icon*. Philadelphia: Temple University Press. 2009. This study of the athlete's life examines his relationship to the Vietnam War and the Nation of Islam.

Fact-Finding Commission on Columbia Disturbances. *Crisis at Columbia: Report of the Fact-Finding Commission Appointed to Investigate the Disturbances at Columbia University in April and May, 1968*. New York, Vintage, 1968. This is the official report on what the Cox Commission found to be underlying causes of the disturbances that took place on the Columbia University campus in April and May 1968.

Fahrenthold, David A. "Bill to Honor Rachel Carson on Hold." *Washington Post*, May, 23, 2007. This newspaper article reports that Oklahoma Sen. Tom Coburn blocked a resolution to honor environmental author Rachel Carson on the 100th anniversary of her birth.

Fairclough, Adam. *To Redeem the Soul of America: The Southern Christian Leadership Conference and Martin Luther King, Jr.* Athens: University of Georgia Press, 1988. This exhaustive study of the Southern Christian Leadership Conference gives secondary and local leaders their due as instruments of change in the civil rights movement.

Fairclough, Rob. *The Prisoner: The Official Companion to the Classic TV Series*. London: Carlton Books, 2002. Tracing the television program's early days in the 1960s, this compendium contains interviews, episode by episode analysis, unpublished photographs, props and memorabilia, production details, cast biographies, and original photography.

Farber, David R. *Chicago '68*. Chicago: University of Chicago Press, 1988. Drawn from underground news sources, films, and interviews, the book explores the main forces behind the protests at the 1968 Chicago Democratic National Convention: the Yippes and Mayor Daley.

Farber, David R. "The Intoxicated State/Illegal Nation: Drugs in the Sixties Counterculture." In Peter Braunstein and Michael William Doyle, eds., *Imagine Nation: The American Counterculture of the 1960s and '70s*. New York: Routledge, 2002. This chapter examines the use of illegal drugs by the counterculture in the 1960s and specifically explores how the use of LSD changed the culture.

Farber, David R, ed. *The Sixties: From Memory to History*. Chapel Hill: University of North Carolina Press, 1994. This collection of essays explores various themes related to the 1960s including the growth of liberalism, the Vietnam War, race and ethnicity, women's liberation, youth culture, the sexual revolution, and more.

Farmer, James. *Lay Bare the Heart: An Autobiography of the Civil Rights Movement*. Ft. Worth: Texas Christian University, 1998. Farmer's account of the civil rights struggle of the 1950s and 1960s includes his establishment of the Congress of Racial Equality in 1942, sit-in mobilizations, and his meetings with leaders such as Franklin and Eleanor Roosevelt, Jack and Bobby Kennedy, Adlai Stevenson, and President Johnson.

Farrell, Gerry. *Indian Music and the West*. Oxford: Clarendon, 1997. This survey of Indian music covers 200 years of representations of the form in the West as well as specific elements that were adopted by Western musicians of the 1960s.

Farrell, James J. *The Spirit of the Sixties: Making Postwar Radicalism*. New York: Routledge, 1997. In this study of the philosophy of personalism, Farrell demonstrates how various social and political movements of the 1960s such as the Catholic Workers, the Beats, students, the counterculture, and the antiwar movement incorporated the philosophy into their structures and goals.

The FBI File on the KKK Murder of Viola Liuzzo. Microfilm. New York: Scholarly Resources, 1990. File coverage includes a background investigation of Viola Liuzzo and her husband; accounts from informants within the Klan; President Johnson's interest in the case; and Alabama governor George Wallace's response to the murder.

Fein, Rashi. *Medical Care, Medical Costs: The Search for a Health Insurance Policy*. Cambridge: Harvard University Press, 1986. Fein surveys the history of U.S. health insurance such as Medicare and Medicaid.

Feldman, Hans. "Kubrick and His Discontents." *Film Quarterly* 30, no. 1 (Autumn 1976): 12–19. This scholarly article argues that Kubrick is one of the best critics of the times via his films such as *Dr. Strangelove, 2001, A Clockwork Orange*, and *Barry Lyndon*.

Fellini, Federico. *Fellini on Fellini*. Translated by Isabel Quigley. New York: Delacorte, 1976. This collection offers boyhood reminiscences and anecdotes alongside his articles, interviews, and essays covering *La Strada, La Dolce Vita, 8 1/2, Juliet of the Spirits, Satyricon*, and *Amarcord*.

Felsenthal, Carol. *Power, Privilege and the Post: The Katharine Graham Story*. New York: Seven Stories, 2003. This gossipy biography covers the subject's life as a publisher and defender of America's free press as she printed the *Pentagon Papers* and ignored Nixon's pressure in her paper's coverage of the Watergate affair.

Felsenthal, Carol. *Phyllis Schlafly: The Sweetheart of the Silent Majority*. Chicago: Regnery Gateway, 1981. This popular biography details the conservative activist leader's early life.

Feminist.com. "Gloria Steinem News." http://www.feminist.com/gloriasteinem/ (accessed April 25, 2010). This webpage contains biographical information about the women's rights activist that chronicles her books, which organizations she is affiliated with, journalism and other awards and recognition she won, as well as links to Steinem in the news.

Ferree, Myra Marx, and Beth B. Hess. *Controversy and Coalition: The New Feminist Movement.* 3rd ed. New York: Routledge, 1995. This third edition includes substantial revision to the work, contributing then-current research and statistics covering the new feminist movement from 1963 to 2000.

Ferriss, Susan, and Ricardo Sandoval. *The Fight in the Fields: Cesar Chavez and the Farmworkers Movement.* Orlando: Harcourt Brace, 1997. This book traces the life of the founder of the United Farm Workers union in 1962 and serves as a companion volume to an eponymous PBS documentary.

Ferruccio, Frank. *Diamonds to Dust: The Life and Death of Jayne Mansfield.* Parker, CO: Outskirts Press, 2007. This self-published ode to the actress covers the basics of her life and death from a fan's perspective.

Field, Marilyn J. et al., eds. *Extending Medicare Coverage for Preventive and Other Services.* Washington, DC: National Academy Press, 2000. Reviews the scientific evidence and estimates the cost to Medicare for covering a variety of services.

Findling, John E., and Kimberly D. Pelle, eds. *Encyclopedia of World's Fairs and Expositions.* Jefferson, NC: McFarland, 2008. This reference work compiles and annotates individual histories of each of the nearly 100 World's Fairs and expositions held in more than 20 countries since 1851.

Fine, Gary Alan. "The Manson Family: The Folklore Traditions of a Small Group." *Journal of the Folklore Institute* 19 no. 1 (January–April 1982): 47–60. This scholarly article describes the folk culture of the Manson Family and explicates features affecting the creation and continuation of small-group folklore generally.

Fine, Sidney. *Violence in the Model City: The Cavanagh Administration, Race Relations and the Detroit Riot of 1967.* Ann Arbor: University of Michigan Press, 1989. This detailed, seminal study of the Detroit Riot of 1967 establishes what happened, why, and what consequences it had for the city, the country, and the civil rights movement.

Finlayson, Andrew R. "A Retrospective on Counterinsurgency Operations: The Tay Ninh Provincial Reconnaissance Unit and Its Role in the Phoenix Program, 1969–70." *Studies in Intelligence* 51 (2007): 59–69. This article is an adaptation of a paper Col. Finlayson gave at a CSI/Texas Tech University Joint Conference on Intelligence and the Vietnam War.

Firestone, Bernard J. "Kennedy and the Test Ban: Presidential Leadership and Arms Control." Edited by Douglas Binkley and Richard T. Griffiths. *John F. Kennedy and Europe.* Baton Rouge: Louisiana State University Press, 1999, 66–94. This chapter places the Test Ban Treaty in a sober context and examines its true significance.

Fisher, James T. "Pirate of the Caribbean," *Commonweal,* October 20, 2006, pp. 34–35. This review of a new biography of Roberto Clemente summarizes the athlete's career highlights and gives a thumbs up to the biography.

Fishman, Diane and Powell, Marcia. *Vidal Sassoon: Fifty Years Ahead.* New York: Rizzoli, 1993. This work surveys the hairdresser's life, influence on popular culture and fashion, and provides photographs of the hairstyles he developed as well as a decade-by-decade chronology of his creative efforts.

Flam, Jack D., ed. *Robert Smithson: Collected Writings.* Berkeley: University of California Press, 1996. This edition updates and expands on the artist's writings and images associated with the antiformalist earth art movement of the 1960s and 1970s.

Flamm, Michael. *Law and Order: Street Crime, Civil Unrest, and the Crisis of Liberalism in the 1960s.* New York: Columbia University Press, 2005. This study considers how crime and civil unrest unsettled Americans in the 1960s and led to the end of the liberal era.

Flammang, Janet A. *Women's Political Voice: How Women are Transforming the Practice and Study of Politics.* Philadelphia: Temple University Press, 1997. This analysis of the history of women's political activism in America centers on a case study of Northern California's Silicon Valley, an area once nicknamed "the feminist capital of the nation'.

Flannery, Austin, ed. *Vatican Council II: The Conciliar and Post-Conciliar Documents.* Northport, NY: Costello, 1975. This volume includes the 16 original constitutions and decrees and 49 documents issued after the close of the council.

Fleming, Peggy. *The Long Program: Skating Toward Life's Victories.* New York: Simon & Schuster, 1999. In this memoir, Fleming recounts her accomplishments as an ice skater who won an Olympic Gold Medal for figure skating in 1968 and as a woman who battled breast cancer.

Flink, Steve. *The Greatest Tennis Matches of the Twentieth Century.* Danbury, CT: Routledge, 1999. Fink highlights 30 historic tennis matches, three of which occurred in the 1960s.

Foley, Michael S. *Dear Dr. Spock: Letters about the Vietnam War to America's Favorite Baby Doctor.* New York: New York University Press, 2005. This volume collects 218 letters from thousands written to Dr. Spock during the Vietnam War—from 1965 to 1972—by parent of soldiers, soldiers themselves, student protesters, WW II veterans, and draft resisters; it present the diversity of public opinion about the war.

Foley, Michael. *Confronting the War Machine: Draft Resistance During the Vietnam War.* Chapel Hill: University of North Carolina Press, 2003. Foley's examination of draft resisters focuses on Boston, one of the movement's most prominent centers.

Follin, Frances. *Embodied Visions: Bridget Riley, Op Art and the Sixties.* London: Thames and Hudson, 2004. The author examines how Riley's op art paintings related to other art of the period, particularly happenings.

Fonda, Jane. *My Life So Far.* New York: Random House, 2005. Fonda's memoir covers her childhood, early films, first marriage, career in film, involvement in the Vietnam War, and marriage to Ted Turner.

"Fonda, Jane Seymour." *The Scribner Encyclopedia of American Lives Thematic Series: The 1960s.* Edited by William L. O'Neill and Kenneth T. Jackson. 2 vols. New York: Scribners, 2003. Reproduced in *Biography Resource Center.* Farmington Hills, MI: Gale, 2010. http://galenet.galegroup.com/servlet/BioRC/ (accessed April 25, 2010). This encyclopedia article provides biographical information on the subject's origins, life, and career, but focuses mainly on her activities during the 1960s.

Foner, Philip S. *The Black Panthers Speak.* Philadelphia: Lippincott, 1970. Foner collects the essential primary documents of the Black Panther Party including cartoons, flyers, and articles by Huey P. Newton, Bobby Seale, and Eldridge Cleaver.

Foreman, James. *The Making of Black Revolutionaries.* Greensboro, NC: Open Hand, 1985. Foreman recounts his role as leader of the Student Nonviolent Coordinating Committee in this memoir.

Foster, L. H. "Race Relations in the South, 1960." *The Journal of Negro Education* 30, no. 2 (Spring 1961): 138–49. This short paper, published as part of a Tuskegee Institute Report, reveals that race relations came closer to a much-needed base of respect for the individual and his rights in 1960 than in previous years.

Fox, Stephen R. *Blood and Power: Organized Crime in Twentieth-Century America.* New York: Penguin, 1989. This encyclopedic popular history of organized crime in twentieth-century America devotes chapters to the Kennedy assassination and its aftermath.

Frady, Marshall. *Jesse: The Life and Pilgrimage of Jesse Jackson.* New York: Simon & Schuster Adult, 2006. This biography of the religious leader delves into Jackson's psychology, his role in the civil right's movement, his relationship with Dr. Martin Luther King Jr., and describes his career highlights.

Frank, Thomas. *The Conquest of Cool: Business Culture, Counterculture, and the Rise of Hip Consumerism.* Chicago: University Press, 1997. Frank delves into the technique by which Madison Avenue co-opted the spirit and values of the 1960s counterculture to modern-day consumer culture.

Frankenthaler, Helen. *Helen Frankenthaler Prints, 1961–1979*. New York: Harper & Row, 1980. This catalog of an exhibition held at Sterling and Francine Clark Art Institute, April 11–May 11, 1980, covers the artist's work during the 1960s and contains biographical information as well as critical analysis of her work in the context of the time and among her peers.

Franklin, Aretha. *Aretha: From These Roots*. Darby, PA: Diane Publishing, 1999. This disappointing autobiography takes the reader through the singer's life and career while settling scores with those in the industry who have maligned her in print.

Franklin, H. Bruce. "Burning Illusions: The Napalm Campaign." In *Against the Vietnam War: Writings by Activists*, ed. Mary Susannah Robbins. Syracuse, NY: Syracuse University Press, 1999, pp. 62–75. In this chapter, Franklin provides evidence that a Stanford University case study of images of napalm-burned Vietnamese was used to change attitudes towards the war in Redwood City, California.

Franklin, H. Bruce. *The Vietnam War in American Stories, Songs, and Poems*. Boston: Bedford Books of St. Martin's 1996. This anthology about the Vietnam War collects 16 stories, five songs, and 63 poems for use by students in college and high school classrooms.

Frantz, Douglas, and David McKean. *Friends in High Places: The Rise and Fall of Clark Clifford*. Boston: Little, Brown, 1992. This biography of the Washington insider hits the career highlights, especially his role as secretary of defense during the Vietnam War.

Frayling, Christopher. *Sergio Leone: Something to Do with Death*. London: Faber & Faber, 2000. As the definitive biographical study of Leone, this hefty volume investigates the director's professional and personal life as well as influences and events that shaped his career.

Freedland, Michael. *Jane Fonda: A Biography*. New York: St. Martin's, 1988. This biography recounts the actor's life up to the age of 60 and examines her role as a cultural icon, her feminist identity, and her business acumen.

Freedlander, Paul. *Rock and Roll: A Social History*. Boulder, CO: Westview Press, 2006. The author sketches how gospel, country, and blues have influenced a variety of British, Canadian, and American musicians.

Freedman, Lawrence. *Kennedy's Wars: Berlin, Cuba, Laos and Vietnam*. New York: Oxford University Press, 2002. This study explores development of President Kennedy's foreign-policy strategy in Berlin, Cuba, Laos, and Vietnam.

Freeman, Jo. *At Berkeley in the Sixties: The Education of an Activist, 1961–1965*. Bloomington: Indiana University Press, 2004. Drawing from her diaries, her letters, and FBI files, the author crafts this memoir and reflects on the student movements—including free speech and women's liberation—she experienced the University of California at Berkeley's campus during the 1960s.

Freeman, Mike. *Jim Brown: The Fierce Life of an American Hero*. New York: HarperCollins World, 2006. This biography of the athlete summarizes his childhood and career while demonstrating Brown's effective advocacy for black causes.

French, Francis, and Colin Burgess. *In the Shadow of the Moon: A Challenging Journey to Tranquility, 1965–1969*. Lincoln: University of Nebraska Press, 2007. New interviews with the astronauts capture the anxiety and fervor surrounding the space race as revealed in these portraits of individuals serving on missions under the Gemini program.

French, Francis, and Colin Burgess. *Into that Silent Sea: Trailblazers of the Space Era, 1961–1965*. Lincoln: University of Nebraska Press, 2007. This account of pioneering astronauts and cosmonauts is based on the authors' interviews with their subjects.

Friedan, Betty. *It Changed My Life: Writings on the Women's Movement*. New York: Random House, 1976. This collection of old and new writings, interviews, magazine articles, and recollections retraces the last dozen years of the second wave of the feminist movement in the United States.

Friedan, Betty. *Life So Far: A Memoir*. New York: Touchstone, 2000. Written as a corrective measure to two biographies published the previous year, this memoir clarifies the author's life as a feminist leader and covers her childhood, her professional accomplishments, and settles old scores.

Friedan, Betty. *The Feminine Mystique*. New York: W. W. Norton, 1963. A classic work that spurred the second wave of the feminist movement by asking questions about women's limited roles in U.S. society and how that undermines and manipulates their ambitions and lives.

Frieden, Bernard J., and Marshall Kaplan. *The Politics of Neglect: Urban Aid from Model Cities to Revenue Sharing*. Cambridge, MA: MIT Press, 1975. This work outlines the Model Cities program from its beginnings to its end in 1974.

Friedland, William H. *Revolutionary Theory*. Totawa, NJ: Allenheld, Osmun, 1982. Drawing on the work of Marx, Engels, Lenin, Trotsky, Luxemburg, Mao, and other important revolutionaries, this book provides a systematic examination of the full range of modern revolutionary theory.

Friedman, Lester D. *Bonnie and Clyde*. London: BFI Publications, 2000. Friedman explores the film's avant-garde handling of youth, fashion, crime, and authority.

Friedman, Milton. *From Galbraith to Economic Freedom*. London: Institute of Economic Affairs, 1977. This pamphlet contains two lectures by the author that critique John Kenneth Galbraith's views in the first and outlines his own tax plan for Great Britain in the second.

Friedman, Myra. *Buried Alive: The Biography of Janis Joplin*. New York: Harmony Books, 1973. As one of the first biographies published after the musician's death, this book served as a primary source of information on Joplin's childhood, musical development, and influences, and career until subsequent works provided more in-depth, scholarly treatment of the subject.

Fry, Joseph A. *Debating Vietnam: Fulbright, Stennis, and Their Senate Hearings*. Lanham, MD: Rowman and Littlefield, 2006. This analysis compares inquiries into the future of the war in Vietnam led by J. William Fulbright and John C. Stennis.

Fulbright, J. William. *The Arrogance of Power*. New York: Random House, 1966. Warning against the practice of being an overconfident and interventionist nation that acts independently of general opinion, Fulbright expands on what he defines as the arrogance of power and how it relates to U.S. foreign policy.

Funicello, Annette. *A Dream Is a Wish Your Heart Makes*. New York: Hyperion, 1994. This modest, heartwarming biography holds no surpises, tells no secrets, and upholds Funicello's good-girl Disney image while charting her rise to stardom, her happy family life, and her struggle with multiple sclerosis.

Fursenko, Aleksandr, and Timothy Naftali. *One Hell of a Gamble: Khrushchev, Castro, and Kennedy 1958–1964*. New York: W. W. Norton, 1997. This study fills the gaps in the historical record regarding international incidents and clarifies the inner workings of the Kremlin based on the authors' access to recently released Soviet records.

Gaddis, John Lewis, ed. *Cold War Statesmen Confront the Bomb: Nuclear Diplomacy Since 1945*. Oxford: Oxford University Press, 1999. This collection of essays examines the careers of 10 leading Cold War statesmen.

Gaillard, Frye. *The Greensboro Four: Civil Rights Pioneers: A Profile*. Charlotte, NC: Main Street Rag, 2001. This short work profiles four university freshmen—Joseph McNeil, Franklin McCain, Ezell Blair Jr. (later known as Jibreel Khazan), and David Richmond—who protested segregation in series of sit-ins in Greensboro, North Carolina in 1960.

Gaines, Steven S. *Heroes and Villains: The True Story of the Beach Boys*. New York: New American Library, 1986. This work catalogs the music group's rise to fame beginning in 1961 and follows their career through the 1980s.

Galbraith, John Kenneth. *The Affluent Society*. London: Penguin, 1999. His original ideas first published in 1958 predicted the widening gulf between the classes and suggested investment in infrastructure such as parks, transportation, education, and other public amenities to remedy the gap and its resultant social issues.

Ganz, Marshall. *Why David Sometimes Wins: Leadership, Organization, and Strategy in the California Farm Worker Movement.* New York: Oxford University Press, 2009. This primer on organizing a successful social movement shares compelling stories from the United Farm Workers' history and approach to organizing and empowering workers around a common cause.

Gardner, Carl. *Andrew Young: A Biography.* New York: Drake, 1978. This study of the activist, politician, and diplomat to U.S. foreign policy begins by examining his early years as a chief assistant to Martin Luther King Jr. in the 1960s where he developed his service philosophy and political strategies.

Gardner, Lloyd C. *Approaching Vietnam: From World War II through Dienbienphu.* New York: W. W. Norton, 1988. Gardner draws on newly unearthed documents that offer a more complex analysis and understanding of the events occurring at Dienbienphu.

Gardner, Lloyd C. *Pay Any Price: Lyndon Johnson and the Wars for Vietnam.* Chicago: I. R. Dee, 1995. Drawing from newly declassified documents at the Johnson Presidential Library, Gardner maps out the course of the Vietnam War from police action to international conflict as conducted by Johnson.

Garrison, Jim. *A Heritage of Stone.* New York: Putnam's, 1970. Garrison argues that President Kennedy was executed by "rogue elements" within the CIA because of his increasing opposition to U.S. involvement in Vietnam, which was against CIA extemists' interests. Reviewers discounted Garrison's theories, sources, and evidence.

Garrison, Jim. *On the Trail of the Assassins: My Investigation and Prosecution of the Murder of President Kennedy.* New York: Warner Books, 1991. Garrison presents the same argument as he did in *A Heritage of Stone,* but implicates members of the FBI, the Dallas Police Department, the Secret Service, and members of the military establishment.

Garrison, Jim. *The Star-Spangled Contract.* New York: McGraw-Hill, 1976. This poorly reviewed novel of political intrigue includes a plot to kill the president.

Garrow, David J. *Bearing the Cross: Martin Luther King, Jr., and the Southern Christian Leadership Conference, 1955–1968.* New York: Morrow, 1986. Drawing on over 700 interviews and King's personal papers, Garrow looks at King's power as a leader and struggles in his personal life.

Garrow, David J., ed. *Birmingham, Alabama, 1956–1963: The Black Struggle for Civil Rights.* Brooklyn, NY: Carlson, 1989. This book highlights the development of civil rights in Birmingham between the Brown decision and the events of the 1963 demonstrations by collecting three previously unpublished studies: Glenn T. Askew's "The Alabama Christian Movement for Human Rights and the Birmingham Struggle for Civil Rights, 1956–1963," Lewis W. Jones's "Fred L. Shuttlesworth, Indigenous Leader," and Lee E. Bains Jr.'s "Birmingham, 1963: Confrontation over Civil Rights."

Garrow, David J. *The FBI and Martin Luther King, Jr.: From "Solo" to Memphis.* New York: W. W. Norton, 1981. Garrow painstakingly chronicles J. Edgar Hoover's fixation on Dr. Martin Luther King Jr. and his lengthy efforts to disgrace paint King as a revolutionary radical who brought violence and unrest to the United States.

Garrow, David J. *Protest at Selma: Martin Luther King Jr. and the Voting Rights Act of 1965.* New Haven, CT: Yale University Press, 1980. Empathizing King as the leader of the Southern Christian Leadership Conference, this book examines the federal voting rights legislation and the civil rights protests in Selma and Birmingham, Alabama, in 1965.

Gaulle, Charles de. *The Complete War Memories.* New York: Simon & Schuster, 1964. This edition contains de Gaulle's personal writings from the fall of France in 1940 to the aftermath of the war in 1946.

Gaulle, Charles de. *Memories of Hope: Renewal and Endeavour.* New York: Simon & Schuster, 1971. De Gaulle imparts his vision of greatness and renewal for the nation of France in this collection of his personal writings.

Gellhorn, Martha. "Suffer the Little Children . . . " *Ladies' Home Journal* 84, no. 1 (Jan., 1967): 57, 107–10. This article advocates for U.S. withdrawal from the war in Vietnam by detailing its effects on innocent Vietnamese children.

Gentile, Thomas. *March on Washington: August 28, 1963.* Washington DC: New Day Publications, 1983. Gentile provides a detailed history and analysis of events leading up to the march and documents the march itself.

George, Edward and Dary Matera. *Taming the Beast: Charles Manson's Life Behind Bars.* New York: St. Martin's, 1998. The author's portrait of the subject covering the eight years of their acquaintance from the late 1970s to the late 1980s confirms that Manson remains a violent madman.

George, Emily. *Martha W. Griffiths.* Lanham, MD: University Press of America, 1982. This biography of the lawyer and politician covers the subject's life and details her work on important victories for equal rights for women and minorities.

George-Warren, Holly, et al. *The Rolling Stone Encyclopedia of Rock and Roll.* New York: Fireside, 2001. This work brings together over 100 new entries and many revisions to the 1,800 entries found in the 1995 edition and establishes an excellent range of coverage of the major rock-and-roll players dating from the 1950s to the present.

Gerber, Robin. *Katharine Graham: The Leadership Journey of an American Icon.* New York: Portfolio Hardcover, 2005. This biography interprets the subject's life using leadership theories popularized by James MacGregor Burns, and the author submits Graham's career as a female model of corporate success.

Gerhard, William D. *Attack on the USS Liberty: An Edited Version of SRH-256.* Walnut Creek, CA: Aegean Park Press, 1996. This text provides an objective examination of the *Liberty* incident. It presents the technical rationale for the *Liberty* mission as well as the particulars of the Israeli explanation, details of U.S. communications failures, a narrative of the attack, and lessons to be learned from the tragic event.

Gherman, Beverly. *Sparky: The Life and Art of Charles Schulz.* New York: Chronicle, 2010. This illustrated biography for children details how the cartoonist based his characters on persons from his own life as well as photographs and Shulz's work.

Giancana, Sam, and Chuck Giancana. *Double Cross: The Explosive Inside Story of the Mobster Who Controlled America.* New York: Warner Books, 1992. Written by the subject's brother and nephew, this biography provides entertainment value.

Gibbons, William Conrad. *The U.S. Government and the Vietnam War: Executive and Legislative Roles and Relationships, Part I: 1945–1960.* Princeton, NJ: Princeton University Press, 1986. This first volume of a five-part policy history of the U.S. government and the Vietnam War covers the period before U.S. involvement.

Gibbons, William Conrad. *The U.S. Government and the Vietnam War: Executive and Legislative Roles and Relationships, Part II: 1961–1964.* Princeton, NJ: Princeton University Press, 1986. This second of a five-part policy history of the U.S. government and the Vietnam War covers the early period prior to U.S. involvement.

Gibbons, William Conrad. *The U.S. Government and the Vietnam War: Executive and Legislative Roles and Relationships, Part III: January-July 1965.* Princeton, NJ: Princeton University Press, 1986. This third volume of a five-part policy history of the U.S. government and the Vietnam War covers the seven-month period between January and July 1965.

Gibbons, William Conrad. *The U.S. Government and the Vietnam War: Executive and Legislative Roles and Partnerships, Part IV: 1965–1968.* Princeton, NJ: Princeton University Press, 1995. This fourth volume of a five-part policy history of the U.S. government and the Vietnam War covers the core period of U.S. involvement from July 1965, when the decision was made to send large-scale U.S. forces, to the beginning of 1968, just before the Tet Offensive and the decision to seek a negotiated settlement.

Gibson, Bob, with Phil Pepe. *From Ghetto to Glory: The Story of Bob Gibson.* Englewood Cliffs, NJ: Prentice-Hall, 1968. This biography recounts Gibson's major career events and provides tips for would-be athletes with pitching grips and how he threw his pitches.

Gibson, Bob, and Reggie Jackson with Lonnie Wheeler. *Sixty Feet, Six Inches: A Hall of Fame Pitcher & a Hall of Fame Hitter Talk About How the Game Is Played.* New York: Doubleday, 2009. This duo discusses controversies in baseball including spitballers, hit batters, steroids, free agency, and racism.

Gibson, Bob, with Lonnie Wheeler. *Stranger to the Game: The Autobiography of Bob Gibson.* New York: Viking, 1994. In this autobiography, Gibson details his youth in Omaha, Nebraska; sketches his battles against racism; reconstructs his prowess as an athlete; and characterizes his adult life in the sports world as complicated.

Giedion, Sigfried. *Walter Gropius: Mensch und Werk.* Stuttgart: 1954. This book provides biographical information as well as examples of Gropius's work.

Gieri, Manuela. *Contemporary Italian Filmmaking: Strategies of Subversion: Pirandello, Fellini, Scola and the Directors of the New Generation.* Toronto: University of Toronto Press, 1995. This postwar critique of Italian filmmaking examines the work of Fellini, Ettore Scola, and many directors of the new generation such as Nanni Moretti, Gabriele Salvatores, Maurizio Nichetti, and Giuseppe Tornatore.

Gifford, Laura Jane. *The Center Cannot Hold: The 1960 Presidential Election and the Rise of Modern Conservatism.* DeKalb: Northern Illinois University Press, 2009. This historiography of American conservatism provides an analysis of interactions between three key party leaders—liberal Nelson Rockefeller, conservative Barry Goldwater, and moderate Richard Nixon—and six key constituencies: liberals, African Americans, conservative intellectuals, youth, Southerners, and ethnic Americans.

Giglio, James. *The Presidency of John F. Kennedy.* 2nd ed. Lawrence: University of Kansas Press, 2006. This volume narrates the major issues Kennedy navigated during his brief presidency.

Gill, Laverne McCain. *African American Women in Congress: Forming and Transforming History.* New Brunswick, NJ: Rutgers University Press, 1997. This work provides in-depth profiles of 15 African American women elected to Congress.

Gillespie, J. David. *Politics at the Periphery: Third Parties in Two Party America.* Columbia: University of South Carolina Press, 1993. This work merges political science, journalism, and history in the author's treatment of third parties in U.S. politics.

Gilpin, Geoff. *The Maharishi Effect: A Personal Journey Through the Movement That Transformed American Spirituality.* New York: Penguin, 2006. This bittersweet memoir discusses the author's return to transcendental meditation and his disenchantment with its disturbing changes.

Gilvey, John A. *Before the Parade Passes By: Gower Champion and the Glorious American Musical.* New York: St. Martin's, 2005. This detailed, well-researched biography explores the director and choreographer's life and career.

Ginsberg, Allen. *Collected Poems, 1947–1997.* New York: Harper Perennial, 2007. This volume offers the first complete collection of the poet's works including exhaustive notes.

Gitlin, Todd. *The Whole World Is Watching.* Berkeley: University of California Press, 1980. Gitlin dissects major news coverage in the early days of the antiwar movement, interviews key activists and news reporters, and develops a novel theory of news coverage as a form of antidemocratic social management.

Gitlin, Todd. *The Sixties: Years of Hope, Days of Rage.* New York: Bantam, 1987. This popular history brings an insider's view of the political, social, and sexual revolutions that characterized the decade.

Gladwell, Malcolm. "The Mosquito Killer." *New Yorker*, July 2, 2001. Gladwell introduces the discovery and manufacture of DDT and its effect on malaria and follows the chemical's evolution into a dangerous pollutant and banned substance.

Gleason, Bill. *Daley of Chicago: The Man, the Mayor, and the Limits of Conventional Politics.* New York: Simon & Schuster, 1970. This readable biography of Daley written by a contemporary lacks the retrospective of more recent biographies but presents a more familiar and amiable chronicle of the subject's life and career.

Glenn, John, and Nick Taylor. *John Glenn: A Memoir*. New York: G. K. Hall, 2000. This simply related memoir lacks depth but appeals to a broad audience and inspires, informs, and grips readers.

Goldberg, Rosalee. *Performance Art: From Futurism to the Present*. London: Thames & Hudson, 2001. This text summarizes conceptual art through the decades from dadaists, Laurie Anderson, John Cage, Cindy Sherman, Mariko Mori, Paul McCarthy, Matthew Barney, Karen Finley, Forced Entertainment, happenings, and Desperate Optimists.

Goldberg, Rosalee. *Performance: Live Art since the '60s*. London: Thames & Hudson, 2004. An essential resource with an international scope on performance art, this work covers artists and experiences since the 1960s from Yves Klein and Piero Manzoni to Joseph Beuys and Robert Wilson, Meredith Monk, Laurie Anderson, Pina Bausch, Matthew Barney, Bill T. Jones, Gilbert & George, Mona Hatoum, and many others.

Goldfarb, Ronald. *Perfect Villains, Imperfect Heroes: Robert Kennedy's War Against Organized Crime*. New York: Random House, 1995. Goldfarb concentrates on Kennedy's tenure as U.S. attorney general and his battle against organized crime in this detailed courtroom memoir.

Goldstein, Joseph., et al. *The My Lai Massacre and Its Cover-Up: Beyond the Reach of Law?* New York: Free Press, 1976. This book is the official report of a U.S. Army inquiry headed by General William R. Peers. Goldstein and his coauthors have added an introductory essay and a selection of relevant documents.

Goldstein, Patrick. "Blasts from the Past." *Los Angeles Times*, August 24, 1997. Available online from http://www.cinetropic.com/bonnieandclyde/times97.html (accessed January 30, 2010). This newspaper article reports the story of how Warren Beatty became involved in the movie *Bonnie and Clyde* and includes interview excerpts from Robert Benton, David Newman, Arthur Penn, Faye Dunaway, Gene Wilder, Dick Lederer, Gene Hackman, and Beatty.

Goldstein, Richard. "Elmo R. Zumwalt Jr., Admiral Who Modernized the Navy Is Dead at 79." *New York Times*, January 3, 2000. This obituary reported the cause of death and provided brief biographical and career information about the admiral.

Goldstein, Warren. *William Sloane Coffin Jr.: A Holy Impatience*. New Haven: Yale University Press, 2006. This book is a compelling biography of an important cultural figure who participated in the Freedom Rides and in various demonstrations of the 1960s.

Goldwater, Barry M., with Casserly, Jack. *Goldwater*. New York: Doubleday, 1988. This straightforward biography chronicles the former senator's achievements and provides a forum in which he attacks his enemies.

Goldwater, Barry M. *With No Apologies: The Personal and Political Memoirs of United States Senator Barry M. Goldwater*. New York: William Morrow, 1979. Goldwater focuses on his losing campaign against Johnson in the 1964 presidential campaign and Nixon's fall from grace in this memoir.

Gomer Pyle, U.S.M.C. http://epguides.com/GomerPyleUSMC/. (accessed January 18, 2011). This website serves as a guide to titles and air dates for episodes of the popular television series *Gomer Pyle U.S.M.C.*

Gomer Pyle, U.S.M.C. http://timstvshowcase.com/gomer.html (accessed January 18, 2011). This website contains cast information, introductory material, stills from the series, audio files to the theme song, photo galleries, and links to other related resources.

Gonos, George. "Go-Go Dancing: A Comparative Frame Analysis." *Urban Life* 5 no. 3 (July 1976): 189–220.

Gonthier, David. *American Prison Film Since 1930: From the Big House to the Shawshank Redemption*. Lewiston, ME: Edwin Mellen Press, 2006. Gonthier studies 12 prison films including *Cool Hand Luke* from a variety of perspectives including the analytical and historical.

Goodman, Mitchell, ed. *The Movement Toward a New America: The Beginnings of a Long Revolution*. Philadelphia: Pilgrim Press, 1970. This compendium collects over 700 pages of art and essays about the U.S. counterculture of the late 1960s and early 1970s.

Goodwin, Doris Kearns. *The Fitzgeralds and the Kennedys: An American Saga*. New York: St. Martin's, 1987. This history of the families stops at 1961 and tells the rich immigrant story that characterized the American spirit.

Goodwin, Doris Kearns. *Lyndon Johnson and the American Dream*. New York: St. Martin's Griffin, 1991. In this popular political biography, Goodwin provides insight into Johnson's humanity as no other biographer could by virtue of her position as a member of his White House staff.

Goossen, E. C. *Helen Frankenthaler*. New York: Praeger, 1969. This volume features the artist's oeuvre through the end of the 1960s and documents her life and creative process in the studio with black-and-white photographs.

Gordon, Alastair. *Spaced Out: Crash Pads, Hippie Communes, Infinity Machines and Other Radical Environments of the Psychedelic Sixties*. New York: Rizzoli, 2008. This richly illustrated book draws readers into the redefined concepts of communities, buildings, and dwellings inspired by the utopian ideals of the 1960s.

Gordon, Leonard. *A City in Racial Crisis: The Case of Detroit Pre- and Post- the 1967 Riot*. New York: William C. Brown, 1971. Gordon assesses the black and white communities in the aftermath of the major 1967 Detroit race riot and suggests multiple ways communities may address the resultant issues confronting the city and its metropolitan area.

Gordon, Linda. *The Moral Property of Women: A History of Birth Control Politics in America*. Champaign: University of Illinois Press, 2007. Gordon follows the movement for legal birth control from the 1870s to the modern era and reasons that attitudes toward birth control are undividable from family values and go hand-in-hand with issues of sexuality and gender equality.

Gorman, Robert. *Michael Harrington: Speaking American*. New York: Routledge, 1995. This biographical portrait appraises the political and intellectual life of a young socialist.

Gosse, Van. *Rethinking the New left: An Interpretative History*. New York: Pargrave Macmillan, 2005. This book synthesizes and chronicles a host of movements from the 1950s to the 1970s but does not focus specifically on the 1960s.

Gottlieb, Robert. *Forcing the Spring: The Transformation of the American Environmental Movement*. Washington, DC: Island Press, 2005. This book provides n historical context for those interested in learning more about the environmental movement that emerged in the 1960s and links that with today's pressing issues of globalization, food, immigration, and sprawl.

Goudsouzian, Aram. *King of the Court: Bill Russell and the Basketball Revolution*. Berkeley: University of California Press, 2010. This book recounts the racial struggles of the first black superstar who later became the first black coach of any major professional team sport.

Goudsouzian, Aram. *Sidney Poitier: Man, Actor, Icon*. Durham: University of North Carolina Press, 2003. This serious, scholarly biography of the actor contextualizes Poitier within his time and identity, offers careful analysis of the actor's films, and chronicles the life and career of the controversial actor.

Gould, Lewis L. *Grand Old Party: A History of the Republicans*. New York: Random House, 2003. This work considers the shifts in GOP policies and attitudes since the party's formation.

Gould, Lewis L. *1968: The Election That Changed America*. 2nd ed. Chicago: Ivan R. Dee, 2010. In this narrative analysis, Gould illustrates how events of one year altered the way Americans thought about politics and their national leaders.

Graham, Hugh Davis. *Civil Rights and the Presidency: Race and Gender in American Politics, 1960–1972*. New York: Oxford University Press, 1992. This text reveals how the classic liberal agenda of nondiscrimination evolved into the controversial program of affirmative action under President Nixon.

Graham, Hugh Davis. *The Civil Rights Era: Origins and Development of National Policy, 1960–1972*. New York: Oxford University Press, 1990. This administrative history of civil rights in the United States examines bureaucratic laws and regulations and shows how they evolved into 1970s affirmative action decisions, which included women as well as blacks.

Graham, Katharine. *Katharine Graham's Washington*. New York: Vintage, 2003. This anthology of writings on Washington, D.C., includes essays from humorists, journalists, novelists, socialites, and political luminaries and their wives.

Graham, Katharine. *Personal History*. New York: Vintage, Reprint ed., 1998. Graham charts her personal life and the lives of her friends and colleagues in this easy-to-read account.

Grant, Joanne. *Ella Baker: Freedom Bound*. New York: John Wiley, 1998. Presumably a biography would focus on the subject named in its title, and this volume does detail the life and activities of Baker, but its greater focus is on the civil rights movement.

Gray, Tara. "Alan B. Shepard, Jr." http://history.nasa.gov/40thmerc7/shepard.htm (accessed January 18, 2011). This website provides biographical information about Shepard that is prepared, authorized, and maintained under the aegis of NASA.

Gray, Timothy. *Gary Snyder and the Pacific Rim: Creating Countercultural Community*. Iowa City: University of Iowa Press, 2006. This critical work survey's Snyder's poetry of the 1950s and 1960s and situates him within his role as spokesperson of the Haight-Ashbury hippie counterculture.

Greenberg, Jack. *Crusaders in the Court: How a Band of Dedicated Lawyers Fought for the Civil Rights Revolution*. New York: Basic Books, 2004. Greenberg melds his personal anecdotes as former head of the NAACP Legal Defense Fund with critical cases of the civil rights movement covering school integration, equal employment, housing and voter registration.

Greene, Eric. *Planet of the Apes as American Myth: Race, Politics, and Popular Culture*. Middletown, CT: Wesleyan University Press, 1998. Greene provides a deep analysis of the television series and the films within the cultural contexts in which they were envisioned, produced, and released.

Greenfieldboyce, Nell. "Pageant Protest Sparked Bra-Burning Myth." National Public Radio, September 5, 2008. This radio news story describes the protest of the 1968 Miss America pageant that spawned the myth associated with bra-burning feminists.

Grogan, Emmett. *Ringolevio: A Life Played For Keeps*. New York; New York Review of Books, 1972. This autobiography of a Haight-Ashbury character captures the bohemian and intellectual attitudes prevalent in the 1960s.

Grose, Peter. *Gentleman Spy: The Life of Allen Dulles*. Boston: Houghton Mifflin, 1994. This full-length biography covers the subject's career and delves into controversial issues in his personal and professional life as director of the CIA.

Gruening, Ernest. *Many Battles: The Autobiography of Ernest Gruening*. New York: Liveright, 1973. This autobiography describes the Alaskan politician's life and career as a journalist.

Guberman, Sidney. *Frank Stella: An Illustrated Biography*. New York: Rizzoli, 1995. This volume blends images of the artist's masterpieces within his biography and gets at the nitty-gritty process behind Stella's creativity in the studio.

Guida, Richard A. "The Costs of Free Information." *Public Interest* 97 (Fall 1989): 87–95. This article describes the number of unintended effects resulting from the Freedom of Information Act (FOIA) as well as the amendments proposed to prevent the use of the FOIA by criminals and foreign agents and to place the cost of administering the law on the user.

Gulbrandsen, Don. *Green Bay Packers: The Complete Illustrated History*. Osceola, WI: Voyageur Press, 2007. This reference guide to the team's statistics, rosters, chalkboard diagrams of key moments, and more offers fans details of the Packers' history.

Guldberg, Horacio Cerutti. *Filosofía de la Liberación Latino Americana*. Mexico: Fondo de Cultura Economica, 1983. This work examines the extent to which the philosophy of

Latin American liberation is an expression of the social and historical reality of Latin America and how resistance and inequality are expressed in speech, as history, sociology, and theology.

Guralnick, Peter. *Careless Love: The Unmaking of Elvis Presley*. New York: Back Bay Books, 2000. This volume covers Presley's tour of duty with the army in Germany, his filmmaking career, marriage to Priscilla, his '68 comeback, and culminates with his death.

Guralnick Peter. *Last Train to Memphis: The Rise of Elvis Presley*. New York: Back Bay Books, 1995. This volume covers Presley's childhood and early adulthood until he enters the army at age 24.

Guthrie, Arlo. *This Is the Arlo Guthrie Book*. New York: Collier, 1969. This musical score contains printed music, melodies for voice and guitar, and lyrics for 20 of Arlo Guthrie's songs.

H. III, C. W. "Federal Legislation to Safeguard Voting Rights: The Civil Rights Act of 1960." *Virginia Law Review* (46): 945–75. This report examines a new attempt by Congress to expand federal authority of judges to protect voting rights.

Hacker, Barton C., and James M. Grimwood. *On the Shoulders of Titans: A History of Project Gemini* (Report SP-4203). Washington, DC: National Aeronautics and Space Administration, 1977. Available online at: http://history.nasa.gov/SP-4203/toc.htm (accessed January 18, 2011). This report outlines the history of the Gemini project.

Hafner, Katie. *Where Wizards Stay Up Late: The Origins of the Internet*. New York: Simon & Schuster, 1996. This work credits a *Sputnik*-era project, ARPANET, as the beginning of the Internet.

Haggard, Merle, and Tom Carter. *Merle Haggard's My House of Memories: For the Record*. New York: Harper Entertainment, 1999. This blunt autobiography recounts the musician's sordid episodes along with his rise to fame and success.

Halberstam, David. *The Best and the Brightest*. New York: Random House, 1972. This comprehensive account of the Vietnam War and the decisions that led to it is easy to read and provides an entrée to an otherwise complex topic.

Halberstam, David. *The Children*. New York: Ballantine, 1998. This overview of the civil rights movement follows the lives of several children—Diane Nash, James Bevel, Jim Lewis, Curtis Murphy, Bernard Lafayette, and James Lawson—as they grow through the movement and ascend to leadership roles.

Halberstam, David. *Ho*. New York: McGraw-Hill, 1986. This short, focused biography offers insight into Ho Chi Minh's public and private life, but focuses mainly on his role during and after the Vietnam War.

Hales, Edward Elton Young. *Pope John and His Revolution*. New York: Doubleday, 1966. This work examines Pope John's work and life and vow to lead the Roman church into the modern era during his time in office.

Haley, Alex. *The Autobiography of Malcolm X*. New York: Ballantine, 1964. This memoir is the classic work on the black experience in America and was dictated to Haley via audiotapes just prior to Malcolm X's assassination.

Hall, Mitchell K. *Because of Their Faith: CALCAV and Religious Opposition to the Vietnam War*. New York: Columbia University Press, 1990. This study focuses on Clergy and Laymen Concerned about Vietnam, an antiwar movement that mobilized the religious community against the war in Vietnam.

Hamby, Alonzo. *Liberalism and Its Challengers: From F.D.R. to Bush*. New York: Oxford University Press, 1985. This survey of political history examines the peaks and valleys of U.S. liberalism in the United States since the Great Depression.

Hamilton, Ian. *Robert Lowell: A Biography*. New York: Vintage, 1983. This biography examines the poet's life and draws from private letters and published works.

Hammel, Eric M. *Six Days in June: How Israel Won the 1967 Arab-Israeli War*. New York: Scribners, 1992. This journalistic approach to the topic narrates how Israel prepared for the war and describes combat situations.

Hammer, Ellen J. *A Death in November: America in Vietnam, 1963*. Oxford: Oxford University Press, 1988. This work chronicles President Ngo Dinh Diem's final 10 months in office.

Hampton, Henry, and Steve Fayer, eds. *Voices of Freedom: An Oral History of the Civil Rights Movement from the 1950s Through the 1980s*. New York: Bantam, 1990. This oral history collection was compiled from 1,000 interviews and documents three decades of civil rights activism for black people.

Hankins, Barry. *Francis Schaeffer and the Shaping of Evangelical America*. Grand Rapids, MI: William B. Eerdmans, 2008. This critical biography explains how Schaeffer's thinking was molded by the contexts of his life.

Hansen, Drew D. *The Dream: Martin Luther King, Jr., and the Speech That Inspired a Nation*. New York: Ecco, 2003. Hansen analyzes King's Dream speech from a variety of viewpoints and draws multiple meanings and interpretations from each in terms of theology, intellectualism, and other topics.

Hansen, Jeffrey Scott. *Digging for the Truth: The Final Resting Place of Jimmy Hoffa*. New York: Spectre, 2009. The author leads readers along step-by-step as he investigates rumors of Hoffa's final resting place.

Harding, James M., and Cindy Rosenthal. *Restaging the Sixties: Radical Theaters and Their Legacies*. Ann Arbor: University of Michigan Press, 2002. This work profiles major political theaters and theater groups that came to prominence in the late '60s and early '70s.

Harland, David M. *How NASA Learned to Fly in Space: An Exciting Account of the Gemini Missions*. Burlington, Ontario, Canada: Apogee Books, 2004. This account of the Gemini Missions details the burgeoning U.S. space program in the fall of 1961.

Harper, Steven J. *Crossing Hoffa: A Teamster's Story*. New York: Borealis Books, 2007. This story reveals the life of a Teamster in the 1960s and what his son discovered many years later when he investigated his father's mysterious death.

Harrington, Michael. *The Long-Distance Runner: An Autobiography*. New York: Henry Holt, 1988. This political autobiography describes the socialist movement and offers insight into the behind-the-scenes mechanics of influencing national policy.

Harrington, Michael. *The Other America: Poverty in the United States*. New York: Macmillan, 1962. This classic work on America's underclass reveals the depth and scope of the poverty crisis.

Harrington, Michael. *Taking Sides: The Education of a Militant Mind*. New York: Henry Holt, 1985. Harrington reflects on his own life and relates issues and debates with which he aligned his beliefs as a political activist.

Harris, Mark. *Pictures at a Revolution: Five Movies and the Birth of the New Hollywood*. New York: Penguin, 2008. This excellent work on filmmaking in the 1960s examines film, actors, themes, new advances in technology, and how cultural and political issues affected the studios.

Harris, W. Edward. *Miracle in Birmingham: A Civil Rights Memoir, 1954–1965*. Indianapolis: Stonework Press, 2004. This memoir examines the small white liberal community in Birmingham, Alabama, during the civil rights movement.

Harrison, Cynthia. *On Account of Sex: The Politics of Women's Issues, 1945–1968*. Berkeley: University of California Press, 1988. This work argues that federal policies of the 1950s gave the burgeoning women's liberation movement a basis to launch their movement from.

Harry, Bill. *The British Invasion: How the Beatles and Other UK Bands Conquered America*. London: Chrome Dreams, 2004. This history includes interviews with key British musicians responsible for exploding onto the American music scene in the 1960s.

Haskell, Barbara. *Donald Judd*. New York: Whitney Museum of American Art, 1988. This catalog accompanied a major exhibition at Tate Modern in early 2004 and includes biographical information on the artist's work as well as critical analysis of his sculpture by Nicholas Serota Rudi Fuchs, Richard Shiff, David Raskin, and David Bachelor.

Hauser, Thomas. *Arnold Palmer: A Personal Journey*. San Francisco: HarperCollins, 1994. This authorized biography traces the golfer's life and career until his 1992 win at the Masters.

Hayden, Tom. *Reunion: A Memoir*. New York: Random House, 1988. In this political autobiography, Hayden hits the highlights of his activities in the 1960s: his cofounding of Students for a Democratic Society, marriage to Jane Fonda, protesting at the 1968 Democratic convention, and more.

Hayman, Ronald. *Edward Albee*. New York: Ungar, 1973. This begins with a chronology of the playwright's life, then examines his 12 plays and mentions their critical reception, lists a chronology of stage productions, and concludes with a bibliography and index.

Haynes, John Earl, and Harvey Klehr. *In Denial: Historians, Communism, and Espionage*. San Francisco: Encounter Books, 2003. The authors rehash major Cold War controversies and assert a new American communist historiography.

Hays, Samuel P. *Beauty, Health, and Permanence: Environmental Politics in the United States, 1955–1985*. New York: Cambridge University Press, 1987. This history of the postwar environmental movement offers a comprehensive treatment of a complex subject.

"He Was a Symbol: Eldridge Cleaver Dies at 62-May 1, 1998." http://www.cnn.com/US/9805/01/cleaver.late.obit/ (accessed January 10, 2010). This newspaper article reports the death of Clever and serves as an obituary.

Hebblethwaite, Peter *Paul VI: The First Modern Pope*. New York: Paulist Press, 1993. This comprehensive biography examines the life and career of Paul VI, pontiff from 1963 to 1978.

Hebblethwaite, Peter. *Pope John XXIII: Shepherd of the Modern World*. Garden City, NY: Doubleday, 1984. This biography of the pope responsible for calling the Second Vatican Council draws from the pontiff's detailed journal and other personal archives.

Heilbrun, Carolyn G. *The Education of a Woman: The Life of Gloria Steinem*. New York: Dial, 1995. This biography emphasizes aspects of Steinem's celebrity and lacks critical treatment of her life as a feminist activist and from a scholarly perspective.

Heineman, Kenneth. *Put Your Bodies upon the Wheels: Student Revolt in the 1960s*. Chicago: Ivan R. Dee, 2001. This work fails to examine student revolt from a class perspective or to make any coherent statement about the subject.

Heitland, Jon. *The Man from U.N.C.L.E. Book: The Behind the Scenes Story of a Television Classic*. New York: St. Martin's, 1987. This comprehensive account of the television show includes a complete episode guide, anecdotes from the cast and crew, and information about its conception, reception, and cancellation.

Heller, Joseph. *Catch-22*. New York: Simon & Schuster, 1996. This classic satire on war was first published in 1961 and deemed the finest novel on the subject to appear in years.

Heller, Steven. *Design Literacy: Understanding Graphic Design*. New York: Allworth, 2004. This self-study course offers case studies and perspectives on trends that allow those new to design to close the gaps in their education on the topic.

Helsing, Jeffrey W. *Johnson's War/Johnson's Great Society: The Guns and Butter Trap*. Santa Barbara, CA: Praeger, 2000. This study examines President Johnson's efforts to curtail the expansion of communism in Southeast Asia while advancing a Great Society at home.

Henderson, Leigh A., and William J. Glass, eds. *LSD: Still with Us After All These Years*. New York: Lexington Books, 1994. An essential resource for parents, counselors, and educators, this guide focuses on current statistics, anecdotes, and research to explore modern LSD use.

Hendrick, George, and Willene Hendrick. *Why Not Every Man? African Americans and Civil Disobedience in the Quest for the Dream*. Chicago: Ivan R. Dee, 2005. The authors sketch the origins and incidences of civil disobedience from Thoreau to Gandhi to King as they relate to African Americans.

Hennessee, Judith Adler. *Betty Friedan: Her Life*. New York: Random House, 1999. This thorough biography presents the subject with all her contradictions and describes her personal and public failures and achievements.

Herman, Jerry, and Marilyn Stacio. *Showtune: A Memoir*. New York: Donald I. Fine, 1996. This memoir discusses the author's controversial lifestyle, HIV status, and remarkable creative career.

Herring, George C. *America's Longest War: The United States and Vietnam, 1950–1975*. 2nd ed. New York: Alfred A. Knopf, 2002. This complete and balanced treatment of the Vietnam War amalgamates military, diplomatic, and political elements in its consideration.

Herring, George C. *LBJ and Vietnam: A Different Kind of War*. Austin: University of Texas Press, 1994. This analysis of President Lyndon Johnson's management of the war in Vietnam suggests that his style of leadership is what caused the war's failure.

Hersey, John. *The Algiers Motel Incident*. Baltimore, MD: Johns Hopkins University Press, 1998. This careful study recounts an event occurring during the Detroit Riot of 1967.

Hersh, Burton. *The Old Boys: The American Elite and the Origins of the CIA*. St. Petersburg, FL: Tree Farm Books, 2002. This history examines the establishment of the CIA and how it influenced the Cold War.

Hersh, Seymour M. *My Lai-4: A Report of the Massacre and Its Aftermath*. New York: Random House, 1970. This thorough survey of the events was released prior to the end of the trial and contains an able synthesis of primary and secondary sources.

Hervey, Ben. *Night of the Living Dead*. New York: Palgrave Macmillan, 2008. This study of the film is the first to provide a detailed critical analysis of its themes, symbols, critical reception, cultural meaning, and cult status.

Hickey, Gerald. *Free in the Forest: Ethnohistory of the Vietnamese Central Highlands, 1954–1976*. New Haven, CT: Yale University Press, 1982. This volume offers a detailed study of the ethnic groups inhabiting the Central Highlands of Vietnam.

Hicks, Michael. *Sixties Rock: Garage, Psychedelic & Other Satisfactions*. Urbana: University of Illinois Press, 1999. This book describes a musical genre whose artists have received little scholarly or popular attention within the context of their affiliation with garage rock and psychedelia.

Hill, Daniel Delis. *As Seen in Vogue: A Century of American Fashion in Advertising*. Lubbock: Texas Tech University Press, 2004. Hill's study of *Vogue* documents the evolution in U.S. fashion and society from as early as 1893.

Hill, Lee. *Easy Rider*. London: BFI Publishing, 1996. This study of the film provides a detailed critical analysis of its themes, symbols, critical reception, cultural meaning, and cult status.

Hillebrand, Henri, ed. *Graphic Designers in the USA*. New York: Universe Books, 1971. This reference source lists biographical and career information of graphic designers in the United States in alphabetical order.

Hilliard, David, and Donald Weise. *The Huey P. Newton Reader*. New York: Seven Stories, 2002. This collection of writings by the founder of the Black Panther Party shows the transformation of the party's ideals and directions as it grew to encompass other concerns such as feminist and gay rights.

Hilliard, David with Keith and Kent Zimmerman. *Huey: Spirit of the Panther*. New York: Thunder's Mouth, 2006. This authorized biography examines Newton's dichotomous nature and introduces readers to his life and legacy.

Hilton, Matthew. *Prosperity for All: Consumer Activism in the Era of Globalization*. Ithaca: Cornell University Press, 2009. This international history of consumerism examines issues of affluence, fair use, free trade, globalization, and changing definitions of consumerism.

Hinckle, Warren. *If You Have a Lemon, Make Lemonade*. New York: Putnam's, 1974. This fascinating, funny memoir charts the editor's private and professional life as he namedrops along the lines of Marshall McLuhan, Timothy Leary, Eldridge Cleaver, Jim Garrison, and Fidel Castro.

Hinckle, Warren. "A Social History of the Hippies." In *West of the West: Imagining California: An Anthology*. Edited Leonard Michaels, David Reid, and Raquel Scherr. Berkeley and Los Angeles: University of California, 1989. This chapter details impressions at a mountain symposium at a Summit Meeting convened in the lowlands of California's High Sierras to discuss the political future of the hippies.

Hirsch, Foster. *Harold Prince and the American Musical Theatre*. New York: Applause Theatre & Cinema Books, 2005. This work examines Prince's complete career.

Hirsch, James S. *Willie Mays: The Life, the Legend*. New York: Scribners, 2010. This authorized and definitive biography draws on interviews with Mays, his family, friends, and colleagues to create a fascinating portrait of an American cultural icon.

Hischak, Thomas S. *Boy Loses Girl: Broadway's Librettists*. Lanham, MD: Scarecrow, 2002. This reference source contains biographical information on major librettists of the American theatre.

Hitchens, Christopher. *The Trial of Henry Kissinger*. New York: Verso, 2001. This prosecutorial document indicts Kissinger as a war criminal.

Hodgkin, Thomas. *Vietnam: The Revolutionary Path*. New York: St. Martin's, 1981. This work places the August 1945 Vietnamese Revolution in the context of Vietnam's long history.

Hodgson, Godfrey. *The Gentleman from New York: Daniel Patrick Moynihan*. New York: Houghton Mifflin, 2000. This biography discusses the politician's career as a legislator and as an intellectual.

Hodson, Joel C. *Lawrence of Arabia and American Culture: The Making of a Transatlantic Legend*. Westport, CT: Greenwood, 1995. Hodson uses the figure or symbol of Lawrence of Arabia to illustrate the power of popular culture and how myths are constructed and propagated.

Home of the Brave. Dir. Paola di Florio. Counterpoint Films, 2004. This documentary focuses on how the murder of civil rights activist Viola Liuzzo affected her family.

"Hoover, J. Edgar (1895–1972)." *Encyclopedia of United States National Security*, http://www.sageereference.com/nationalsecurity/Article_n279.html (accessed February 26, 2010). This encyclopedia article gives biographical information about Hoover and details his early life and career.

Hopkins, Jerry, and Daniel Sugerman. *No One Here Gets Out Alive*. New York: Warner Books, 1980. This biography of Jim Morrison covers the musician's childhood, adulthood, film education at UCLA, and musical career as the vocalist for the Doors.

Horn, Barbara Lee. *David Merrick: A Bio-Bibliography*. Westport, CT: Greenwood, 1992. This work compiles and annotates writings about and by Merrick, as well as providing biographical information about his life and career.

Horn, Barbara Lee. *The Age of Hair: Evolution and the Impact of Broadway's First Rock Musical*. New York: Greenwood, 1991. This comprehensive and academic investigation of *Hair* includes essentials such as cast and credits for the three New York productions and the film, an extensive bibliography, 1960s cultural context, staging, and nudity.

Horn, Robert. *Soviet-Indian Relations: Issues and Influence*. New York: Praeger, 1982. This study examines the acceleration of relations between the Soviet Union and India at mid-century.

Horowitz, Daniel. *The Anxieties of Affluence: Critiques of the American Consumer Culture, 1939–1970*. Boston: University of Massachusetts Press, 2004. This book charts American consumer habits from the end of the Great Depression until 1979.

Horowitz, Daniel. *Betty Friedan and the Making of the Feminine Mystique: The American Left, The Cold War, and American Feminism*. Amherst: University of Massachusetts Press, 1998. This work draws on her papers to trace Friedan's feminist genealogy.

Horton, Andrew. *The Films of George Roy Hill*. Jefferson, NC: McFarland, 2005. This work examines the director's films chapter by chapter, giving detailed study to the art, craft, and style of each.

Houston, Joe. *Optic Nerve: Perceptual Art of the 1960s*. London and New York: Merrell, 2007. This comprehensive survey of the art movement includes work by as Josef Albers, Bridget Riley, and Victor Vasarely.

Houston, Kay. "The Detroit Housewife Who Moved a Nation Toward Racial Justice." "Rearview Mirror," *Detroit News* http://web.archive.org/web/19990427180231/http://www.detroitnews.com/history/viola/viola.htm) (accessed January 18, 2011). This website provides biographical information about Viola Liuzzo, a civil rights worker who was murdered.

Hudson, Berkley, and Rebecca Townsend. "Unraveling the Webs of Intimacy and Influence: Willie Morris and *Harper's Magazine*, 1967–71." *Literary Journalism Studies* 1, no. 2 (2009): 63–78. This scholarly journal article characterizes Morris's editorship as promoting a creative, defiant culture that produced radical examples of New Journalism.

Hughes, Howard. *Stagecoach to Tombstone: The Filmgoers' Guide to the Great Westerns*. New York: Palgrave Macmillan, 2008. This guide to the Western genre includes a complete filmography, trivia, and insight into 27 key films.

Hughes, Langston. *Fight for Freedom: The Story of the NAACP*. New York: W. W. Norton, 1962. This history of the establishment of the organization emphasizes the human element and the personal stories of its founders rather than the dates and locations typically associated with organizational histories.

Hull, N. E. H., and Peter Charles Hoffer. *Roe v. Wade: The Abortion Rights Controversy in American History*. Lawrence: University Press of Kansas, 2001. This work covers the history of abortion laws in the United States over the centuries and provides information about social movements and forces that had an effect in changing or reforming them.

Hulsey, Byron C. *Everett Dirksen and His Presidents: How a Senate Giant Shaped American Politics*. Lawrence: University Press of Kansas, 2000. This comprehensive biography of the senator gathers widespread primary documents and blends them into a study of Dirksen's public career.

Hummel, Karl-Joseph. *Vatikanische Ostpolitik unter Johannes XXIII. und Paul VI. 1958–1978*. Paderborn: Schöningh, 1999. This German-language work examines the Vatican's foreign policy in Eastern Europe under the leadership of two pontiffs.

Humphrey, Hubert. *Education of a Public Man: My Life and Politics*. Minneapolis: University of Minnesota Press, 1991. This readable autobiography, while not the most comprehensive, recounts the life, career, and vice presidency of Humphrey.

Hunt, Andrew E. *The Turning: A History of Vietnam Veterans Against the War*. New York: New York University Press, 1999. This volume examines the history of the Vietnam Veterans Against the War, which placed veterans protesting alongside students in the U.S. antiwar movement in the 1960s.

Hunt, Michael H. *Lyndon Johnson's War: America's Cold War Crusade in Vietnam: 1945–1968*. New York: Hill and Wang, 1996. This scholarly study of U.S. involvement in Vietnam is based on documents gathered at Hanoi, Washington, and the Johnson Presidential Library.

Huntley, Horace, and McKerley, John W, eds. *Foot Soldiers for Democracy: The Men, Women, and Children of the Birmingham Civil Rights Movement*. Urbana: University of Illinois Press, 2009.

Huxley, Aldous. *The Doors of Perception/Heaven and Hell*. New York: Harper Colophon, 1963. This is Huxley's argument for the use of hallucinogens as a means to opening the mind to new ideas and perceptions.

Icons: A Portrait of England, "The V Sign: The Japanese Version." http://www.icons.org.uk/theicons/collection/the-v-sign/a-harvey-smith-to-you/the-asian-v-sign-in-progress), (accessed June 27, 2010). This website includes photos and text identifying and describing the meaning of the Japanese version of the V sign.

Icons: A Portrait of England, "The V Sign: V for Victory." http://www.icons.org.uk/theicons/collection/the-v-sign/biography/v-for-victory), (accessed 27 June 2010). This website includes photos and text identifying and describing the meaning of the V is for Victory sign.

Ingham, Chris. *The Rough Guide to the Beatles*. London: Rough Guides, 2003. This companion to the musical group contains biographical and career highlights of each Beatle and the group, their solo years, facts, statistics, and critical commentary on all their combined creative works.

Ingham, Zita. "Edward Abbey." *American Nature Writers*. Edited by John Elder. 2 vols. New York: Scribner-Simon & Schuster Macmillan, 1996. 1–19. This chapter includes a black-and-white photograph, a bibliography of Abbey's works, a list of biographical and critical studies, and profiles his life as well as themes of nature in his writing.

Ingram, Robert, and Paul Duncan. *François Truffaut: Film Author 1932–1984*. New York: Taschen, 2004. This book outlines the director's career and is special for its rare images from Truffaut's personal archives.

Insdorf, Annette. *François Truffaut*. Boston: Twayne, 1978. This guide to the director's films offers insight into his influences and his approaches to filmmaking.

Internet Movie Database (IMDB). "Annette Funicello." http://www.imdb.com (accessed July 30, 2010). This website offers brief biographical information but an in-depth filmography for Funicello.

Internet Movie Database (IMDB). "The Graduate." http://www.imdb.com (accessed July 30, 2010). This website offers brief plot summary of the movie and information about director, producer, cast, crew, credits, etc.

Isaacson, Walter, and Evan Thomas. *The Wise Men: Six Friends and the World They Made*. New York: Simon & Schuster, 1997. This group biography focuses on the lives of six men who ran the State Department during World War II and the Cold War: Dean Acheson, Charles Bohlen, Averell Harriman, George Kennan, Robert Lovett, and John Jay McCloy.

Isaacson, Walter. *Kissinger: A Biography*. New York: Simon & Schuster, 1992. This massive biography provides insight into the political scientist and diplomat's early childhood and details his exploits as a Washington insider.

Isserman, Maurice. *If I Had a Hammer: The Death of the Old Left and the Birth of the New Left*. New York: Basic Books, 1987. This scholarly history traces the roots of the New Left to the 1950s and 1960s.

Isserman, Maurice. *The Other American: The Life of Michael Harrington*. New York: Public Affairs, 2000. This study argues that the Socialist Party under Harrington's leadership in the early 1960s was not so different in its operations from the Communist Party that he despised.

Isserman, Maurice, and Michael Kazin. *America Divided: The Civil War of the 1960s*. New York: Oxford University Press, 2000. This survey of the 1960s offers a standard and conventional summary with no surprises.

Jackson, Jean-Pierre. *Miles Davis*. Arles: Actes-Sud, 2007. This French-language biography questions the stereotypes of Davis in his later years that marked him as a rock star.

Jackson, John. *American Bandstand: Dick Clark and the Making of a Rock 'n' Roll Empire*. New York: Oxford University Press, 1999. This work sketches the 40-year history of Clark's run as host of the popular television show and gives insight into its cultural influence and relevance in each decade.

Jackson, Thomas F. *From Civil Rights to Human Rights: Martin Luther King, Jr., and the Struggle for Economic Justice*. Philadelphia: University of Pennsylvania Press, 2006. This study cements King's commitment to social justice as a means of addressing and correcting America's race- and class-based socioeconomic hierarchy.

Jaffe, Philip J. *The Rise and Fall of American Communism*. New York: Horizon Press, 1975. This work examines the American Communist Party in the 1930s and 1940s, but adds little that prior histories of the party have not covered better.

James, Daniel. *Che Guevara: A Biography*. New York: Stein and Day, 1969. This biography examines Guevara's childhood, quickly segues into a treatment of his military maneuvers, and concludes with his death as a soldier.

Jamieson, Kathleen Hall, and David S. Birdsell. *Presidential Debates: The Challenge of Creating an Informed Electorate*. New York: Oxford University Press, 1988. This guide provides further information about the purpose of a political debate and examines its origins in the eighteenth century, its evolution, and strategies for updating it.

Jamieson, Neil L. *Understanding Vietnam*. Berkeley: University of California Press, 1993. This introduction to Vietnamese people, their culture, and their history allows readers to experience the diversity of expression and thought as articulated in the poems, prose, essays, essays, reports, interviews, and anecdotes included in this book.

Janken, Kenneth Robert. *Walter White: Mr. NAACP*. Chapel Hill: University of North Carolina Press, 2006. In this blend of scholarship and popular history, White's life and legacy as a civil rights champion are given their due.

Jeffreys-Jones, Rhodri. *The CIA and American Democracy*, 3rd ed. New Haven, CT: Yale University Press, 2003. This complete history of the CIA examines its significance from 1947 to the present.

Jeffries, Judson L., ed. *Black Power in the Belly of the Beast*. Urbana: University of Illinois, 2006. This in-depth look at the black power movement covers 1963 until the mid-1970s in 12 chapters devoted to specific organizations.

Jeffries, Judson L. *Huey P Newton: The Radical Theorist*. Jackson, MS: University Press of Mississippi, 2002. This work argues that Newton was an important political thinker of America's civil rights movement.

Jellinek, George. *Callas: Portrait of a Prima Donna*. New York: Dover, 1986. This biography of the opera personality chronicles her life, creative roles, and controversial choices.

Jensen & Walker. *The Pritzker Architecture Prize: 1991, Robert Venturi*. Los Angeles: Jensen & Walker, 1991. This work was published as part of the formal program and award presentation, Palacio de Iturbide, Mexico City, Mexico, May 16, 1991.

Jodidio, Philip, and Janet Adams Strong. *I.M Pei: Complete Works*. New York: Rizzoli, 2008. This volume showcases over 50 of the architect's works with rich photographs, sketches, and plans; scholarly text accompanies each structure.

John F. Kennedy Presidential Library and Museum, Historical Resources, http://www.jfklibrary.org.

John XXIII, Pope. *Journal of a Soul*. Garden City, NY: Doubleday, 1980. This record traces the Pope's thoughts and spiritual development, contains a biographical portrait written by his personal secretary, several of his moving prayers, several letters, his last will and testament, 60 brief thoughts and aphorisms, as well as other items.

Johnson, Lady Bird. *A White House Diary*. New York: Holt, Rinehart, and Winston, 1970. This behind-the-scenes account of the Johnson White House records critical events of the times and the First Lady's own interests such as her environmental activism.

Johnson, Lyndon B. *My Hope for America*. New York: Random House, 1964. This short book served as campaign literature for the 1964 election and listed Johnson's domestic and foreign policies.

Johnson, Lyndon B. *The Vantage Point: Perspectives of the Presidency 1963–1969*. New York: Holt, Rinehart, and Winston, 1971. This memoir devotes a great deal of space to Vietnam and highlights issues in his presidency that were close to his heart such as civil rights and the War on Poverty.

Johnson, Robert David. *Ernest Gruening and the American Dissenting Tradition*. Cambridge: Harvard University Press, 1998. This excellent congressional biography chronicles Gruening's 60-year public career as a dissenter.

Joint Chiefs of Staff. Historical Division, Joint Secretariat. *The History of the Joint Chiefs of Staff, The Joint Chiefs of Staff and the War in Vietnam: 1960–1968, Part I & II.* Washington, DC: July 1970. This work chronicles the mission, objectives, and role of the Joint Chiefs of Staff over an eight-year period in Vietnam.

Jonas, Gilbert. *Freedom's Sword: The NAACP and the Struggle Against Racism in America, 1909–1969.* New York: Taylor and Francis, 2004. This work chronicles the organization's first 60 years through the efforts of grassroots citizens and regional and national leaders.

Jones, Charles E. "From Protest to Black Conservatism: The Demise of the Congress of Racial Equality." In *Black Political Organizations in the Post-Civil Rights Era*, Ollie and A. Johnson III and Karin L. Stanford, eds. New Brunswick, NJ: Rutgers University Press, 2002. Part of a larger work, this chapter narrates the ideological transformation of CORE.

Jones, Howard. *Death of a Generation: How the Assassinations of Diem and JFK Prolonged the Vietnam War.* Oxford: Oxford University Press, 2003. This book links America's escalating entrenchment in Vietnam with the aftermath of the death of each country's leader.

Jones, Howard. *The Bay of Pigs.* Oxford: Oxford University Press, 2008. This definitive history of the invasion posits that it initiated a new trend in U.S. foreign policy by blending military force with assassination.

Jones, John Bush. *Our Musicals, Ourselves: A Social History of the American Musical Theatre.* Lebanon, NH: University Press of New England, 2003. This encyclopedic social history of American theater examines the social issues that affected the development of the Broadway musical.

Jones, Tom, and Harvey Schmidt. *The Fantasticks: The Complete Illustrated Text Plus The Official Fantasticks Scrapbook and History of the Musical.* New York: Applause, 2002. This work includes Tom Jones's recollections; the show's lyrics and music; drawings of the stage settings; and concludes with a scrapbook section providing biographical information about cast, crew, authors, producers, etc.

Joplin, Laura. *Love, Janis.* New York: Villard Books, 1992. This revealing and even-handed account of the musician's life written by her sister offers insights into Joplin's childhood, personality, and personal struggles that no "official" biographer could understand.

Jowitt, Deborah. *Jerome Robbins: His Life, His Theater, His Dance.* New York: Simon & Schuster, 2004. This biography covers Robbins's struggle with sexual and ethnic identity, his inspired choreography, his testimony before the House Committee on Un-American Activities in the 1950s, and his work on popular Broadway shows of the 1950s and '60s.

Judd, Donald. *Complete Writings 1959–1975: Gallery Reviews, Book Reviews, Articles, Letters to the Editor, Reports, Statements, Complaints.* Halifax: Press of the Nova Scotia College of Art and Design, 2005. This volume collects the artist and critic's complete writings, which provide critical analysis of this groundbreaking era in American art.

Kackman, Michael. *Citizen Spy: Television, Espionage, and Cold War Culture.* Minneapolis: University of Minnesota Press, 2005. Kackman considers how media representations of the spy are entrenched in the American imagination.

Kagan, Norman. *The Cinema of Stanley Kubrick.* New York: Continuum, 2000. This study summarizes plots of each of Kubrick's films, offers details from each, and documents scholarly and popular criticism as well.

Kahin, George McT. *Intervention: How America Became Involved in Vietnam.* New York: Alfred A. Knopf, 1986. This work summarizes the expansion of U.S. involvement in Vietnam, 1945–1966.

Kaiser, Charles. *1968 in America: Music, Politics, Chaos, Counterculture, and the Shaping of a Generation.* New York: Weidenfeld & Nicolson, 1988. This book reflects the author's perspective as a supporter of Eugene McCarthy and focuses on the 1968 campaign trail and political life.

Kaiser, David. *American Tragedy: Kennedy, Johnson, and the Origins of the Vietnam War.* Cambridge, MA: Harvard University Press, 2000. This governmental history tracks the origins of the Vietnam War through the administration of two presidents and places them with the Eisenhower administration.

Kaliss, Jeff. *I Want to Take You Higher: The Life and Times of Sly and the Family Stone.* Hal Leonard, 2008. This work reflects on the band from its origins to current plans for a comeback.

Kamitsuka, David G. *Theology and Contemporary Culture: Liberation, Postliberal and Revisionary Perspectives.* Cambridge, MA: Cambridge University Press, 1999. This scholarly work presents Christian theology and methodology from a Latin American liberation theology perspective as a response to needs generated by contemporary culture.

Kantor, Seth. *Who Was Jack Ruby?* New York: Everest House, 1978. This sketch of the man who shot President Kennedy gathers information about Ruby's origins, childhood, livelihood, and habits, and intersperses that with conspiracy theories about whether he acted alone or with others.

Kaplan, Lawrence M. *Nike Zeus: The U.S. Army's First Antiballistic Missile.* Falls Church, VA: Missile Defense Agency, 2009. This 18-page document chronicles the history of the U.S. Army's first antiballistic missile; the report was approved for public release 09-MDA-4885 (October 20, 2009).

Kaplan, Marshall, and Cuciti, Peggy L. *The Great Society and Its Legacy: Twenty Years of U.S. Social Policy.* Duke University Press, 1986. This inspection of the Great Society and its aftermath describes and evaluates America's key social policy initiatives from Presidents Johnson to Reagan.

Kaplan, Marshall. *The Model Cities Program: The Planning Process in Atlanta, Seattle, and Dayton.* New York: Praeger, 1970. This work provides a brief description and evaluation of the planning experience in the first round of planning grants to illustrate factors influencing the content, direction, product, and impact of the model cities planning process.

Karnow, Stanley. *Vietnam: A History.* New York: Viking, 1983. This monumental history traces the decisions U.S. foreign policy makers reached to bring troops into Southeast Asia and out again.

Kastner, Jeffrey and Brian Wallis. *Land and Environmental Art.* New York: Phaidon, 1998. This survey of the art form defines and examines the movement and places it in its historical context, then surveys major examples of the form beginning with works as early as 1947, and concludes with articles, reviews, and artists' statements in support of land and environmental art.

Katzman, Robert A., ed. *Daniel Patrick Moynihan: The Intellectual in Public Life.* Washington, DC: Woodrow Wilson Center Press, 2004. This *festschrift* was compiled in celebration of the subject's 70th birthday and expounds on his ideas in essays written by persons such as Bill Bradley, Nathan Glazer, Stephen Hess, Suzanne R. Garment, Robert A. Peck, Seymour Martin Lipset, and Nicholas N. Eberstadt.

Kelly, Richard. *The Andy Griffith Show.* Winston-Salem, NC: John F. Blair, 1981. This definitive study of the television series contains a working script, episode summaries, interviews with the cast and crew, and other items.

Keniston, Kenneth. "Review: Counter-Culture: Cop Out . . . ." In *Life* magazine 67 no. 19 (November 7, 1969): 10–11. This book review of Theodore Roszak's *The Making of a Counter Culture* presents the author's argument that the youth culture of today is so radical it scarcely looks like a culture at all.

Kennedy, Edward M. *True Compass.* New York: Grand Central Publishing, 2009. This memoir shares the senator's life story, demonstrates the powerful influence that his family had on his life, examines controversies that plagued him, and surmises career highlights and disappointments.

Kennedy, Robert F. *The Enemy Within*. New York: Harper, 1960. This volume relates the corruption within the Teamsters and other unions that Kennedy investigated as part of his role as chief counsel of the 1957–1959 Senate Labor Rackets Committee.

Kenneth Hamilton. *God Is Dead: The Anatomy of a Slogan*. Grand Rapids, MI: William B. Eerdmans, 1966. This book examines Christian atheism as promoted by William Hamilton and Thomas Altizer.

Keough, Pamela Clark: *Jackie Style*. NY: HarperCollins, 2001. This volume establishes Jackie as a fashion icon, recreates her personal fashion style via black-and-white photographs, personal letters, memos, and essays, allowing readers to examine the progression of her taste in clothing designers and accessories and how her choices influenced women in the 1960s and today.

Kerr, Clark. *The Gold and the Blue: A Personal Memoir of the University of California, 1949–1967*. Berkeley: University of California Press, 2001. This memoir of a faculty member, administrator, and president of the University of California traces the growth of that institution from an insider's perspective and provides insight into his decisions regarding student demonstrations on campus in 1964.

Kesey, Ken. *One Flew Over the Cuckoo's Nest: Text and Criticism*. Edited by John Clark Pratt. New York: Viking Penguin, 1973. This edition includes sketches the author completed while institutionalized and a new introduction to this classic novel of a man who faked insanity to escape a jail term for vandalism.

Keyser, Herbert H. *Geniuses of the American Musical Theatre: The Composers and Lyricists*. New York: Applause Theatre & Cinema Books, 2009. This work collects 28 biographical entries of outstanding songwriters and lyricists of Broadway musicals.

Kezich, Tullio. *Federico Fellini: His Life and Work*. Translated by Minna Proctor with Viviana Mazza. New York: Faber & Faber, 2006. This work's primary focus is the director's work, not his life, though elements of his biography appear in anecdotes related by the author who is a personal friend to Fellini.

Kiley, Frederick, and Stuart Rochester. *Honor Bound: The History of American Prisoners of War in Southeast Asia, 1961–1973*. Washington, DC: Historical Office, Office of the Secretary of Defense, 1998. This comprehensive, balanced, and authoritative account investigates what happened to almost 800 Americans captured during the Vietnam War.

Kimball, Jeffrey. *Nixon's Vietnam War*. Lawrence: University of Kansas Press, 1998. This work reassesses the "peace with honor" myth that Nixon argued characterized his foreign policy approach.

Kimball, Penn. *Keep Hope Alive: Super Tuesday and Jesse Jackson's 1988 Campaign for the Presidency*. Washington, DC: Joint Center for Political and Economic Studies. 1991. This work traces Jackson's 1988 presidential campaign across the United States.

King, Billie Jean, and Frank Deford. *Billie Jean*. New York: Penguin Group USA, 1982. This autobiography records King's childhood, training as an athlete, and her first doubles win at Wimbledon in 1961 and other career highlights as a professional tennis player.

King, Desmond S. *Making Americans: Immigration, Race, and the Origins of the Diverse Democracy*. Cambridge, MA: Harvard University Press, 2000. This study presents the issues surrounding immigration policies and how they affect our notions and experiences of democracy.

King, Larry L. *In Search of Willie Morris: The Mercurial Life of a Legendary Writer and Editor*. New York: Public Affairs, 2006. This biography of the editor who revitalized America's oldest magazine, *Harper's*, describes how he modernized the magazine, his relationships with the literati, and his resignation in 1971.

King, Martin Luther. *I Have A Dream: Writings and Speeches That Changed the World*. San Francisco: HarperCollins, 1982. This work collects King's most important writings and orations.

King, Martin Luther, and Clayborne Carson, ed. *The Autobiography of Martin Luther King, Jr.* New York: Grand Central Publishing, 1998. This posthumous autobiography draws on King's essays, notes, letters, speeches, and sermons.

Kingston Victoria. *Simon & Garfunkel: The Biography.* New York: Fromm International, 1998. This work chronicles the friendship and creative partnership of Paul Simon and Art Garfunkel.

Kirkwood, James. *American Grotesque: An Account of the Clay Shaw-Jim Garrison-Kennedy Assassination Trial in New Orleans.* New York: Harper Perennial, 1992. This interesting study of the Garrison investigation documents police corruption in the state of Louisiana, contains inaccurate information, questionable sources, and skewed perspectives.

Kissel, Howard. *David Merrick, the Abominable Showman: The Unauthorized Biography.* New York: Applause, 1993. This portrait documents the producer's behavior and business practices and chronicles the his popular Broadway shows.

Kissinger, Henry A. *White House Years.* Boston: Little, Brown, 1979. This work provides Kissinger's insights into the politics of the diplomatic process.

Kissinger, Henry A. *Years of Upheaval.* Boston: Little, Brown, 1982. In this work, Kissinger recalls the chaotic years of the second administration of Richard Nixon.

Klagsbrun, Francine, and David C. Whitney. *Assassination: Robert F. Kennedy, 1925–1968.* New York: Cowles, 1968. This work collects photographs and newspaper articles published at the time of Kennedy's assassination.

Klehr, Harvey, and John Earl Haynes. *The American Communist Movement: Storming Heaven Itself.* New York: Twayne, 1992. This account of the communist movement in the United States provides useful information on the party's activities and how the party line shifted, but otherwise fails to explain regular turnover in leadership.

Klima, John. *Willie's Boys: The 1948 Birmingham Black Barons, the Last Negro League World Series, and the Making of a Baseball Legend.* Hoboken, NJ: John Wiley, 2009. This history of the Black Barons touches on Willie Mays's experience of Birmingham segregation, baseball's intuitional racism, and signing with the New York Giants.

Kluger, Richard. *Simple Justice: The History of Brown v. Board of Education and Black America's Struggle for Equality.* New York: Knopf Doubleday, 2004. This history of the Supreme Court case and decision examines race relations in America, details the cases that culminated in *Brown*, and explicates the judicial process by which the Court reached their decision.

Knox, E. Kitzes. *Gomer Pyle, U.S.M.C.* New York: Pyramid, 1965. This novel was based on the television series.

Kofsky, Frank. *John Coltrane and the Jazz Revolution of the 1960s.* New York: Pathfinder, 1998. This book compiles articles about Coltrane originally published in *Jazz Review*.

Kolko, Gabriel. *Anatomy of a War: Vietnam, the United States, and the Modern Historical Experience.* New York: Pantheon, 1985. This study represents a thorough Marxist contextualization of the war.

Kosc, Grzegorz. *Robert Lowell: Uncomfortable Epigone of the Grands Maîtres.* New York: Peter Lang, 2005. This book offers a radical reexamination of Lowell's entire oeuvre, concluding that he sought a crypto-modernist confessionalism style characteristic of the 1960s.

Kosygin, Aleksey Nikolayevich. *Selected Speeches and Writings.* Oxford: Pergamon, 1981. This Russian translation collects selected speeches and writings of the statesman who led Soviet Russia's economic reform.

Kozol, Jonathan. *Death at an Early Age: The Destruction of the Hearts and Minds of Negro Children in the Boston Public Schools.* Boston: Houghton Mifflin, 1967.

Kramer, Stanley. *A Mad, Mad, Mad, Mad World: A Life in Hollywood.* New York: Harcourt Brace, 1997. In this candid memoir, Kramer documents his life in Hollywood; readers may find his exploits during the McCarthy era noteworthy.

Krepinevich, Andrew F. *The Army in Vietnam.* Baltimore, MD: Johns Hopkins University Press, 1986. This study argues that the army's refusal to change its standard operating procedures doomed its operations in Vietnam until civilian strategists intervened after the Tet Offensive.

Krinsky, Carol Herselle. *Gordon Bunshaft of Skidmore, Owings & Merrill*. New York and Cambridge, MA: MIT Press, 1988. This analysis of the architect's work draws from interviews with the subject and considers his pioneering technological innovations as well.

Kruse, Kevin M. *White Flight: Atlanta and the Making of Modern Conservatism*. Princeton, NJ: Princeton University Press, 2005. This study draws connections between race, poverty, class, conservative politics, and real estate in Atlanta.

Kushner, Harvey W. "Federal Bureau of Investigation." *Encyclopedia of Terrorism*. California Oaks: SAGE Publications, 2003, pp. 132–134. This encyclopedia entry provides an overview of the FBI and chronicles its development, history, and expertise in handling domestic terrorist attacks.

Ky, Nguyen Cao. *Buddha's Child: My Fight to Save Vietnam*. New York: St. Martin's, 2002. This autobiography recounts the former South Vietnamese prime minister's rise to and fall from power.

Lacayo, Richard. "A Piece of Our Time." *Time*, March 27, 2008. http://www.time.com/time/magazine/article/0,9171,1725969,00.html (accessed June 27, 2010). This article examines the origins of the peace symbol on the 50th anniversary of its birth and examines its popularity amongst 1960s youth.

Lacouture, Jean. De Gaulle. New York: W. W. Norton, 1990–1992. This two-volume work covering the life and times of France's president presents his family background, education, military career, his election as president, resignation, and return to power.

LaFeber, Walter. *The Deadly Bet: LBJ, Vietnam, and the 1968 Election*. Lanham, MD: Rowman & Littlefield, 2005. This study discusses the election of 1968 and its implications for American culture and history.

Lahr, John, ed. *The Diaries of Kenneth Tynan*. New York: Bloomsbury, 2001. This rollicking recollection of Britain's foremost drama critic chronicles the international theater scene of the twentieth century.

Lake, John. "Two for the Football Show: The Swinger and the Square." *New York Times*, November 5, 1967, p. SM21. This newspaper article reports on Joe Namath's style, career, and influence on football.

Lambert, Patricia. *False Witness: The Real Story of Jim Garrison's Investigation and Oliver Stone's Film JFK*. New York: M. Evans, 2000. This work argues that Jim Garrison's 1969 prosecution of Clay Shaw was a red herring.

Lanagan, David. "Surfing in the Third Millennium: Commodifying the Visual Argot." *Australian Journal of Anthropology* 13 (2002): 283–91. This scholarly article outlines how the sport of surfing was appropriated by big business and commodified to create a lucrative market for lifestyle clothing.

Lansdale, Edward. *In the Midst of Wars: An American's Mission to Southeast Asia*. New York: Harper & Row, 1972. The first part of this book chronicles Lansdale's work as advisor to Phillipine President Ramon Magsaysay, and the second half covers his role as advisor to Vietnam's Ngo Dinh Diem.

Lassiter, Matthew D. *The Silent Majority: Suburban Politics in the Sunbelt South*. Princeton, NJ: Princeton University Press, 2006. Lassiter puts forward the argument that Republicans gained in the South because of a population boom, not because of regional racism.

Laver, Rod, with Bud Collins. *The Education of a Tennis Player*. 1971. Reprint. New York: New Chapter Press, 2009. This autobiography narrates the athlete's childhood, early career, important matches, and highlights his historic 1969 Grand Slam sweep of all four major tennis titles.

Lavezzoli, Peter. *The Dawn of Indian Music in the West: Bhairavi*. New York: Continuum, 2006. This work examines the influence of Indian music on American musicians beginning in the 1960s with artists such as Ravi Shankar, George Harrison of the Beatles, and John Coltrane.

Lawrence, Greg. *Dance with Demons: The Life of Jerome Robbins*. New York: Putnam's, 2001. This full-length biography seems gossipy at times, but the number of photographs and quotations makes for a rounded portrait of the subject.

Lawrence, Mark Atwood. *The Vietnam War: A Concise International History*. New York: Oxford University Press, 2008. Though brief, this work offers little new analysis, criticism, or interpretation that previous treatments of the war have not covered.

Le Beau, Bryan. *The Atheist: Madalyn Murray O'Hair*. New York: New York University Press, 2003. This study examines O'Hair's work to ban school prayer in her son's school and chronicles her efforts to separate church and state, the philosophical arguments behind her actions, and her bizarre disappearance and discovery of her body.

Leadership Conference on Civil Rights. "About LCCR and LCCREF." http://www.civilrights.org/about/ (accessed January 11, 2010.) This webpage provides basic information about LCCR and LCCREF such as the year it was founded and its mission and goals.

Leaming, Barbara. *Marilyn Monroe*. New York: Three Rivers Press, 1998. This book written by a leading celebrity-biographer gives brief discussion of Monroe's early years and focuses on her last 11 years; 1951–1962.

Lear, Linda. *Rachel Carson: Witness for Nature*. New York: Henry Holt, 1997. This biography investigates Carson's childhood, college education, federal government job, scientific training, and writing career.

Lee, Chana Kai. *For Freedom's Sake: The Life of Fannie Lou Hamer*. Chicago: University of Illinois Press, 1999. This biography is less concerned with Hamer's personal life than with her development as an activist via the Mississippi Freedom Democratic Party and leader of the civil rights movement.

Lee, Laura. *Arlo, Alice, and Anglicans: The Lives of a New England Church*. New York: W. W. Norton, 2000. This history covers the Trinity Church in western Massachusetts, which became a haven for East Coast hippies when it was deconsecrated in the early 1960s.

Lee, M. A., and Shlain, B. *Acid Dreams: The Complete Social History of LSD: The CIA, the Sixties and Beyond*. New York: Pan Books, 1985. This work includes profiles of Timothy Leary and Ronald Stark, and demonstrates the CIA's secret testing of LSD on Greenwich Village and San Francisco residents.

Lehman, Peter. *Roy Orbison: Invention of an Alternative Rock Masculinity*. Philadelphia: Temple University Press, 2003. This book accomplishes the typical goals of biography but offers a new model that considers Orbison's atypical masculinity as a factor in his creativity and career longevity.

Lehmann-Haupt, Christopher. "What Made Allard Lowenstein Run." *New York Times*, November 22, 1993. This article is a book review of William H. Chafe's *Never Stop Running*, which examines Allard K. Lowenstein's role in three liberal crusades of the 1960s and 70s.

Lemov, Michael R. "John Moss and the Battle for Freedom of Information, 41 Years Later." *Nieman Watchdog*, July 3, 2007. http://niemanwatchdog.org/index.cfm?fuseaction=background.view&backgroundid=00191 (accessed January 18, 2011). This commentary illustrates how Moss overcame many obstacles to win the American people access to information about the activities of their government.

Lerner, Mitchell B. *The Pueblo Incident: A Spy Ship and the Failure of American Foreign Policy*. Lawrence: University Press of Kansas, 2003. Lerner posits that North Korea acted on its own in the *Pueblo* Incident for completely domestic reasons and documents the crew's torture and imprisonment for almost a year.

Levine, Robert. *Maria Callas: A Musical Biography*. New York: Black Dog and Leventhal, 2003. This work covers Callas's career and personal life; photos and CDs accompanying the book allow readers to immerse themselves in a multimedia experience as they read about her accomplishments.

Levitan, Sar A., and Benjamin H Johnson. *The Job Corps: A Social Experiment That Works*. Baltimore, MD: Johns Hopkins University Press, 1975. This quasi-memoir provides a

Seydor, Paul. *Peckinpah: The Western Films—A Reconsideration.* Urbana and Chicago: University of Illinois Press, 1999. This book locates Peckinpah's work in the central tradition of American art.

Shabecoff, Philip. *Fierce Green Fire: The American Environmental Movement.* New York: Island Press, 2003. The new edition of this definitive history of U.S. environmentalism analyzes the Bush administration's record of antienvironmentalism.

Shankar, Ravi. *My Music, My Life.* New York: Simon & Schuster, 1968. This book chronicles the extraordinary career of India's best-known musician.

Shannon, David. *The Decline of American Communism: A History of the Communist Party of the United States Since 1945.* New York: Chatham Bookseller, 1959. This is a first-rate history of the party in which Shannon examines the Wallace Progressive Party, the defeat and expulsion of Browder, and other crucial moments in the party's history.

Shapiro, Andrew, and John Striker. *Mastering the Draft: A Comprehensive Guide for Solving Draft Problems.* Boston: Little, Brown, 1970. This work offers guidelines for dealing with issues of selective service and the draft.

Shapiro, David. *Jasper Johns Drawings, 1954–1984.* New York: Harry N. Abrams, 1984. This work is illustrated with more than 150 color, black-and-white, and other images of Johns's drawings and also includes an introductory text, notes, biography, and a list of his exhibitions.

Shaw, Randy. *Beyond the Fields: Cesar Chavez, the UFW, and the Struggle For Justice in the 21st Century.* Berkeley: University of California Press, 2008. This work narrates the story of the labor rights activist and the United Farm Workers in winning rights for workers.

Shayler, David J. *Gemini Steps to the Moon.* New York: Springer-Verlag, 2001. This book describes the Gemini program in vivid detail, especially in the context of NASA's response to Russia's dominance of space at the time.

Sheehan, Neil. *A Bright Shining Lie: John Paul Vann and America in Vietnam.* New York: Random House, 1988. This history of U.S. involvement in Vietnam centers on Vann's activities as a field advisor in the army during the early years.

Shellard, Dominic. *Kenneth Tynan: A Life.* New Haven: Yale University Press, 2003. This biography offers the first complete appraisal of Tynan's powerful contribution to postwar British theater, set against the context of the '50s, '60s, and '70s and his own turbulent life.

Shepard, Alan, and Deke Slayton, with Jay Barbree and Howard Benedict. *Moon Shot: The Inside Story of America's Race to the Moon.* Atlanta: Turner Publishing, 1994. This book recounts U.S. astronauts' experiences in the early days of the space program.

Shepherd, Donald, and Robert Slatzer. *Duke: The Life and Times of John Wayne.* New York: Zebra Books, Kensington, 1985. This work chronicles Wayne's life and film career.

Sheridan, Walter. *The Fall and Rise of Jimmy Hoffa.* New York: Saturday Review Press, 1972. This work chronicles the life and career of Hoffa and examines his role as an organizer and president of the International Brotherhood of Teamsters

Sherman, Janann. *No Place for a Woman: A Life of Senator Margaret Chase Smith.* New Brunswick, NJ: Rutgers University Press, 2000. This biography charts the personal and public arc of the senator's life.

Sheward, David. *Rage and Glory: The Volatile Life and Career of George C. Scott.* New York: Applause Theatre & Cinema Books, 2008.This work explores Scott's creative vision as well as his tumultuous career.

Shires, Preston. *Hippies of the Religious Right.* Waco, TX: Baylor University Press, 2007. This study argues that the hippie counterculture movement of the 1960s evolved into the Jesus Movement of the 1970s.

"Shirley Anita Chisholm." In *Black Americans in Congress, 1870–2007.* Washington, DC: U.S. government Printing Office, 2008. This encyclopedia entry features biographical and career highlights.

Shore, Michael. *The History of American Bandstand*. New York: Ballantine, 1985. This work uses the music show to chart evolving trends in U.S. popular culture of interest to teenagers.

Short, Bob. *Everything Is Pickrick: The Life of Lester Maddox*. Macon, GA: Mercer University Press, 1999. This revealing biography chronicles Maddox's paradoxical life and career as a businessman and politician.

Short, Philip. *Mao: A Life*. New York: Henry Holt, 2000. This book demonstrates how Mao's leadership modernized China.

Siegel, Deborah. *Sisterhood, Interrupted: From Radical Women to Girls Gone Wild*. New York: Macmillan, 2007. This book examines past struggles for women's equality and suggests that young women today must reconcile past history and create new theories applicable to their lives.

Sigler, David B. *Vietnam Battle Chronology: U.S. Army And Marine Corps Combat Operations, 1965–1973*. Jefferson, NC: McFarland, 1992. This reference tool is a chronological listing of over 600 army and marine combat operations from 1965 through 1973.

Simmons, Garner. *Peckinpah: A Portrait in Montage*. New York: Limelight, 2004. This work offers a balanced look at the life and work of director Sam Peckinpah.

Sinclair, Mick. *San Francisco: A Cultural and Literary History*. Northampton, MA: Interlink Books, 2004. This volume examines the city's literary, popular, social, and cultural evolution.

Singh, Robert. *The Congressional Black Caucus: Radical Politics in the U.S. Congress*. London: SAGE Publications, 1998. This history demonstrates that the Congressional Black Caucus has had a marginal impact on public policy.

Sitkoff, Harvard. *The Struggle for Black Equality, 1954–1980*. New York: Hill and Wang, 1981. This history of the civil rights movement shows that it has not lived up to its expectations.

Skidmore, Thomas et al. *Modern Latin America*, 7th ed. New York: Oxford University Press, 2010. This overview offers a timeline of key events, analyses of major news developments, lists of heads of state, and case studies that discuss the major countries and themes of the region over the past 150 years.

Sloane, Arthur. *Hoffa*. Cambridge, MA: MIT Press, 1992. This biography of the labor leader and union president offers a comprehensive portrait that focuses on how he influenced the industry.

Slotkin, Richard. *Gunfighter Nation: The Myth of the Frontier in Twentieth-Century America*. New York: Macmillan, 1992. This work appraises the significance of the frontier in the American imagination through its examination of film and pulp novels.

Slusser, Robert M. *The Berlin Crisis of 1961; Soviet-American Relations and the Struggle for Power in the Kremlin, June-November 1961*. Baltimore, MD: Johns Hopkins University Press, 1973. This book focuses on the factors influencing the strength of Khrushchev's leadership and illustrates the complex military issues at play during the crisis.

Small, Melvin. *Johnson, Nixon, and the Doves*. New Brunswick, NJ: Rutgers University Press, 1988. This history examines whether the antiwar movement had any effect on the presidents or their advisors.

Smith, Jeremy, and Melanie Ilic, eds. *Khrushchev in the Kremlin: Policy and Government in the Soviet Union, 1956–64*. London: Routledge, 2010. This book presents a new picture of the politics, economics, process of government in the Soviet Union under the leadership of Nikita Khrushchev.

Smith, Larry David. *Elvis Costello, Joni Mitchell, and the Torch Song Tradition*. London: Praeger, 2004. This work explores how the torch song tradition combined with the force of personality in two major singer-songwriters, examining their respective life's work and the ways in which that work reflect the artists' world-views.

Smith, Patti. *Just Kids* New York: HarperCollins, 2010. This memoir traces the love affair that began in New York City in the 1960s and evolved into a lifelong friendship between rocker Patti Smith and photographer Robert Mapplethorpe.

Smith, Paul. *Clint Eastwood: A Cultural Production*. Minneapolis: University of Minnesota Press, 1993. This work interprets and critiques Eastwood's films and demonstrates their complex and problematic relationship to American culture.

Smith, Peter H. *Talons of the Eagle: Latin America, the United States, and the World*. 3rd ed. New York: Oxford University Press, 2008. This work explores the relationship between the United States and Latin America through three stages: imperial, Cold War, and uncertainty.

Smith, Suzanne. *Dancing in the Street: Motown and the Cultural Politics of Detroit*. Cambridge, MA: Harvard University Press, 2001. This history of Motown uses the label and its artists as a means of examine its role in the civil rights movement.

Smurthwaite, Nick, and Paul Gelder. *Mel Brooks and the Spoof Movie*. London and New York: Proteus Books, 1982. This work examines Brooks's filmography and provides an introduction to and critical analysis of the genre.

Smyser, R. W. *Kennedy and the Berlin Wall: A Hell of a Lot Better Than a War*. Lanham, MD: Rowman & Littlefeld, 2009. This work examines the Berlin Wall crisis and chronicles the tensions between President Kennedy and General Lucius Clay.

Snead, James A. *White Screens/Black Images: Hollywood from the Dark Side*. London: Routledge, 1994. Essays in this collection offer thoughtful inquiry into the intricate modes of racial coding in Hollywood cinema from 1915 to 1985.

Snodgrass, Mary Ellen. *Civil Disobedience: An Encyclopedic History of Dissidence in the United States*. 2 vols. Armonk, NY: Sharpe Reference, 2009. This work explores the philosophies, themes, concepts, and practices of activist groups and individuals, as well as the legislation they influenced. A detailed chronology of civil disobedience, listings of acts of conscience and civil disobedience by act and by location, a bibliography of primary and secondary sources, and a comprehensive index complete the set.

Solberg, Carl. *Hubert Humphrey: A Biography*. St. Paul, MN: Borealis Books, 2003. This biography presents a portrait of a vivacious, complex man, the leading orator and most productive legislator of his age.

Solinger, Rickie, ed. *Abortion Wars: A Half Century of Struggle, 1950–2000*. Berkeley: University of California Press, 1998. This collection of 18 essays written by abortion supporters scrutinize the current political and social trends regarding the issue and present a variety of experiences and opinions across the pro-choice spectrum.

Sorsensen, Theodore C. *Kennedy*. New York: Harper & Row, 1965. This biography, penned by Kennedy's speechwriter, covers the president's life and career.

Sousa, William H. "Federal Bureau of Investigation." In *Encyclopedia of Crime and Punishment*, ed. by David Levinson. California Oaks, CA: SAGE Publications, 2002, pp. 684–85. This entry provides basic information about the agency such as its mission, directors, criminal proceedings, etc.

Southern Poverty Law Center. "Council of Conservative Citizens." http://www.splcenter.org/get-informed/intelligence-files/groups/council-of-conservative-citizens (accessed July 3, 2010). This webpage provides information about the white nationalist group including its date of organization, location, leader, ideology, background, and narrative of its activities.

Southern, Eileen. *The Music of Black America: A History*. New York: W. W. Norton, 1997. This work examines the development of black music from 1619 to the present and covers genres as diverse as gospel, blues, jazz, classical, crossover, Broadway, and rap as they relate to African American music.

The Southern Historical Collection. "Shelby Foote Papers." http://www.lib.unc.edu/mss/inv/f/Foote,Shelby.html (accessed November 6, 2010).

Spector, Ronald H. *Advice and Support: The Early Years of the United States Army in Vietnam 1941–1960*. New York: Free Press, 1985. describes the activities of the U.S. Army in Vietnam during World War II, military advice and assistance to the French government during the immediate postwar years, and the advisory program that developed after the Geneva Agreements of 1954.

Spikes, Michael P. "Willie Morris and the Power of Memory." *Arkansas Review: A Journal of Delta Studies* 35, no. 3 (December 2004): 168–78. This article profiles Morris and examines the influence of his southern childhood on his life and work.

Spock, Benjamin, and Mitchell Zimmerman. *Dr. Spock on Vietnam*. New York: Dell, 1968. Spock writes about his opposition to the Vietnam war in this book.

Spoto, Donald. *Stanley Kramer, Film Maker*. New York: Putnam's, 1978. This biography examines the filmmaker's life and work.

Srodes, James. *Allen Dulles: Master of Spies*. Washington, DC: Regnery, 1999. This biography outshine its predecessor for its access to restricted family papers.

St. Charnez, Casey. *The Films of Steve McQueen*. Secaucus, NJ: Citadel, 1984. This work examines the life and films of actor.

Stackpoole, Alberic, ed. *Vatican II by Those Who Were There*. London: Geoffrey Chapman, 1986. This volume gathers the recollections of men from the council who participated in it or were closely involved in its work.

Stancioff, Nadia. *Maria: Callas Remembered*. New York: Dutton, 1987. This work chronicles the eight-year friendship between the author and Callas.

Stanton, Mary. *From Selma to Sorrow: The Life and Death of Viola Liuzzo*. Athens: University of Georgia Press, 1998. This book examines the life and civil rights activities of Liuzzo before she was murdered.

Stanton, Shelby. *The Rise and Fall of an American Army: U.S. Ground Forces in Vietnam, 1965–1973*. Novato, CA: Presidio, 1985. This study describes the U.S. Army's actions in Vietnam from 1965–1973.

Stanton, Shelby. *Vietnam Order of Battle*. New York: Galahad, 1986. This reference work details U.S. Army and allied forces that fought in the Vietnam War from 1962 through 1973.

Stanton, Tom. *Hank Aaron and the Home Run That Changed America*. New York: It Books, 2005. This book details the year that Aaron hit his 715th home run and broke Babe Ruth's record, which America viewed problematically since Aaron was a black man.

Starr, Michael. *Mouse in the Rat Pack: The Joey Bishop Story* USA: Taylor Trade Publishing, 2002. This biography chronicles the life and times of Bishop.

Stassinopoulos, Arianna. *Maria Callas: The Woman Behind the Legend*. New York: Simon & Schuster, 1981. This biography charts Callas's creative development, career accomplishments, and personal life.

State of Illinois. "Gwendolyn Brooks—Bio." http://www2.illinois.gov/poetlaureate/Pages/brooks.aspx (accessed April 24, 2010). This website provides biographical and career information about the famous poet.

Stavros, George. "An Interview with Gwendolyn Brooks." *Contemporary Literature* 11 (1970): 1–20. This interview details Brooks's life, career, literary accomplishments and themes, and hopes for the future.

Steel, Ronald. *In Love with Night: The American Romance with Robert Kennedy*. New York: Simon & Schuster, 2000. This work deconstructs the man and the myth.

Stein, Jean, and George Plimpton. *Edie: American Girl*. New York: Alfred A. Knopf, 1982. This oral biography of Edie Sedgwick examines the life of a '60s icon who died at age 28.

Steinem, Gloria. *Moving Beyond Words*. New York: Simon & Schuster, 1994. This work presents six essays—three new and three reworked—that demonstrate the author's eloquence and commitment to feminism.

Steinem, Gloria. *Outrageous Acts and Everyday Rebellions*. New York: Holt, Rinehart, and Winston, 1983. This book collects Steinem's essays and articles that were previously published elsewhere.

Steinem, Gloria *The Revolution from Within*. Boston: Little, Brown, 1992. This book reflects on the spiritual struggles that women face.

Steiner, Gilbert Yale. *Constitutional Inequality: The Political Fortunes of the Equal Rights Amendment*. Washington, DC: Brookings Institution, 1985. This study surveys the history of the equal rights movement, beginning with the 1848 Seneca Falls Convention and the ratification of the Nineteenth Amendment, but primarily focuses on the struggle to enact the ERA.

Stern, Mark. *Calculating Visions: Kennedy, Johnson, and Civil Rights*. New Brunswick, NJ: Rutgers University Press, 1992. This study explains how Kennedy and Johnson pursued power and votes, and ultimately redirected their own course of action and altered the nation's future.

Steuding, Bob. *Gary Snyder*. Twayne's United States Authors Series. Boston: Twayne, 1976. This volume provides criticism and interpretation of Snyder's poems.

Stevens, Jay. *Storming Heaven: LSD and the American Dream*. New York: Grove Press, 1987. This work recounts the remarkable science story in which Harvard professors become drug gurus.

Stewart, Richard W. *American Military History: The United States Army in a Global Era, 1917–2003*. Washington, DC: Center of Military History, United States Army, 2005. This work contains a historical survey of the organization and accomplishments of the U.S. Army from the eve of World War I to the war against terrorism still under way.

Stokes, Geoffrey. *The Beatles*. New York: Rolling Stone Press, 1980. This group biography charts the musical group's beginnings, early years of success, rocketing stardom, and solo projects.

Stolarik, M. Mark. *The Prague Spring and the Warsaw Pact Invasion of Czechoslovakia, 1968: Forty Years Later*. Mundelein, IL: Bolchazy-Carducci, 2010. This volume offers fresh interpretations from eight scholars regarding the aftermath of forces of the Warsaw pact invading Czechoslovakia, ending the "Prague Spring."

Story, Rosalynn M. *And So I Sing: African American Divas of Opera and Concert*. New York: Grand Central Publishing, 1990. This work includes portraits of the greatest African American artists in the genre and rescues the legacies of those that might otherwise be lost.

Stossel, Scott. *Sarge: The Life and Times of Sargent Shriver*. Washington, DC: Smithsonian Books, 2004. This biography of the public servant tends toward hagiography.

Stripes, James. "A Strategy of Resistance: The 'Actorvism' of Russell Means from Plymouth Rock to the Disney Studios." *Wicazo Sa Review* 14, no. 1 (Spring 1999) 87–101. This article examines the acts of resistance in Means's life.

Stuart, Gary L. *Miranda: The Story of America's Right to Remain Silent*. Tucson: University of Arizona Press, 2004. This work chronicles the history of the law that give crime suspects the right to remain silent so that they may not incriminate themselves.

Sugrue, Thomas J. *The Origins of the Urban Crisis: Race and Inequality in Postwar Detroit*. Princeton, NJ: Princeton University Press, 1996. This study examines the economic rise and fall of Detroit.

Sugrue, Thomas J. *Sweet Land of Liberty: The Forgotten Struggle for Civil Rights in the North*. New York: Random House, 2009. This work focuses on the civil rights movement in the north.

Sullivan, Patricia. *Lift Every Voice: The NAACP and the Making of the Civil Rights Movement*. New York: New Press, 2009. This work highlights a century of civil rights activism.

Sullivan, Will. "Summer in the City: Detroit and Newark Are Still Recovering from the Violence That Erupted 40 Years Ago." *U.S. News and World Report* 143:3 (July 23, 2007): 34. This article examines the effect that riots in the 1960s still have on the urban centers of Detroit and Newark.

Suri, Jeremy. *Henry Kissinger and the American Century*. Cambridge, MA: Belknap Press, 2007. This work explores the philosophical roots of Henry Kissinger's actions.

Swanberg, W. A. *Luce and His Empire*. New York: Scribners, 1972. This work chronicles the life and career of the founder of *Time* magazine.

Swenson, Loyd, James M. Grimwood, and Charles C. Alexander. *This New Ocean: A History of Project Mercury* (SP-4201). Washington, DC: National Aeronautics and Space Administrations, 1966. Available online at: http://history.nasa.gov/SP-4201/toc.htm (accessed January 18, 2011). This website provides the complete text of the history of Project Mercury, the first human spaceflight program of the United States.

Swerdlow, Amy. *Women Strike for Peace: Traditional Motherhood and Radical Politics in the 1960s*. Chicago: University of Chicago Press, 1993. This work details the formation of the group in 1961 and its relationships with other groups, activities, and achievements.

Szatmary, David. *Rockin' in Time: A Social History of Rock and Roll*. Upper Saddle River, NJ: Pearson Prentice Hall, 1987. This work provides brief sketches of the era's seminal musicians placed well within the context of their particular decade/genre/syle.

Szulc, Tad. *Fidel: A Critical Portrait*. New York: Morrow, 1986. This work reconstructs Castro's ideological evolution toward Marxism-Leinism.

Szulc, Tad. *The Illusion of Peace: Foreign Policy in the Nixon Years*. New York: Viking, 1978. This work offers a narrative history and analysis of U.S. foreign policy during the Nixon years.

Tai, Hue-Tam Ho. *Radicalism and the Origins of the Vietnamese Revolution*. Cambridge, MA: Harvard University Press, 1992. This study focuses on Vietnamese politics of the 1920s and 1930s to examine radicalism and its displacement by Marxism-Leninism by 1930.

Tamony, Peter. "'Hootenanny': The Word, Its Content and Continuum." *Western Folklore* 22, no. 3 (July 1963): 165–70. This article expounds on the practice and production of the hootenanny.

Tang, Truong Nhu, David Chanoff, and Doan Van Toai. *A Viet Cong Memoir: An Inside Account of the Vietnam War and Its Aftermath*. New York: Random House, 1985. This memoir explains the political and military impossibilities of Tang's fight to save his country from the United States and the North Vietnamese.

Tanham, George K. *Communist Revolutionary Warfare: The Vietminh in Indochina*. New York: Praeger, 1961. This book examines the organization, logistics, and tactics of the insurgency mounted by the Viet Minh in Indochina and the French military response.

Taraborrelli, J. Randy. *The Secret Life of Marilyn Monroe*. New York: Rose Books, 2009. This work reveals new information Monroe's life, drawing from interviews and files retrieved via the Freedom of Information Act.

Tate, Greg. *Midnight Lightning: Jimi Hendrix and the Black Experience*. Chicago: Lawrence Hill Books, 2003. This work relates the life and creative development of Hendrix and explores the social meaning of his blackness.

Tatu, Michel. *Power in the Kremlin: From Khrushchev to Kosygin*. Translated by Helen Katel. New York: Viking, 1969. This work examines the political power of the Soviet Union's leaders.

Taubman, William. *Khrushchev: The Man and His Era*. New York: W. W. Norton, 2004. This full-length biography details the leader's life by drawing on newly opened archives.

Tavard, George. *Vatican II and the Ecumenical Way*. Milwaukee, WI: Marquette University Press, 2006. This work expounds on principles outlines at the Second Vatican Council.

Taylor, John. *The Rivalry: Bill Russell, Wilt Chamberlain, and the Golden Age of Basketball*. New York: Random House, 2005. This work offers an account of the rivalry between Russell and Chamberlian.

Temple, Michael, and James S. Williams, eds. *The Cinema Alone: Essays on the Work of Jean-Luc Godard, 1985–2000*. Amsterdam: Amsterdam University Press, 2000. This volume of essays constitutes a comprehensive and interdisciplinary engagement with Jean-Luc Godard's current film and video work.

Tentler, Leslie Woodcock. *Catholics and Contraception: An American History*. Ithaca, NY: Cornell University Press, 2004. This work examines the American Catholic Church's historical relationship with contraception in light of the need to promote responsible birth control to its membership.

Thakur, Ramesh, and Carlyle Thayer. *Soviet Relations with India and Vietnam*. New York: St. Martin's, 1992. This book analyzes the political, military, and economic relationships among India, Vietnam, and the (former) Soviet Union as three Asian powers. It seeks to understand the dynamics of foreign policy interactions that could have a major impact on shaping the "new world order" in Asia and the Pacific

Theoharis, Athan G., Tony G. Poveda, Susan Rosenfeld, and Richard Gid Powers. *The FBI: A Comprehensive Reference Guide*. Phoenix: Oryx Press, 1999. This reference work covers traditions, controversies, facilities, organizational structure, the bureau's image in popular culture, and much more.

Thomas, Evan. *Robert Kennedy: His Life*. New York: Simon & Schuster, 2000. This biography chronicles the senator's life and political accomplishments.

Thomas, Hugh. *Cuba: The Pursuit of Freedom*. New York: Harper & Row, 1971. This work describes and analyzes Cuba's history from the English capture of Havana in 1762 through Spanish colonialism, U.S. imperialism, the Cuban Revolution, and the Missile Crisis to Fidel Castro's defiant but precarious present state.

Thomas, Richard L. *Admiral Elmo R. Zumwalt Jr: An Enlisted Man's Officer*. Quantico, VA: Marine Corps Command and Staff College, Marine Corps Combat Development Command, 1989. This work chronicles the life and military career of the youngest man to serve as chief of naval operations.

Thompson, Neal. *Light This Candle: The Life and Times of Alan Shepard—America's First Spaceman*. New York: Crown, 2004. This biography charts the life and accomplishments of U.S. astronaut Alan Shepard.

Tofel, Richard J. *Sounding the Trumpet: The Making of John F. Kennedy's Inaugural Address*. Chicago: Ivan R. Dee, 2005. This work describes the full story of the ideas behind, the drafting, and revisions of Kennedy's inaugural address.

Tompson, William. *The Soviet Union Under Brezhnev*. London: Longman, 2000. This work examines politics and policy under Brezhnev, including chapters on leadership politics, domestic policy, and foreign policy. Additional sections discuss economy and society, and individual chapters cover economic performance, demographic and social change, and culture.

Tong, Rosemarie. *Feminist Thought: A More Comprehensive Introduction*, 3rd ed. New York: Westview Press, 2008. This work provides clear, comprehensive, and indispensable introduction to the major traditions of feminist theory.

Tosa, Marco. *Barbie: Four Decades of Fashion, Fantasy, and Fun*. New York: Harry N. Abrams, 1998. This study includes description of how the dolls are made, a family tree, a chart of the dolls' occupations, the dates of issue of each Barbie doll discussed, and photographs of original packaging.

Tovo, Ken. 2005. *From the Ashes of the Phoenix: Lessons for Contemporary Counterinsurgency Operations*. Carlisle Barracks, PA: U.S. Army War College, 2005. This paper argues that the United States must neutralize militant Islamic infrastructure that enables insurgency's global attacks.

"Toward a Hidden God." *Time*, April 8, 1966. This lengthy article examines the new quest for God and ponders the theological question of the age, "Is God dead?"

Trachtenberg, Marc. *A Constructed Peace: The Making of the European Settlement, 1945–1963*. Princeton, NJ: Princeton University Press, 1999. This work describes how a stable international system came into being during the Cold War period.

Transcript. George W. Ball Oral History Interview I, II, III, and IV. April 12 and 16, 1965; February 16 and March 29, 1968. Interviews by Joseph Kraft and Larry J. Hackman. JFK Library. http://www.jfklibrary.org/Historical+Resources/Archives/Summaries/col

_ball.htm (accessed August 10, 2010). This is a transcript of an oral history interview with George Ball who served during the Johnson administration as secretary of state.

Trinidad, David. "The Valley of No Return." *Chronicle of Higher Education*. May 30, 2008, B28. This article describes the cultural effect that Jacqueline Susann's *Valley of the Dolls* had on the 1960s.

Tropiano, Stephen. *Obscene, Indecent, Immoral and Offensive: 100+ Years of Censored, Banned and Controversial Films*. New York: Limelight, 2009. This work offers astute and accessible analysis of such films as *The Birth of a Nation, Who's Afraid of Virginia Woolf?, Baby Doll, Blackboard Jungle, Bonnie and Clyde, A Clockwork Orange, Natural Born Killers, Rosemary's Baby, Life of Brian*, and *The Passion of the Christ*.

Troy, Tevi. *Intellectuals and the American Presidency: Philosophers, Jesters or Technicians?* Lanham, MD: Rowman & Littlefield, 2002. This study demonstrates the role of intellectuals as advisors to presidents beginning with Kennedy.

Truffaut, François. *The Films in My Life*. Translated by Leonard Mayhew. New York: Simon & Schuster, 1978. This collection of 100 essays ranges widely over the history of film and pays tribute to Truffaut's particular heroes, among them Hitchcock, Welles, Chaplin, Renoir, Cocteau, Bergman, and Buñuel.

Tsai, Eugene, ed. *Robert Smithson: A Retrospective*. Berkeley: University of California Press, 2002. This work accompanies an exhibition held Feb. 27–May 2, 1999, at The National Museum of Contemporary Art, Oslo; Modern Museum, Stockholm, June 19, 1999–Sept. 12, 1999.

Tuchman, Phyllis. *George Segal*. New York: Abbeville, 1983. This work examines the life and career of the famous sculptor.

Tucker, Spencer. *Vietnam*. Lexington: University Press of Kentucky, 1999. This volume of Vietnamese military history focuses on the French and American twentieth-century conflicts.

Ture, Kwame, and Charles V. Hamilton. *Black Power: The Politics of Liberation in America*. New York: Vintage, 1967. This work exposed the depths of systemic racism in this country and provided a radical political framework for reform.

Turley, William S. *The Second Indochina War: A Concise and Military History*, 2nd ed. Lanham, MD: Rowman & Littlefield, 2009. This work provides a comprehensive overview of the second Indochina War.

Turner, James Morton. *The Promise of Wilderness: A History of American Environmental Politics*. PhD diss., Princeton University, 2004. This dissertation offers a history of environmental politics focusing on the internal changes at the Wilderness Society from 1964 to 1994.

Turner, William W., and John Christian. *The Assassination of Robert F. Kennedy: The Conspiracy and the Cover-Up, 1968–1978*. New York: Random House, 1978. This work was one of the first, and best, books detailing the core facts of the assassination.

Tushnet, Mark V. *Making Civil Rights Law: Thurgood Marshall and the Supreme Court, 1936–1961*. New York: Oxford University Press, 1994. This work recounts Marshall's efforts to achieve civil rights for African Americans just prior to the passage of the Civil Rights Act of 1964.

Tushnet, Mark V. *Making Constitutional Law: Thurgood Marshall and the Supreme Court, 1961–1991*. New York: Oxford University Press, 1997. This book chronicles Marshall's efforts to achieve civil rights for African Americans just prior to the passage of the Civil Rights Act of 1964, during that time period, afterwards, and concludes with an overview of the justice's career accomplishments.

Tushnet, Mark V. *The NAACP's Legal Strategy Against Segregated Education, 1925–1950*. Chapel Hill: University of North Carolina Press, 1987. This work emphasizes the internal workings of the organization as revealed in its own documents and argues that the dedication and political and legal skills of staff members such as Walter White, Charles

Hamilton Houston, and Thurgood Marshall were responsible for the ultimate success of public interest law.

Tytell, John. *Naked Angels: The Lives & Literature of the Beat Generation*. New York: McGraw-Hill, 1976. This volume profiles the lives and writings of Burroughs, Kerouac, and Ginsberg, with extensive commentaries on their works.

U.S. Department of Defense. *Pentagon Papers: The Defense Department History of United States Decision-Making on Vietnam, the Senator Gravel ed., Vols. 1–5*, Boston: Beacon Press, 1971. This massive five-volume set details the U.S. government's policy on Vietnam.

U.S. News and World Report. "The People's Vote: Voting Rights Act (1965)." http://www.usnews.com/usnews/documents/docpages/document_page100.htm (accessed January 11, 2010). This website contains the act enforcing the Fifteenth Amendment to the U.S. Constitution that eased obstacles that prevented blacks from voting.

Ueda, Reed. *Postwar Immigrant America: A Social History*. Boston: Bedford Books of St. Martin's, 1994. This study focuses on the global and international forces that prompted the large-scale uprooting and transplanting of people following World War II.

Underwood, James E., and William J. Daniels. *Governor Rockefeller in New York: The Apex of Pragmatic Liberalism in the United States*. Westport, CT.: Greenwood, 1982. This volume analyzes Rockefeller's political philosophy and his gubernatorial performance.

Ungar, Sanford J. *The Papers & the Papers: An Account of the Legal and Political Battle over the Pentagon Papers*. New York: Columbia University Press, 1989, 1972. This work recounts the *Pentagon Papers* controversy.

Unger, Irwin. *The Best of Intentions: The Triumphs And Failures of the Great Society Under Kennedy, Johnson, and Nixon*. New York: Doubleday, 1996. This work argues that the Great Society initiative was in fact intended for the advantage of the middle class.

United States, Department of State. *Foreign Relations of the United States*. Johnson Administration, Volumes XI and XVIII, published 1997 and 2000. These volumes chronicle the U.S. government's foreign relations with other countries during President Lyndon B. Johnson's administration.

United States. *Immigration: Hearings Before the Subcommittee on Immigration and Naturalization of the Committee on the Judiciary, United States Senate, Eighty-Ninth Congress, First Session on S. 500 to Amend the Immigration and Nationality Act, and for Other Purposes*. Washington, DC: U.S. Government Printing Office, 1965. This work stands an official record of a hearing on immigration policy of the U.S. Senate.

University of Missouri, Kansas City, Faculty Law Project. http://www.law.umkc.edu/faculty/projects/ftrials/nuremberg/JudgmentAtNuremberg.html (accessed January 18, 2011). This website provides information about Stanley Kramer's film *Judgment at Nuremberg*.

Unterberger, Richie. *Eight Miles High: Folk-Rock's Flight from Haight-Ashbury to Woodstock*. San Francisco: Backbeat Books, 2003. This book explores the folk-rock scene from mid-1966 to the end of that decade, when folk-rock began spinning and splintering into many different directions that continue to influence music today.

Unterberger, Richie. *Turn! Turn! Turn! The '60s Folk-Rock Revolution*. San Francisco: Backbeat Books, 2002. This volume traces the evolution in the 1960s of a new form of popular music that blended poetic lyricism, social awareness, and rock-and-roll rebellion.

U.S. Environmental Protection Agency. "DDT Ban Takes Effect." http://www.epa.gov/history/topics/ddt/01.htm (accessed August 10, 2010). This website contains a press release from the EPA announcing the ban of DDT.

Valentine, Douglas. *The Phoenix Program*. New York: William Morrow, 1990. This work examines the CIA plot to destroy the Viet Cong infrastructure.

Vallin, Marlene Boyd. *Margaret Chase Smith: Model Public Servant*. Westport, CT: Greenwood, 1998. This biography examines the life and career of the inspirational senator.

Van Deburg, William L., ed. *Modern Black Nationalism: From Marcus Garvey to Louis Farrakhan*. New York: New York University Press, 1997. This volume collects the most influential speeches, pamphlets, and articles that trace the development of black nationalism in the twentieth century.

VanDeMark, Brian. *Into the Quagmire: Lyndon Johnson and the Escalation of the Vietnam War*. New York: Oxford University Press, 1991. This study documents America's deepening involvement in Vietnam during November '64 to July '65.

Varnedoe, Kirk, ed. *Jasper Johns: Writings, Sketchbook Notes, Interviews*. New York: Museum of Modern Art, 1996. This book explores Johns's art and thought, from all periods of his career, through interviews, published writings, working notes he kept in his sketchbooks, and recorded conversations with critics and friends.

Varnedoe, Kirk, et al. *Jasper Johns: A Retrospective*. New York: Museum of Modern Art, 1996. This volume contains 264 color plates illustrating Johns's paintings, drawings, sculptures, and prints along with essays that review his essential themes, analyze his references to other artists, and explore how his contemporaries have, in turn, seen and absorbed his own work.

Vaughn, Wally G., and Mattie Campbell Davis, eds. *The Selma Campaign, 1963–1965: The Decisive Battle of the Civil Rights Movement*. Dover, MA: Majority Press, 2006. This work examines a neglected aspect of the U.S. civil rights movement.

Velez-Sainz, Julio, and Nieves Romero-Diaz. *Cervantes and/on/in the New World*. Newark, DE: Juan de la Cuesta 2007. This work was published as part of a symposium held at University of Massachusetts and Mount Holyoke College that aimed to frame Cervantes within the lens of Trans-Atlanticism in a variety of forms.

Verney, Kevern, ed. *Long Is the Way and Hard: One Hundred Years of the NAACP*. Little Rock: University of Arkansas Press, 2009. This work collects 16 original essays that offer new and invaluable insights into the work and achievements of the association.

Viagas, Robert, and Donald C. Farber. *The Amazing Story of the Fantasticks: America's Longest-Running Play*. New York: Limelight, 2002. This book explores the musical's roots in an 1865 play by Edmund Rostand and its 1960 opening at Manhattan's Sullivan Theater.

Viagas, Robert. *I'm the Greatest Star: Broadway's Top Musical Legends from 1900 to Today*. New York: Applause Theatre & Cinema Books, 2009. This work surveys Broadway musical theatre stars and tells the life stories of 40 stage luminaries from Al Jolson, Fanny Brice, and Gwen Verdon to Nathan Lane, Patti Lupone, and Audra McDonald.

Vineburg, Steve. *High Comedy in American Movies: Class and Humor from the 1920s to the Present*. Lanham, MD: Rowman & Littlefield, 2005. This study examines the ways in which class comedy's inside view of the aristocratic lifestyle has been influenced by the culture and times in which the movies are produced.

Vollers, Maryanne. *Ghosts of Mississippi: The Murder of Medgar Evers, the Trials of Byron De La Beckwith, and the Haunting of the New South*. New York: Little, Brown, 1995. This history of the civil rights movement in the deep South is told from the perspective of the Byron De La Beckwith trials and reveals new insights into the case as provided by trial prosecutors and the widow of NAACP official Evers.

Von Hallberg, Robert. *American Poetry and Culture, 1945–1980*. Cambridge: Harvard University Press, 1985. This book examines poetry inspired by the American experience since 1945. Chapters on the political poems of the 1950s and 1960s may be of greatest interest to the readership of this book.

Vonnegut, Kurt. *Slaughterhouse-Five*. New York: Dell, 1991. This novel follows a U.S. prisoner of war who witnesses the firebombing of Dresden.

Vreeland, Diana. *D.V.* New York: A Borzoi Book, Alfred A. Knopf, 1984. This autobiography reveals insights into Vreeland's life and career as a fashion arbiter.

Wagenheim, Kal. *Clemente!* Chicago: Olmstead Press, 2001. This book exemplifies Clemente's dramatic life from his childhood in Puerto Rico to his career with the Pittsburgh Pirates.

Wainstock, Dennis D. *The 1968 Presidential Campaign and Election*. PhD diss., West Virginia University, 1984. This dissertation examines the history and legacy of the 1968 presidential campaign and election.

Waldman, Diane. *Roy Lichtenstein*. New York: Solomon R. Guggenheim Museum, 1993. This comprehensive monograph focuses on the artist's painting and sculpture from the '60s to the present

Wallace, Patricia Ward. *Politics of Conscience: A Biography of Margaret Chase Smith*. Westport, CT: Praeger, 1995. This biography examines the senator's legacy in light of women's rights and women's history.

Wallis, Hal, and Charles Higham. *Starmaker: The Autobiography of Hal Wallis*. New York: Berkley Books, 1980. This autobiography chronicles the life and career of the American motion picture producer.

Ward, Christopher. *Brezhnev's Folly: The Building of BAM and Late Soviet Socialism*. Pittsburgh: Pittsburgh University Press, 2009. This study is a groundbreaking social history of the BAM railway project.

Warhol, Andy, and Pat Hackett. *Popism: The Warhol Sixties*. Orlando, FL: Harcourt, Brace and Co, 1980. Warhol provides his personal view of the pop phenomenon in New York in the 1960s and a look back at the relationships that made up the scene at the Factory.

Wasserman, Dale. *The Impossible Musical*. New York: Applause Theatre & Cinema Books, 2003. This work details the full story of *Man of La Mancha*, before Broadway and beyond.

Watson, Bruce. *Freedom Summer: The Savage Season That Made Mississippi Burn and Made America a Democracy*. New York: Penguin, 2010. This overview of the Mississippi civil rights movement during the summer of 1964 features more than 50 personal accounts from activists who participated in the historic event.

Watson, Steven. 2003. *Factory Made: Warhol and the Sixties*. New York: Pantheon Books. This work focuses on marginal characters who crossed paths with Warhol during the Silver Factory period, stretching roughly from 1960 to 1968.

Wedin, Carolyn. *Inheritors of the Spirit: Mary White Ovington and the Founding of the NAACP*. New York: John Wiley, 1998. This history of the NAACP highlights the life and accomplishments of one of its key leaders, Ovington, by discussing her work in settlement houses with poor blacks.

Weiner, Tim. *Legacy of Ashes: A History of the CIA*. New York: Doubleday, 2007. This work examines the CIA's history and blames all presidential administrations for its slide into mediocrity.

Weisbrot, Robert. *Freedom Bound: A History of America's Civil Rights Movement*. New York: Plume, 1990. This work examines three decades of America's civil rights movement and argues that black collaboration with white liberals was ineffective.

Weiss, Jeffrey, et al. *Jasper Johns: An Allegory of Painting, 1955–1965*. New Haven, CT: Yale University Press, 2006. This publication approaches Johns's work of this 10-year period through a thematic framework. It examines the artist's interest in the condition of painting as a medium, a practice, and an instrument of encoded meaning.

Weisser, Thomas. *Spaghetti Westerns: The Good, the Bad, and the Violent*. Jefferson, NC: McFarland, 1992. This work contains a filmography covering 558 Spaghetti Westerns, followed by filmographies of personnel—actors and actresses, directors, musical composers, scriptwriters, and cinematographers.

Welk, Lawrence, and Bernice McGeehan. *Ah-One, Ah-Two! Life with My Musical Family*. Boston: G. K. Hall, 1974. This book provides anecdotes and narrative covering the decades that *The Lawrence Welk Show* aired on U.S. television.

Welk, Lawrence. *Lawrence Welk's Musical Family Album*. Englewood Cliffs, NJ: Prentice-Hall, 1977. This work contains photos, cast biographies, and information about the popular television series' run.

Wellock, Thomas Raymond. *Critical Masses: Opposition to Nuclear Power in California, 1958–1978*. Madison: University of Wisconsin Press, 1998. This study recounts how the citizens of California from the tiny town of Wasco in the Central Valley to the vast suburbs of Los Angeles challenged the threat of nuclear power, transformed the antinuclear movement, and helped changed the face of U.S. politics

Wells, Tom. *The War Within: America's Battle Over Vietnam*. Berkeley: University of California Press, 1994. This work details the successes of the antiwar movement in the United States.

Whalen, Charles, and Barbara Whale. *The Longest Debate: A Legislative History of the 1964 Civil Rights Act*. Cabin John, MD: Seven Locks Press, 1985. This work examines the role of House Republicans in the passage of the Civil Rights Act of 1964.

Whalen, Thomas J. *Kennedy Versus Lodge: The 1952 Senate Race*. Boston: Northeastern University Press, 2000. This history demonstrates the importance of this Senate race.

White, Mark J. *The Cuban Missile Crisis*. New York: New York University Press, 1995. This study offers new interpretation of Khrushchev's motives for putting missiles in Cuba.

White, Theodore H. *The Making of the President, 1968*. New York: Atheneum, 1969. This history offers a compelling account of one of the most turbulent presidential campaigns in history: the 1968 election that put Richard M. Nixon in the White House

Whiteley, Sheila. *The Space Between the Notes: Rock and the Counter-Culture*. London: Routledge, 1992. This study of '60s and '70s popular music and its related counterculture illuminates its theories with analysis of key recordings by artists such as the Rolling Stones, Cream, and Jimi Hendrix.

Whitfield, Stephen E., and Gene Roddenberry. *The Making of Star Trek*. New York: Ballantine, 1968. This book outlines the complete history of the TV series, from conception, design, and scripting to how the finished product was produced and sold.

Who's Who in America. Vol. 36, 1970–71. Chicago: Marquis-Who's Who Incorporated, 1970. This reference work offers biographical information on outstanding Americans.

Wilhelms, Don E. *To a Rocky Moon: A Geologist's History of Lunar Exploration*. Tucson: University of Arizona Press, 1994. This work presents background information about how our ideas about the moon have evolved and how Apollo cemented our notions of it.

Wilk, Max. *The Making of The Sound of Music*. New York: Routledge, 2007. This volume tells the full story of the making of the show, from the first rough ideas through the tryouts, fine tuning, and eventual triumph.

Wilkinson, Alec. *The Protest Singer: An Intimate Portrait of Pete Seeger*. New York: Vintage, 2010. This intimate biography of the social activist, environmentalist, and musician highlights Seeger's modesty, folksiness, and legacy.

Williams, Juan. *Eyes on the Prize: America's Civil Rights Years, 1954–1965*. New York: Penguin, 1988. This work detailing the struggles of the civil rights movement highlights stories of unrecognized activists.

Williams, Juan. *Thurgood Marshall: American Revolutionary*. New York: Times Books, 1998. This biography of Marshall presents a balanced and critical analysis of his life and career.

Williams, Tony. *The Cinema of George A. Romero, Knight of the Living Dead*. New York: Wallflower, 2003. This book explores the relevance of the director's films within American cultural traditions and thus explains the potency of such work beyond "splatter movie" models.

Williamson, Allan. *Pity the Monsters: The Political Vision of Robert Lowell*. New Haven: Yale University Press, 1974. This work examines Lowell's career from 1944 to 1970.

Willis, Ellen. 1980. "Janis Joplin." In Jim Miller, ed. *The Rolling Stone Illustrated History of Rock and Roll*. New York: Random House and Rolling Stone Press, pp. 275–79. This entry details the life, career, and musical development of Joplin.

Wills, Garry. *John Wayne's America: The Politics of Celebrity*. New York: Simon & Schuster, 1997. This work provides critical analysis of Wayne's film career.

Wilson, J. R. "Fifty Years of Inventing the Future." *Aerospace America*, February 2008, pp. 30–43. Available http://www.aiaa.org/aerospace/images/articleimages/pdf/AA_Feb2008_DARPA%20Anniversary.pdf (accessed November 15, 2010). This work provides an overview of the Defense Advanced Research Projects Agency.

Wilson, Paula, and Humphrey, Hubert H. *The Civil Rights Rhetoric of Hubert H. Humphrey: 1948–1964*. Lanham, MD: Rowman & Littlefield, 1996. This study provides a comprehensive examination of Humphrey's civil rights rhetoric.

Wilson, William Julius. *The Truly Disadvantaged: The Inner City, the Underclass, and Public Policy*. Chicago: University of Chicago Press, 1987. In his sociological analysis of black inner-city poverty, the author targets the loss of manufacturing jobs as the main cause.

Wirtz, James J. *The Tet Offensive: Intelligence Failure in War*. Ithaca, NY: Cornell University Press, 1991. This study examines how the United States missed the Tet Offensive.

Wiseman, Carter. *I. M. Pei: A Profile in American Architecture*. New York: Harry N. Abrams, 2001. This comprehensive record of the architect's work present Pei's buildings in all their splendid variety, while scores of revealing drawings, plans, and models, as well as personal and documentary photographs provide additional insight.

Witcover, Jules. *Very Strange Bedfellows: The Short and Unhappy Marriage of Richard Nixon and Spiro Agnew*. New York: Public Affairs, 2007. This study examines the five-years relationship of the two men.

Wofford, Harris. *Of Kennedys and Kings: Making Sense of the Sixties*. New York: Farrar, Straus, and Giroux, 1996. Wofford's recollections and reflections shed light on the '60s and on the dramatic domestic and international politics of the era.

Wolfe, Tom. *The Right Stuff*. New York: Farrar, Straus, and Giroux, 1979. This study of the U.S. space program presents the astronauts as heroes.

Wolff, Miles. *Lunch at the Five and Ten: The Greensboro Sit-Ins: A Contemporary History*. New York: Stein and Day, 1970. This work recounts the 1960 sit-in at a Woolworth's lunch counter in Greensboro, North Carolina, which ignited the civil rights movement in the United States.

Wollman, Elizabeth Lara. *The Theatre Will Rock: A History of the Rock Musical from Hair to Hedwig*. Ann Arbor: University of Michigan Press, 2006. This study chronicles the rock musical's evolution over 50 years.

Woods, Randall Bennett. *Fulbright: A Biography*. Cambridge: Cambridge University Press, 1995. This evenhanded biography chronicles the senator's career and legacy.

Woods, W. David. *How Apollo Flew to the Moon*. Chichester, UK: Praxis, 2008. This work traces the development of America's postwar astronautical research facilities, describes early launches through manned orbital spaceflights, and details each step.

Woodson, John. *A Study of Joseph Heller's Catch-22: Going Around Twice*. New York: Peter Lang, 2001. This work illustrates Heller's heavy influence by the New Criticism and myth criticism that he studied in graduate school and demonstrates that *Catch-22* is a faithful and inclusive retelling of the ancient epic of Gilgamesh.

Woodstock: Three Days of Peace and Music. DVD. Dir. by Michael Wadleigh. 1970. Burbank, CA: Warner Home Video, 2009. This documentary uses wide-screen and split-screen techniques and stereo sound to recreate the experience of the festival in all its peace-loving, mud-splattered glory.

Wyden, Peter. *Bay of Pigs: The Untold Story*. New York: Simon & Schuster, 1980. This work details each development in the crisis from planning to invasion and present theories for its failure.

Wyman, Bill. *Rolling with the Stones*. New York: DK Publishing, 2002. This coffee-table-sized memoir includes photographs and ephemera that illustrate the band's cultural influence and historical observation.

Yogi, Maharishi Mahesh. *Science of Being and Art of Living: Transcendental Meditation.* New York: Meridian, 1995. This work introduces practitioners to the technique of transcendental meditation.

Young, Marilyn Blatt. *The Vietnam Wars, 1945–1990.* New York: HarperCollins, 1991. This work excoriates the U.S. for its involvement in Vietnam.

Zaroulis, Nancy, and Gerald Sullivan. *Who Spoke Up? American Protest Against the War in Vietnam, 1963–1975.* Garden City, NY: Doubleday, 1984. This compendium attempts a year-by-year and month-by-month chronology of the antiwar protests and draws information from secondary and primary sources and interviews.

Zeffirelli, Franco. *Zeffirelli: An Autobiography.* New York: Weidenfeld & Nicolson, 1986. This autobiography charts the filmmaker's origins, life, and career achievements.

Zeiler, Thomas W. *Dean Rusk: Defending the American Mission Abroad.* Wilmington, DE: SR Books, 1999. This work reflects on the uses and abuses of predominant power in diplomacy, and interprets well-known events and issues in the comparative framework of idealism and realism.

Zeskin, Leonard. *Blood and Politics: The History of the White Nationalist Movement from the Margins to the Mainstream.* New York: Farrar, Straus, and Giroux, 2009. Ths work focuses on the lives, activities, and groups led by three men: Willis Carto, William Pierce, and David Duke.

Ziegler, Mel, ed. *Bella! Ms. Abzug Goes to Washington.* New York: Saturday Review Press, 1972. This book relates anecdotes from Azbug's first term as a congresswoman.

Zinn, Howard. *SNCC, The New Abolitionists.* Boston: Beacon Press, 1964. This work provides an indispensable study of the organization, of the 1960s, and of the process of social change.

Zumwalt, Elmo M Jr. *On Watch: A Memoir.* New York: Quadrangle, 1978. This memoir focuses on Zumwalt's experience as chief of naval operations in Washington between 1970 and 1974.

About the Editors and Contributors

THE EDITORS

JAMES S. BAUGESS earned his undergraduate degrees from North Greenville College in South Carolina and Carson-Newman College in Tennessee. He has three graduate degrees, two from Ohio State University, and a master of divinity from Southeastern Baptist Theological Seminary in Wake Forest, North Carolina. Currently, he is PhD candidate at the Southern Baptist Theological Seminary in Louisville, Kentucky. In addition, he is an ordained Southern Baptist minister and has served in pastoral ministry in churches in Ohio and South Carolina. Jim has written numerous entries for other encyclopedias, including ABC-Clio's *Encyclopedia of the American Civil War*. Since 1991, he has taught American and Western Civilization at Columbus State Community College in Columbus, Ohio. In addition, Jim is a proud son, brother, husband, father, and grandfather. He lives (but mostly dies) by his beloved Cleveland Indians and has hope that the University of Tennessee Volunteers football team will be better next year. His great ambition is to teach until the end of his life at a Baptist college in the South. Jim enjoys reading classic British mysteries, is a devotee of the BBC's *Law & Order U.K.*, *Masterpiece Theatre*, *Mystery*, and all things pertaining to Jane Austen.

ABBE ALLEN DeBOLT is a graduate of Miami University in Oxford, Ohio, and has earned two graduate degrees at The Ohio State University and one from Ohio University. After several years teaching Western Civilization courses at Columbus State Community College (where she remains as an online instructor), Abbe moved to North Carolina and now serves as full-time instructor in the Social and Behavioral Sciences Department at Sandhills Community College in Pinehurst, North Carolina, where her husband Steve is the Village Manager for Whispering Pines. At Sandhills, Abbe teaches Western Civilization, World Civilization, Introduction to Comparative Political Science, and the Introduction to International Relations. She has published articles in several books and encyclopedias. Abbe brings an eclectic background to the project. She has visited Europe, the old Soviet Union, Ukraine, Turkey, Greece, and China, where she has toured the finest art museums in the world; therefore, her knowledge of art is vast and she has served as volunteer docent at the Columbus Museum of Art. Abbe remains loyal to her alma mater, Miami University, and the Ohio State Buckeyes.

Currently, Jim and Abbe are editing a Civil War journal entitled *Glorious Victory: The Journal of John A. Gillis, Sixty-Fourth Ohio Volunteer Infantry, Company K,* for the University of Tennessee Press.

THE CONTRIBUTORS

Reynaldo Anderson
PhD, University of Nebraska-Lincoln
Howe-Stowe State University

Jonathan Anuik
PhD, University of Saskatchewan
Lakehead University

Stephen Azzi
PhD, University of Waterloo
Laurentian University

Mark Barringer
PhD, Texas Christian University
Stephen F. Austin State University

James S. Baugess
Doctoral candidate, Southern Baptist Theological Seminary
Columbus State Community College

Devan Bissonette
PhD, University of Binghampton
Strayer University

Nicola Davis Bivens
EdD, Nova Southeastern University

Lee Blanding
Doctoral candidate, University of Victoria
John C. Smith University

Anne Blaschke
Doctoral candidate and lecturer, Boston University

Jeffrey H. Bloodworth
PhD, Ohio University
Gannon University

Sarah Boslaugh
PhD, City University of New York Graduate Center
Washington University School of Medicine

Brittany Bounds
Doctoral candidate, Texas A&M

J. A. Brown-Rose
PhD, Stony Brook University
Western New England College

Joshua W. Butler
Graduate student, Valdosta State University

Heath W. Carter
Doctoral candidate, University of Notre Dame

Caitlin Casey
Doctoral candidate, Yale University

Daphne R. Chamberlain
PhD, University of Mississippi
Jackson State University

Todd Chappell
BA, University of North Carolina at Charlotte

Boyd Childress
MLS, University of Alabama
Auburn University Libraries

Rodger D. Citron
JD, Yale Law School
Turo Law Center

Emily Suzanne Clark
Doctoral candidate, Florida State University

Brian Cogan
PhD, New York University
Molloy College

Darron R. Darby
Doctoral candidate, Florida State University

Thomas S. Darragh
Doctoral candidate, Central Michigan University

Susan de Gaia
PhD, University of Southern California
Independent Scholar

Rosemary Deller
MA, Central European University

Elizabeth Demers
PhD, Michigan State University
Senior Editor, Potomac Books

Anitha Deshamudre
Master of Architecture, University of North Carolina at Charlotte School
of Architecture

Mariadele Di Blasio
Doctoral candidate, University of Bologna

Christopher Dietrich
Doctoral candidate, University of Texas

Micha Gerrit Philipp Edlich
Doctoral candidate, Johannes Gutenberg-Universität Mainz
Columbia University

Mark Thomas Edwards
PhD, Purdue University
Ouachita Baptist University

Rebecca S. Feind
MALS, University of Missouri-Columbia
San Jose State University

Amy L. Fletcher
PhD, University of Georgia
University of Canterbury

Christos G. Frentzos
PhD, University of Houston
Austin Peay State University

Justin D. Garcia
PhD candidate, Temple University
Millersville University

Carla W. Garner
MLIS, San Jose State University

Matthew R. Garrett
PhD, Arizona State University
Bakersfield College

Anca Gata
PhD, University of Bucharest
Université Dunărea de Jos, Galaţi

Carine S. Germond
PhD, University de Strasbourg
Maastricht University

Mohammad Gharipour
MA, University of Tehran
Visiting Professor, University of North Carolina at Charlotte

Laura Jane Gifford
PhD, University of California, Los Angeles
Independent Scholar

M. Carmen Gomez-Galisteo
Doctoral candidate, Universidad de Alcala

Herbert R. Hartel Jr.
PhD, City University of New York
John Jay College of Criminal Justice, CUNY

Patrick J. Hayes
PhD, Catholic University of America
Assistant Archivist, Redemptorists of the Baltimore Province, Brooklyn,
New York

Tuan Hoang
Doctoral candidate, University of Notre Dame

Marilyn K. Howard
PhD, Ohio State University
Columbus State Community College

Matt D. Jacobs
PhD, Ohio University

Kate Keane
PhD, University of Maryland

Caroline E. Kelley
DPhil, University of Oxford
Umea Universitet, Sweden

Ryan J. Kirkby
Doctoral candidate, University of Waterloo

Grzegorz Kosc
PhD, University of Lodz
University of Warsaw

Chris Kostov
PhD, University of Ottawa

Helga Lenart-Cheng
PhD, Harvard University

Courtney Lyons
Doctoral candidate, Baylor University

Martin J. Manning
MSLS, Catholic University of America
Research Librarian, U.S. State Department

Jeffrey T. Manuel
PhD, University of Minnesota
Southern Illinois University, Edwardsville

Karen Mason
MLIS, Rutgers University
Serials Librarian, Medgar Evers College,
City University of New York

Daniel Robert McClure
Doctoral candidate, University of California, Irvine

MaryKate McMaster
PhD, College of William and Mary
Anna Maria College

Brendan McQuade
Doctoral candidate, Binghamton University

Sarah Katherine Mergel
PhD, George Washington University
Dalton State College

Cynthia J. Miller
PhD, McGill University
Emerson College

Elizabeth Bryant Morgenstern
Doctoral candidate, Florida State University

Lincoln Mullen
Doctoral candidate, Brandeis University

Caryn Murphy
PhD, University of Wisconsin-Madison
University of Wisconsin-Oshkosh

Theresa Napson-Williams
BA, American University
Richard Stockton College of New Jersey

Caryn E. Neumann
PhD, Ohio State University
Miami University

Melanie D. Newport
Doctoral candidate, Temple University

Miles Adam Park
Doctoral candidate, Florida State University

R. Joseph Parrott
Doctoral candidate, University of Texas

Joshua R. Pate
Doctoral candidate, University of Tennessee

Adam Pearson
BA, Northumbria University

Christopher John Pennington
PhD, University of Toronto
University of Toronto-Scarborough

Rachel Pierce
Doctoral candidate, University of Virginia

Patryk Polec
Doctoral candidate, University of Ottawa

Andrew Polk
Doctoral candidate, Florida State University

Caleb Puckett
MLIS, University of Oklahoma
Emporia State University

Kasper Grotle Rasmussen
Doctoral candidate, University of Aarhus

Andrew Rath
Doctoral candidate, McGill University

Lindon Ratliff
PhD, University of Mississippi

Christopher J. Richmann
PhD, Baylor University

Jason D. Roberts
PhD, George Washington University

Oliver A. Rosales
Doctoral candidate, University of California at Santa Barbara

Ricardo Santhiago
PhD, Universidade de São Paulo

Giulia Savio
Doctoral candidate, University of Genoa

Brooke Sherrard
Doctoral candidate, Florida State University

Christopher D. Stone
PhD, Indiana University
University of Wisconsin-Manitowoc

Tracy R. Szczepaniak
U.S. Air Force Academy
Independent Scholar

Steven Wayne Teske
MDiv, Concordia Theological Seminary
Central Arkansas Library System

Robert J. Thompson III
Doctoral candidate, University of Southern Mississippi

Jennifer Thomson
Doctoral candidate, Harvard University

Rebecca Tolley-Stokes
MLIS, University of North Carolina-Greensboro
Sherrod Library, East Tennessee University

Jinny Turman-Deal
Doctoral candidate, West Virginia University

A. Bowdoin Van Riper
PhD, University of Wisconsin-Madison
Southern Polytechnic University

Kimberly Wilmot Voss
PhD, University of Maryland
University of Central Florida

Marsha Walker
Doctoral candidate, Indiana University
Johnson C. Smith University

Robert Walsh
MALS, Southern Connecticut State University
Three Rivers Community College

Kathleen Warnes
PhD, University of Toledo

Julia Watson
PhD, University of California-Irvine
Ohio State University

Tim J. Watts
MLS, Indiana University
Kansas State University Library

Stan C. Weeber
PhD, University of North Texas
McNeese State University

Seth Weitz
PhD, Florida State University
Dalton State College

Grant T. Weller
PhD, Temple University
Independent Scholar

William Whyte
MA, East Stroudsburg University
Northampton Community College

Hettie V. Williams
MA, Monmouth University
Monmouth University

Kevin Wilson
Doctoral candidate, Ohio University

Brett F. Woods
PhD, University of Essex
American Military University

Katheryn Wright
PhD Florida State University

Ben Wynne
PhD, University of Mississippi
Gainesville State College

Ronald E. Young Jr.
PhD, University of California at Los Angeles
Canterbury School

Index

Page numbers in **bold** type refer to main entries in the encyclopedia.

introduction

Weeknights at about 6 p.m. can be make-or-break time when it comes to eating well. We've all been there: hungry after a long, busy day, faced with the burning question of "What's for dinner?" and without a plan. At that vulnerable point, you are forced to make a pivotal decision: Order takeout, pop a meal into the microwave, or cook something. Sure, what you choose on any one evening won't have a big impact on your well-being, but opting to cook dinner at home most of the time has more power than you may realize. Simply fixing food from scratch means you will likely be eating smarter portions with fewer calories, and much less saturated fat and sodium and more nutrients than if you went the restaurant or prepared-food route. That, of course, can ultimately lead to a fitter, healthier life for you and your loved ones. You also get to enjoy fresher food, prepared exactly to your taste, and save money.

With all that upside, why doesn't everyone cook dinner more often? "I don't have time." "I am out of ideas and bored eating the same thing over and over." "I have nothing in the house." "I don't feel like cooking." Sound familiar? I hear these excuses (ahem . . . reasons) from many people I speak with and, I confess, they sometimes run through my head too. Once in a while they compel me to go out to eat or call for delivery, and there is nothing wrong with that now and then. I live in New York City, after all, the mecca of great restaurants and take-out menus, which I enjoy exploring. But I cook at home most nights because, despite all the exciting options, it is by far the most desirable and healthful way to eat. When I cook, I know I am getting the best-quality ingredients prepared just the way my family and I like them. When negative thoughts arise, the thing that tips the scale in favor of cooking is having an arsenal of absolutely delicious, inspiring, fast dinner ideas at my fingertips. It makes cooking feel less overwhelming and it becomes a pleasure and high point of my day rather than a chore. That is exactly what I hope this collection of recipes will do for you.

This book a treasure trove of delicious, healthy dinner solutions—150 recipes that take 30 minutes or less to get on the table—and a fountain of fresh, new ideas designed to de-stress cooking, knock out mealtime boredom, and ultimately help keep you and your family on track for a healthy life.

As a passionate food lover, taste is number one for me, and each of these dishes is full-out delicious. But they are good for you too, something that is important to me as a nutritionist and mom. By focusing on fresh, minimally processed ingredients, following my tried and true "Usually-Sometimes-Rarely" food philosophy, and using a few smart shortcuts, the recipes here hit that sweet spot where taste and health meet, and quickly, so they are doable on the busiest weekdays.

I introduced my "Usually-Sometimes-Rarely" food lists in my very first book, *Small Changes, Big Results*, and they have been a guiding force for all my work and every recipe I have created since. My golden rule: No food is ever off-limits. Rather, I categorize food under the headings of Usually, Sometimes, or Rarely. "Usually" foods are those I use most plentifully and are the backbone of healthy eating: vegetables, whole fruits, beans, nuts and seeds, lean protein, low-fat dairy, whole grains, and healthy oils. I sprinkle in "Sometimes" foods here and there for flavor and variety. They are a bit more processed and less nutrient rich, like white flour or dark chocolate, or a little higher in saturated fat, like chicken thighs. "Rarely" foods—like sugar, cream, full-fat cheese, and butter—are the foods that many nutritionists forbid and many cooks use with a heavy hand. I have found the ideal midpoint by using these foods in small amounts, but strategically for maximum impact.

The idea is that there is no need to deprive yourself or go to extremes to be healthy. In fact, extremes are usually unhealthy and trap us into a dieting mentality. Rather, balance is key. If you are eating mostly nutrient-rich whole foods, there is room for some butter in your mashed potatoes, some sugar on your strawberries, or even a slice of rich chocolate cake.

I also believe in using pure, minimally processed ingredients and steering clear of artificial additives. I will use reduced-fat foods only if they work taste-wise and are not laden with chemical additives. So I use low-fat milk and yogurt, for example, but you won't get me within a yard of fat-free whipped topping. (Have you ever read the ingredient list on that stuff?) I'll take a little good-old-fashioned whipped cream any day. And when it comes to cheeses like Parmesan, blue cheeses, and sharp cheddar, there is just no substitute. Besides, they are so flavorful that just a bit goes a long way. The truth is, sometimes what's best is a little of the real thing.

When it comes to saving time in the kitchen, in keeping with my food philosophy, I might suggest a smart shortcut, like prewashed greens, frozen peas, or canned beans (more on that later), but I steer clear of anything that is highly processed or has artificial additives. No instant fat-free puddings or bottled salad dressings with a laundry list of preservatives here. I also make a point of sticking to common, easy-to-find ingredients and making them shine by pulling them together in fast, innovative ways.

time on your side

On a busy weeknight you want food fast, so each of these recipes takes 30 minutes or less to get on the table. That includes preheating the oven, boiling the water, chopping, and cooking—everything.

To make that 30-minute window truly realistic, I took a totally different approach when writing these recipes. Most recipes list ingredients as they should be prepared (for example, "1 medium onion, diced," or "5 mushrooms, stemmed and sliced"), implying you should have them lined up and ready to go, in what chefs call mise en place. That prep, of course, takes time and, frankly, no one I know really cooks like that at home. Instead, we dice the onion as the oil is heating in the pan, and chop the herbs while the meat cooks, and so on. To help make the most of your time in the kitchen, I call for whole ingredients ("1 medium onion" or "5 mushrooms") and write the chopping and slicing instructions into the method when there are windows of time during the cooking process. (For example, "While the mixture simmers, stem and dice the mushrooms.")

For maximum efficiency, I recommend that before you start cooking you read the recipe all the way through so that you have a good mental picture of what needs to happen, and so you can get all of your ingredients and tools out.

the weeknight wonders pantry

A well-stocked pantry takes the stress out of meal planning and saves you time because you don't have to be constantly running to the store. This list covers all the nonperishable items you need to make any recipe in this book. With these on hand, all you need to do is fill in with perishable items—which you can do on a weekly basis— and you will have paved the way to make fast, fabulous home-cooked dinners a regular part of your life.

OILS AND VINEGARS

Canola oil
Cooking spray
Extra-virgin olive oil
Olive oil
Toasted sesame oil
Balsamic vinegar
Cider vinegar
Red wine vinegar
Rice vinegar, unseasoned
Sherry vinegar
White wine vinegar

CONDIMENTS, SAUCES, AND OTHER FLAVOR
BOOSTERS

Asian fish sauce
Capers
Chipotle chiles in adobo sauce
Chili-garlic sauce (sriracha)
Chocolate, chocolate chips, dark (60% to 70% cocoa
solids or bittersweet)
Cocoa powder, unsweetened, natural
Hot pepper sauce
Jams and preserves (apricot)
Jarred sauces (basil pesto, tomatillo salsa)
Ketchup

Mayonnaise

Mustard (Dijon)

Olives (green, pimento-stuffed, calamata)

Soy sauce, reduced-sodium

Spirits: beer (stout), orange-flavored liqueur, port (tawny and ruby), rum (light), sherry (dry), white wine (dry)

Tea (Earl Grey)

Thai red curry paste

Worcestershire sauce

VEGETABLES, FRUITS, FISH, BEANS, AND BROTHS

Applesauce, unsweetened, natural

Baby corn

Bamboo shoots, sliced

Beans and peas, canned, preferably low-sodium (black, black-eyed peas, cannellini, chickpeas, kidney, pinto, red, white)

Broth and stock, low-sodium (beef, chicken, fish, vegetable)

Coconut milk, unsweetened, light

Fish, anchovies, sardines, tuna (light, Italian-style olive oil–packed)

Lentils, dried red

Pumpkin, solid pack

Roasted red peppers in water

Sun-dried tomatoes, not oil-packed

Tomatoes, preferably no-salt-added (diced, fire-roasted diced, crushed, tomato sauce, tomato paste)

SWEETENERS AND LEAVENERS

Baking powder

Baking soda

Honey

Pure maple syrup

Sugar (granulated, dark brown, light brown)

Unsulfured molasses

NUTS, SEEDS, AND DRIED FRUITS

Peanut butter, creamy, natural-style

Tahini (sesame paste)

Variety of shelled, unsalted nuts and seeds (almonds, cashews, hazelnuts, peanuts, pecans, pine nuts, pistachios, pumpkin seeds, sesame seeds, sunflower seeds, walnuts)

Dried fruits (Turkish apricots, cherries, dried coconut, cranberries, dates, figs, prunes, raisins)

GRAINS

Amaretti cookies

Bread crumbs, unseasoned, preferably whole wheat, panko

Brown rice, quick cooking "instant" (parboiled)

Bulgur wheat, quick cooking or fine

Cornstarch

Couscous, whole-wheat

Egg noodles, whole-wheat

Flour (whole-wheat, whole-wheat pastry, all-purpose)

Ladyfinger cookies

Oats, quick cooking

Pasta (whole-wheat or whole-wheat blend: spaghetti, penne, and orzo)

Polenta

Popcorn kernels

Quinoa (prerinsed)

Thai rice noodles (wide)

IN THE FREEZER

Artichoke hearts

Broccoli

Bread (whole-wheat sandwich bread, crusty whole-wheat bread, pita, whole-wheat hamburger buns)

Cheese ravioli, whole-wheat

Corn (kernels, ears)

Edamame, shelled

Fruit, unsweetened (cherries, mangos, peaches)

Ice cream (light) or frozen yogurt, vanilla

Pearl onions

Peas

Pizza dough, whole-wheat

Spinach, chopped

THE SPICE RACK

Almond extract
Bay leaf
Caraway seeds
Cayenne pepper
Chili powder
Cinnamon sticks
Creole seasoning
Crushed red pepper flakes
Cumin seeds
Curry powder
Dried basil
Dried oregano
Dried tarragon
Dried thyme
Garlic powder
Ground allspice
Ground cinnamon
Ground cloves
Ground coriander
Ground cumin

Ground fennel seeds
Ground ginger
Ground nutmeg
Ground oregano
Ground turmeric
Ground white pepper
Herbes de Provence
Mustard powder
Old Bay seasoning
Onion powder
Paprika
Peppercorns, black
Salt
Smoked paprika
Vanilla extract
Wasabi powder
Whole cloves
Whole mustard seeds

quick and simple accompaniments

Many of the recipes in this book are complete meals in themselves, while others are meant to be the star of the plate served with simply prepared accompaniments alongside, like rice or steamed green beans or grilled chicken. For each recipe, I provide specific serving suggestions to make for a balanced meal, both taste- and health-wise. Here is an at-a-glance guide for quick and simple grains, vegetables, and proteins to pair with some of the recipes while keeping you in the 30-minute zone.

express whole grains

Sometimes all you need is a basic steamed or boiled grain to make one of the skillet suppers or stir-fries in this book a complete,

satisfying meal. These quick-cooking whole grains are ideal for the weeknight dinner rush. Other whole grains that require no cooking at all include whole-grain wheat or corn tortillas and whole-grain breads such as pita or crusty Italian or French bread.

fresh steamed vegetables

A simply steamed vegetable is often the ideal way to round out a meal, adding color, nutrition, and a crisp, clean flavor element. Steaming is the best way to cook vegetables to preserve their nutritional value, and you can do it in one of two ways: on the stove using a steamer basket or in the microwave. Both methods are equally beneficial and easy.

To steam the old-fashioned way, on the stove, simply bring a few inches of water to a boil in a pot that can be fitted with a steamer basket and has a tight-fitting lid. Place the cut, washed vegetable in the

GRAIN	AMOUNT DRY (CUPS)	WATER/ LIQUID (CUPS)	COOK TIME (MINUTES, AFTER LIQUID BOILS)	DIRECTIONS	YIELD (CUPS)
Bulgur, fine	1	1¾	10	Bring liquid to a boil, add bulgur, cover, remove from heat to steam.	3
Couscous, whole-wheat	1	1¼	5–10	Bring liquid to a boil, add couscous, cover, remove from heat to steam.	3
Egg noodles, whole-wheat	8 ounces	5 quarts	4–6	Bring water to a boil, stir in noodles, return to a boil. Cook until tender, drain.	4
Pasta, whole-grain	8 ounces	5 quarts	6–12 minutes, depending on shape	Bring water to a boil, stir in pasta, return to a boil. Cook until tender, drain.	4
Polenta, grits	1	4	20	Bring liquid to a boil, add polenta gradually, whisking. Cook until creamy, stirring frequently.	4
Quinoa	1	1¾	15–20	Bring liquid to boil, add quinoa, cover and simmer until water is absorbed.	3
Rice, brown instant (parboiled)	1	1¾	10–12	Combine rice and liquid, bring to a boil, cover, simmer until water is absorbed.	4

basket, place the basket over the water, making sure the water doesn't touch the basket, cover, and steam over high heat.

For microwave steaming, wash and cut the vegetable, and then, with the water still clinging to it, place the vegetable in a microwave-safe bowl that has a tight-fitting lid. Cover and microwave on high power for about the same amount of time as you would with a regular steamer.

Once the vegetable is steamed to crisp-tender, drain, then toss with a little extra-virgin olive oil or a couple of teaspoons of butter and a sprinkle of salt. It is simply delicious just like that. If you'd like, you can take the seasoning a step further with a spritz of lemon juice and/or some chopped fresh herbs.

VEGETABLE	STEAM TIME FOR CRISP-TENDER (MINUTES)
Asparagus, medium thickness	4
Green beans, medium thickness	5
Broccoli, 1-inch florets	5–6
Carrots, ¼-inch-thick coins	5–6
Cauliflower, 1-inch florets	5
Snap peas	3–4
Snow peas	1–2
Spinach	30 seconds

fast, lean proteins

You don't have to do much to these proteins to make them delicious, and they are perfect for turning some of the fabulous salads and sides here into substantial suppers. Simply season them with salt and freshly ground pepper; spray a grill, grill pan, or nonstick skillet with cooking spray and preheat it over medium-high heat, or preheat the broiler and position the rack about 4 inches from the heat source; and cook according to the directions below, turning only once. Allow meat and poultry to rest for 3 to 5 minutes before serving so the juices can redistribute. Squeeze some lemon or lime juice over chicken or seafood, if desired.

POULTRY, MEAT	GRILL/ BROIL/SKILLET-GRILL COOK TIME (MINUTES PER SIDE)
Fish fillet, white such as cod, halibut, tilapia, mahi-mahi	4–5 per inch thickness (broil or skillet-grill)
Salmon fillet	4–5, per inch thickness
Shrimp, large (about 20 per pound)	2–3 (skewer if grilling)
Chicken breast, skinless, boneless, ¼ inch thick	3
Chicken breast, skinless, boneless ½ inch thick	3–5
Chicken thigh, skinless boneless	5
Sirloin or tenderloin steak, boneless, 1 inch thick	5, for medium rare
Lamb chop, loin, ¾ inch thick	3–5, for medium rare
Pork chop, loin, ¾ inch thick	3–5, for medium rare

healthy shortcuts

Sure, the best way to buy ingredients is at your local farmer's market—whole, just picked, with the dirt still clinging to them—and prep them yourself right before cooking. But let's get real—life's hectic pace doesn't always allow for that. Luckily there are plenty of healthy shortcuts available that make it a lot more doable to get a great meal on the table on busy weeknights. Don't hesitate to take advantage of them.

prewashed greens

You can get just about any green leafy vegetable in prewashed packages these days. Mixed lettuces make for instant salads, spinach and arugula are perfect for tossing into pasta and other sauces, and you can even get washed and cut kale and chard. Just be sure to check the sell-by date on the package and keep them refrigerated at home.

prepped produce

From cubed butternut squash and pomegranate seeds (arils) to sliced mushrooms and peeled and cored pineapple, there are a multitude of prepped fresh produce items in stores today that let you walk into your kitchen as if your very own sous chef has done the knife work already. Sure, once you cut a fruit or vegetable it begins to lose nutrition, but precut produce will still have plenty, and it could make the difference between cooking something healthy or not, so go for it when time is tight.

frozen fruits and vegetables

Frozen fruits and vegetables are comparable nutritionally to their fresh, cooked counterparts, and they work really well in many recipes. Stock up on the selection on the pantry list (page 17) to have healthy produce at your fingertips anytime. Just remember to buy it fresh-frozen, without added sauces, seasonings, or sweeteners.

precooked whole grains

Precooked whole grains like brown rice, quinoa, and grain mixes are now being sold in pouches on supermarket shelves and in the freezer section. It takes just minutes to reheat them. Here too, be sure to buy them without added seasonings, which are often high in sodium.

about the nutrition facts

I don't cook with a calculator at hand to get a certain nutrient profile from a recipe. Rather, I set out to make a delicious dish with all the familiar tastes and textures you expect, using the principles laid out in my "Usually-Sometimes-Rarely" food philosophy. Incredibly, when I do so, the numbers tend to work out on their own. But while I prefer to focus on the balance and quality of the food, because numbers can be a helpful guide I have included the nutrition facts for each recipe, with the amount of calories, fat, protein, carbohydrate, fiber, cholesterol, and sodium in each serving. Since some fats are beneficial and others detrimental, I further break down the fat content into saturated (bad fat), monounsaturated, and polyunsaturated (both good fats).

I have also listed "excellent" and "good" sources of essential nutrients in each recipe. To qualify as an excellent source, a serving must provide at least 20 percent of the Daily Value (the standard daily recommended intake), and to be called a good source, a serving must contain at least 10 percent of the Daily Value. I encourage you not to get hung up on these values, but to factor them in when planning your meals and let them serve as a reminder that vitamins and minerals are not just found in powders and pills, as so many marketers would have us believe. They are bountifully present in delicious, wholesome foods.

Keep in mind that the nutrition information excludes optional ingredients or anything added to taste, and if there is a choice of ingredients, like "nonfat or low-fat yogurt," I always use the first option listed for the analysis.

To help put the nutrition breakdown in perspective, here are some daily total numbers to shoot for based on a 2,000-calorie diet (the maintenance calorie level for most moderately active women):

Total Fat: 65g
(Saturated fat: 20g or less, monounsaturated fat: 25g, polyunsaturated fat: 20g)
Protein: 90g
Carbohydrate: 275g
Fiber: 28g or more
Cholesterol: 300mg or less
Sodium: 2,300mg or less

Regarding portion size, since everyone has different appetites and different calorie needs, there will always be a range of how many people a given recipe serves. But in order to do the nutrition analysis, I had to pick one number. So I chose to base the serving sizes on amounts that would satisfy most moderately active women. If you are serving a group of high-school football players, if you are training for a marathon, or if you are not as active as you'd like to be, adjust the portions accordingly.

ready, set, cook! and enjoy!

You may need to get dinner on the table fast—and the recipes here will certainly help you do that—but once you are ready eat, make a point of putting the rush and stress of the day behind you. Set the table nicely, even if you are dining solo; turn off the TV and computer and put your phone away. Put on some soothing music, sit down, and take a little time to relax and really taste each bite. If you are with friends and family, enjoy sharing the meal and conversation with them. Be sure to take a moment to fully savor your delicious weeknight wonder!

salads

STARTERS AND SIDE SALADS

BLACK AND RED SALAD WITH WALNUTS AND GOAT CHEESE | 43
SUGAR SNAP PEA, TOMATO, AND WATERMELON SALAD WITH FETA | 44

MAIN-COURSE SALADS

STEAK AU POIVRE SALAD | 47
SHRIMP PAD THAI SALAD | 48
CEVICHE SALAD WITH AVOCADO AND GRAPEFRUIT | 49
"FALAFEL" SALAD | 51
TUNA AND WHITE BEAN SALAD WITH RADICCHIO | 52
GRILLED GREEK SALAD WITH CHICKEN | 54
ANCHO CHICKEN SALAD WITH JÍCAMA, ORANGE, AND AVOCADO | 56

Sometimes you need an accompaniment that provides cool, crisp contrast to the main course, with clear, elemental flavors that complement, not compete. That's what this salad is made for. It is simply chopped lettuce and scallion, dressed with olive oil and lemon or lime juice. I use lime when I am pairing it with Asian and Central or South American–inspired dishes and lemon for Mediterranean and European fare.

cool and crisp
shredded romaine salad

MAKES 4 SERVINGS

Chop the lettuce into ½-inch-thick ribbons and thinly slice the scallion. Place them in a large bowl. Juice the lemon or lime (about 1½ tablespoons) and add to the bowl along with the oil, salt, and pepper. Toss to coat.

SERVING SIZE: 1½ CUPS
CALORIES 80; Total Fat 7g (Sat Fat 1g, Mono Fat 5.4g, Poly Fat 0.6g); Protein 1g; Carb 3g; Fiber 1g; Cholesterol 0mg; Sodium 150mg
EXCELLENT SOURCE OF Vitamin A, Vitamin C
GOOD SOURCE OF Vitamin K

1½ hearts of romaine lettuce
1 large scallion
½ medium lemon or 1 small lime
2 tablespoons extra-virgin olive oil
¼ teaspoon salt
¼ teaspoon freshly ground black pepper

In the summer, when tomatoes are at their best, this salad is a go-to in my home. It was one of the first dishes my daughter learned to make on her own—that's how easy it is. And she usually takes charge of getting it on the table to this day. However easy, it is absolutely delicious and versatile too. Serve it as a starter or alongside sandwiches, hummus and pita, pizza, or anything with a Mediterranean flair you might be tossing on the grill.

mediterranean chopped salad

MAKES 4 SERVINGS

3 medium tomatoes

1 medium yellow or orange bell pepper

1 medium English cucumber or 1 large regular cucumber

2 tablespoons extra-virgin olive oil

1 tablespoon red wine vinegar

2 teaspoons dried oregano

½ teaspoon salt

¼ teaspoon freshly ground black pepper

Core the tomatoes and core and seed the bell pepper. Cut the tomato, bell pepper, and cucumber into ½-inch chunks and place in a large bowl. Add the oil, vinegar, oregano, salt, and black pepper, and toss to coat.

SERVING SIZE 1½ cups
CALORIES 100; Total Fat 7g (Sat Fat 1g, Mono Fat 5.4g, Poly Fat 0.7g); Protein 2g; Carb 8g; Fiber 2g; Cholesterol 0mg; Sodium 300mg
EXCELLENT SOURCE OF Vitamin C
GOOD SOURCE OF Manganese, Potassium, Vitamin A, Vitamin K

FORGET FAT-FREE SALAD DRESSINGS. You need some fat to absorb all the valuable nutrients in produce. And studies show your body gets the most out of salad when prepared with monounsaturated fat–rich oils, like olive oil or canola.

Magic happens when you put your everyday ingredients together in this new and exciting way. By chopping the usual salad staples—tomato, bell pepper, and cucumber—and stirring them into a creamy base of yogurt and buttermilk with some fresh dill and scallion, you wind up with a refreshing summer soup that is anything but ordinary. It is one of those flexible dishes that allows you to use whatever produce you have on hand—chopped fresh fennel, radish, and sweet onion; grated carrot; already cooked peas or corn; and herbs like basil or parsley would all work well. It makes for a satisfying no-cook summer dinner served with hummus and pita.

summer vegetable yogurt soup

MAKES 4 SERVINGS

2½ cups low-fat buttermilk

⅔ cup plain low-fat Greek yogurt

1 large tomato

1 medium yellow bell pepper

½ English cucumber

2 scallions

3 tablespoons fresh dill fronds

½ teaspoon salt

¼ teaspoon freshly ground black pepper

2 teaspoons extra-virgin olive oil

In a large bowl, whisk the buttermilk and yogurt until smooth. Seed and dice the tomato, yellow pepper, and cucumber and add them to the bowl. Separate the scallion greens from the whites. Finely slice the scallion greens and add them to the bowl (reserve the whites for another use). Chop the dill and add 2 tablespoons to the bowl, reserving the rest for garnish. Stir in the salt and black pepper. Before serving, drizzle each bowl with ½ teaspoon oil and top with a bit of the remaining dill.

SERVING SIZE 1¼ cups
CALORIES 140; Total Fat 5g (Sat Fat 1.5g, Mono Fat 2.2g, Poly Fat 0.3g); Protein 10g; Carb 16g; Fiber 2g; Cholesterol 10mg; Sodium 470mg
EXCELLENT SOURCE OF Calcium, Iodine, Vitamin C, Vitamin K
GOOD SOURCE OF Folate, Manganese, Molybdenum, Phosphorus, Potassium, Protein, Riboflavin, Vitamin A, Vitamin B6

THE ACTIVE CULTURES IN YOGURT are not only good for your digestion, but studies show they can also boost your immune system and may even help prevent respiratory infections like the common cold.

You have probably heard of wedding soup, an Italian-American favorite that gets its name not because it is served at weddings, but because it is a marriage of meat (in the form of tiny meatballs) and vegetables (usually a green, like spinach or escarole). I call this version Shotgun Wedding Soup because it is so quick to the altar. Instead of fussing with mini meatballs, you simply brown the meat (I keep it lean with ground poultry), and using baby spinach means there's little prep needed for the greens, making the dish completely weeknight friendly. Serve it with Parmesan-Herb Flatbread Crackers (page 265) or Tomato Bread (page 266).

shotgun wedding soup

MAKES 4 SERVINGS

Dice the onion and mince the garlic. Heat the oil in a large soup pot over medium-high heat. Add the onion and chicken or turkey and cook, breaking up the meat as you stir, until it is just no longer pink, about 2 minutes. Stir in the garlic, salt, and pepper and cook for 1 minute more.

Add the broth, cover, and bring to a boil over high heat. Meanwhile, finely chop the parsley and grate the cheese. Place the parsley and cheese in a medium bowl, add the eggs, and whisk to combine. Then chop the spinach coarsely and set aside.

Once the soup is boiling, uncover and reduce the heat to medium-low. Stir the broth in a circular motion, then slowly drizzle in the egg mixture, stirring all the while, to form thin strands. Stir in the spinach and cook until the spinach is just wilted, about 30 seconds. Season with additional salt and pepper, if desired.

- ½ medium onion
- 2 cloves garlic
- 1 tablespoon olive oil
- ½ pound ground chicken or turkey
- ½ teaspoon salt, plus more to taste
- ¼ teaspoon freshly ground black pepper, plus more to taste
- 8 cups low-sodium chicken broth
- 2 tablespoons fresh Italian parsley leaves
- ½ ounce Parmesan cheese (3 tablespoons grated)
- 2 large eggs
- 3 cups lightly packed baby spinach leaves (about 3 ounces)

SERVING SIZE 2 cups
CALORIES 260; Total Fat 14g (Sat Fat 4g, Mono Fat 7.1g, Poly Fat 2.2g); Protein 25g; Carb 10g; Fiber 1g; Cholesterol 160mg; Sodium 600mg
EXCELLENT SOURCE OF Niacin, Phosphorus, Potassium, Protein, Riboflavin, Selenium, Vitamin A, Vitamin B6, Vitamin B12, Vitamin K
GOOD SOURCE OF Calcium, Copper, Iron, Pantothenic Acid, Vitamin C, Zinc

This delightful soup is a perfect example of the extraordinary flavor that can happen when you take two common ingredients and put them together in an exciting new way. Here, creamy pumpkin puree reveals its savory side as it is brightened by diced tomatoes and simmered in a curry-spiced broth to make a sumptuous soup. You can keep it rustic and chunky as I did here, or puree it if you'd like a smooth, creamy consistency. Either way, don't forget the cool contrast of a dollop of yogurt on top. Pair it up with a hearty green salad that has nuts and dried fruit, like Shaved Brussels Sprout Salad (page 31) or Tuscan Kale Salad (page 41).

curried pumpkin and tomato soup

MAKES 4 SERVINGS

1 medium onion

1 tablespoon canola oil

3 cloves garlic

One 1-inch piece fresh ginger

2 teaspoons yellow curry powder

¼ teaspoon crushed red pepper flakes

One 15-ounce can solid-pack pure pumpkin

One 14.5-ounce can no-salt-added diced tomatoes

3 cups low-sodium chicken broth or vegetable broth

½ teaspoon salt

¼ teaspoon freshly ground black pepper

¼ cup plain low-fat Greek yogurt

Dice the onion. Heat the oil in a large (4-quart) saucepan over medium heat. Add the onions and cook, stirring occasionally, until they are soft and golden, about 10 minutes. While the onions cook, mince the garlic and finely grate the ginger. Add the garlic, ginger, curry powder, and crushed red pepper flakes to the pan and cook, stirring, until the spices are fragrant, 1 minute. Add the pumpkin puree, tomatoes with their juice, broth, salt, and black pepper; stir to incorporate. Turn the heat to high and bring to a boil, then lower the heat to medium and simmer until thickened slightly, 5 minutes. Serve each bowl with a dollop of yogurt.

SERVING SIZE 1½ cups
CALORIES 150; Total Fat 5g (Sat Fat 1g, Mono Fat 2.8g, Poly Fat 1.3g); Protein 7g; Carb 20g; Fiber 5g; Cholesterol 0mg; Sodium 370mg
EXCELLENT SOURCE OF Vitamin A, Vitamin C, Vitamin K
GOOD SOURCE OF Copper, Fiber, Iron, Manganese, Niacin, Phosphorus, Potassium, Protein

You may know this hearty, comforting soup as "pasta fazool"—an American twist on the word *fagioli* (fah-JOH-lee), which means "beans" in Italian. One thing for sure, there won't be much talking at all when you serve it, because everyone will be too busy eating the savory, belly-warming combination of tender elbow pasta and white beans fortified with an extra helping of zucchini and a punch of Parmesan. Serve it with a simple salad, like Celery, Radish, and Herb Salad (page 34), and whole-grain Italian bread with some extra-virgin olive oil for dipping.

pasta fagioli with zucchini

MAKES 4 SERVINGS

Chop the onion and mince the garlic. Heat the oil in a medium pot over medium-high heat. Add the onion and cook, stirring, until softened, about 3 minutes. Add the garlic and cook for 1 minute more. Meanwhile, chop the zucchini.

Drain and rinse the beans and add to the pot along with the tomatoes, broth, salt, and pepper. Bring to a boil. Add the zucchini and macaroni, return to a boil, then reduce the heat to medium and cook, stirring occasionally, until the pasta is tender, about 12 minutes. While the pasta is cooking, grate the cheese and chop the parsley.

Remove the pot from the heat and stir in the cheese. Serve garnished with the chopped parsley.

SERVING SIZE 1½ cups
CALORIES 290; Total Fat 11g (Sat Fat 2.5g, Mono Fat 6.0g, Poly Fat 1.1g); Protein 15g; Carb 36g; Fiber 7g; Cholesterol 5mg; Sodium 510mg
EXCELLENT SOURCE OF Fiber, Magnesium, Manganese, Phosphorus, Protein, Thiamin, Vitamin C, Vitamin K
GOOD SOURCE OF Calcium, Copper, Iron, Molybdenum, Niacin, Potassium, Riboflavin, Vitamin A, Vitamin B6, Zinc

- 1 small onion
- 2 cloves garlic
- 2 tablespoons olive oil
- 2 medium zucchini (about ½ pound each)
- One 15-ounce can low-sodium white beans
- One 14.5-ounce can no-salt-added diced tomatoes
- 3 cups low-sodium chicken broth
- ½ teaspoon salt
- ¼ teaspoon freshly ground black pepper
- ½ cup whole-wheat elbow macaroni
- 1 ounce Parmesan cheese (⅓ cup grated)
- 2 tablespoons fresh Italian parsley leaves

This divinely creamy soup has a familiar, comforting quality to it, but its extraordinary flavor truly sets it apart. The combination of artichoke hearts, a dash of sherry, and aged Manchego cheese gives it a savory Spanish flair. And it gets its thick creaminess not from cups of cream, as you would usually find in a soup like this, but as a result of pureeing the artichokes with reduced-fat milk and a little potato. Serve it with Tomato Bread (page 266) in keeping with the Spanish sensibility.

velvety artichoke soup

MAKES 4 SERVINGS

3 cups low-sodium chicken broth

3 tablespoons olive oil

1 large onion

2 cloves garlic

1 medium white potato (about 5 ounces)

¼ cup dry sherry or dry white wine

Two 9-ounce packages frozen artichoke hearts

¾ teaspoon salt, plus more to taste

¼ teaspoon ground white pepper

2 ounces aged Manchego cheese or Parmesan cheese (¼ cup grated)

1 cup 2% milk

Bring the broth to a boil in a medium (3-quart) covered saucepan over high heat.

While the broth is heating, heat the oil in a large (4-quart) saucepan over medium-high heat. Meanwhile, chop the onion. Add the onion to the saucepan and cook until softened, about 3 minutes. While the onion is cooking, mince the garlic and peel and dice the potato into ½-inch dice. Add the garlic to the saucepan and cook for 1 minute.

Stir in the sherry or wine, then add the potatoes, artichokes, salt, pepper and hot broth to the pot. Cover and return to a boil over high heat, then lower the heat to medium and simmer until the potatoes have softened, about 8 minutes. Meanwhile, finely grate the cheese.

Remove the soup from the heat, stir in the milk, then puree in 3 batches in a blender, transferring the puree to the saucepan that held the broth. (Alternatively, use an immersion blender.) Heat the puree over medium heat until hot but not boiling. Add the cheese and stir until melted, 30 seconds. Season with additional salt, if desired.

SERVING SIZE 2 cups
CALORIES 320; Total Fat 18g (Sat Fat 4.5g, Mono Fat 9.5g, Poly Fat 1.5g); Protein 15g; Carb 27g; Fiber 9g; Cholesterol 15mg; Sodium 830mg
EXCELLENT SOURCE OF Calcium, Fiber, Phosphorus, Protein, Vitamin C
GOOD SOURCE OF Niacin, Potassium, Riboflavin, Vitamin B6, Vitamin B12

HERE'S A SURPRISING FACT: Artichoke hearts are the number one most antioxidant-rich vegetable! They rank right up there with the super-berries in healing power.

There is a Chinese take-out place by me that makes a simple soup chock-full of crisp-tender vegetables in a clear chicken broth that I just love. I have turned it into a main course here by adding slices of lean pork to the mix and heightening the flavor of the broth with fresh ginger so that it doesn't need quite as much salt. (I am sure theirs has about a day's worth!) Not only do I like my version even better, but it is also on the table faster than if I ordered it. Make a bowl of Sesame Quinoa (page 260) to serve alongside, or if you have leftover cooked rice, put some in each bowl and pour the hot soup over it.

chinese vegetable soup with pork

MAKES 4 SERVINGS

Heat 1 tablespoon of the oil in a large soup pot over medium-high heat. Slice the pork into ¼-inch-thick slices and cook until browned, about 2 minutes per side. Transfer the pork to a plate. While the pork is cooking, slice the mushrooms.

Add the remaining 1 tablespoon oil to the pot, add the mushrooms, and cook, stirring occasionally, until they release their water and begin to brown, 6 to 7 minutes. Meanwhile, chop the scallions and grate the ginger, then add them to the pot and cook until the scallions begin to soften, 1 minute. Add the broth, turn the heat to high, cover, and bring to a boil.

While the broth is heating, trim and chop the bok choy, trim the snow peas, and drain and rinse the baby corn and bamboo shoots. Halve the baby corn if large.

When the broth is boiling, add the bok choy, snow peas, baby corn, bamboo shoots, and salt and return to a boil. Cook until the snow peas and bok choy are just crisp-tender, about 1 minute.

- 2 tablespoons canola oil
- ½ pound pork tenderloin
  One 10-ounce package button mushrooms
- 4 scallions
  One 2-inch piece fresh ginger
- 8 cups low-sodium chicken broth
- 1 bunch baby bok choy (½ pound)
- 2 cups snow peas (½ pound)
  One 15-ounce can baby corn
  One 8-ounce can sliced bamboo shoots
- ¾ teaspoon salt

SERVING SIZE 3 cups
CALORIES 260; Total Fat 12g (Sat Fat 2g, Mono Fat 6.2g, Poly Fat 2.9g); Protein 26g; Carb 16g; Fiber 3g; Cholesterol 35mg; Sodium 860mg
EXCELLENT SOURCE OF Copper, Manganese, Niacin, Phosphorus, Potassium, Protein, Riboflavin, Selenium, Thiamin, Vitamin A, Vitamin B6, Vitamin C, Vitamin K
GOOD SOURCE OF Fiber, Folate, Iron, Pantothenic Acid, Vitamin B12, Zinc

This Italian-style chicken soup is as delicious and comforting as it is fun, fast, and easy. It has tender chunks of chicken and is packed with vegetables and aromatics like onions and garlic. A few handfuls of chopped escarole add Mediterranean flair and a layer of savory flavor to the broth, but fresh spinach leaves would work well too, if you prefer. The fun part comes when you get to break the spaghetti into the pot to make bite-sized pieces and give it a rustic, playful touch. Serve with Tomato Bread (page 266) or the Parmesan-Herb Flatbread Crackers (page 265).

chicken and broken noodle soup

MAKES 4 SERVINGS

- 2 tablespoons canola oil
- 1 pound skinless boneless chicken breast
- ¾ teaspoon salt, plus more to taste
- ½ teaspoon freshly ground black pepper
- 1 medium onion
- 1 large carrot
- 2 stalks celery
- 2 cloves garlic
- ½ bunch escarole
- 6 cups low-sodium chicken broth
- 1 teaspoon dried basil
- ¼ teaspoon crushed red pepper flakes
- 2 ounces whole-wheat spaghetti

Heat 1 tablespoon of the oil in a large (6-quart) stockpot over medium heat. Dice the chicken and season it with ¼ teaspoon each of the salt and black pepper. Cook the chicken, turning occasionally, until just cooked through, 5 minutes. Transfer to a plate along with any accumulated juices.

While the chicken is cooking, chop the onion, carrot, and celery. Add the remaining 1 tablespoon oil to the pot, then add the onion, carrot, celery, and the remaining ½ teaspoon salt and ¼ teaspoon black pepper. Cook, stirring occasionally, until the onions become translucent and the carrots begin to soften, 6 minutes.

Meanwhile, mince the garlic and then separate the escarole leaves from the white ribs, discarding the ribs. Slice the escarole leaves into thin ribbons and reserve. When the onions and carrot are ready, add the garlic to the pot and cook for 1 minute more.

Add the broth, basil, and crushed red pepper flakes to the stockpot, then add the spaghetti, breaking it into thirds before adding it to the pot. Stir to combine. Turn the heat to high, cover, and bring to a boil. Then uncover, lower the heat to medium to maintain a vigorous simmer, and cook until the spaghetti is firm-tender, about 9 minutes. During the last 2 minutes of cooking, return the cooked chicken to the pot to warm through. Season with additional salt if desired.

SERVING SIZE 2¼ cups
CALORIES 330; Total Fat 13g (Sat Fat 2g, Mono Fat 6.3g, Poly Fat 3.1g); Protein 35g; Carb 22g; Fiber 4g; Cholesterol 75mg; Sodium 720mg
EXCELLENT SOURCE OF Folate, Manganese, Niacin, Pantothenic Acid, Phosphorus, Potassium, Protein, Selenium, Vitamin A, Vitamin B6, Vitamin K
GOOD SOURCE OF Copper, Fiber, Iron, Magnesium, Riboflavin, Thiamin, Vitamin C, Zinc

Pureeing buttery cashews into a savory carrot-ginger soup takes it from delicious but somewhat expected to a richly satisfying main course that makes you say "wow!" The nuts add a lovely texture and body to the soup, not to mention protein and healthy fats. Their subtle sweetness plays off the sweetness of the carrots, while the ginger and allspice provide a fragrant, warming effect. This soup pairs beautifully with Chicory Salad with Green Apple, Cranberries, and Blue Cheese (page 37).

savory carrot-cashew soup

MAKES 4 SERVINGS

Bring the broth to a boil in a medium saucepan. While the broth is heating, chop the onion and mince the garlic and ginger. Slice all but one-quarter of one of the carrots into ¼-inch-thick coins.

Heat the oil in another medium pot over medium-high heat. Add the onion and cook, stirring occasionally, until softened, 3 to 4 minutes. Add the garlic and ginger and cook for 1 minute more. Stir in the allspice and cook for 30 seconds.

Stir the carrot coins into the pot with the onions, then add the boiling broth, cover and return to a boil over a high heat. Lower the heat to medium, uncover, and simmer until the carrots are tender, 8 to 9 minutes. Meanwhile, grate the remaining carrot quarter and chop 2 tablespoons of the cashews to use for garnish.

Remove the pot from the heat, stir in the whole cashews, honey, salt, and pepper, and then puree the soup in 3 batches in a blender until smooth. (Alternatively, use an immersion blender.)

Serve garnished with the grated carrot and chopped cashews.

- 4 cups low-sodium chicken broth
- 1 medium onion
- 2 cloves garlic
- One 1-inch piece fresh ginger
- 1½ pounds carrots (5 large)
- 1 tablespoon olive oil
- ¼ teaspoon ground allspice
- ½ cup unsalted roasted cashews
- 2 teaspoons honey
- ¾ teaspoon salt
- ¼ teaspoon ground white pepper

SERVING SIZE 1½ cups
CALORIES 250; Total Fat 13g (Sat Fat 2.5g, Mono Fat 7.8g, Poly Fat 2.2g); Protein 9g; Carb 29g; Fiber 5g; Cholesterol 0mg; Sodium 620mg
EXCELLENT SOURCE OF Copper, Fiber, Manganese, Niacin, Phosphorus, Potassium, Vitamin A, Vitamin K
GOOD SOURCE OF Folate, Iron, Magnesium, Molybdenum, Protein, Riboflavin, Thiamin, Vitamin B6, Vitamin C, Zinc

This hearty meal in a bowl is so loaded with savory goodies that it could easily be considered a stew. Whatever you call it, I know you will call it wonderful, with its tender hunks of chicken, pinwheels of corn on the cob, potatoes, and plantains simmered in a fragrant tomato broth. If you can't find plantains, unripe (yes, green!) bananas work well too. They soften when cooked and impart a slight sweetness to the soup, um stew ... whatever!

colombian chicken soup with corn, potatoes, and plantains

MAKES 4 SERVINGS

Cut the chicken thighs in half, then thinly slice the onion into half-moons and mince the garlic. Heat the oil in a large (4-quart) saucepan over medium heat, add the chicken and onion, and cook until the onions begin to soften, 3 to 4 minutes, turning the chicken midway through cooking. Add the garlic, cumin, and salt and cook for 1 minute more. Add the broth, cover, and bring to a boil.

Meanwhile, halve the potatoes, peel and roughly chop the carrot, peel the plantain or banana and cut it crosswise into 8 chunks, and cut the corn crosswise into 8 wheels, adding the vegetables to the soup as you cut them.

Add the diced tomatoes, cover, and return the soup to a boil. Reduce the heat and simmer, covered, until the vegetables are tender, 10 to 12 minutes. Season with additional salt if desired. Coarsely chop the cilantro and garnish each bowl of soup with it right before serving.

- 4 skinless boneless chicken thighs (about ¼ pound each)
- 1 medium onion
- 2 cloves garlic
- 1 tablespoon canola oil
- ¼ teaspoon ground cumin
- ¾ teaspoon salt, plus more to taste
- 5 cups low-sodium chicken broth
- 8 multicolored fingerling or baby potatoes (7 ounces total)
- 1 large carrot
- 1 large green plantain or unripe (green) banana
- 1 ear corn, thawed if frozen
- 1 cup canned no-salt-added diced tomatoes
- ¼ cup fresh cilantro leaves

SERVING SIZE 2¼ cups
CALORIES 470; Total Fat 18g (Sat Fat 4.5g, Mono Fat 7.9g, Poly Fat 4.4g); Protein 39g; Carb 41g; Fiber 4g; Cholesterol 110mg; Sodium 660mg
EXCELLENT SOURCE OF Niacin, Phosphorus, Potassium, Protein, Riboflavin, Selenium, Vitamin A, Vitamin B6, Vitamin C, Zinc
GOOD SOURCE OF Copper, Fiber, Folate, Iron, Magnesium, Manganese, Pantothenic Acid, Thiamin, Vitamin B12, Vitamin K

GREEN BANANAS are rich in a type of starch called resistant starch, which is not broken down by our digestive enzymes, so it acts more like a fiber than a true starch. Eating it may help control blood sugar, manage weight, and lower cholesterol.

I will never forget my first roti sandwich, at a tiny food shack on the Caribbean island of Anguilla: island music playing, the heady aroma of curry filling the little shop, and a hot wrap sandwich stuffed with a spicy, saucy chickpea stew in my hands. The first messy bite confirmed I was in paradise. This sandwich takes me right back there every time I need an island fix. Buying pre-cut butternut squash makes this recipe a breeze, but you will likely have to cut it a bit further to get 1-inch pieces.

caribbean chickpea curry wraps (roti)

MAKES 4 SERVINGS

- 1 medium onion
- 1 small Scotch bonnet pepper or 1 medium jalapeño pepper
- 2 cloves garlic
- 1 tablespoon canola oil
- One 15-ounce can low-sodium chickpeas
- 4 cups cubed butternut squash (1¼ pounds)
- 2 teaspoons ground turmeric
- 2 teaspoons ground coriander
- 1 teaspoon ground cumin
- 1 teaspoon mustard powder
- 1 teaspoon ground fennel
- 1 teaspoon ground allspice
- ¼ teaspoon cayenne pepper
- 1¼ cups low-sodium chicken broth
- ¾ teaspoon salt
- ¼ teaspoon freshly ground black pepper
- 2 scallions
- Four 10-inch whole-wheat tortillas or wrap breads

Chop the onion, seed and chop the pepper, and mince the garlic.

Heat the oil in a large skillet over medium-high heat. Add the onions and pepper and cook, stirring occasionally, until softened, about 5 minutes. Meanwhile, drain and rinse the chickpeas and, if necessary, cut the butternut squash cubes further into 1-inch pieces.

When the onions are soft, add the garlic to the skillet and cook for 1 minute more. Stir in the turmeric, coriander, cumin, mustard powder, fennel, allspice, and cayenne and cook, stirring, until fragrant, 1 minute.

Add the chickpeas and butternut squash to the skillet and cook until the squash begins to soften, 3 to 4 minutes. Add the broth, salt, and black pepper, bring to a boil, then lower the heat to medium, cover, and cook until the squash is softened and about half the liquid is absorbed, 10 to 12minutes. Chop the scallions.

Place a tortilla or wrap bread on each plate, scoop a cup of the stew onto the center of each, sprinkle with scallions, and then wrap. Alternatively, you can serve the stew in bowls garnished with scallion and the tortilla or bread on the side.

SERVING SIZE 1 cup stew and 1 tortilla
CALORIES 470; Total Fat 9g (Sat Fat 0.5g, Mono Fat 2.6g, Poly Fat 1.3g); Protein 15g; Carb 69g; Fiber 11g; Cholesterol 0mg; Sodium 710mg
EXCELLENT SOURCE OF Copper, Fiber, Iron, Magnesium, Manganese, Potassium, Protein, Vitamin A, Vitamin C, Vitamin K
GOOD SOURCE OF Calcium, Folate, Molybdenum, Niacin, Phosphorus, Thiamin, Vitamin B6

This sumptuous supper has layers of exciting flavors and textures, all piled high on warm flatbread: first, crunchy cucumber ribbons; then a mound of aromatically spiced sautéed onions; third, flakes of freshly broiled salmon; and finally, a cool, creamy lemon-yogurt sauce. It's like no sandwich you have had before, but it's one you'll make again and again.

open-face mediterranean salmon sandwiches

MAKES 4 SERVINGS

2 tablespoons olive oil

1½ teaspoons ground cumin

¾ teaspoon ground turmeric

½ teaspoon ground coriander

½ teaspoon salt

½ teaspoon freshly ground black pepper

¼ teaspoon cayenne pepper

2 large onions

4 cloves garlic

1 pound skinless salmon fillets

1 large English cucumber

2 scallions

½ large lemon

¾ cup plain low-fat yogurt

4 whole-grain flatbreads or pita breads (about 6 inches in diameter)

Preheat the broiler.

In a small bowl, stir together the oil, cumin, turmeric, coriander, salt, black pepper, and cayenne until well combined. Thinly slice the onions and garlic. Heat 1½ tablespoons of the oil-spice mixture in a very large nonstick skillet over medium-high heat. Add the onions and garlic, then reduce the heat to medium and cook, stirring occasionally, until softened and slightly charred, 13 to 14 minutes.

While the onions are cooking, place the salmon on an aluminum foil–lined baking sheet and rub the top with the remaining oil-spice mixture. Broil about 5 inches from the heat source for 10 minutes per inch of thickness for medium doneness. Remove from the broiler, allow to cool for 5 minutes, then flake with a fork.

While the salmon is cooking, slice the cucumber in half crosswise, then slice each half lengthwise into thin ribbons using a sharp knife, mandoline, or vegetable peeler. Chop the scallions and place them in a medium bowl. Squeeze the lemon juice into the bowl (about 2 tablespoons), add the yogurt, and whisk to combine.

Heat the flatbreads or pita in the broiler for 30 seconds. To serve, top each piece of bread with about ¾ cup cucumber slices, then ⅓ cup of the onions and ¾ cup of the flaked salmon. Drizzle each with ¼ cup of the yogurt sauce.

SERVING SIZE 1 sandwich
CALORIES 470; Total Fat 17g (Sat Fat 3g, Mono Fat 7.7g, Poly Fat 4.3g); Protein 33g; Carb 49g; Fiber 8g; Cholesterol 65mg; Sodium 710mg
EXCELLENT SOURCE OF Copper, Fiber, Iron, Magnesium, Manganese, Molybdenum, Niacin, Pantothenic Acid, Phosphorus, Potassium, Protein, Riboflavin, Selenium, Thiamin, Vitamin B6, Vitamin B12, Vitamin C, Vitamin D, Vitamin K
GOOD SOURCE OF Calcium, Folate, Iodine, Zinc

Grilling vegetables concentrates their flavor and makes them meaty and satisfying, so even carnivores will be happy with this substantial open-face sandwich for dinner. It is like a French bread pizza: piled with tender, charred vegetables, seasoned with a spread of basil pesto, and topped with mozzarella cheese, which melts all bubbly and browned under the broiler. Feel free to mix it up when it comes to the vegetables you use: Portobello mushrooms, sliced eggplant, and wedges of fennel would all be delicious.

open-face grilled vegetable sandwiches

MAKES 4 SERVINGS

If using a grill, spray it with cooking spray and preheat it over medium-high heat. Otherwise, wait to preheat a grill pan.

Trim the stem ends off the zucchini, then slice them lengthwise into ¼-inch-thick slices. Slice the peppers lengthwise into 4 pieces, discarding the core and seeds, and slice the onion into ¼-inch-thick rounds. If using a grill pan, spray it with cooking spray and preheat it over medium-high heat.

Brush both sides of the vegetables lightly with the oil, then cook until tender and grill marks have formed, 2 to 3 minutes per side for the zucchini and onions and about 4minutes per side for the peppers. You may need to cook the vegetables in 2 or more batches depending on the size of your grill or grill pan.

While the vegetables are cooking, slice the bread in half lengthwise and then again in half crosswise so you have 4 long pieces. Scoop the soft center out of the bread and discard. Shred the mozzarella cheese if not pre-shredded.

Preheat the broiler.

Slice the grilled peppers into ½-inch-thick strips.

Spread each piece of bread with 1 tablespoon of the pesto. Top with about 4 slices of zucchini, 6 slices of peppers, and 5 or 6 onion rings and sprinkle each with about ¼ cup of the cheese. Broil about 4 inches from the heating element until the cheese is melted and beginning to brown and the bread is crisp, 1 to 2 minutes.

Cooking spray

2 medium zucchini (½ pound each)

2 medium red bell peppers

1 large red onion

2 tablespoons olive oil

One 16-ounce (about 16 inches long) whole-grain French baguette or Italian bread

4 ounces part-skim mozzarella cheese (1 cup shredded)

¼ cup prepared basil pesto

SERVING SIZE 1 sandwich
CALORIES 490; Total Fat 23g (Sat Fat 7g, Mono Fat 12.0g, Poly Fat 2.0g); Protein 24g; Carb 48g; Fiber 9g; Cholesterol 20mg; Sodium 680mg
EXCELLENT SOURCE OF Calcium, Copper, Fiber, Folate, Magnesium, Manganese, Molybdenum, Niacin, Phosphorus, Potassium, Protein, Riboflavin, Selenium, Thiamin, Vitamin A, Vitamin B6, Vitamin C, Vitamin K, Zinc
GOOD SOURCE OF Iron, Pantothenic Acid, Vitamin B12

This sandwich has all the elements of a classic French dip sandwich—crusty bread, tender slices of roast beef, and a savory au jus gravy—only here it is served open-face, so the gravy is poured over the sandwich rather than served as a dip alongside. That keeps the carb portion smart and allows the toasted bread to soak in the luscious gravy on the plate. A layer of garlicky spinach makes it a complete meal, vegetables and all.

open-face "french dip" sandwiches

MAKES 4 SERVINGS

Heat 1 tablespoon of the oil in a medium (9-inch) skillet over medium-high heat. Thinly slice the onion and cook, stirring occasionally, until it is tender and lightly golden, 5 to 7 minutes. Add the sherry and cook until reduced by half, 2 to 3 minutes. Add the broth, soy sauce, and pepper. Turn the heat to high and return to a boil, then lower the heat to medium and simmer until the sauce reduces by about one-third, about 10 minutes more.

While sauce simmers, thinly slice the garlic. Heat the remaining 1 tablespoon oil in a large skillet over medium-high heat and cook the garlic until fragrant, 1 minute. Add the spinach and cook until just wilted, 2 minutes.

Toast the bread until crispy and golden. Place a slice of bread on each of 4 plates. Top each with the wilted spinach, then layer with slices of roast beef and pour the gravy on top.

- 2 tablespoons canola oil
- 1 medium onion
- ½ cup dry sherry
- 1½ cups low-sodium beef broth
- 4 teaspoons reduced-sodium soy sauce
- ¼ teaspoon freshly ground black pepper
- 3 cloves garlic
- 5 cups lightly packed baby spinach leaves (5 ounces)

  Four ½-inch-thick slices from a round loaf of crusty whole-grain bread (about 2½ ounces each)
- ¾ pound lean roast beef, thinly sliced

SERVING SIZE 1 sandwich and about ½ cup gravy
CALORIES 490; Total Fat 17g (Sat Fat 3.5g, Mono Fat 8.6g, Poly Fat 2.8g); Protein 42g; Carb 38g; Fiber 7g; Cholesterol 85mg; Sodium 640mg
EXCELLENT SOURCE OF Copper, Fiber, Iron, Magnesium, Manganese, Niacin, Phosphorus, Protein, Riboflavin, Selenium, Thiamin, Vitamin A, Vitamin B6, Vitamin B12, Zinc
GOOD SOURCE OF Calcium, Folate, Pantothenic Acid, Potassium, Vitamin C, Vitamin K

Frozen veggie burgers are OK in a pinch, but they can't hold a candle to a freshly made one, brimming with tender, fresh vegetables, meaty beans, nuts, whole grains, and sumptuous seasonings. This recipe gives you all that, and fast, thanks to the use of quick-cooking whole-grain couscous and canned beans. You can make it even faster by buying pre-sliced mushrooms if you want. While veggie burgers can be seasoned in any number of ways, from Middle Eastern to Mexican, I purposely kept this one out of any specific ethnic realm. Rather, I wanted it to be an all-purpose, go-to burger full of savory flavors—like sautéed onion, mustard, and Worcestershire sauce—that you can't pin down to a specific ethic cuisine. I also made it without eggs so I'd be able to serve it to my vegan friends. Think of it as the anytime, for everybody, all-American veggie burger.

all-american veggie burgers

MAKES 4 SERVINGS

FOR THE BURGERS:

¼ cup whole-grain couscous

¼ cup pine nuts

One 15-ounce can low-sodium chickpeas

7 medium button mushrooms (about ¼ pound)

2 tablespoons olive oil

1 small onion

1 stalk celery

½ medium red bell pepper

2 cloves garlic

2 tablespoons dried unseasoned bread crumbs

1 tablespoon Worcestershire sauce

2 teaspoons yellow mustard or Dijon mustard

½ teaspoon salt

¼ teaspoon freshly ground black pepper

Cooking spray

FOR SERVING:

4 whole-grain burger buns

2 medium tomatoes

4 romaine lettuce leaves

Ketchup, optional

To make the burgers, cook the couscous according to directions on the package, then set aside. While the couscous is cooking, toast the pine nuts in a small dry skillet over medium-high heat, stirring frequently, until they are fragrant and golden brown, 2 minutes. Drain and rinse the chickpeas and set them aside.

Slice the mushrooms. Heat the oil in a large nonstick skillet over medium-high heat. Add the mushrooms and cook, stirring occasionally, until they release their water, about 4 minutes. Meanwhile, dice the onion, celery, and bell pepper. Add to the skillet with the mushrooms and cook for 2 minutes. While they are cooking, mince the garlic, then add it to the skillet and cook until all the vegetables are firm-tender and beginning to brown, about 1 minute more.

continued on page 86

continued from page 85

Transfer the mushroom mixture to a food processor. Add the couscous, pine nuts, chickpeas, bread crumbs, Worcestershire, mustard, salt, and black pepper and pulse until mostly finely chopped but you still have some larger chunks, 12 to 15 pulses. Be careful not to overprocess or the burgers will become mushy. Add an additional tablespoon of breadcrumbs if the mixture seems too wet. Form the mixture into 4 large patties. (Patties can be made ahead up to this point up and kept in an airtight container in the refrigerator for up to 3 days.)

Spray the same nonstick skillet with the cooking spray and heat over medium-high heat. Cook the patties until browned on one side, about 3 minutes, then spray the top of the patties with cooking spray, turn gently, and cook until the other side is browned, about 3 minutes more.

While the burgers cook, toast the buns, slice the tomatoes, and remove the spines from the lettuce leaves. Serve the patties on the buns with lettuce, tomato, and ketchup, if desired.

SERVING SIZE 1 burger
CALORIES 440; Total Fat 16g (Sat Fat 2.0g, Mono Fat 5.0g, Poly Fat 3.6g); Protein 15g; Carb 62g; Fiber 11g; Cholesterol 0mg; Sodium 690mg
EXCELLENT SOURCE OF Copper, Fiber, Magnesium, Manganese, Molybdenum, Niacin, Phosphorus, Protein, Selenium, Vitamin A, Vitamin C, Vitamin K
GOOD SOURCE OF Calcium, Folate, Iron, Potassium, Riboflavin, Thiamin, Vitamin B6, Zinc

Here pumpkin seeds take a star turn, whirred in the food processor into a rich, spreadable kind of pesto that's creamy but retains an appealing crunch. It has a wonderful depth of flavor from sautéed onions, garlic, jalapeño, and spices, and a bright zing of lime and herbal freshness from cilantro leaves. Slathered generously on a whole-grain wrap and rolled with lettuce, tomato, and avocado, it makes a filling meal you can hold in your hand.

pumpkin seed pesto wraps

MAKES 4 SERVINGS

- 1 small onion
- 2 tablespoons canola oil
- 1 medium jalapeño pepper
- 3 cloves garlic
- ¼ teaspoon ground cumin
- 1½ large limes
- 1 cup unsalted pumpkin seeds (pepitas)
- ½ cup packed fresh cilantro leaves
- ½ teaspoon salt
- ¼ teaspoon freshly ground black pepper
- 4 large red leaf lettuce leaves
- 1 medium tomato
- 1 medium avocado
- 4 whole-wheat wraps or flour tortillas (about 9 inches in diameter)

Dice the onion. Heat 1 tablespoon of the oil in a medium skillet over medium-high heat. Add the onion and cook, stirring occasionally, until softened, about 3 minutes. Meanwhile, seed and finely chop the jalapeño and mince the garlic. Add the jalapeño, garlic, and cumin to the skillet and cook until the jalapeño begins to soften, 1 minute more.

Transfer the onion mixture to a food processor. Finely zest and juice the limes (3 tablespoons juice) into the processor. Add the pumpkin seeds, cilantro, salt, black pepper, the remaining 1 tablespoon oil, and ½ cup water and process until creamy.

Remove and discard the spines of the lettuce leaves. Slice the tomato into half-moons and pit, peel, and slice the avocado. Spread ¼ cup of the pumpkin seed pesto on each wrap. Top each with 2 lettuce leaf halves, 2 tomato slices, and a few slices of avocado, then wrap up burrito-style.

SERVING SIZE 1 wrap
CALORIES 480; Total Fat 32g (Sat Fat 4g, Mono Fat 14.0g, Poly Fat 8.8g); Protein 15g; Carb 36g; Fiber 8g; Cholesterol 0mg; Sodium 480mg
EXCELLENT SOURCE OF Copper, Fiber, Iron, Magnesium, Manganese, Phosphorus, Protein, Vitamin A, Vitamin C, Vitamin K
GOOD SOURCE OF Folate, Niacin, Potassium, Vitamin B6, Zinc

PUMPKIN SEEDS are one of the best vegetarian sources of zinc, an essential mineral that helps with fertility, mood, and bone health.

There is a reason Vietnamese banh mi sandwiches have become all the rage lately. They are ridiculously good—with layers of savory, titillating flavors all piled into a crusty roll. They are easy to make too, and this healthy version is ideal for a quick and satisfying weeknight meal. In it, a whole-grain roll is slathered with a spicy-creamy spread (made with Greek yogurt to keep it light), then layered with lean yet succulent pork, a simple Asian-seasoned radish and carrot slaw, slices of cooling cucumbers, and fresh cilantro. It is a tricked-out combination that turns a sandwich into an exciting taste discovery.

pork banh mi sandwiches

MAKES 4 SERVINGS

¼ cup unseasoned rice vinegar

3 tablespoons honey

1 tablespoon fish sauce

1 large carrot

⅓ medium daikon radish (about 5 ounces)

2 cloves garlic

2 teaspoons chili-garlic sauce, such as sriracha

One 1-pound pork tenderloin

Cooking spray

½ English cucumber

½ small bunch fresh cilantro (1 cup cilantro leaves)

4 whole-wheat mini baguettes or sandwich rolls (about ¼ pound each)

2 tablespoons plain low-fat Greek yogurt

2 tablespoons mayonnaise

In a medium bowl, whisk together the vinegar, 1 tablespoon of the honey, and 2 teaspoons of the fish sauce. Grate the carrot and radish in a food processor or on a box grater. Add to the bowl with the sauce and toss to combine.

Mince the garlic and add to another medium bowl. Add the remaining 2 tablespoons honey, remaining 1 teaspoon fish sauce, and 1 teaspoon of the chili-garlic sauce and stir to combine. Slice the pork into ½-inch medallions. Add the pork to the bowl with the garlic-honey sauce and toss to coat.

Spray a large nonstick skillet or grill pan with cooking spray and preheat over medium-high heat. Add the pork and cook until browned and just cooked through, about 2 minutes per side.

While the pork is cooking, use a vegetable peeler to cut the cucumber into thin ribbons. Rinse the cilantro and pick leaves from stalks.

Slice each roll lengthwise, scoop out and discard the soft insides, and toast lightly.

continued on page 90

continued from page 89

In a small bowl, whisk together the yogurt, mayonnaise, and remaining 1 teaspoon chili-garlic sauce, and spread 1 tablespoon on the bottom side of each bun. Layer one-quarter each of the carrot-radish slaw and the cucumber ribbons on each bun and top each with about 4 slices of the grilled pork. Top with the cilantro leaves and cap with the remaining bun half.

SERVING SIZE 1 sandwich
CALORIES 470; Total Fat 10g (Sat Fat 2g, Mono Fat 2.6g, Poly Fat 3.6g); Protein 34g; Carb 64g; Fiber 8g; Cholesterol 75mg; Sodium 930mg
EXCELLENT SOURCE OF Fiber, Magnesium, Manganese, Niacin, Phosphorus, Potassium, Protein, Riboflavin, Selenium, Thiamin, Vitamin A, Vitamin B6, Vitamin C, Zinc
GOOD SOURCE OF Calcium, Copper, Iron, Pantothenic Acid, Vitamin B12, Vitamin K

These salmon burgers are fresh, moist, and mouthwatering, seasoned with Far East flavors like ginger, soy, and sesame and served on a bun garnished with a creamy, spicy Asian sauce and crisp carrot and cucumber. The food processor makes them a breeze to prepare in half an hour, but you can make the burgers ahead if you prefer, keeping them in an airtight container in the refrigerator for up to a day so that they are ready to go when you come home the next evening.

pacific rim salmon burgers

MAKES 4 SERVINGS

FOR THE SAUCE:

- ⅓ cup plain low-fat Greek yogurt
- 2 tablespoons mayonnaise
- 1 teaspoon chili-garlic sauce, such as sriracha
- ½ teaspoon toasted sesame oil
- ¼ teaspoon salt
- ¼ teaspoon freshly ground black pepper

FOR THE BURGERS:

Cooking spray

- 2 slices whole-wheat sandwich bread (3 ounces)
- 1 pound skinless salmon fillets
- ½ medium red bell pepper
- 3 scallions

One 2-inch piece fresh ginger

- 3 medium garlic cloves
- 1 large egg white
- 2 tablespoons reduced-sodium soy sauce
- 1 teaspoon toasted sesame oil
- ¼ teaspoon freshly ground black pepper

FOR SERVING:

- 1 small carrot

One 3-inch piece English cucumber (about 2½ ounces)

- 4 whole-grain hamburger buns
- 8 butter or Bibb lettuce leaves

To make the sauce, in a small bowl, whisk together the yogurt, mayonnaise, chili-garlic sauce, oil, salt, and black pepper.

To make the burgers, if using a grill, spray it with cooking spray and preheat it over medium-high heat. Otherwise, wait to heat a grill pan.

Place the bread in the food processor and process into fine crumbs (you should wind up with about 1⅓ cups crumbs). Transfer them to a large bowl. Roughly chop the salmon, then place it in the processor and pulse until chopped but some pieces still remain visible, about 15 pulses; add to the bowl with the bread crumbs.

Seed and finely mince the red pepper, thinly slice the scallions (both white and green parts), peel and finely grate

continued on page 92

continued from page 91

the ginger, and finely mince the garlic, adding them each to the bowl. Lightly beat the egg white and add it to the bowl along with the soy sauce, sesame oil, and black pepper.

If using a grill pan, spray it with cooking spray and preheat over medium-high heat. Form the salmon mixture into 4 burgers and grill until just cooked through, 2 to 3 minutes per side.

While the burgers are cooking, use a vegetable peeler to cut the carrot into ribbons. Thinly slice the cucumber. Spread each bun half with 1 tablespoon of the sauce. Serve the salmon burgers on the buns layered with lettuce leaves, cucumber slices, and carrot ribbons.

SERVING SIZE 1 burger
CALORIES 420; Total Fat 15g (Sat Fat 2.5g, Mono Fat 4.7g, Poly Fat 6.1g); Protein 33g; Carb 39g; Fiber 6g; Cholesterol 65mg; Sodium 810mg
EXCELLENT SOURCE OF Copper, Fiber, Folate, Magnesium, Manganese, Molybdenum, Niacin, Pantothenic Acid, Phosphorus, Potassium, Protein, Riboflavin, Selenium, Thiamin, Vitamin A, Vitamin B6, Vitamin B12, Vitamin C, Vitamin K
GOOD SOURCE OF Calcium, Iron, Zinc

Mushrooms have such a meaty texture and savory flavor. They are a great way to get big beefiness, either on their own in vegetarian dishes or mixed with modest amounts of meat to amp up portion sizes and boost vegetable intake. I often use finely chopped sautéed mushrooms in dishes that call for ground beef, so it dawned on me that they would make a perfect base for a veggie sloppy Joe. And do they ever! These have all the classic, saucy, tangy-sweet taste of the crowd-pleasing favorite, and the mushrooms and beans work perfectly in their meaty role. Making good use of the food processor for mincing the vegetables makes them a cinch to prep. Serve with a simple, colorful salad like Mediterranean Chopped Salad (page 29).

mushroom sloppy joes

MAKES 4 SERVINGS

- 1 medium onion
- 1 large green bell pepper
- 2 tablespoons canola oil
- 3 cloves garlic
- ¾ pound cremini mushrooms
- One 15-ounce can low-sodium pinto beans
- One 16-ounce can no-salt-added tomato sauce
- 2 tablespoons tomato paste
- 2 tablespoons molasses
- 1 tablespoon chili powder
- 1½ teaspoons cider vinegar
- 1 teaspoon mustard powder
- ½ teaspoon salt
- ¼ teaspoon freshly ground black pepper
- 4 whole-wheat hamburger buns

Roughly chop the onion; seed and roughly chop the bell pepper. Place the onions and peppers in the bowl of a food processor and pulse until they are finely chopped but a few larger pieces remain, 10 to 15 pulses. Heat the oil in a very large skillet over medium-high heat. Add the onions and peppers and cook, stirring occasionally, until the onions are golden and peppers are soft, about 7 minutes.

While the peppers and onions cook, mince the garlic. Remove the stems from the mushrooms, clean the mushroom caps, and then place them in the food processor and pulse until finely minced, 10 to 15 pulses.

When the peppers and onions are done, add the garlic and cook for 1 minute more, then add the mushrooms and cook, stirring once or twice, until they release their water, about 5 minutes. Drain and rinse the beans and add them to the skillet along with the tomato sauce, tomato paste, molasses, chili powder, vinegar, mustard powder, salt, and black pepper.

Bring to a boil, then lower heat to medium and simmer until the sauce thickens and most of the liquid is evaporated, 10 to 12 minutes. To serve, pile about ¾ cup of the mixture onto each hamburger bun.

SERVING SIZE 1 sandwich
CALORIES 380; Total Fat 10g (Sat Fat 1g, Mono Fat 5.2g, Poly Fat 3.2g); Protein 12g; Carb 64g; Fiber 12g; Cholesterol 0mg; Sodium 640mg
EXCELLENT SOURCE OF Copper, Fiber, Iron, Magnesium, Manganese, Niacin, Phosphorus, Potassium, Protein, Riboflavin, Selenium, Thiamin, Vitamin A, Vitamin B6, Vitamin C
GOOD SOURCE OF Calcium, Pantothenic Acid, Vitamin K, Zinc

BESIDES HAVING A BEEFY TEXTURE, mushrooms make a great meat substitute because, like meat, they are packed with umami, the fifth basic taste that can best be described as savory deliciousness.

meat dishes

BEEF

PORK

This dish offers the ultimate in home-cooked contentment. It is a perfect winter supper that makes the most of the season's flavors. It is humble yet also has a kind of rich elegance to it—with juicy pork loin chops and hearty root vegetables in a tasty apple cider–based sauce. A touch of honey in the sauce enhances the vegetables' sweet earthiness, and a punch of fresh sage and mustard provides tasty balance. Serve it with Spinach Salad with Mushrooms and Red Onion (page 30) as a starter.

pork chops with carrots, parsnips, and sage

MAKES 4 SERVINGS

- 1 tablespoon canola oil
- 4 boneless pork loin chops (about 5 ounces each)
- ½ teaspoon salt
- ½ teaspoon freshly ground black pepper
- ¾ pound carrots (2 medium-large)
- ¾ pound parsnips (2 medium-large)
- 4 fresh sage leaves
- 1 cup apple cider
- 1 cup low-sodium chicken broth
- 2 teaspoons Dijon mustard
- 1 tablespoon honey

Heat the oil in a very large skillet that has a cover over medium-high heat. Season the pork with ¼ teaspoon each of the salt and pepper. Add the pork to the skillet and cook until browned and just slightly blush in the center, 4 to 5 minutes per side. Transfer to a plate and cover with aluminum foil to keep warm.

While the pork is cooking, trim the carrots and parsnips and cut them into ½ x 3-inch batons. Thinly slice the sage leaves.

After transferring the pork to the plate, add the cider, broth, mustard, honey, sage, and remaining ¼ teaspoon each salt and pepper to the skillet, scraping the bottom to incorporate any browned bits into the sauce. Bring to a boil over a high heat and cook until the liquid thickens slightly, 1 minute. Add the carrots and parsnips, lower the heat to medium-low, cover, and simmer until the vegetables are tender, 8 to 10 minutes. Return the pork to the skillet and warm through, 1 to 2 minutes.

Divide the carrots, parsnips, and pork among 4 plates, then drizzle some sauce on top.

SERVING SIZE 1 pork chop, 1 cup vegetables, and 1½ tablespoons sauce
CALORIES 380; Total Fat 12g (Sat Fat 3.5g, Mono Fat 6.1g, Poly Fat 1.8g); Protein 32g; Carb 34g; Fiber 6g; Cholesterol 85mg; Sodium 500mg
EXCELLENT SOURCE OF Fiber, Manganese, Niacin, Phosphorus, Potassium, Protein, Selenium, Thiamin, Vitamin A, Vitamin B6, Vitamin C, Vitamin K
GOOD SOURCE OF Copper, Folate, Iron, Magnesium, Molybdenum, Pantothenic Acid, Riboflavin, Zinc

Just thinking about the sweet-and-sour sauce in this dish gets my mouth watering. It's the old-world, classic combination of pork and cabbage taken to new, healthier heights, with medallions of lean, tender pork mingling with ruby red cabbage that's braised until tender with dried cherries in sauce spiked with honey and cider vinegar. It's an easy, down-to-earth dish that is absolutely heavenly. Try it with whole-wheat egg noodles or step it up a notch and make Egg Noodles with Onions, Caraway, and Parsley (page 264).

pork tenderloin with sweet-and-sour red cabbage and dried cherries

MAKES 4 SERVINGS

¼ cup all-purpose flour

½ teaspoon salt

½ teaspoon freshly ground black pepper

1 pound pork tenderloin

2 tablespoons canola oil

½ small head red cabbage

⅓ cup dried cherries

¾ cup low-sodium chicken broth

¾ cup cider vinegar

3 tablespoons honey

Place the flour and ¼ teaspoon each of the salt and pepper in a sealable plastic bag. Slice the pork into ½-inch-thick medallions, place in the bag, and shake to coat.

Heat the oil in a very large skillet (not nonstick) with a cover over medium-high heat. Add the pork and cook until browned and cooked through, 2 to 3 minutes per side. Transfer the pork to a plate.

Meanwhile, thinly slice the cabbage and roughly chop the cherries.

Add the broth, vinegar, and honey to the skillet and stir, scraping up and incorporating any browned bits that formed from cooking the meat. Bring to a boil over a high heat, and add the cabbage, cherries, and remaining ¼ teaspoon each salt and pepper. Lower the heat to medium, cover, and cook until the cabbage is tender and the cherries begin to plump,

11 to 12 minutes. Return the pork to pan and cook until warmed through, about 2 minutes more.

SERVING SIZE 1¼ cups
CALORIES 370; Total Fat 10g (Sat Fat 1.5g, Mono Fat 5.5g, Poly Fat 2.6g); Protein 28g; Carb 44g; Fiber 6g; Cholesterol 75mg; Sodium 400mg
EXCELLENT SOURCE OF Fiber, Manganese, Niacin, Phosphorus, Potassium, Protein, Riboflavin, Selenium, Thiamin, Vitamin A, Vitamin B6, Vitamin C, Vitamin K
GOOD SOURCE OF Folate, Iron, Magnesium, Pantothenic Acid, Vitamin B12, Zinc

EATING DRIED CHERRIES could help you get a better night's sleep, since they are one of the richest sources of natural melatonin, a compound that helps regulate sleep patterns. They could even help you beat jet lag. Studies show that eating ½ cup of the dried fruit an hour or so before your desired sleep time when traveling could help reset your body's sleep clock.

As these foil packets cook, the chicken poaches in a flavorful liquid at the bottom, while the steam that accumulates on top cooks the colorful vegetables to crisp-tender perfection. The oven does most of the work, and quickly at that. All you need to do is pile up the fuss-free ingredients and seal the packets, and in less than 15 minutes you have your delightfully seasoned protein, vegetables, and sauce just waiting to be revealed.

Get a pot of instant brown rice or soba noodles started as soon as you preheat the oven for a whole-grain bed to serve it on. You can also make the packets up to 12 hours ahead of time and store them in the refrigerator. If you do so, just give them an extra 3 minutes cooking time.

asian chicken and vegetables in foil packets

MAKES 4 SERVINGS

- 4 large scallions
- 1 medium red bell pepper
- 1 medium yellow bell pepper
- 1 large carrot
- 4 thin-cut skinless boneless chicken breasts (¼ inch thick, about 5 ounces each)
- 2 tablespoons reduced-sodium soy sauce
- 1 tablespoon unseasoned rice vinegar
- 1 tablespoon dark brown sugar
- 1 tablespoon toasted sesame oil
- 1 teaspoon chili-garlic sauce, such as sriracha
- 4 teaspoons sesame seeds

Preheat the oven to 400°F.

Trim the roots off the scallions, then cut the whites off about 4 inches from the bottom so you have four 4-inch-long pieces. Then slice each of those pieces lengthwise into quarters. Thinly slice the greens, keeping the whites and greens separate. Thinly slice the peppers. Slice the carrot into thin ribbons using a vegetable peeler.

Cut 4 pieces of heavy-duty aluminum foil about 18 inches long. Place 1 piece of chicken at the center of each piece of foil. Layer the carrots on top of the chicken pieces and arrange the peppers on top of the carrots. Scatter the scallion whites on top.

In a small bowl, whisk together the soy sauce, vinegar, brown sugar, oil, and chili-garlic sauce, and drizzle about 1 tablespoon of the sauce onto each stack. Tightly seal the foil into packets, leaving several inches of space inside each packet for the chicken and vegetables to steam. Place the packets on a baking sheet and cook until the chicken is cooked through and the vegetables are crisp-tender, 12 minutes.

continued on page 144

continued from page 143

Meanwhile, toast the sesame seeds in a small dry skillet over medium-high heat until they are golden and begin to pop. When the chicken is done, carefully open the packets. Use tongs to transfer the contents of each packet to a plate, then pour the accumulated juices on top. Sprinkle each portion with 1 teaspoon sesame seeds and garnish with some of the scallion greens.

SERVING SIZE I packet (I chicken breast, ¾ cup vegetables, 2 tablespoons sauce, and I teaspoon sesame seeds)
CALORIES 260; Total Fat 9g (Sat Fat 1.5g, Mono Fat 3.0g, Poly Fat 2.7g); Protein 32g; Carb 11g; Fiber 2g; Cholesterol 90mg; Sodium 480mg
EXCELLENT SOURCE OF Niacin, Pantothenic Acid, Phosphorus, Potassium, Protein, Selenium, Vitamin A, Vitamin B6, Vitamin C, Vitamin K
GOOD SOURCE OF Copper, Folate, Iron, Magnesium, Manganese, Riboflavin, Thiamin

SWEET BELL PEPPERS are one of the best sources of vitamin C, and the brighter the pepper, the more you get. A green bell pepper has more vitamin C than a medium orange, a red one has more than twice that, and a yellow pepper has a whopping three times the vitamin C of an orange!

A couple of smart shortcuts and an extraordinary yet simple sauce make this one of the quickest, easiest, most delicious meals imaginable. The shortcuts are using the meat from a rotisserie chicken and seasoning it with store-bought tomatillo salsa before folding it into a warm corn tortilla. The sauce is as easy to make as your morning smoothie. Just blend avocado, buttermilk, lime, and cilantro until smooth and you wind up with a decadently creamy, tasty, stunning pale green sauce that transforms the simply stuffed tortillas into a luscious dish. Serve with Cool and Crisp Shredded Romaine Salad (page 28) or Zucchini, Spinach and Corn Sauté (page 254)

chicken enchiladas with avocado sauce

MAKES 4 SERVINGS

½ medium rotisserie chicken (about 1¼ pounds)

1 large avocado

1 cup low-fat buttermilk

1 cup lightly packed fresh cilantro leaves

1 small lime

⅛ teaspoon salt

⅛ teaspoon freshly ground black pepper

1 cup store-bought tomatillo salsa

¼ small red onion

8 small corn tortillas (5 inches in diameter)

Remove and discard the skin from the chicken. Take the meat off the bones (both white and dark meat) and pull it apart with your fingers or forks to shred it.

Pit and peel the avocado and put it in the bowl of a food processor along with the buttermilk, ¼ cup of the cilantro leaves, the juice of the lime (about 1½ tablespoons), 1 tablespoon water, and the salt and pepper. Process until smooth.

Put the salsa in a medium skillet and heat over medium heat until warm. Stir in the shredded chicken and cook until warmed through, about 3 minutes. Meanwhile, thinly slice the onion.

Wrap the tortillas in a damp paper towel and microwave for 45 to 60 seconds, until heated through. Place 2 tortillas on each of 4 serving plates. Spoon about ¼ cup of the chicken mixture onto each tortilla and top with about 1 tablespoon each sliced onion and some cilantro leaves. Roll the tortillas, then pour about ⅓ cup avocado sauce on top of each plate and garnish with the remaining cilantro leaves.

SERVING SIZE 2 enchiladas and ⅓ cup sauce
CALORIES 390; Total Fat 17g (Sat Fat 3g, Mono Fat 9.4g, Poly Fat 2.6g); Protein 27g; Carb 38g; Fiber 9g; Cholesterol 75mg; Sodium 620mg
EXCELLENT SOURCE OF Protein, Fiber, Riboflavin, Niacin, Vitamin B6, Vitamin C, Folate, Vitamin K, Pantothenic Acid, Calcium, Phosphorus, Potassium, Selenium
GOOD SOURCE OF Copper, Iodine, Iron, Magnesium, Manganese, Thiamin, Zinc

This dish is beautiful and bold, with chicken in a tomato-based sauce infused with glorious aromatic flavors—fennel, onions, garlic, and cumin—and studded with green olives. The highlight, though, is the thinly sliced lemon rounds, simmered so that they soften and absorb some sauce and their rinds become deliciously edible. Besides being visually stunning, they add an unforgettable dimension of flavor and texture. Serve over whole-grain couscous.

moroccan-style chicken with lemon, fennel, and olives

MAKES 4 SERVINGS

4 skinless boneless chicken breasts (about 6 ounces each)

¼ teaspoon salt

¼ teaspoon freshly ground black pepper

2 tablespoons olive oil

1 medium onion

1 medium bulb fennel

2 cloves garlic

½ cup pitted green olives

½ teaspoon ground cumin

½ teaspoon crushed red pepper flakes

One 28-ounce can no-salt-added diced tomatoes

2 medium lemons

¼ cup packed fresh cilantro leaves

Place the chicken between pieces of plastic wrap and pound to an even ½-inch thickness. Sprinkle with the salt and black pepper. Heat 1 tablespoon of the oil in a very large (12- or 14-inch) skillet with a cover over medium-high heat. Add the chicken and cook until lightly browned, about 2 minutes per side. Transfer the chicken to a plate.

Meanwhile, slice the onion and fennel thinly into half-moons. Add the remaining 1 tablespoon oil to the same skillet, then add the onions and fennel and cook, stirring occasionally, until they begin to soften, 3 to 4 minutes. While they are cooking, mince the garlic and slice the olives. Add the garlic, cumin, and crushed red pepper flakes to the skillet and cook, stirring, for 1 minute more.

Stir in the olives and the tomatoes with their juice. Return the chicken to the skillet, cover, and bring to a boil. Slice one of the lemons very thinly and arrange the lemon slices evenly on top of the chicken mixture. Simmer, covered, over medium-low heat until the lemons soften a bit and the ingredients meld, about 5 minutes. Squeeze the juice from the remaining lemon on top and simmer, uncovered, stirring gently once or twice, until the liquid is reduced somewhat and the chicken is cooked through, about 5 minutes more. Serve garnished with the cilantro.

SERVING SIZE 1 chicken breast and 1 cup sauce
CALORIES 400; Total Fat 17g (Sat Fat 2.5g, Mono Fat 10.9g, Poly Fat 2.1g); Protein 39g; Carb 20g; Fiber 4g; Cholesterol 110mg; Sodium 740mg
EXCELLENT SOURCE OF Niacin, Pantothenic Acid, Phosphorus, Potassium, Protein, Selenium, Vitamin A, Vitamin B6, Vitamin C
GOOD SOURCE OF Fiber, Iron, Magnesium, Riboflavin

A sumptuous stuffing of spinach and soft goat cheese, jeweled with sun-dried tomatoes and basil, is all it takes to turn plain ol' chicken breast into a magnificent craveable main. It pairs perfectly with Lemon-Thyme Orzo Pilaf (page 263) for a meal that is colorful, elegant, and satisfying.

chicken florentine roll-ups

MAKES 4 SERVINGS

Preheat the oven to 400°F.

Thaw the spinach in the microwave or on the stove as per the directions on the package, then place it in a strainer and squeeze out as much liquid as possible, discarding the liquid.

Chop the sun-dried tomatoes, grate the Parmesan cheese, and chop the basil, and place them in a medium bowl with ²/₃ cup of the spinach, the goat cheese, egg white, ¹/₈ teaspoon of the salt, and ¹/₄ teaspoon of the pepper. Stir with a fork until well incorporated.

Spread 3 tablespoons of the filling on the top half of each chicken breast, roll up, and secure with 2 toothpicks. Sprinkle the chicken rolls with the remaining ¹/₈ teaspoon salt and ¹/₄ teaspoon pepper.

Heat the oil in a large ovenproof skillet with a cover over medium-high heat. Brown the chicken rolls until golden, 2 minutes per side. Pour the chicken broth over the rolls, cover, and transfer the skillet to the oven. Bake until the chicken is cooked through, 12 to 14 minutes. Serve drizzled with the liquid from the skillet.

- One 10-ounce package frozen chopped spinach
- 4 medium sun-dried tomatoes
- ½ ounce Parmesan cheese (3 tablespoons grated)
- ¼ cup lightly packed fresh basil leaves
- 3 ounces soft goat cheese (chèvre)
- 1 large egg white
- ¼ teaspoon salt
- ½ teaspoon freshly ground black pepper
- 4 thin-cut skinless boneless chicken breasts (about 5 ounces each)
- 1 tablespoon olive oil
- ¼ cup low-sodium chicken broth

SERVING SIZE 1 roll-up
CALORIES 300; Total Fat 13g (Sat Fat 5g, Mono Fat 4.9g, Poly Fat 1.2g); Protein 39g; Carb 6g; Fiber 2g; Cholesterol 105mg; Sodium 500mg
EXCELLENT SOURCE OF Folate, Magnesium, Manganese, Niacin, Pantothenic Acid, Phosphorus, Potassium, Protein, Riboflavin, Selenium, Vitamin A, Vitamin B6, Vitamin K
GOOD SOURCE OF Calcium, Copper, Iron, Thiamin, Vitamin C, Zinc

In this dish, juicy morsels of chicken thigh, onions, garlic, and green bell pepper are simmered in a sauce that is, in essence, a showcase of the pleasures of paprika, with its mild but deep, earthy flavor and glorious red color. A dollop of reduced-fat sour cream at the end gives the sauce a velvety creaminess. Serve it over whole-grain egg noodles so you don't miss a drop, and steamed green beans or broccoli for a fresh, crisp accompaniment.

chicken paprikash

MAKES 4 SERVINGS

Cut the chicken into 1-inch chunks. Slice the onion into half-moons.

Heat the oil in a large skillet with a lid over medium-high heat. Add the onions and cook, stirring occasionally, until they begin to soften, 3 minutes. Meanwhile, seed the bell pepper and chop it into ½-inch pieces. Add the pepper to the skillet and cook, stirring, until softened slightly, an additional 2 minutes. Thinly slice the garlic, add to the skillet, and cook for 1 minute more.

Add the chicken, paprika, salt, black pepper, and cayenne to the skillet, and cook, stirring, until fragrant, 1 minute. Stir in the broth, raise the heat to high, and bring to a boil, then reduce the heat to medium-low, cover, and simmer until the chicken is cooked through, 8 to 10 minutes. Meanwhile, chop the parsley.

Stir in the sour cream and cook, uncovered, until incorporated, 1 minute. Serve garnished with the parsley.

1¼ pounds skinless boneless chicken thighs

1 large onion

2 tablespoons olive oil

1 large green bell pepper

2 cloves garlic

1 tablespoon plus 2 teaspoons paprika (preferably sweet Hungarian)

¾ teaspoon salt

¼ teaspoon freshly ground black pepper

¼ teaspoon cayenne pepper

½ cup low-sodium chicken broth

3 tablespoons lightly packed fresh Italian parsley leaves

½ cup reduced-fat sour cream

SERVING SIZE 1 cup
CALORIES 320; Total Fat 15g (Sat Fat 4.5g, Mono Fat 7.4g, Poly Fat 1.7g); Protein 34g; Carb 10g; Fiber 3g; Cholesterol 100mg; Sodium 640mg
EXCELLENT SOURCE OF Niacin, Pantothenic Acid, Phosphorus, Potassium, Protein, Selenium, Vitamin A, Vitamin B6, Vitamin C, Vitamin K
GOOD SOURCE OF Fiber, Magnesium, Riboflavin, Thiamin

Romesco is a Spanish pureed sauce made with almonds and roasted peppers. It has a lovely smoky undertone from the peppers, smoked paprika, and, in this version, fire-roasted tomatoes, plus a rich, full-bodied texture from the almonds. It is incredibly versatile: It can be made ahead and kept in the refrigerator for up to a week, served heated or at room temperature, and used as a sauce for cooked vegetables, seafood, or poultry or as a dip for anything from crudités to shrimp cocktail. It is so quick and easy to make that it is also ideal for a rush-hour dinner, spooned over grilled chicken as it is here. I like to serve the dish with Parsley Potatoes (page 255) alongside, after a starter of Cool and Crisp Shredded Romaine Salad (page 28).

chicken romesco

MAKES 4 SERVINGS

Cooking spray

2 tablespoons slivered almonds

1 small onion

2 tablespoons olive oil

3 cloves garlic

One 7-ounce jar roasted red peppers

1 teaspoon smoked paprika

One 14-ounce can fire-roasted diced tomatoes

1½ tablespoons sherry vinegar

¼ teaspoon salt

¼ teaspoon freshly ground black pepper

4 thin-cut skinless boneless chicken breasts (about 5 ounces each)

2 teaspoons extra-virgin olive oil, optional

1 tablespoon packed fresh Italian parsley leaves

If using a grill, spray it with cooking spray and preheat it over medium-high heat. Otherwise, wait to preheat a grill pan.

Place the almonds in a small dry skillet and toast over medium-high heat, stirring frequently, until golden and fragrant, 3 to 4 minutes.

Chop the onion. Heat the olive oil in a large skillet over medium heat. Add the onions and cook until tender and lightly golden, stirring occasionally, about 6 minutes. While the onions cook, mince the garlic and drain and rinse the roasted peppers.

Add the garlic and paprika to the skillet and cook, stirring, for 1 minute more. Add the peppers and tomatoes with their juice; bring to a boil over a high heat, then reduce the heat to medium-low and simmer until about half of the liquid is evaporated, 10 to 12 minutes. Remove from the heat, stir in the vinegar, almonds, and ⅛ teaspoon each salt and black pepper. Transfer to a food processor or blender and process until smooth yet still retaining some texture.

continued on page 152

continued from page 151

While the sauce is cooking, if using a grill pan, spray it with cooking spray and preheat it over medium-high heat. Sprinkle the chicken with the remaining ⅛ teaspoon each salt and black pepper. Grill until cooked through and grill marks form, about 3 minutes per side. Top each piece of chicken with some of the sauce, then drizzle with the extra-virgin olive oil, if using. Coarsely chop the parsley and sprinkle on top.

SERVING SIZE 1 chicken breast and ⅓ cup sauce
CALORIES 300; Total Fat 13g (Sat Fat 2g, Mono Fat 7.1g, Poly Fat 1.7g); Protein 32g; Carb 11g; Fiber 3g; Cholesterol 90mg; Sodium 620mg
EXCELLENT SOURCE OF Niacin, Pantothenic Acid, Phosphorus, Protein, Selenium, Vitamin A, Vitamin B6, Vitamin C, Vitamin K
GOOD SOURCE OF Fiber, Iron, Magnesium, Potassium, Riboflavin

I have a definite penchant for savory, sweet-tangy sauces. It seems I am in good company, as you find that kind of tongue-tingling condiment in every culture around the world. Barbecue sauce and ketchup are prime examples that are close to home. This easy tomato-based chutney hits that spot perfectly with an Indian flair, incorporating deep flavor from onion, garlic, cumin, and coriander, sweetness from dried apricots and a touch of brown sugar, and a puckery essence from mustard seeds and cider vinegar. I could eat it by the spoonful on its own, but I hold myself back because it is really good on chicken—and the rest of my family has to eat too!

chicken with tomato-onion chutney

MAKES 4 SERVINGS

1 small onion
1 medium clove garlic
2 tablespoons canola oil
½ teaspoon mustard seeds
4 medium ripe tomatoes (1¼ pounds)
6 dried apricots
2 tablespoons cider vinegar
1 tablespoon tomato paste
1 tablespoon packed dark brown sugar
½ teaspoon salt
½ teaspoon freshly ground black pepper
½ teaspoon ground cumin
½ teaspoon ground coriander
Cooking spray
4 thin-cut skinless boneless chicken breasts (about 5 ounces each)

Preheat the oven to 350°F.

Finely chop the onion and mince the garlic. Heat 1 tablespoon of the oil in a medium saucepan over medium-high heat. Add the onions and cook, stirring occasionally, until translucent, 3 to 4 minutes. Add the garlic and mustard seeds and cook until fragrant, 1 minute more. Meanwhile, chop the tomatoes and finely chop the apricots.

Add the tomatoes, apricots, vinegar, tomato paste, brown sugar, and ¼ teaspoon each of the salt and pepper to the pan. Bring to a boil, then lower the heat to medium-low and simmer, stirring occasionally, until thickened and a chunky sauce is formed, about 15 minutes.

While the sauce simmers, in a small bowl, combine the remaining 1 tablespoon oil with the cumin, coriander, and the remaining ¼ teaspoon each salt and pepper. Rub the mixture onto the chicken. Spray a baking dish with cooking spray, place the chicken in the dish, and bake until cooked through, 11 to 13 minutes. Serve the chutney on top of the chicken or alongside.

SERVING SIZE 1 chicken breast and ½ cup chutney
CALORIES 300; Total Fat 11g (Sat Fat 1.5g, Mono Fat 5.6g, Poly Fat 2.7g); Protein 32g; Carb 20g; Fiber 3g; Cholesterol 90mg; Sodium 500mg
EXCELLENT SOURCE OF Niacin, Pantothenic Acid, Phosphorus, Potassium, Protein, Selenium, Vitamin A, Vitamin B6, Vitamin C, Vitamin K
GOOD SOURCE OF Fiber, Magnesium, Manganese, Molybdenum, Riboflavin, Thiamin

This dish has the savory, crispy-coated appeal of breaded chicken cutlets, minus the messy, unhealthy frying and with the added bonus of a sweet peach topping. The chicken is dipped in a homemade Italian dressing, then coated in freshly toasted seasoned bread crumbs, topped with the peaches, and baked until delightfully browned and crisp but still lusciously moist from the fruit. Toss some asparagus with a little olive oil and salt and pop it in the oven for a few minutes before you put the chicken in for a roasted asparagus side, or try it with Asparagus "Pasta" (page 246) or Pan-Steamed Broccoli with Lemon, Garlic, and Parsley Gremolata (page 253).

peach chicken with crispy bread crumbs

MAKES 4 SERVINGS

- 4 large ripe fresh peaches or one 1-pound bag unsweetened frozen sliced peaches
- 4 pieces whole-wheat sandwich bread (¼ pound)
- 1 tablespoon sesame seeds
- ¾ teaspoon paprika
- ½ teaspoon salt
- ½ teaspoon freshly ground black pepper
- 3 cloves garlic
- ¼ cup olive oil
- ⅓ cup white wine vinegar
- 1 teaspoon dried oregano
- 1 teaspoon sugar
- ½ teaspoon onion powder
  Cooking spray
- 4 skinless boneless chicken breasts (about 6 ounces each)

Preheat the oven to 375°F.

If using fresh peaches, pit them and slice each one into 8 slices. Otherwise, thaw frozen peaches in the microwave or in a saucepan on the stove.

Place the bread in the bowl of a food processor and process until fine crumbs form. Place them in a large nonstick skillet over medium heat and cook, stirring frequently, until they are crisp and toasted, 3 to 4 minutes.

Combine the bread crumbs, sesame seeds, ½ teaspoon of the paprika, and ¼ teaspoon each of the salt and pepper in a shallow dish. Mince the garlic and place it in a small bowl along with the oil, vinegar, oregano, sugar, onion powder, and remaining ¼ teaspoon each paprika, salt, and pepper. Whisk well to combine.

continued on page 156

continued from page 155

Spray a 9 x 13-inch baking dish with cooking spray. Dip the chicken in the vinaigrette, then press it into the bread crumb mixture and place it in the baking dish. Sprinkle any remaining bread crumbs into the pan, on and around the chicken, then drizzle the remaining vinaigrette on top to moisten the crumbs.

Distribute the peaches evenly across the top of the chicken and drizzle with any accumulated peach juices. Bake until the chicken is cooked through and begins to brown, 12 to 13 minutes.

SERVING SIZE 1 chicken breast, ½ cup peaches, and ¼ cup additional crumb mixture
CALORIES 480; Total Fat 20g (Sat Fat 3g, Mono Fat 12.2g, Poly Fat 3.0g); Protein 42g; Carb 32g; Fiber 5g; Cholesterol 110mg; Sodium 620mg
EXCELLENT SOURCE OF Fiber, Magnesium, Manganese, Niacin, Pantothenic Acid, Phosphorus, Potassium, Protein, Selenium, Vitamin B6, Vitamin C, Vitamin K
GOOD SOURCE OF Copper, Iron, Riboflavin, Thiamin, Vitamin A, Zinc

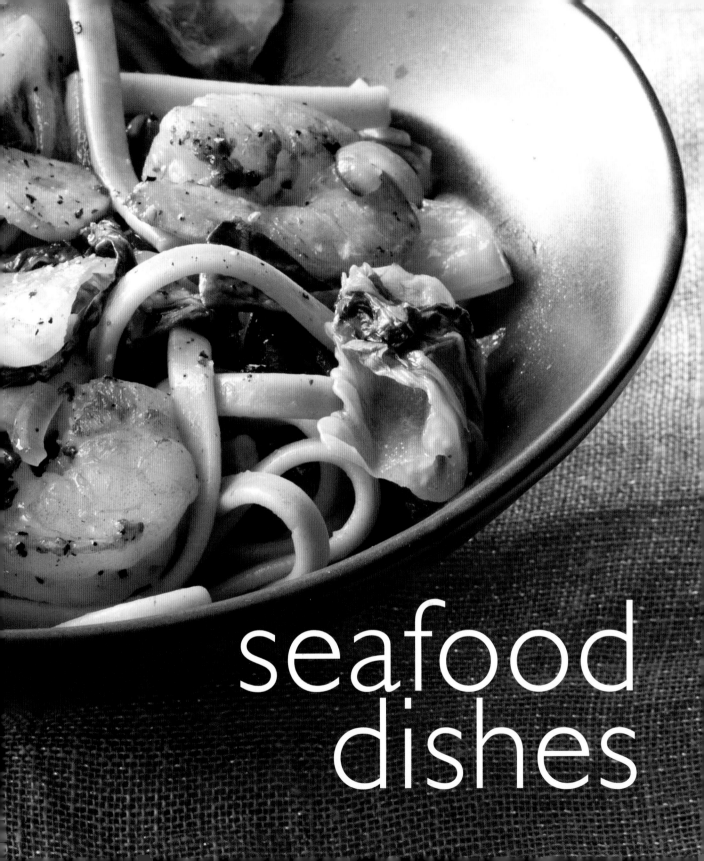

seafood
dishes

SHELLFISH

FISH

If you have yet to discover the glory of smoked paprika, this is your official invitation. Made from smoked red peppers, it is a key ingredient in Spanish cooking (where it is called *pimentón*). It imparts a deep ruby color and distinctive smoky flavor and aroma, instantly giving the simplest foods, like eggs, potatoes, or grilled chicken, a huge wow factor. In this dish, it teams up with golden toasted garlic for doubly exciting seasoning for sautéed shrimp and spinach. You can buy smoked paprika in sweet or hot varieties, but I buy the sweet because I figure you can always add some heat if you want it—and I do add a touch here. Make this with Tomato Bread (page 266) for a classic Spanish supper, *rápidamente*.

shrimp with spinach, garlic, and smoked paprika

MAKES 4 SERVINGS

Rinse the shrimp and pat dry with a paper towel. Thinly slice the garlic. Coarsely chop the spinach.

Place the oil in a large nonstick skillet and heat over medium-high heat. Lower the heat to medium-low, add the garlic, and cook, stirring frequently, until the garlic is golden, about 5 minutes. Watch closely so the garlic does not burn. Transfer the garlic to a small dish using a slotted spoon, leaving the oil in the skillet.

Raise the heat to medium-high, add the shrimp, paprika, salt, and cayenne to the skillet, and cook until the shrimp turns pink and is nearly cooked though, about 3 minutes. Stir in the spinach, return the garlic to the pan, and cook until the shrimp is opaque throughout and the spinach is wilted, 1 to 2 minutes more.

1¼ pounds large shrimp (about 20 per pound), peeled and deveined, tails on

3 large cloves garlic

5 cups lightly packed baby spinach leaves (5 ounces)

3 tablespoons olive oil

2 teaspoons smoked paprika

¼ teaspoon salt

Pinch cayenne pepper

SERVING SIZE 1¼ cups (6 or 7 shrimp)
CALORIES 260; Total Fat 13g (Sat Fat 2g, Mono Fat 7.8g, Poly Fat 2.1g); Protein 30g; Carb 6g; Fiber 2g; Cholesterol 215mg; Sodium 410mg
EXCELLENT SOURCE OF Iron, Phosphorus, Protein, Selenium, Vitamin A, Vitamin B12
GOOD SOURCE OF Calcium, Copper, Magnesium, Niacin, Vitamin B6, Vitamin C, Zinc

When I was a kid, my dad used to pack me sardine sandwiches in my lunch box. I admit I actually liked them, but oh, how I wished I could have had peanut butter and jelly like the other kids! Now I am thankful that he exposed me to this underrated fish, which is delicious, sustainable, and one of the best sources of omega-3 fat.

This dish really gives the humble sardine its due. It is packed with full, earthy flavors that meet the fish on its bold level—pleasantly bitter broccoli rabe, buttery pine nuts, sweet plump raisins, and nutty whole-grain pasta. Because it calls for canned sardines rather than fresh, it is extra quick and accessible. It's the kind of meal you might find at a small trattoria or in a nonna's kitchen in Sicily—humble and homey yet totally sublime.

pasta with sardines and broccoli rabe

MAKES 4 SERVINGS

3 tablespoons pine nuts

1 small bunch broccoli rabe (about ¾ pound)

4 cloves garlic

Two 3½-ounce cans olive oil–packed sardines

12 ounces whole-wheat fusilli or rotini

3 tablespoons olive oil

¼ cup raisins

½ teaspoon salt

½ teaspoon freshly ground black pepper

¼ teaspoon crushed red pepper flakes, optional

Bring a large pot of water to a boil. While the water is heating, toast the pine nuts in a small dry skillet over medium-high heat until fragrant, about 4 minutes. Transfer to a plate to cool. Trim the tough ends from the broccoli rabe, and then chop the rest, including the leaves, into ½-inch pieces. Roughly chop the garlic and drain the sardines.

Cook the pasta for 1 minute less than it says on the package directions; drain, reserving 1 cup of the cooking water. While the pasta is cooking, heat the oil in a large skillet over medium-high heat. Add the broccoli rabe, raise the heat to high, and cook, stirring, until it is crisp-tender, 2 to 3 minutes. Add the garlic and cook for 1 minute more. Remove from the heat and cover to keep warm.

Return the drained pasta to the large pot, add the broccoli rabe mixture, the sardines, the raisins, pasta cooking water, salt, black pepper, and crushed red pepper flakes, if using. Turn the heat to medium-high and toss to warm through, 1 to 2 minutes. The sardines will break up as you toss. Serve each bowl sprinkled with about 2 teaspoons of the pine nuts.

SERVING SIZE 1¾ cups
CALORIES 620; Total Fat 23g (Sat Fat 2.5g, Mono Fat 10.6g, Poly Fat 6.0g); Protein 28g; Carb 77g; Fiber 8g; Cholesterol 75mg; Sodium 600mg
EXCELLENT SOURCE OF Calcium, Fiber, Iron, Manganese, Phosphorus, Protein, Selenium, Vitamin A, Vitamin B12, Vitamin C, Vitamin D
GOOD SOURCE OF Copper, Magnesium, Niacin, Potassium, Vitamin K

continued from page 196

black pepper. Cook the salmon for 10 minutes total per inch of thickness, flipping once. While the fish is cooking, cut the basil leaves into ribbons. Right before serving, stir all but 2 tablespoons of the basil into the sauce.

To serve, spoon about ¼ cup of the sauce onto each plate. Top each with a salmon fillet and garnish with the remaining basil.

SERVING SIZE ¼ cup sauce and 1 salmon fillet
CALORIES 370; Total Fat 14g (Sat Fat 2g, Mono Fat 6.1g, Poly Fat 4.8g); Protein 35g; Carb 20g; Fiber 1g; Cholesterol 95mg; Sodium 230mg
EXCELLENT SOURCE OF Copper, Molybdenum, Niacin, Pantothenic Acid, Phosphorus, Potassium, Protein, Riboflavin, Selenium, Thiamin, Vitamin B6, Vitamin B12, Vitamin C, Vitamin K
GOOD SOURCE OF Folate, Iron, Magnesium, Manganese

EAT SALMON, BE HAPPY. One 6-ounce salmon fillet covers you for the daily recommended amount of both vitamin D and omega-3 fat. Not only does getting enough of those nutrients keep you healthy, but they can also help improve your mood.

Salmon gets the royal treatment here, slathered in a sweet and tangy honey-mustard sauce that bubbles and browns in the broiler and then presented on a bed of crisp and lemony endive and apple salad. The bright tartness of the green apple and the pleasant bitterness of the endive balance the buttery richness of the fish beautifully. I like to serve this with some whole-grain bread with a luxurious extra-virgin olive oil for dipping.

honey-mustard glazed salmon with endive and green apple

MAKES 4 SERVINGS

3 tablespoons Dijon mustard
2 tablespoons honey
½ medium lemon
4 skinless salmon fillets (about 6 ounces each)
½ teaspoon freshly ground black pepper
5 medium Belgian endives (about 1 pound)
½ large Granny Smith apple
20 chives
2 tablespoons olive oil
¼ teaspoon salt

Preheat the oven to 400°F.

In a small bowl, mix together the mustard, honey, and ½ teaspoon juice from the lemon. Line a baking sheet with aluminum foil and place the salmon on top. Sprinkle the salmon with ¼ teaspoon of the pepper, then drizzle a heaping tablespoon of the honey-mustard sauce on top of each fillet. Bake for 10 minutes per inch thickness. Turn on the broiler and broil 5 inches from the heat until the top is caramelized, 1½ to 2 minutes.

Meanwhile, juice the rest of the lemon (about 1½ tablespoons juice) into a medium bowl. Cut the endives crosswise into ½-inch pieces, discarding the cores. Put them into the bowl and toss with the lemon juice. Thinly slice the apple into wedges, then cut the wedges into ½-inch pieces; add to the bowl and toss. Cut the chives into ½-inch pieces, add to the bowl along with the oil, salt, and remaining ¼ teaspoon pepper, and toss to combine.

Serve the salmon on top of the endive-apple salad.

SERVING SIZE 1 salmon fillet and 1 cup salad
CALORIES 380; Total Fat 18g (Sat Fat 2.5g, Mono Fat 8.5g, Poly Fat 5.1g); Protein 35g; Carb 20g; Fiber 4g; Cholesterol 95mg; Sodium 490mg
EXCELLENT SOURCE OF Copper, Folate, Molybdenum, Niacin, Pantothenic Acid, Phosphorus, Potassium, Protein, Riboflavin, Selenium, Thiamin, Vitamin B6, Vitamin B12
GOOD SOURCE OF Fiber, Iron, Magnesium, Vitamin C, Vitamin K

This pizza is a celebration of the rich colors and tastes of fall, with slices of golden-sweet butternut squash balancing big-flavored Gorgonzola cheese, along with red onion, sage, and a scattering of crunchy walnuts. It is important to slice the squash very thinly since it cooks right on the pizza as it bakes. Serve with Spinach Salad with Mushrooms and Red Onion (page 30) for even more autumnal pleasure.

butternut squash, gorgonzola, and sage pizza

MAKES 4 SERVINGS

⅓ cup cubed butternut squash (about 2½ ounces)

1 tablespoon olive oil

¼ small red onion

5 large fresh sage leaves

1 tablespoon cornmeal

¾ pound whole-wheat pizza dough, thawed if frozen

Cooking spray

4 ounces Gorgonzola cheese (⅔ cup crumbled)

¼ cup walnut pieces

Preheat the oven to 475°F.

Thinly slice each cube of butternut squash and toss in a small bowl with the oil. Thinly slice the onion and sage.

Sprinkle a work surface with the cornmeal and use a rolling pin and/or your hands to stretch the dough into a 12-inch circle. Spray a baking sheet with cooking spray and place the dough onto it. Crumble the Gorgonzola and sprinkle it evenly all over the dough, leaving a 1-inch border for the crust. Scatter the squash and onions on top of the cheese. Sprinkle the sage on top of the pizza. Bake until the cheese is melted, the squash is softened, and the crust is almost browned, 11 minutes. Scatter the walnuts over the pizza and bake until they are lightly toasted, an additional 2 minutes.

Slice the pizza into 8 wedges.

SERVING SIZE 2 slices
CALORIES 390; Total Fat 19g (Sat Fat 8g, Mono Fat 5.1g, Poly Fat 3.9g); Protein 14g; Carb 42g; Fiber 6g; Cholesterol 25mg; Sodium 860mg
EXCELLENT SOURCE OF Fiber, Protein, Vitamin A
GOOD SOURCE OF Calcium, Folate, Manganese

Oh, there really is so much you can do with pizza dough. The proof is in this inspired supper full of flavorful goodness: spinach and basil leaves, fresh and sun-dried tomatoes, ricotta and mozzarella cheese all easily folded into a rolled-out sheet of pizza dough. The final product is sure to elicit ooohhs and ahhhhs, as it is absolutely beautiful and enticing with all the ingredients melded and the cheese melted inside a golden brown crust. Your family and friends will think you slaved for hours in the kitchen. You don't need to let on that it was a breeze to make in less than 30 minutes. I like to serve this with something green and fresh like Cool and Crisp Shredded Romaine Salad (page 28) or Pan-Steamed Broccoli with Lemon, Garlic, and Parsley Gremolata (page 253).

pizza "strudel"

MAKES 4 SERVINGS

3 cups lightly packed baby spinach leaves

4 ounces part-skim mozzarella cheese (1 cup shredded)

6 sun-dried tomato halves

8 fresh basil leaves

1 large ripe tomato

1 tablespoon cornmeal

½ pound whole-wheat pizza dough, thawed if frozen

Cooking spray

¾ cup part-skim ricotta cheese

1 large egg white

Preheat the oven to 450°F.

Finely chop the spinach and shred the mozzarella. Finely chop sun-dried tomatoes and cut the basil into ribbons. Slice the ripe tomato into thin half-moons.

Sprinkle a work surface with the cornmeal. Using your hands and/or a rolling pin, stretch the dough into a 10 x 16-inch rectangle. Spray a baking sheet with cooking spray and transfer the dough to the baking sheet

Spread the ricotta along the middle of the dough, leaving a 3-inch border on each long side and a ½-inch border on the top and the bottom. Sprinkle the spinach and sun-dried tomatoes over the cheese. Arrange the tomato slices on top, then top with the mozzarella and basil. Whisk the egg white, and brush it along each side of the dough. Fold the two short sides of the dough over the filling then roll the whole thing up lengthwise like a jelly roll. Press with your fingers to seal the top and bottom firmly. Position the roll so it is seam side down (diagonally if needed to fit).

continued on page 222

continued from page 221

Brush the entire surface of the dough with the remaining egg white, and cut four 1-inch slits into the top of the dough, spaced about 2 inches apart.

Bake until the crust has browned and the cheese has melted and bubbles slightly from the slits, 14 to 15 minutes. Using a serrated knife, slice into 8 pieces and serve.

SERVING SIZE two 2 x 4-inch pieces
CALORIES 320; Total Fat 12g (Sat Fat 6g, Mono Fat 3.8g, Poly Fat 0.4g); Protein 20g; Carb 37g; Fiber 5g; Cholesterol 30mg; Sodium 720mg
EXCELLENT SOURCE OF Calcium, Fiber, Phosphorus, Protein, Selenium, Vitamin A
GOOD SOURCE OF Folate, Iodine, Manganese, Potassium, Riboflavin, Vitamin B12, Vitamin C, Vitamin K, Zinc

My daughter loves pumpkin ravioli, but while delicious, it has little of the actual winter squash stuffed into it. I created this dish as a way to get those same autumnal flavors but with more healthy pumpkin. Not only does it do the trick on that front, but its colorful and creamy sauce also adds tremendous appeal. Although inspired by a child, don't think of this as just kid food. It is sophisticated enough to impress eaters of all ages. I like to serve it with Spinach Salad with Mushrooms and Red Onion (page 30).

ravioli with savory pumpkin sauce

MAKES 6 SERVINGS

- 3 cloves garlic
- 1 tablespoon olive oil
- 1½ cups 1% milk
- 1 cup canned solid-pack pure pumpkin
- ⅓ cup low-sodium chicken broth
- ½ teaspoon ground nutmeg
- ½ teaspoon salt
- ¼ teaspoon freshly ground black pepper, plus more for garnish

  Two 9-ounce packages whole-wheat cheese ravioli
- 1½ ounces Parmesan cheese (½ cup grated)

Put a large pot of water on the stove to boil. While the water is heating, mince the garlic. Heat the oil in a large saucepan over medium heat. Add the garlic and cook until golden, 1 minute. Add the milk, pumpkin, broth, nutmeg, salt, and pepper. Whisk to combine and cook, whisking occasionally, until it comes to a simmer; continue to cook, stirring occasionally, until slightly thickened, 4 minutes more. Decrease the heat to low to keep warm until the ravioli is ready.

Cook the ravioli according to the package directions, until al dente. Meanwhile, grate the cheese. Drain the cooked ravioli and return to the pot; add the sauce and toss gently to combine. Serve each dish sprinkled with a heaping tablespoon of Parmesan.

SERVING SIZE about 1 cup
CALORIES 350; Total Fat 14g (Sat Fat 7g, Mono Fat 2.4g, Poly Fat 0.3g); Protein 18g; Carb 40g; Fiber 5g; Cholesterol 65mg; Sodium 910mg
EXCELLENT SOURCE OF Calcium, Fiber, Protein, Vitamin A
GOOD SOURCE OF Iron, Phosphorus, Vitamin K

PUMPKIN, along with other winter squashes, sweet potatoes, carrots, and mango, get their glorious orange hue from beta-carotene, an antioxidant form of vitamin A that helps protect the heart and keep skin and eyes healthy. Eating ample amounts can give your skin a beautiful golden glow, which, according to one study, was rated as more attractive than a suntan.

This dish showcases what I love most about Italian food: wholesome, fresh ingredients pulled together in a simple but flavorful way that the whole family enjoys. The key to this recipe is the way the garlic is cooked: It's thinly sliced and sautéed gently in olive oil until just golden, so it infuses the dish with a deep, toasted flavor and aroma. The rest is minimal prep for maximum reward, with bursting bite-sized tomatoes and just-wilted spinach. I know it will be as much of a regular on your dinner table as it is on mine.

penne with grape tomatoes, spinach, and toasted garlic

MAKES 4 SERVINGS

Put a large pot of water on the stove to boil. While the water heats, peel and thinly slice the garlic and halve the tomatoes.

Put the oil and garlic in a large skillet over medium heat. Cook, stirring frequently, until the garlic is golden brown, about 5 minutes. Be careful not to let the garlic burn.

Add the tomatoes to the skillet, turn the heat up to medium-high, cover, and cook, stirring once or twice, until the tomatoes are warm and softened but still retain their shape, about 4 minutes. Coarsely chop the spinach and stir it into the tomatoes. Remove the skillet from the heat and cover to keep warm until the pasta is ready. Grate the cheese and set aside.

Meanwhile, once the water comes to a boil, add the pasta and cook according to the directions on the package, then drain.

Add the pasta to the skillet along with ¼ cup of the cheese, the salt, and pepper and toss to combine. Serve garnished with the remaining cheese.

- 4 medium cloves garlic
- 4 cups grape tomatoes
- 3 tablespoons olive oil
- 3 cups lightly packed baby spinach (3 ounces)
- 1 ounce Parmesan cheese (⅓ cup grated)
- ¾ pound whole-grain penne
- ½ teaspoon salt
- ¼ teaspoon freshly ground black pepper

SERVING SIZE 2 cups
CALORIES 480; Total Fat 15g (Sat Fat 2.5g, Mono Fat 8.0g, Poly Fat 1.2g); Protein 15g; Carb 73g; Fiber 10g; Cholesterol 5mg; Sodium 460mg
EXCELLENT SOURCE OF Fiber, Protein, Vitamin A, Vitamin C, Vitamin K
GOOD SOURCE OF Calcium, Iron, Manganese, Potassium

CONCENTRATED CARBOHYDRATES (pasta, breads, grains, and so on) boost the brain chemical serotonin, which has a calming, relaxing effect. So opt for protein and vegetables midday when you want to stay sharp and save your carbs for dinnertime when you are ready to unwind. Also, research shows that eating most of your daily carbs at your evening meal might even benefit your metabolism.

I adore a classic basil–pine nut pesto, full of pasta-coating flavor and healthful ingredients, but I see that formula as a jumping-off point for even more exciting variations. This one shakes things up deliciously by using a mix of basil (for sweet, floral essence) and arugula (for peppery punch), along with lots of almonds for their body and toothsome crunch, not to mention their protein and nutrients. The big flavor of this pesto stands up beautifully to the earthy whole-grain spaghetti. Try it with Mediterranean Chopped Salad (page 29) to start.

spaghetti with almond-arugula pesto

MAKES 4 SERVINGS

Put a large pot of water on the stove to boil.

Toast the almonds in a small dry skillet over medium-high heat, stirring frequently, until golden brown and fragrant, about 3 minutes. Coarsely chop the garlic and grate the Parmesan cheese.

Place the almonds and garlic in the bowl of a food processor and process until finely ground. Add the Parmesan cheese, arugula, basil, the juice from the lemon (about 2 tablespoons), the salt, and pepper and begin to process. While the processor is running, gradually drizzle in the oil until the pesto is smooth. It will be somewhat thick.

Cook the pasta according to the directions on the package, then drain, reserving 1/4 cup of the cooking water. Return the pasta to the pot, add the pesto and the reserved cooking water, and toss until well coated.

- 1/3 cup unsalted sliced almonds, preferably skin on
- 1 clove garlic
- 3/4 ounce Parmesan cheese (1/4 cup grated)
- 3 cups lightly packed baby arugula leaves (3 ounces)
- 1 cup lightly packed fresh basil leaves
- 1/2 large lemon
- 1/2 teaspoon salt
- 1/2 teaspoon freshly ground black pepper
- 1/4 cup extra-virgin olive oil
- 12 ounces whole-grain spaghetti

SERVING SIZE 1½ cups
CALORIES 500; Total Fat 21g (Sat Fat 3.5g, Mono Fat 13.7, Poly Fat 2.8g); Protein 17g; Carb 68g; Fiber 12g; Cholesterol 5mg; Sodium 390mg
EXCELLENT SOURCE OF Copper, Fiber, Iron, Magnesium, Manganese, Niacin, Phosphorus, Protein, Selenium, Thiamin, Vitamin K
GOOD SOURCE OF Calcium, Folate, Pantothenic Acid, Potassium, Riboflavin, Vitamin A, Vitamin B6, Vitamin C, Zinc

This is a quick, savory skillet meal that my Israeli friends taught me how to make. They call it shakshuka, but it could also be considered a Middle Eastern version of "eggs in purgatory." It is a sumptuous mix of tomatoes and red bell peppers cooked with garlic and spices with whole eggs nestled into it and simmered to slightly runny perfection. I added a smattering of creamy goat cheese on top, just for the fun and deliciousness of it. Enjoy with warm pita.

eggs in a skillet with spicy tomato and bell pepper sauce (shakshuka)

MAKES 4 SERVINGS

1 medium onion

2 large red bell peppers

1 tablespoon olive oil

3 cloves garlic

1 teaspoon paprika

1 teaspoon ground cumin

1 teaspoon crushed red pepper flakes

½ teaspoon ground coriander

½ teaspoon salt

Two 14.5-ounce cans no-salt-added diced tomatoes

4 large eggs

2 ounces soft goat cheese (chèvre)

¼ cup packed fresh Italian parsley leaves

Chop the onion and thinly slice the bell peppers. Heat the oil in a large (12-inch) skillet with a cover over medium-high heat. Add the onions and peppers and cook, stirring occasionally, until softened, about 6 minutes. Meanwhile, mince the garlic. When the onions and peppers have softened, add the garlic, paprika, cumin, crushed red pepper flakes, coriander, and salt and cook, stirring, until the spices are fragrant, about 1 minute.

Stir in the tomatoes with their juice, lower the heat to medium, cover, and cook, stirring occasionally, until the ingredients meld and the peppers soften further, 5 minutes.

Using a wooden spoon, form a 3-inch crater in the sauce in one quarter of the skillet; crack 1 egg directly into the crater. Repeat the process with the remaining 3 eggs. Sprinkle the cheese around the eggs. Cook, covered, until whites of the eggs are set but the yolks are still runny, 4 to 5 minutes.

While the eggs are cooking, coarsely chop the parsley. Serve garnished with the parsley.

SERVING SIZE 1 egg and 1¼ cups sauce
CALORIES 230; Total Fat 12g (Sat Fat 4g, Mono Fat 5.1g, Poly Fat 1.3g); Protein 12g; Carb 19g; Fiber 4g; Cholesterol 220mg; Sodium 440mg
EXCELLENT SOURCE OF Protein, Riboflavin, Selenium, Vitamin A, Vitamin B6, Vitamin C, Vitamin K
GOOD SOURCE OF Calcium, Fiber, Folate, Iodine, Iron, Manganese, Molybdenum, Pantothenic Acid, Phosphorus, Vitamin B12

A frittata (basically a crust-free quiche) is a reliably good, fast, nutritious main course, but this one comes together in a way that, almost magically, gives it a certain wow factor. It is just beautiful! It's slightly puffed and golden yellow flecked with green and white, with whole chives gracing the top. The taste is extraordinary too, somehow both rich and light, bursting with herbal flavor enhanced by creamy goat cheese. By splitting the difference and using half whole eggs and half egg whites, you get that sunny yellow and all the nutrients of the egg yolks without overdoing the cholesterol. Serve it with Parsley Potatoes (page 255) or some crusty bread and slices of fresh tomato drizzled with extra-virgin olive oil.

spinach, herb, and goat cheese frittata

MAKES 4 SERVINGS

Preheat the broiler.

Combine the whole eggs, egg whites, and 2 tablespoons water in a medium bowl and whisk well.

If using leek, slice off the dark green top and discard. Slice the remaining white and light green parts in half lengthwise and rinse well between each layer to remove any trapped dirt, then finely chop. Otherwise, dice the onion. Coarsely chop the spinach, parsley, and all but about 8 of the chives.

Heat the oil in a medium (10-inch) cast-iron or nonstick ovenproof skillet over medium heat. Add the leek or onion and cook, stirring, until it begins to soften, about 3 minutes. Add the spinach, parsley, chives, salt, and pepper and cook until the spinach is just wilted, 1 minute.

Pour the egg mixture over the greens in the skillet, covering them evenly. Lower the heat to medium-low and cook until the egg mixture has set around the edges of the pan but not in the middle, 8 to 10 minutes.

5 large eggs

5 large egg whites

1 medium leek or 1 small onion

3 cups baby spinach leaves

½ cup fresh Italian parsley leaves

40 chives

1 tablespoon olive oil

¼ teaspoon salt

¼ teaspoon freshly ground black pepper

2 ounces soft goat cheese (chèvre)

continued on page 230

continued from page 228

Distribute the cheese over the top of the eggs in 10 to 12 dollops and scatter the reserved whole chives on top. Place the skillet under the broiler about 2 inches from the heat and broil until the surface is set and golden brown, 1 to 2 minutes. Be careful not to overcook or the egg mixture will become tough.

Cut the frittata into 4 wedges and serve.

SERVING SIZE 1 wedge
CALORIES 200; Total Fat 13g (Sat Fat 4.5g, Mono Fat 5.6g, Poly Fat 1.3g); Protein 16g; Carb 7g; Fiber 2g; Cholesterol 270mg; Sodium 390mg
EXCELLENT SOURCE OF Iodine, Protein, Riboflavin, Selenium, Vitamin A, Vitamin C, Vitamin K
GOOD SOURCE OF Copper, Folate, Iron, Molybdenum, Pantothenic Acid, Phosphorus, Vitamin B12

FAST, EASY, AFFORDABLE, AND SATISFYING, eggs are a perfect dinnertime protein, yolks and all. While the yolks contain all the egg's cholesterol (186mg, a little more than half the 300mg recommended daily limit), they also contain almost all the valuable vitamins, minerals, and antioxidants. To get all the egg goodness without overdoing cholesterol, stick to about one whole egg per day.

This is just like the hash and eggs you know and love—except totally different, in the best possible way. This hash is deeply satisfying, sizzling, and skillet-browned, but with much healthier ingredients and fun Asian seasonings. In it, moist sweet potatoes and tender green edamame are cooked up together in a skillet with a slightly spicy soy-sesame seasoning to bring them all together. I like to add a smattering of smoky lean Canadian bacon, but you can simply omit it to keep the dish vegetarian. Topping it with a perfectly runny "fried" egg makes it a super supper.

sweet potato and edamame hash and eggs

MAKES 4 SERVINGS

2 large sweet potatoes (1½ pounds)

1 small onion

4 scallions

3 slices Canadian bacon (2 ounces), optional

3 medium cloves garlic

1 tablespoon canola oil

One 10-ounce package frozen shelled edamame, thawed (1½ cups)

2 tablespoons reduced-sodium soy sauce

2 teaspoons chili-garlic sauce, such as sriracha

2 teaspoons toasted sesame oil

Cooking spray

4 large eggs

Bring 3 inches of water to a boil in a large pot fitted with a steamer basket and lid. Cut the sweet potatoes into ½-inch cubes. Place them in the steamer basket and steam, covered, until just tender but not fully cooked, 7 minutes.

Chop the onion, slice the scallions (keeping the green and white parts separate), dice the Canadian bacon, if using, and mince the garlic.

Heat the canola oil in a very large skillet over medium-high heat. Add the onions and scallion whites and cook, stirring occasionally, until they soften and begin to brown, 4 to 5 minutes. Add the garlic and Canadian bacon, if using, and cook for 1 minute more. Add the sweet potatoes and edamame and cook, stirring once or twice, until the potatoes begin to brown, 4 minutes.

continued on page 232

Asian eggplants are long and slim, with a thinner skin, fewer seeds, and a sweeter, more delicate flavor than other varieties—qualities that practically guarantee success with them in the kitchen, no peeling or salting necessary. Here, they are slathered in a savory miso-peanut spread that has just the right kick of heat and touch of sweetness, which forms a lusciously caramelized crown for the meltingly tender vegetable. It pairs especially well with teriyaki-seasoned grilled or broiled steak. If you can't find Asian eggplant, you can use small Italian eggplant instead.

broiled miso-peanut eggplant

MAKES 4 SERVINGS

1½ pounds Asian (Japanese or Chinese) eggplant (8 eggplant)

1 tablespoon canola oil

One 1-inch piece fresh ginger

2 tablespoons blond (shiro) miso paste

2 tablespoons creamy natural-style peanut butter

2 tablespoons packed dark brown sugar

1 tablespoons unseasoned rice vinegar

1 tablespoon fresh orange juice

½ teaspoon chili-garlic sauce, such as sriracha

2 scallions

Preheat the broiler.

Trim the eggplant, then slice in half lengthwise. Brush lightly on both sides with the oil and place, cut side up, on an aluminum foil–lined baking sheet. Broil about 5 inches from the heat until the eggplant begins to soften, 3 to 4 minutes.

Meanwhile, peel the ginger, then grate it into a small bowl. Add the miso, peanut butter, brown sugar, vinegar, orange juice, and chili-garlic sauce and whisk until well combined.

Flip the eggplant and broil until further softened, about 2 minutes more. Flip the eggplant again so it is cut side up and brush the tops with the miso-peanut sauce. Return to the broiler until charred and the sauce begins to bubble, 1 to 2 minutes. While the eggplant is cooking, thinly slice the scallions. Serve the eggplant sprinkled with the scallions.

SERVING SIZE 4 eggplant halves
CALORIES 170; Total Fat 8g (Sat Fat 1g, Mono Fat 2.4g, Poly Fat 1.4g); Protein 5g; Carb 21g; Fiber 7g; Cholesterol 0mg; Sodium 420mg
EXCELLENT SOURCE OF Fiber, Manganese, Vitamin K
GOOD SOURCE OF Folate, Molybdenum, Potassium, Vitamin C

The dressing in this dish is my version of the one that adorns crisp green salads in Japanese restaurants——it is enticingly fresh in flavor and bright orange in color, subtly sweet-tart with a warming zing of ginger. I am only slightly exaggerating when I say I could practically drink it. I hold back, though, because I want to ensure that I have plenty to serve with wedges of napa cabbage that are charred until crisp-tender on the grill. Pair with simply grilled fish, shrimp, or chicken.

grilled napa cabbage wedges with carrot-ginger dressing

MAKES 4 SERVINGS

Peel the carrot and ginger. Coarsely chop the white and light green parts of the scallions. Reserve the dark green parts for garnish.

Grate the carrot and ginger in a food processor using the shredding disk. Switch to the chopping blade and add the chopped scallions, orange juice, vinegar, soy sauce, and sesame oil to the carrot and ginger in the bowl of the processor. While processing, drizzle 3 tablespoons of the canola oil into the bowl until incorporated, then continue processing until the dressing is fairly smooth. It will be somewhat thick and maintain some texture from the carrot.

Spray a grill or grill pan with cooking spray, then preheat over medium-high heat. Cut the cabbage lengthwise into quarters so that each piece has some of the core to keep it intact. Brush the cut sides of the cabbage with the remaining 1 tablespoon canola oil. Grill until slightly wilted and grill marks have formed, about 2 minutes per cut side. While the cabbage is cooking, finely slice the scallion greens.

Pour about ⅓ cup of the dressing onto each of 4 serving plates, place a wedge of cabbage on top of the sauce, and garnish with the scallion greens.

- 1 large carrot (about 7 ounces)
  One 2-inch piece fresh ginger
- 2 medium scallions
- ¼ cup fresh orange juice
- 2 tablespoons unseasoned rice vinegar
- 2 teaspoons reduced-sodium soy sauce
- 2 teaspoons toasted sesame oil
- ¼ cup canola oil
  Cooking spray
- 1 large head napa cabbage (about 2½ pounds)

SERVING SIZE 1 wedge cabbage and ⅓ cup dressing
CALORIES 230; Total Fat 16g (Sat Fat 1.5g, Mono Fat 9.8g, Poly Fat 5.0g); Protein 4g; Carb 17g; Fiber 5g; Cholesterol 0mg; Sodium 160mg
EXCELLENT SOURCE OF Calcium, Vitamin A, Vitamin C, Vitamin K
GOOD SOURCE OF Fiber

Swiss chard just may be the most underappreciated of the dark green leafy vegetables. Spinach is on everyone's list and kale is the trendy hotshot, but while Swiss chard offers the best of both of them, it hardly gets any attention. It's time for a chard awakening, and this is just the lip-smacking recipe to do the trick.

Chard leaves are tender and quick cooking like spinach, but they lean toward having the sturdiness and slightly deeper flavor of kale. Their stems are delicious too and add nuggets of crisp-tender texture and color when cooked with the leaves. Like its leafy green cousins, chard loves to be paired with dried fruit and nuts—this recipe steps scrumptiously out of the ordinary with sweet plump figs and crunchy sunflower seeds. If you haven't tried chard, I know you will love it, and if it is already part of your repertoire, this recipe offers a new and exciting perspective. Try it alongside grilled or broiled meat or poultry.

rainbow chard with sunflower seeds and dried figs

MAKES 4 SERVINGS

Toast the sunflower seeds in a very large dry skillet, stirring frequently, until fragrant, 3 to 4 minutes. Transfer to a plate.

Thinly slice the figs. Slice the leaves from the chard stalks. Chop the stalks into ¼-inch pieces. Slice the leaves into ¼-inch ribbons. Thinly slice the garlic.

Heat the oil in the same skillet over medium-high heat. Add the garlic and chard stalks and cook until the garlic is golden and fragrant and the chard stalks begin to soften, 1 to 2 minutes. Add chard leaves in 2 batches, allowing 1 to 2 minutes between additions, stirring. Then add the broth, salt, black pepper, and crushed red pepper flakes and cook, stirring, until the chard wilts, 3 to 4 minutes total. Add the figs and cook for 1 minute more. Remove from the heat. Finely zest the lemon over the chard, then squeeze the lemon juice (about 1½ tablespoons) over and stir in the sunflower seeds.

- ¼ cup hulled unsalted sunflower seeds
- 5 or 6 dried black Mission figs
- 2 bunches rainbow chard (1½ pounds)
- 4 medium cloves garlic
- 2 tablespoons olive oil
- ½ cup low-sodium chicken broth
- ¼ teaspoon salt
- ¼ teaspoon freshly ground black pepper
- ¼ teaspoon crushed red pepper flakes
- ½ medium lemon

SERVING SIZE 1 cup
CALORIES 190; Total Fat 12g (Sat Fat 1.5g, Mono Fat 6.7g, Poly Fat 3.0g); Protein 6g; Carb 19g; Fiber 5g; Cholesterol 0mg; Sodium 520mg
EXCELLENT SOURCE OF Copper, Fiber, Iron, Magnesium, Manganese, Potassium, Vitamin A, Vitamin C, Vitamin K
GOOD SOURCE OF Calcium, Folate, Molybdenum, Phosphorus, Protein, Riboflavin, Thiamin, Vitamin B6

ADDING A SQUIRT OF LEMON OR LIME JUICE to green vegetables not only tastes wonderful, but it also helps your body absorb the iron they contain.

This unique tapenade, a savory-sweet-salty-crunchy delight, truly dances in your mouth. It always gets raves when I make it as a spread for crackers or toasts at parties, and since it is so easy to make, I thought it would be an ideal way to enliven a weeknight dinner. Does it ever! Here it transforms simply steamed cauliflower into a remarkable dish that is special enough to be the centerpiece of the meal. I like to serve it with simply grilled or roasted meat or poultry, or with a chunk of Manchego cheese and crusty whole-grain bread. Leftovers are also a treat, chilled and served at room temperature.

cauliflower with almond-olive tapenade

MAKES 6 SERVINGS

- 1 large head cauliflower
- ¼ cup golden raisins
- ½ cup whole natural almonds
  One 8-ounce jar roasted red peppers
- 1 medium clove garlic
- ½ cup pitted green olives
- ⅓ cup fresh Italian parsley leaves
- 1 tablespoon extra-virgin olive oil
- 2 teaspoons sherry vinegar or white wine vinegar
- ⅛ teaspoon freshly ground black pepper
  Salt, to taste

Put a pot of water that can be fitted with a large steamer basket on the stove to boil.

While the water is heating, trim and core the cauliflower and cut it into 1-inch florets. Place the raisins in a small bowl, then transfer ½ cup of the hot water from the pot to the bowl with the raisins and soak the raisins until they are plump, about 5 minutes; then drain. Place the cauliflower in the steamer basket, cover, and cook until firm-tender, 5 to 6 minutes, then transfer to a large bowl.

While the cauliflower is cooking, toast the almonds in a dry skillet over medium-high heat, stirring frequently, until lightly browned and fragrant, about 5 minutes. Drain and rinse the red peppers. Mince the garlic. Put the raisins, almonds, peppers, garlic, olives, parsley, oil, vinegar, and black pepper in a food processor and pulse until the ingredients are finely minced but still somewhat chunky, 12 to 15 pulses.

Add the tapenade to the cauliflower and toss until well combined. Taste and season with salt if necessary, depending on the saltiness of the olives.

SERVING SIZE 1 cup
CALORIES 200; Total Fat 13g (Sat Fat 1.5g, Mono Fat 8.6g, Poly Fat 2.1g); Protein 6g; Carb 18g; Fiber 6g; Cholesterol 0mg; Sodium 380mg
EXCELLENT SOURCE OF Fiber, Folate, Manganese, Vitamin C, Vitamin K
GOOD SOURCE OF Magnesium, Molybdenum, Pantothenic Acid, Phosphorus, Potassium, Protein, Riboflavin, Vitamin A, Vitamin B6

This 6-minute technique for cooking broccoli is a revelation. It gives you the health benefits of steaming without having to wait for a big pot of water to boil. Once your broccoli is steamed you can season it however you like, but this tasty combo of lemon, garlic, and parsley—a traditional Italian combination known as gremolata—is pretty unbeatable.

pan-steamed broccoli with lemon, garlic, and parsley gremolata

MAKES 6 SERVINGS

- 1 large head broccoli (1½ pounds)
- 1 medium lemon
- ⅓ cup fresh Italian parsley leaves
- 1 small clove garlic
- 1½ tablespoons extra-virgin olive oil
- ¼ teaspoon salt
- ¼ teaspoon freshly ground black pepper

Cut the large stems off the broccoli, peel them, then slice into ⅛-inch-thick coins. Cut the broccoli top into florets about 2 inches in diameter.

Arrange the broccoli coins on the bottom of a large deep skillet with a lid. Place the florets on top. Add ½ cup water, cover, and cook over high heat for 3 minutes. Lower the heat to medium and cook for an additional 3 minutes. Do not remove the lid during cooking. When the broccoli is done, it will be cooked to crisp-tender. If you prefer it a bit softer, remove it from the heat and allow it to sit, covered, for another minute or two.

While the broccoli is cooking, zest the lemon into a large bowl. Juice half of the lemon into the bowl (about 1½ tablespoons). Chop the parsley and finely mince the garlic; add them to the bowl along with the oil, salt, and pepper. Stir to combine.

Using a slotted spoon, transfer the broccoli to the bowl with the lemon mixture and toss to combine.

SERVING SIZE 1 cup
CALORIES 70; Total Fat 4g (Sat Fat 0.5g, Mono Fat 2.5g, Poly Fat 0.4g); Protein 3g; Carb 8g; Fiber 3g; Cholesterol 0mg; Sodium 135mg
EXCELLENT SOURCE OF Vitamin C, Vitamin K
GOOD SOURCE OF Fiber, Folate, Manganese, Potassium, Vitamin A, Vitamin B6

This dessert has the same decadent effect as a chocolate fondue, without the fuss of having to keep the chocolate warm once served. Instead, you melt it quickly in the microwave and then drizzle it over a bowl of bite-sized pieces of banana and angel food cake. The chocolate is spiced Mexican-style with some cinnamon and a hint of cayenne for a subtle but definite flair that pairs especially well with the banana and cake.

cake and banana toss with spiced chocolate drizzle

MAKES 4 SERVINGS

¼ pound store-bought angel food cake (about one-quarter of a 10-inch angel food cake)

4 medium-ripe bananas

2 ounces dark chocolate (60% to 70% cocoa solids)

¼ teaspoon ground cinnamon

⅛ teaspoon cayenne pepper, optional

Cut the cake into 1-inch cubes and place in a large bowl. Peel and cut the bananas into 1-inch chunks, add them to the bowl, and toss to combine. Divide among 4 dessert bowls.

Place the chocolate in a microwave-safe bowl and heat on high power for 90 seconds. Stir, then heat for an additional 30 seconds and stir again. Microwave for one or two more 30-second intervals, as needed, until the chocolate is melted and smooth. Stir well between each interval. Stir the cinnamon and cayenne, if using, into the chocolate, then drizzle it over the bowls of cake and banana. Serve immediately.

SERVING SIZE 1 banana, ½ cup cake, and 2 teaspoons chocolate drizzle
CALORIES 240; Total Fat 6g (Sat Fat 3.5g, Mono Fat 1.7g, Poly Fat 0.3g); Protein 3g; Carb 47g; Fiber 5g; Cholesterol 0mg; Sodium 160mg
EXCELLENT SOURCE OF Manganese, Vitamin B6
GOOD SOURCE OF Copper, Fiber, Magnesium, Phosphorus, Potassium, Riboflavin, Vitamin C

These sweet dessert pizzas are so sumptuous and special that you can hardly believe how quick and easy they are to make. In the oven, the juicy fig slices meld into the creamy ricotta, which warms and softens as the pita crust crisps. A drizzle of balsamic vinegar and honey provides sweet-tart contrast, and a sprinkle of basil tops it off with fragrant freshness. They are ideal for a weeknight treat, but they also make a perfect finger food at a party, cut into wedges and served as a dessert or an appetizer.

fig and ricotta pita pizzas

MAKES 4 SERVINGS

- 2 whole-wheat pita pocket breads, about 6 inches in diameter
- 8 medium fresh figs (about 7 ounces)
- 1 tablespoon olive oil
- ½ cup part-skim ricotta cheese
- 1 tablespoon honey
- 1 teaspoon balsamic vinegar
- 8 large or 16 small fresh basil leaves

Preheat the oven to 450°F. Line 2 baking sheets with parchment paper.

Slice the pita pockets in half so each forms 2 rounds and you have 4 rounds in all. Remove the stems from the figs and slice into ⅛-inch rounds.

Place the pita rounds on the baking sheets, cut side up, and brush the top of each with the oil.

Spread 2 tablespoons ricotta cheese on each pita, leaving about a ½-inch border around the edges, then top with the sliced figs. Bake until edges are crisped and the cheese is warmed, 5 to 7 minutes.

While the pizzas bake, in a small bowl stir together the honey and balsamic vinegar until combined. When the pizzas are done, drizzle each with a teaspoon of the honey-balsamic mixture. Tear the basil leaves into small pieces and arrange on top of the pizzas. Serve immediately.

SERVING SIZE 1 pizza
CALORIES 210; Total Fat 7g (Sat Fat 2g, Mono Fat 3.3g, Poly Fat 0.8g); Protein 7g; Carb 33g; Fiber 4g; Cholesterol 10mg; Sodium 210mg
EXCELLENT SOURCE OF Manganese, Selenium
GOOD SOURCE OF Calcium, Fiber, Phosphorus, Protein, Vitamin K

The heavenly pairing of peaches and cream is made all the more scrumptious when infused with almond essence and layered with crunchy-sweet amaretti cookies in this stunning parfait. Folding Greek yogurt into fresh whipped cream makes for a perfect balance of decadence and health. If you can't find amaretti cookies, almond biscotti work well too.

amaretti-peach parfait

MAKES 4 SERVINGS

Squeeze the lemon juice (about 2 tablespoons) into a large bowl. Add the honey and cinnamon and whisk to combine. Pit and thinly slice the peaches, add them to the bowl, and gently toss to coat.

Place the cream, sugar, and almond extract in a large bowl and whip with an electric mixer on high speed until soft peaks form, about 2 minutes. Using a spatula, gently fold in the yogurt.

Place the cookies in a sealable plastic bag and crush into large crumbs using a rolling pin or mallet.

To make the parfaits, dollop 1 tablespoon of the cream into each of 4 large wine goblets or parfait glasses. Top each with 2 tablespoons of the cookie crumbs and 1/3 cup of the peaches. Then add another layer of 2 tablespoons cream, 1 tablespoon cookie crumbs, and 1/3 cup peaches. Top each with 1 tablespoon cream and an additional tablespoon of cookie crumbs. Garnish with the mint.

1/2 large lemon
1 tablespoon honey
1/8 teaspoon ground cinnamon
4 medium firm ripe peaches (2 pounds)
1/3 cup cold heavy cream
2 tablespoons granulated sugar
1/4 teaspoon almond extract
1/3 cup plain low-fat Greek yogurt
14 small amaretti cookies (2 ounces)
Mint sprigs, for garnish

SERVING SIZE 1 parfait
CALORIES 260; Total Fat 10g (Sat Fat 5g, Mono Fat 2.3g, Poly Fat 0.4g); Protein 5g; Carb 42g; Fiber 4g; Cholesterol 30mg; Sodium 40mg
EXCELLENT SOURCE OF Vitamin C
GOOD SOURCE OF Potassium, Protein, Vitamin A

The essence of orange, a touch of honey, and 10 minutes is all it takes to transform a basic bowl of berries into a true dessert. The berries soften slightly as they marinate, and their flavors meld with the sweet citrus glaze. It is a refreshing and light sweet-tooth satisfier.

orange-honey glazed berries

MAKES 4 SERVINGS

Finely grate the outer peel of the orange until you wind up with 1 teaspoon zest. Cut a large wedge out of the orange and squeeze it to extract 1 tablespoon juice.

In a small bowl, stir together the orange zest, orange juice, honey, and orange liqueur (if using) until the honey is dissolved.

Trim and quarter the strawberries. Place the berries in a medium bowl, drizzle with the orange-honey glaze, and toss gently to coat. Let marinate for 10 minutes. Meanwhile, chop the mint leaves. Stir in the mint right before serving.

1 medium orange
1 tablespoon honey
1 tablespoon orange liqueur, such as Grand Marnier, optional
½ pound strawberries
6 ounces blueberries
6 ounces raspberries
3 tablespoons fresh mint leaves

SERVING SIZE about ¾ cup
CALORIES 80; Total Fat 0.5g (Sat Fat 0g, Mono Fat 0.1g, Poly Fat 0.3g); Protein 1g; Carb 21g; Fiber 5g; Cholesterol 0mg; Sodium 0mg
EXCELLENT SOURCE OF Fiber, Manganese, Vitamin C
GOOD SOURCE OF Vitamin K

A cheese-and-fruit plate is a fine dessert—you won't catch me complaining about being served one, especially if there is a drizzle of good honey on it too. But why settle for ordinary when a few small steps easily elevate the same elements to a fabulous grand finale? Tossing the juicy, ruby red fruits with a simple, sweet-tart mix of balsamic vinegar, honey, and fresh thyme and topping that with a dollop of goat cheese that's gently sweetened and whipped into a light mousse (a technique that's easier than whipping cream) makes it an absolutely heady treat.

red plums and cherries with goat cheese cream

MAKES 4 SERVINGS

- 4 medium-ripe red plums (about 1¼ pounds)
- ½ pound fresh or frozen cherries, thawed if frozen
- ½ teaspoon fresh thyme leaves
- ¼ cup honey
- 1 tablespoon balsamic vinegar
- 4 ounces soft goat cheese (chèvre)
- ¼ cup 2% milk

Pit the plums and cut them into wedges. If using fresh cherries, pit and halve them. Chop the thyme leaves. In a medium bowl, toss the fruit with 2 tablespoons of the honey, the vinegar, and the thyme, and allow to marinate at room temperature for 15 minutes.

While the fruit is marinating, place the goat cheese, the remaining 2 tablespoons honey, and the milk in a bowl and whip using an electric mixer until creamy, 1 to 2 minutes.

Divide the fruit and its liquid among 4 dessert bowls and top each with ¼ cup of the goat cheese cream.

SERVING SIZE 1 cup fruit and ¼ cup goat cheese cream
CALORIES 250; Total Fat 6g (Sat Fat 4.5g, Mono Fat 1.5g, Poly Fat 0.2g); Protein 7g; Carb 46g; Fiber 3g; Cholesterol 15mg; Sodium 115mg
EXCELLENT SOURCE OF n/a
GOOD SOURCE OF Copper, Fiber, Phosphorus, Potassium, Protein, Vitamin A, Vitamin C

This recipe is stunning in more ways than one. It looks gorgeous: a bright yellow-orange soft-serve tropical sorbet flecked with bits of basil. But it will also stun you when you realize how easy and practically instantaneous it is to make. And the fact that it is made with whole fruit sweetened only with a touch of honey is pretty stunning too. Isn't it nice to know you are just four ingredients, two minutes, and one blender away from a truly special and deliciously refreshing frozen dessert?

two-minute mango-coconut sorbet

MAKES 4 SERVINGS

1 pound frozen mango chunks (3 cups)

¼ cup honey

½ cup light coconut milk

2 tablespoons lightly packed fresh basil leaves

Place the mango in a blender with the honey and ¼ cup of the coconut milk. Blend for 15 seconds, pulsing if necessary, then scrape down the sides of the blender with a spatula. Add the remaining ¼ cup coconut milk and first pulse, then blend, until the mixture is nearly smooth, about 20 seconds. Add the basil and blend until the basil is integrated and the mixture has the texture of sorbet, 10 to 15 seconds more. Serve immediately, or for firmer sorbet, freeze in an airtight container for 15 to 20 minutes. The mixture may be stored in the freezer for up to 1 week. Allow to soften slightly at room temperature before scooping.

SERVING SIZE ¾ cup
CALORIES 160; Total Fat 2g (Sat Fat 1.5g, Mono Fat 0g, Poly Fat 0g); Protein 1g; Carb 38g; Fiber 2g; Cholesterol 0mg; Sodium 5mg
EXCELLENT SOURCE OF Vitamin C
GOOD SOURCE OF Vitamin A

COCONUT has been getting a lot of superfood hype, most of which is unfounded. But research shows that this sumptuous tropical fruit may be better for us than we once thought. Although it is high in saturated fat, the type it contains, medium-chain triglycerides (MCTs), may not have as negative an effect on heart health as other forms. Plus, coconut is rich in antioxidants. Saturated fat does raise cholesterol, though, so while the jury's out I use dried coconut sparingly, go for light coconut milk, and although I occasionally use virgin coconut oil, I cook mostly with olive and canola oils.

Just like a versatile dress that goes easily from day to evening with a change of accessories, bananas are transformed here from a daytime snack into a sexy dessert. A few minutes under the broiler with a bit of sugar and spice renders them luxuriously softened and deeply flavored, with a caramelized coating. Add a scoop of frozen yogurt to melt on top and a sprinkle of toasted coconut and you will see that this favorite everyday fruit has a serious party side.

bananas brûlée à la mode with coconut

MAKES 4 SERVINGS

Preheat the broiler.

Toast the coconut in a dry nonstick skillet over medium heat until fragrant and golden, stirring occasionally, 3 to 4 minutes. Transfer to a plate to cool.

Peel and slice the bananas lengthwise. Place them cut side up on an aluminum foil–lined baking sheet, then sprinkle evenly with the brown sugar, nutmeg, and cinnamon. Broil about 3 inches from the heat source until the sugar is caramelized and bubbly, 2 to 3 minutes. Divide among 4 plates and top each with ¼ cup scoop frozen yogurt and 2 tablespoons toasted coconut.

- ½ cup unsweetened coconut flakes
- 4 firm ripe medium bananas
- ¼ cup lightly packed light brown sugar
- ½ teaspoon ground nutmeg
- ¼ teaspoon ground cinnamon
- 1 cup vanilla frozen yogurt

SERVING SIZE 1 banana, ¼ cup frozen yogurt, and 2 tablespoons toasted coconut
CALORIES 260; Total Fat 8g (Sat Fat 7g, Mono Fat 0.3g, Poly Fat 0.2g); Protein 3g; Carb 47g; Fiber 5g; Cholesterol 5mg; Sodium 25mg
EXCELLENT SOURCE OF Manganese, Vitamin B6
GOOD SOURCE OF Fiber, Magnesium, Potassium, Vitamin C

Every holiday season, my sister (who is an incredible, passionate cook) slices a wheel of Brie in half, stuffs it with nuts and sugar or jam, and bakes it until it is melted and bubbling. It is always immediately devoured, and I certainly do my share of the damage, but I consider it a once-or-twice-a-year treat. This dessert, of sweet ripe pears baked until fragrant and topped with crunchy, sugar-spiced pecans and a blanket of melted Brie, captures the luxurious essence of my sister's special dish in a way that is healthy enough to enjoy anytime.

pears baked with sweet pecan and brie topping

MAKES 4 SERVINGS

- **2** firm ripe pears, such as Bosc (1¼ pounds)
- ¼ cup unsalted pecans
- **4** ounces Brie cheese
- **4** teaspoons lightly packed dark brown sugar
- ½ teaspoon ground cinnamon
- ¼ teaspoon ground nutmeg

Preheat the oven to 375°F.

Halve the pears lengthwise, then core them using a melon baller or paring knife. Toast the pecans in a small dry skillet over medium-high heat, stirring frequently, until fragrant and lightly browned, 3 to 4 minutes. Allow to cool slightly, then roughly chop them. Cut the Brie into 4 slices.

Arrange the pears, cut side up, on an aluminum foil–lined baking sheet (cut a notch into the bottom of the pears if necessary to steady them) and sprinkle the tops evenly with the brown sugar, cinnamon, and nutmeg. Then top each pear halve with 1 tablespoon of the pecans and a slice of the cheese. Bake until the cheese is melted and slightly bubbly and the pears are tender but still retain their shape, 9 to 10 minutes.

Serve immediately.

SERVING SIZE 1 pear half
CALORIES 230; Total Fat 13g (Sat Fat 5g, Mono Fat 4.8g, Poly Fat 1.6g); Protein 7g; Carb 26g; Fiber 5g; Cholesterol 30mg; Sodium 180mg
EXCELLENT SOURCE OF Fiber, Manganese
GOOD SOURCE OF Protein, Riboflavin, Vitamin C

This dessert combines the comforting pleasure of a warm, fragrant cup of tea with a sweet and satisfying dessert. Earl Grey tea, with its delightful floral essence and pleasantly tannic undertone, infuses and plumps the dried fruit and brings layers of flavor to this compote, effortlessly. Serve it warm or chilled, on its own or with a dollop of Greek yogurt.

earl grey spiced fruit compote

MAKES 4 SERVINGS

Bring 1¼ cups water to a boil in a medium saucepan. Stir in the honey, then immerse the tea bag in the water. Add the apricots, prunes, raisins, the juice from the lemon, the cinnamon stick, and cloves to the saucepan and return to a boil.

Lower the heat to medium and simmer, uncovered, for 4 minutes. Remove the tea bag, then continue to simmer, stirring occasionally, until the liquid thickens to a loose syrup, about 8 minutes more. Remove the cinnamon and cloves and discard. Transfer the compote to a bowl and allow to cool slightly, about 5 minutes. The compote will keep in the refrigerator in an airtight container for up to 1 week.

- 3 tablespoons honey
- 1 Earl Grey tea bag
- ½ cup dried apricots
- ½ cup pitted prunes
- ½ cup golden raisins
- ¼ large lemon
- 1 cinnamon stick
- 4 whole cloves

SERVING SIZE ⅓ cup
CALORIES 190; Total Fat 0g (Sat Fat 0g, Mono Fat 0.0g, Poly Fat 0.1g); Protein 2g; Carb 52g; Fiber 3g; Cholesterol 0mg; Sodium 10mg
EXCELLENT SOURCE OF n/a
GOOD SOURCE OF Fiber, Potassium, Vitamin A, Vitamin K

TEA AND DRIED FRUITS rank among the most powerful of beauty foods. They contain concentrated amounts of compounds that protect the skin from sun damage, and they are linked with less skin wrinkling as we age.

This dish is a celebration of grapes that is delightfully elegant yet incredibly simple to make. Boiling port wine with orange zest and juice along with honey and cinnamon reduces it to a thick, sumptuous dessert sauce that infuses plump, fresh grapes, softening them as they simmer. An inexpensive port works perfectly here—just be sure to use a ruby port, which is sweeter than a tawny port. It is one of those bottles that you can keep in the refrigerator for several weeks at least, and you will be glad you have it because you will want to make this again and again. This dessert is also delicious served chilled, and it can be stored in the refrigerator for up to a week in an airtight container.

grapes simmered in port wine sauce

MAKES 4 SERVINGS

1 orange
1 cup ruby port wine
1 cinnamon stick
1 tablespoon honey
2½ cups seedless red grapes
1 cup vanilla frozen yogurt or plain low-fat Greek yogurt, optional

Using a vegetable peeler, strip off one ½ x 2-inch strip of the orange peel, being careful not to include any of the white pith. Juice enough of the orange to yield 2 tablespoons juice and reserve the rest of the orange for another use.

Put the strip of orange peel and the 2 tablespoons juice in a medium saucepan along with the wine, cinnamon stick, and honey and bring to a boil over high heat, stirring to dissolve the honey. Continue cooking over high heat until the liquid is reduced to about ⅓ cup, about 12 minutes. Meanwhile, halve the grapes.

Remove the orange peel and cinnamon stick from the saucepan and discard. Stir in the grapes, return to a boil, then lower the heat to medium and simmer, stirring occasionally, for 3 minutes, until the grapes have softened slightly. Set aside to cool for 5 minutes.

Serve in a small dish on its own, or top each serving with a ¼-cup scoop of frozen or Greek yogurt, if using.

SERVING SIZE about ½ cup
CALORIES 180; Total Fat 0g (Sat Fat 0g, Mono Fat 0g, Poly Fat 0.1g); Protein 1g; Carb 30g; Fiber 1g; Cholesterol 0mg; Sodium 5mg
EXCELLENT SOURCE OF Vitamin C
GOOD SOURCE OF Vitamin K

Sweet-salty-crunchy Cracker Jack synergy is the flavor inspiration for these popcorn balls, which are held together with a scrumptiously sticky mix of peanut butter and honey instead of the usual caramel. They are not only a joy to eat, but they are fun to make too. I call for a brown paper lunch bag to make the popcorn in the microwave, but you can also pop it in a pan on the stove if you prefer.

"caramel" popcorn-peanut balls

MAKES 4 SERVINGS

In a small bowl, toss together the popcorn kernels, oil, and ⅛ teaspoon of the salt. Transfer the mixture to a brown paper lunch bag and fold the bag over three or four times to close. Place the bag in the microwave on top of a plate and cook on high power until the kernels stop popping, about 2 minutes.

In a medium bowl, stir together the honey, peanut butter, and remaining ⅛ teaspoon salt. Add the popcorn, removing and discarding any unpopped kernels. Add the peanuts and stir until well combined. Place the bowl in the freezer for 5 minutes to help solidify the mixture.

Spray your hands with cooking spray. Using your hands, form 4 baseball-sized clusters out of the mixture. Squeeze each cluster firmly, holding for several seconds, so the cluster adheres into a ball. Spray your hands with cooking spray again if the mixture begins to stick to your hands. Place the balls on a plate and place in the refrigerator for 5 to 10 minutes to solidify further. Serve immediately, or wrap in aluminum foil and store in the refrigerator for up to 4 hours.

- 2 tablespoons popcorn kernels
- ½ teaspoon canola oil
- ¼ teaspoon salt
- ¼ cup honey
- 1 tablespoon natural-style peanut butter
- ⅓ cup roasted unsalted peanuts
- Cooking spray

SERVING SIZE 1 ball
CALORIES 180; Total Fat 8g (Sat Fat 1g, Mono Fat 3.3g, Poly Fat 0.5g); Protein 4g; Carb 25g; Fiber 2g; Cholesterol 0mg; Sodium 160mg
EXCELLENT SOURCE OF Vitamin K
GOOD SOURCE OF Fiber, Iron, Niacin, Protein, Thiamin, Vitamin C

Dried fruits and nuts are a famously perfect match: the dried fruit provides intense, chewy-soft sweetness and the nuts counter harmoniously with a substantial, rich crunch. This recipe takes the partnership to another level entirely with plump dates and buttery pistachios ground with warming spices and then rolled in toasted coconut, to create an exotic, sweet-tooth-satisfying candy with health benefits.

coconut-date truffles

MAKES 4 SERVINGS

Toast the pistachios in a small dry skillet over medium-high heat until slightly darker in color and fragrant, 3 minutes. Place the coconut on a small plate.

Pit the dates, then place them in the small bowl of a food processor along with the pistachios, cinnamon, cloves, and salt. Process until finely chopped.

Form the mixture into eight 1-inch balls with your fingers, then roll each ball in the coconut, pressing down somewhat so the coconut adheres.

¼ cup shelled unsalted pistachios

2 tablespoons unsweetened coconut flakes

½ cup Medjool dates (5 large)

¼ teaspoon ground cinnamon
Pinch of ground cloves
Pinch of salt

SERVING SIZE 2 truffles
CALORIES 110; Total Fat 5g (Sat Fat 1.5g, Mono Fat 2.1g, Poly Fat 1.2g); Protein 2g; Carb 18g; Fiber 2g; Cholesterol 0mg; Sodium 75mg
EXCELLENT SOURCE OF n/a
GOOD SOURCE OF Manganese

Recipes for cakes made in a mug or jar in the microwave have gone viral on the Internet, and the idea intrigued me so much that I thought I'd give it a try my way, with healthier ingredients. Now I know what all the fuss is about—they are truly amazing! All you do is whip up a simple batter and in less than a minute you have your very own perfectly portioned warm cake. These fragrant pumpkin cakes turn out almost like a tender pumpkin-spiced bread pudding. A scoop of vanilla frozen yogurt tops them off perfectly.

mini pumpkin "jar cakes"

MAKES 6 SERVINGS

Cooking spray
2 large eggs
2 large egg whites
½ cup canned solid-pack pure pumpkin
⅔ cup lightly packed light brown sugar
¼ cup canola oil
¼ cup 1% milk
1 teaspoon pure vanilla extract
⅓ cup all-purpose flour
⅓ cup whole-wheat pastry flour
½ teaspoon baking powder
½ teaspoon ground cinnamon
¼ teaspoon ground nutmeg
¼ teaspoon ground ginger
⅛ teaspoon salt
¾ cup vanilla frozen yogurt

Spray six 6-ounce glass jars or ramekins with cooking spray.

In a large bowl, whisk together the whole eggs, egg whites, pumpkin, sugar, oil, milk, and vanilla until smooth. In a medium bowl, whisk together the all-purpose and whole-wheat flours, baking powder, cinnamon, nutmeg, ginger, and salt. Add the dry ingredients to the wet ingredients and stir until just combined.

Place ⅓ cup of the batter in one prepared jar or ramekin and microwave on high power until set, 45 seconds. (The cake will puff up dramatically, like a soufflé, but will fall to below the level of the jar once completely cooked. The cakes must be cooked one at a time.) Allow to cool for 1 to 2 minutes before topping with a small scoop (2 tablespoons) of frozen yogurt.

SERVING SIZE 1 cake
CALORIES 260; Total Fat 12g (Sat Fat 1.5g, Mono Fat 6.6g, Poly Fat 2.9g); Protein 6g; Carb 32g; Fiber 2g; Cholesterol 75mg; Sodium 150mg
EXCELLENT SOURCE OF Vitamin A
GOOD SOURCE OF Iodine, Protein, Selenium, Vitamin K

index